1997
Banned Books
resource guide

Robert P. Doyle

Sponsored by:
American Booksellers Association
American Booksellers Foundation for Free Expression
American Library Association
American Society of Journalists and Authors
Association of American Publishers
National Association of College Stores

Endorsed by the Center for the Book of the Library of Congress.

American Library Association, Chicago, Illinois

Celebrate The Freedom To Read

1997 Design and publication composition by Jade Publishing Services, Chicago

Printed on 60# Williamsburg offset (a pH-neutral paper) by Wagner Printing Company, Freeport, IL

Colophon: This publication was composed using QuarkXPress, Adobe Illustrator and Adobe Photoshop for the Macintosh. The primary typefaces used are Franklin Gothic and Adobe Garamond, from Adobe Systems, Inc.

ISBN 0-8389-7886-X   ISSN 0888-0123   LCCN 88-659709

Celebrate The Freedom To Read

Contents

Introduction

Censorship has gone "Hollywood" and, as seems to be typical with media depictions of freedom of expression issues, the result is rife with irony. The film *The People vs. Larry Flynt* has received both critical acclaim and condemnation. Critics claim that the movie glorifies a pornographer. The film's fans claim it is a tribute to freedom of speech. Director Milos Forman defends the work saying, "it's important to separate the pro-free expression message of the film from the 'uncomfortable character' who perhaps fittingly, delivers that message: it's the speech we dislike that's the most in need of protection," (*Free Expression,* Winter 1997, American Booksellers Association).

Forman noted, "I've lived in two societies where it was the pornographers and perverts who were publicly attacked and censored first — the Nazis and the Communists. We all applauded — who wants perverts running through the streets, after all? It's the easiest thing for the government to find support for censorship of pornography. But they are smart; they have ways of formulating the laws so that you suddenly learn that Shakespeare was a pervert, Jesus was a pervert…that, in fact, everyone who does not conform with the government is a super-pervert."

In fact, Shakespearean works are have been frequently targeted. Over the last four centuries, *Hamlet, King Lear, The Merchant of Venice,* and the *Tragedy of King Richard II* have been banned and challenged for political and religious reasons. This year, *Twelfth Night* was removed from a New Hampshire library in accordance with a policy that bans instruction that has the "effect of encouraging or supporting homosexuality as a positive lifestyle alternative."

Sex, profanity, violence, and racism remained the primary targets, but challenges also were directed at books considered "dreary" (Shel Silverstein's *A Light in the Attic*), books that contained "armpit farts" (Bruce Coville's *My Teacher Glows in the Dark*), books some believed handled suicide inappropriately (Judith Guest's *Ordinary People*), and books which depicted teen smoking (*Ryan White: My Own Story*). In Lindale, Texas, classics such as Nathaniel Hawthorne's *Scarlet Letter,* Harper Lee's *To Kill a Mockingbird,* Herman Melville's *Moby Dick,* and Mark Twain's *The Adventures of Huckleberry Finn* were removed from the high school's reading list because they "conflicted with the values of the community."

In 1996, there were hundreds of formal challenges to materials in schools, school libraries and public libraries. These challenges were not just someone expressing their point of view regarding these materials; rather, the challengers were asking that the material be removed from the curriculum or library, thereby restricting the access of others. The positive message of Banned Books Week: Celebrating the Freedom to Read is that due to the commitment of librarians, teachers, parents, students and other concerned citizens, most of these challenges were unsuccessful and the materials were retained in the school curriculum or library collection.

These books were challenged or banned with the intention of protecting someone, frequently children. And, while this cause can be considered noble and commendable, this method of protection contains hazards far greater than exposure to the "evil" against which the protection is leveled. Supreme Court Justice William Brennan, in *Texas v. Johnson*, said most eloquently, "If there is a bedrock principle underlying the First Amendment, it is that the Government may not prohibit the expression of an idea simply because society finds the idea itself offensive or disagreeable." Individuals may restrict what they themselves or their children read, but they must not call on governmental or public agencies to prevent others from reading or seeing that material.

Banned Books Week 1997 is the sixteenth annual promotion celebrating the freedom to read. Firmly rooted in the First Amendment of the U.S. Constitution, the rights to freedom of speech and freedom of press require continuing vigilance in order to keep them vital. Threats against the freedom to read come from many quarters, and many political persuasions are represented in the spectrum of those who would limit the freedom of others to choose what they read, see, or hear.

Banned Books Week is sponsored by the American Booksellers Association, the American Booksellers Foundation for Free Expression, the American Library Association, the American Society of Journalists and Authors, the Association of American Publishers and the National Association of College Stores. It is also endorsed by the Center for the Book of the Library of Congress. These groups sponsor this week to draw attention to the danger that exists when restraints are imposed on the availability of information in a free society.

The message of Banned Books Week is more than the freedom to choose or the freedom to express one's opinion even if that opinion might be considered unorthodox or unpopular. The essential message of Banned Books Week is the importance of ensuring the availability of those unorthodox or unpopular viewpoints to all who wish to read them.

Banned Books Week—Celebrating the Freedom to Read is an opportunity to conduct or sponsor positive educational programs, including exhibits, lectures, discussions, plays, and films demonstrating the harms of censorship. This publication can help bookstores, libraries, and schools organize their programs in support of the First Amendment. It includes factual information about banned books, specific suggestions for activities for Banned Books Week, and clip art to help launch a successful publicity campaign.

Books Challenged or Banned in 1996-1997. This short list makes it easier for you to identify material that

has been challenged within the past year. These titles are also included in the longer list, described below. Reprints of the short list are available for distribution to customers and patrons.

Caution! Some People Consider These Books Dangerous. This list includes books that have been banned or considered controversial from 387 B.C. to the present. Browsing through this list can provide valuable ideas for preparing an exhibit or preparing for discussions, presentations, and writings.

Notable First Amendment Court Cases. This section describes some noted legal precedents concerning freedom of speech and can be used to support your programs, presentations, articles, and displays.

Quotes on the First Amendment. Summing up the value of the First Amendment can be difficult for the layperson, especially compared to these effective and memorable expressions by notable individuals! Use these quotes to illustrate your displays or to provide an inspiration for your celebration; or sprinkle your press materials with these words of wisdom. You can even print quotes on T-shirts or tote bags.

Action Guide. This section features suggested activities. From ordering lapel buttons to sponsoring a community-wide forum on censorship, some creative ways to draw attention to your bookstore/library and the freedom to read are presented here. Success stories of activities from the field over the past fifteen years are included, as well as information on how to order T-shirts, books, educational materials—and even copies of the U.S. Constitution. Also included are display ideas, basic public relations tips, an annotated bibliography of publications on the topic and list of concerned national organizations.

Indexes. The three indexes to the comprehensive list can help customize an exhibit or program by identifying challenged books by title, location, and category. For example, if you wanted to create an exhibit of books banned or challenged in your state or city, use the geographic index to find the titles. Or, if you want to have a program on children's literature or gay literature, check the topical index. Using these tools will create an event targeted for your audience or community. Please note that the bibliography entries are numbered sequentially and the entry number (not the page number) is used in all three indexes.

Clip Art. Camera-ready art is provided to illustrate flyers, posters, newsletters and bibliographies; to spruce up invitations to performances or forums; to tie together the look of your Banned Books Week celebration by using the graphics on bookbags, bookmarks, table tents, and so on, as well as on all your press material.

Books Challenged or Banned in 1996-97

Books challenged or banned as reported in the *Newsletter on Intellectual Freedom* from March 1996 through March 1997.

Adoff, Arnold, ed. *Poetry of Black America*. Harper Collins. Challenged at the Fort Walton Beach, Fla. school libraries (1996) because it "promotes violence" and contains "expletives and a reference to abortion." Source: July 1996, p. 133.

Allison, Dorothy. *Bastard Out of Carolina*. NAL. Removed from the Mt. Abram High School English classes in Salem, Maine (1996) because the language and subject matter (incest and rape) were inappropriate for fifteen-year-olds. Source: Mar. 1996, p. 49; Nov. 1996, p. 196; Mar. 1997, p. 39.

Anaya, Rudolfo A. *Bless Me, Ultima*. TQS Pubns. Retained on the Round Rock, Tex. Independent High School reading list (1996) after a challenge that the book was too violent. Source: May 1996, p. 99.

Andrews, V. C. *Garden of Shadows*. Pocket Bks. Removed from Oconee County, Ga. school libraries (1994) "because the book encouraged sexual activity and the result of reading or seeing it might be 'incestuous relationships' and 'aggressive sexual behavior.'" The book was removed despite a recommendation from a committee of parents and teachers to retain it. The action stemmed from a complaint filed in May 1994 when eight other V. C. Andrews books were removed. Source: Nov. 1994, p. 188; Jan. 1995, p. 6; July 1996, p. 117.

Angelou, Maya. *I Know Why the Caged Bird Sings*. Bantam. Challenged, but retained in the Volusia County, Fla. County Schools (1995). The complainants wanted the book removed because "it is sexually explicit and promotes cohabitation and rape." Challenged, but retained on an optional reading list at the East Lawrence High School in Moulton, Ala. (1996). The book was challenged because the School Superintendent decided "the poet's descriptions of being raped as a little girl were pornographic." Removed from the curriculum pending a review of its content at the Gilbert, Ariz. Unified School (1995). Complaining parents said the book did not represent "traditional values." Retained on the Round Rock, Tex. Independent High School reading list (1996) after a challenge that the book was too violent. Pulled from the reading list at Lakota High School in Cincinnati, Ohio (1996) because of parents' claims that its is too graphic. Source: Mar. 1996, pp. 47, 63; May 1996, pp. 84, 99; July 1996, p. 120; Sept. 1996, pp. 152-53; Nov. 1996, pp. 197-98; Jan. 1997, p. 26.

Anonymous. *Go Ask Alice.* Avon; Prentice-Hall. Removed from a supplemental reading list for sophomore English students in Warm Springs, Va. (1995) because of its "profanity and indecent situations." Source: Mar. 1996, p. 50.

Armstrong, William Howard. *Sounder.* Harper. Challenged, but retained in the Rockingham County, N.C. schools (1996). A parent had problems with the use of the word "nigger" on page 21 and a reference to the main character, a black sharecropper, as "boy." Source: Sept. 1996, p. 169; Nov. 1996, p. 212.

Blume, Judy. *Deenie.* Bradbury Pr. Challenged by a parent in the Cornelius Elementary School library in Charlotte, N.C. (1996) due to the novel's sexual content. Source: May 1996, p. 83.

———. *Forever.* Bradbury Pr. Challenged at the Wilton, Iowa School District for junior and senior high school students (1996) because of its sexual content. Source: May 1996, p. 97.

Bode, Janet and Mack, Stan. *Heartbreak and Roses: Real Life Stories of Troubled Love.* Delacorte. Pulled from the Ouachita Parish school library in Monroe, La. (1996) because of sexual content. The Louisiana chapter of the ACLU filed a lawsuit in the federal courts on October 3, 1996, claiming that the principal and the school superintendent violated First Amendment free speech rights and also failed to follow established procedure when they removed the book. Source: Sept. 1996, pp. 151-52; Jan. 1997, p. 7.

Carle, Eric. *Draw Me a Star.* Philomel Bks. Challenged in the elementary school libraries in the Edmonds, Wash. School District (1996). The book is illustrated with highly stylized representations of a naked woman and man. Source: Nov. 1996, pp. 211-12.

Carter, Forrest. *The Education of Little Tree.* Univ. of New Mex. Pr. Challenged, but retained at the Astoria, Oreg. Elementary School (1995). Complainants wanted the book removed because it includes profanity, mentions sex and portrays Christians as "liars, cheats and child molesters." Source: Jan. 1996, p. 17; Mar. 1996, p. 64.

Chute, Carolyn. *The Beans of Egypt.* Harcourt; Warner. Challenged at the Oxford Hills High School in Paris, Maine (1996). A parent stated that "teachers are not qualified to explore the issues of rape, incest, suicide and mental illness contained in Chute's novel." Source: Nov. 1996, p. 212.

Collier, James Lincoln, and Collier, Christopher. *Jump Ship to Freedom.* Delacorte; Dell. Challenged at the Nathan Hale Middle School in Crestwood, Ill. (1996) because it "was damaging to the self-esteem of young black students. Source: Mar. 1997, p. 39.

———. *My Brother Sam Is Dead.* Scholastic. Challenged in the Jefferson County Public Schools in Lakewood, Colo. (1996) because of "the persistent usage of profanity" in the book, as well as references to rape, drinking, and battlefield violence. Retained in the Antioch, Calif. elementary school libraries (1996) after a parent complained about the profanity and violence in the Newbery Award-winning novel. Source: July 1996, p. 121; Jan. 1997, p. 25.

———. *War Comes to Willy Freeman.* Delacorte. Pulled from two classes at Western Avenue School in Flossmoor, Ill. (1996) after a parent complained that the book "represents totally poor judgment, a complete lack of racial sensitivity and is totally inappropriate for fifth-graders. This book is an education in racism, a primer for developing prejudice." Source: Jan. 1997, p. 9.

Comfort, Alex. *The Joy of Sex: The Cordon Bleu Guide to Lovemaking.* Crown; Pocket Bks. Removed from the Clifton, N.J. Public Library (1996) and replaced with a dummy book made of styrofoam. The library's new policy restricts to adults any material containing "patently offensive graphic illustrations or photographs of sexual or excretory activities or contact as measured by contemporary community standards for minors." Source: July 1996, pp. 118-19.

———. *More Joy of Sex.* Crown. Restricted to patrons over 18 years of age at the Main Memorial Library in Clifton, N.J. (1996). The book is hidden behind the checkout counter and on the shelves is a dummy book jacket. The book was described as hardcore pornography by the complainant. Source: Mar. 1996, p. 63; May 1996, p. 83.

Conley, Jane Leslie. *Crazy Lady.* Harper. Challenged at the Prospect Heights, Ill. school libraries (1996) because of "swear words." Source: Mar. 1996, p. 46.

Cormier, Robert. *The Chocolate War.* Dell; Pantheon. Removed from the East Stroudsburg, Pa. ninth grade curriculum (1996) after complaints about the novel's language and content. Removed from the middle school libraries in the Riverside, Calif. Unified School District (1996) as inappropriate for seventh- and eighth- graders to read without class discussion due to mature themes, sexual situations, and smoking. Source: May 1996, p. 99; July 1996, p. 82; Nov. 1996, p. 198.

Courtney, Bryce. *The Power of One.* Ballantine. Retained on the Round Rock, Tex. Independent High School reading list (1996) after a challenge that the book was too violent. Source: May 1996, p. 99.

Coville, Bruce. *The Dragonslayers.* Pocket Bks. Challenged in the Berkeley County, S.C. School District (1995) because of the "witchcraft" and "deception" and because a "main character openly disobeys his parents." Source: Mar. 1996, p. 63.

_____. *My Teacher Glows in the Dark.* Pocket Bks. Contested in the classrooms and school libraries in Palmdale, Calif. (1995) because the book includes the words "armpit farts" and "farting." Source: Mar. 1996, p. 45.

Forster, E. M. *Maurice.* Norton. Banned from the Mascenic Regional High School in New Ipswich, N.H. (1995) because it is about gays and lesbians. An English teacher was fired for refusing to remove the book. An arbitrator ruled in April 1996 that she can return to work in September without a year's back pay. The Mascenic Regional School Board is appealing the ruling. The teacher was eventually reinstated after a decision by the state's Public Employee Labor Relations Board. Source: Sept. 1995, p. 166; Jan. 1996, p. 15; July 1996, pp. 130-31; Jan. 1997, p. 27.

Fox, Paula. *The Slave Dancer.* Bradbury Pr. Challenged, but retained by the Fayette County, Ga. school system (1996). The 1974 Newbery Medal winner about a 13-year-old boy who is snatched from the docks of New Orleans and put on a slave ship bound for Africa. The book was considered objectionable because of language that is "insensitive and degrading." Source: May 1996, p. 99.

Friday, Nancy. *Women on Top: How Real Life Has Changed Women's Fantasies.* Pocket Bks. Challenged at the Chester County Library at Charlestown, Pa. (1996) because of graphic details about sex acts and fantasies. Source: Nov. 1996, p. 194; Jan 1997, p. 8; Mar. 1997, p. 49.

Fuentes, Carlos. *The Old Gringo.* Farrar. Retained in the Guilford County, N.C. school media centers (1996) after a parent wanted the book removed because of its explicit language. Source: Jan. 1997, p. 25.

George, Jean Craighead. *Julie of the Wolves.* Harper. Challenged in the classrooms and school libraries in Palmdale, Calif. (1995) because the book describes a rape. Removed from the sixth-grade curriculum of the New Brighton Area School District in Pulaski Township, Pa. (1996) because of a graphic marital rape scene. Challenged at the Hanson Lane Elementary School in Ramona, Calif. (1996) because the award-winning book includes an attempted rape of a 13-year-old girl. Source: Mar. 1996, p. 45; May 1996, p. 88; Jan. 1997, p. 9.

Greene, Bette. *The Drowning of Stephan Jones.* Bantam. Banned from the Mascenic Regional High School in New Ipswich, N.H. (1995) because it is about gays and lesbians. An English teacher was fired for refusing to remove the book. Source: Sept. 1995, p. 166; Jan. 1996, p. 15.

_____. *Summer of My German Soldier.* Bantam; Dial. Temporarily removed from an eighth-grade supplemental reading list in Cinnaminson, N.J. (1996) because it contains offensive racial stereotypes. Source: Jan. 1997, p. 10.

Grisham, John. *The Client.* Doubleday. Challenged in a sixth-grade high-level reading class in Hillsborough,

N.J. (1996) because of its violence and use of "curse words." Source: July 1996, p. 122; Sept. 1996, p. 155.

Guest, Judith. *Ordinary People.* Ballantine; Hall; Viking. Temporarily pulled from the Lancaster, N.Y. High School curriculum (1996) because two parents contended it contained foul language, graphic references to sex and inappropriate handling of the subject of suicide. A Lancaster student took the matter to the New York Civil Liberties Union which sent a letter to the school board saying that were "greatly dismayed" with the board's action. Source: Sept. 1996, pp. 155-56; Nov. 1996, p. 197.

Hahn, Mary Downing. *Wait Till Helen Comes.* Clarion Bks. Challenged in the Lawrence, Kans. School District curriculum (1996) because the book presents suicide as a viable, "even attractive way of dealing with family problems. Ghosts, poltergeists and other supernatural phenomena are presented as documented reality and these are capable of deadly harm to children." Source: May 1996, pp. 87-88.

Harris, Robie H. *It's Perfectly Normal: A Book about Changing Bodies, Growing Up, Sex, and Sexual Health.* Candlewick Pr. Challenged at the Provo, Utah Library (1996) because it contains discussions of intercourse, masturbation and homosexuality. Removed from the Clover Park, Wash. School District library shelves (1996) because parents charged that it was too graphic and could foster more questions than it answers. Challenged at the Chester County, Pa. Library (1996) because the "book is an act of encouragement for children to begin desiring sexual gratification ... and is a clear example of child pornography." Source: Sept. 1996, p. 152; Jan. 1997, p. 8; Mar. 1997, p. 49.

Hawthorne, Nathaniel. *The Scarlet Letter.* Bantam; Dell; Dodd; Holt; Houghton; Modern Library; NAL; Norton. Banned from the Lindale, Tex. advanced placement English reading list (1996) because the book "conflicted with the values of the community." Source: Nov. 1996, p. 199.

Homes, A. M. *Jack.* Vintage. Placed on the Spindale, N.C. school library's (1996) reserve shelf. This meant parental permission was required for a student to check it out. A parent did not find the novel "proper to be in the library due to the language." Source: Nov. 1996,

pp. 193-94.

Isensee, Rick. *Love Between Men.* Prentice-Hall; Alyson Pubns. Challenged at the Chester County Library at Charlestown, Pa. (1996) because it was "pornographic and smutty." Source: Nov. 1996, p. 194.

Jennings, Kevin, ed. *Becoming Visible: A Reader in Gay and Lesbian History for High School and College Students.* Alyson Pubns. Banned from the two high school libraries in Mehlville, Mo. (1996) by order of the superintendent. The donated book was removed because it "does not meet the needs of the curriculum." Source: May 1996, pp. 82-83.

Jimenez, Carlos M. *The Mexican-American Heritage.* TQS Pubs. Challenged in the Santa Barbara, Calif. schools (1996) because the book promotes "Mexican nationalism." Source: May 1996, p. 98.

Johnson, Earvin (Magic). *What You Can Do to Avoid AIDS.* Times Books. Removed from the Horace Greeley High School in Chappaqua, N.Y. (1996) because a group of parents complained that the basketball player's written description of oral and anal sex were inappropriate for 14- and 15-year-olds. Johnson's book is endorsed by the American Medical Association and the Children's Defense Fund. Source: May 1996, p. 88; July 1996, p. 119.

Keehn, Sally. *I Am Regina.* Philomel Bks. Challenged as optional fifth-grade reading at the Orland Park, Ill. School District 135 (1996) because the book uses unflattering stereotypes to depict Native Americans and uses the word "squaw" which was offensive. Source: Jan. 1997, p. 10.

Keyes, Daniel. *Flowers for Algernon.* Bantam; Harcourt. Challenged, but retained in the Yorktown, Va. schools (1996). A parent complained about the profanity and references to sex and drinking in the novel. Source: May 1996, p. 100.

Knowles, John. *A Separate Peace.* Bantam; Dell; Macmillan. Challenged at the McDowell County, N.C. schools (1996) because of "graphic language." Source: Jan. 1997, p. 11.

Koontz, Dean R. *Watchers.* Putnam. Removed from the Hickory High School curriculum in Sharon, Pa. (1996) by the superintendent because the language was offensive. Source: Mar. 1997, p. 50.

Kroll, Ken. *Enabling Romance: A Guide to Love, Sex and Relationships for the Disabled.* First Woodline House. Removed from the Clifton, N.J. Public Library (1996) and replaced with a dummy book made of styrofoam. The library's new policy restricts to adults any material containing "patently offensive graphic illustrations or photographs of sexual or excretory activities or contact as measured by contemporary community standards for minors." Source: July 1996, pp. 118-19.

Lee, Harper. *To Kill a Mockingbird.* Lippincott/Harper; Popular Library. Challenged at the Moss Point, Miss. School District (1996) because the novel contains a racial epithet. Banned from the Lindale, Tex. advanced placement English reading list (1996) because the book "conflicted with the values of the community." Source: Nov. 1996, pp. 196-97, 199.

L'Engle, Madeleine C. *A Wrinkle in Time.* Dell. Challenged, but retained by the Catawba County School Board in Newton, N.C. (1996). A parent requested the book be pulled from the school libraries because it allegedly undermines religious beliefs. Source: May 1996, pp. 97-98.

Lowry, Lois. *The Giver.* Dell; Houghton. Challenged at the Lakota High School in Cincinnati, Ohio (1996). Source: Nov. 1996, p. 198.

Lundgren, Astrid. *The Runaway Sleigh Ride.* Viking. Challenged in the Kokomo-Howard County, Ind. Public Library (1995) because it makes "light of a drinking situation." The book is by the author of the Pippi Longstocking series. Source: Mar. 1996, p. 46.

Lynch, Chris. *Iceman.* Harper. Challenged at the Haysville, Kans. Middle School library (1996) when a parent counted 36 places where profanity was used in the book. Source: Mar. 1997, p. 49.

Mathabane, Mark. *Kaffir Boy.* NAL. Temporarily pulled from the Greensboro, N.C. high school libraries (1996) after a resident sent letters to school board members and some administrators charging that the book could encourage young people to sexually assault children. Challenged at the Lewis S. Mills High School (1996) in Burlington, Conn. because of brutal and graphic language. Source: July 1996, p. 119; Mar. 1997, p. 38.

McFarland, Philip J., et al. *Themes in World Literature.* Houghton. Challenged, but retained at the Tempe Union High School District in Mesa, Ariz. (1995). The story, "A Rose for Emily," by William Faulkner was objectionable because it uses the word "nigger" six times as well as other demeaning phrases. Source: Jan. 1996, p. 13; May 1996, p. 98.

Melville, Herman. *Moby Dick.* Modern Library. Banned from the advanced placement English reading list at the Lindale, Tex. schools (1996) because it "conflicts with the values of the community." Source: Nov. 1996, p. 199.

Moe, Barbara A. *Everything You Need to Know About Sexual Abstinence.* Rosen. Pulled from the Ouachita Parish school library in Monroe, La. (1996) because of sexual content. The Louisiana chapter of the ACLU filed a lawsuit in the federal courts on October 3, 1996, claiming that the principal and the school superintendent violated First Amendment free speech rights and also failed to follow established procedure when they removed the book. Source: Sept. 1996, pp. 151-52; Jan. 1997, p. 7.

Mohr, Richard D. *A More Perfect Union: Why Straight America Must Stand Up for Gay Rights.* Beacon Pr. Challenged, but retained at the Belfast, Maine Free Library (1996) because "homosexuality destroys marriages and families; it destroys the good health of the individual and the innocent are infected by it." Source: May 1996, p. 97.

Momaday, N. Scott. *House Made of Dawn.* Harper; NAL; Penguin. Retained on the Round Rock, Tex. Independent High School reading list (1996) after a challenge that the book was too violent. Source: May 1996, p. 99.

Morrison, Toni. *Beloved.* Knopf; NAL. Retained on the Round Rock, Tex. Independent High School reading list (1996) after a challenge that the book was too violent. Source: May 1996, p. 99.

Myers, Walter Dean. *Fallen Angels.* Scholastic. Removed from a twelfth-grade English class in Middleburg Heights, Ohio (1995) after a parent complained of its sexually explicit language. The novel won the Coretta Scott King Award and was named Best Book of 1988 by School Library Journal. Source: Mar. 1996, p. 49.

O'Malley, Kevin, illus. *Froggy Went A-Courtin'.* Stewart, Tabori and Chang. Restricted at the Baltimore County, Md. school libraries (1996) because of Froggy's nefarious activities including burning money, and speeding away from the cat police, as well as robbery and smoking. The book is to be kept in restricted areas of the libraries where only parents and teachers will be allowed to check it out and read it to children. Source: Jan. 1997, p. 7; Mar. 1997, p. 35.

Orenstein, Peggy. *Schoolgirls: Young Women, Self-esteem and the Confidence Gap.* Doubleday. Challenged in Courtland, Ohio High School (1996) because of its "rotten, filthy language." The teacher offered the parents a black marker with which to delete offending passages, but the parents wanted it banned. The school board voted to continue the book. Source: Mar. 1997, p. 50.

Paterson, Katherine. *Bridge to Terabithia.* Crowell. Removed from the fifth-grade classrooms of the New Brighton Area School District in Pulaski Township, Pa. (1996) due to "profanity, disrespect of adults, and an elaborate fantasy world they felt might lead to confusion." Source: May 1996, p. 88.

Peck, Robert Newton. *A Day No Pigs Would Die.* ABC-Clio; Dell; Knopf. Pulled from an Anderson, S.C. middle school library (1995) because of the "gory" descriptions of two pigs mating, a pig being slaughtered, and a cow giving birth. Challenged at the Anderson, Mo. Junior High School (1996) because of its content. Source: Mar. 1996, p. 46; Jan. 1997, p. 10.

Ray, Ron. *Gays in or Out of the Military.* Brassey's. Pulled from the Ouachita Parish school library in Monroe, La. (1996) because of sexual content. The Louisiana chapter of the ACLU filed a lawsuit in the federal courts on October 3, 1996, claiming that the principal and the school superintendent violated First Amendment free speech rights and also failed to follow established procedure when they removed the book. Source: Sept. 1996, pp. 151-52; Jan. 1997, p. 7.

Reed, Rick. *Obsessed.* Dell. Permanently removed from the East Coweta County, Ga. High School library (1996) because of several sexually and violently graphic passages. Source: Jan. 1997, p. 7; Mar. 1997, p. 35.

Reiss, Johanna. *The Upstairs Room.* Bantam; Harper. Challenged as assigned reading for sixth grade students in Sanford, Maine (1996) because of profanity. Source: July 1996, p. 118.

Rodriguez, Luis J. *Always Running.* Curbstone Pr. Challenged as an optional reading at the Guilford High School in Rockford, Ill. (1996) because it is "blatant pornography." Source: July 1996, p. 118.

Roquelaire, A. E. [Anne Rice]. *Beauty's Punishment.* NAL. Removed from the Columbus, Ohio Metropolitan Library (1996) as hardcore pornography. Source: July 1996, pp. 119-20.

_____. *Beauty's Release.* NAL. Removed from the Columbus, Ohio Metropolitan Library (1996) as hardcore pornography. Source: July 1996, pp. 119-20.

_____. *The Claiming of Sleeping Beauty.* NAL. Removed from the Columbus, Ohio Metropolitan Library (1996) as hardcore pornography. Source: July 1996, pp. 119-20.

Salinger, J. D. *Catcher in the Rye.* Bantam; Little. Challenged at the Oxford Hills High School in Paris, Maine (1996). A parent objected to the use of "the 'F' word." Source: Nov. 1996, p. 212.

Sarton, May. *The Education of Harriet Hatfield.* Norton. Removed from the Mascenic Regional High School in New Ipswich, N.H. (1995) because it is about gays and lesbians. An English teacher was fired for refusing to remove the book. Source: Sept. 1995, p. 166; Jan. 1996, p. 15.

Shakespeare, William. *Twelfth Night.* Airmont; Cambridge Univ. Pr.; Methuen; NAL; Penguin; Pocket Bks.; Washington Square. Removed from a Merrimack, N.H. high school English class (1996) because of a policy that bans any instruction which has "the effect of encouraging or supporting homosexuality as a positive lifestyle alternative." Source: May 1996, p. 96.

Silko, Leslie Marmon. *Ceremony.* Viking; Penguin. Retained on the Round Rock, Tex. Independent High School reading list (1996) after a challenge that the book was too violent. Source: May 1996, p. 99.

Silverstein, Charles, and Picano, Felice. *The New Joy of Gay Sex.* Harper. Restricted to patrons over 18 years of age at the Main Memorial Library in Clifton, N.J. (1996). The book is hidden behind the checkout counter and on the shelves is a dummy book jacket. The book was described as hardcore pornography by the complainant. Source: Mar. 1996, p. 63; May 1996, p. 83.

Silverstein, Shel. *A Light in the Attic.* Harper. Challenged, but retained on the Webb City, Mo. school library shelves (1996). A parent had protested that the book imparts a "dreary" and "negative" message. Source: May 1996, p. 97.

Simon, Neil. *Brighton Beach Memoirs.* NAL; Random. Removed from the required reading and optional reading lists from the Dallas, Tex. schools (1996) because of passages containing profanity and sexually explicit language. Source: May 1996, p. 88.

Sinclair, April. *Coffee Will Make You Black.* Hyperion. Removed from the curriculum at the Julian High School in Chicago, Ill. (1996) because the book was not appropriate for freshman as required reading because of sexually explicit language. Source: May 1996, p. 87.

Smiley, Jane. *A Thousand Acres.* Fawcett; Knopf; Thorndike Pr. Retained on the Round Rock, Tex. Independent High School reading list (1996) after a challenge that the book was too violent. Source: May 1996, p. 99.

Spies, Karen Bornemann. *Everything You Need to Know About Incest.* Rosen. Pulled from the Ouachita Parish school library in Monroe, La. (1996) because of sexual content. The Louisiana chapter of the ACLU filed a lawsuit in the federal courts on October 3, 1996, claiming that the principal and the school superintendent violated First Amendment free speech rights and also failed to follow established procedure when they removed the book. Source: Sept. 1996, pp. 151-52; Jan. 1997, p. 7.

Stanway, Andrew. *The Lovers' Guide.* St. Martin. Removed from the Clifton, N.J. Public Library (1996) and replaced with a dummy book made of styrofoam. The library's new policy restricts to adults any material containing "patently offensive graphic illustrations or photographs of sexual or excretory activities or contact as measured by contemporary community standards for minors." Source: July 1996, pp. 118-19.

Steel, Danielle. *The Gift.* Delacorte. Challenged at a Coventry, Ohio school (1996) because "the schools had no business teaching his children about sex, that it was the job of the parents." Source: Jan. 1997, p. 11.

Steinbeck, John. *Of Mice and Men.* Bantam; Penguin; Viking. Challenged at the Stephens County High School library in Toccoa, Ga. (1995) because of "curse words." Challenged, but retained in a Warm Springs, Va. High School (1995) English class. Source: Mar. 1996, pp. 50, 63.

_____. *Red Pony.* Viking. Challenged, but retained on a recommended reading list at Holmes Middle School in Eden, N.C. (1996). A parent complained that there were curse words on ten different pages of the book. Source: Sept. 1996, p. 170.

Stern, Howard. *Miss America*. Regan. Challenged at the Prince William County, Va. Library (1996). Two newly appointed members of the library board want to limit young people's access to books by removing them from the collection or by creating an "adults-only" section of the library. Source: Nov. 1996, p. 194.

Stine, R. L. *Beach House*. Pocket Bks. Challenged at the Pulaski Heights Elementary School library in Little Rock, Ark. (1996) along with similar Stine titles. The book, part of the "Fear Street" series, includes graphic descriptions of boys intimidating and killing girls. Source: Nov. 1996, p. 211.

_____. *Goosebumps*. Scholastic. Challenged at the Bay County, Fla. elementary schools (1996) because of "satanic symbolism, disturbing scenes and dialogue." *The Barking Ghost,* for satanic symbolism and gestures, possession and descriptions of dogs as menacing and attacking; *Night of the Living Dummy II,* for spells or chants, violence and vandalism; *The Haunted Mask,* for graphic description of the ugly mask, demonic possession, violence, disturbing scenes and dialogue; *The Scarecrow Walks at Midnight,* for satanic acts and symbolism, and disturbing scenes; and *Say Cheese and Die!,* for promoting mischief, demonic possession, a reference to Satan and his goals, a disturbing scene describing a death, and a scene that tells of a child disappearing from a birthday party. Challenged at the Anoka-Hennepin, Minn. school system (1997) because "children under the age of twelve may not be able to handle the frightening content of the books." Source: July 1996, p. 134; Mar. 1997, p. 35.

Stoppard, Miriam. *The Magic of Sex*. Newspaper Guild. Restricted to patrons over 18 years of age at the Main Memorial Library in Clifton, N.J. (1996). The book is hidden behind the checkout counter and on the shelves is a dummy book jacket. The book was described as hardcore pornography by the complainant. Source: Mar. 1996, p. 63; May 1996, p. 83.

Tan, Amy. *The Joy Luck Club*. Putnam. Banned from the Lindale, Tex. advanced placement English reading list

(1996) because the book "conflicted with the values of the community." Source: Nov. 1996, p. 199.

Taylor, William. *Agnes the Sheep*. Scholastic. Removed from the Nesbit Elementary School in Gwinnett County, Ga. (1995) because it "overused" the words "hell, damn, and God." After other parents wanted the book restored in the elementary school, the County Board of Education refused to reinstate the book. Source: Jan. 1996, p. 11; Mar. 1996, p. 64.

Twain, Mark [Samuel L. Clemens]. *The Adventures of Huckleberry Finn*. Bantam; Bobbs-Merrill; Grosset; Harper; Holt; Houghton; Longman; Macmillan; NAL; Norton; Penguin; Pocket Bks. Challenged in the Kenosha, Wis. Unified School District (1995). The complaint was filed by the local NAACP which cited the book as offensive to African-American students. Challenged as required reading in an honors English class at the McClintock High School in Tempe, Ariz. (1996). Demonstrators called for the ouster of the principal. In May 1996, a class-action lawsuit was filed in U.S. District Court in Phoenix, alleging that the district has deprived minority students of educational opportunities by requiring them to read racially offensive literature or allowing them to go the library if they objected. Dropped from the mandatory required reading list at the Upper Dublin, Pa. schools (1996) because of its allegedly insensitive and offensive language. Banned from the Lindale, Tex. advanced placement English reading list (1996) because the book "conflicted with the values of the community." Challenged for being on the approved reading list in the Federal Way, Wash. schools (1996) because it "perpetuates hate and racism." Challenged as required reading at the Cherry Hill, Pa. High Schools (1996) because of language. Source: Mar. 1996, pp. 64-65; May 1996, p. 98; July 1996, p. 120; Sept. 1996, pp. 153, 157; Nov. 1996, pp. 198-99; Jan. 1997, p. 12; Mar. 1997, p. 40.

Updike, John. *Rabbit is Rich*. Knopf. Removed from the library at Sun Valley High School in Aston, Pa. (1996) because it contains "offensive language and explicit sexual scenes." The novel won the Pulitzer Prize for fiction in 1982. Source: May 1996, pp. 83-84.

Van Lustbader, Eric. *White Ninja.* Fawcett. Challenged at the Prince William County, Va. Library (1995) because of passages that describe the vicious rape and flaying of a young woman. Source: Jan. 1996, p. 12; Nov. 1996, pp. 194, 211; Jan. 1997, p. 26.

Vonnegut, Kurt, Jr. *Breakfast of Champions.* Dell. Challenged in the Monmouth, Ill. School District Library (1995) because it is "pornographic trash." Source: Mar. 1996, p. 45.

_____. *Slaughterhouse-Five.* Dell; Dial. Retained on the Round Rock, Tex. Independent High School reading list (1996) after a challenge that the book was too violent. Source: May 1996, p. 99.

Walker, Alice. *The Color Purple.* Harcourt. Retained on the Round Rock, Tex. Independent High School reading list (1996) after a challenge that the book was too violent. Challenged as part of the reading list for Advanced English classes at Northwest High School in High Point, N.C. (1996) because the book is "sexually graphic and violent." Source: May 1996, p. 99; Mar. 1997, p. 50.

Welch, James. *Winter in the Blood.* Harper. Retained on the Round Rock, Tex. Independent High School reading list (1996) after a challenge that the book was too violent. Source: May 1996, p. 99.

Wieler, Diane. *Bad Boy.* Delacorte. Challenged at the State College, Pa. area middle school libraries (1996). Three parents requested the book's removal, charging that it was full of profanity and portrayed underage drinking

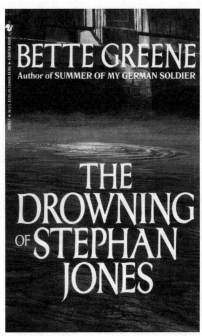

and other problems. In addition, the portrayal of the homosexual relationship between two secondary characters "conveys a wrong message." Source: Nov. 1996, p. 211; Jan. 1997, p. 9.

Wilder, Laura Ingalls. *Little House in the Big Woods.* Buccaneer; Harper; Transaction. Removed from the classrooms, but later reinstated for third-graders at the Lincoln Unified School District in Stockton, Calif. (1996). Complainants also want the book removed from the library because it "promotes racial epithets and is fueling the fire of racism." Source: Jan. 1997, p. 9; Mar. 1997, p. 50.

White, Ryan and Cunningham, Ann Marie. *Ryan White: My Own Story.* Dial. Removed from the curriculum, but placed on library shelves, with restricted access, at the Stroudsburg, Pa. middle school (1996) because a section "uses a gutter term for sodomy and another approves of teen smoking." Source: Mar. 1997, p. 37.

Wright, Richard. *Black Boy.* Harper. Retained on the Round Rock, Tex. Independent High School reading list (1996) after a challenge that the book was too violent. Source: May 1996, p. 99.

_____. *Native Son.* Harper. Challenged as part of the reading list for Advanced English classes at Northwest High School in High Point, N.C. (1996) because the book is "sexually graphic and violent." Source: Mar. 1997, p. 50.

Some People Consider These Books Dangerous

This list of books some people consider dangerous was compiled from the following sources:

1. Geller, Evelyn. *Forbidden Books in American Public Libraries, 1876-1939: A Study in Cultural Change.* Westport, Conn.: Greenwood Pr., 1984.

2. Green, Jonathon. *The Encyclopedia of Censorship.* New York, N.Y.: Facts On File, 1990.

3. Haight, Anne Lyon, and Grannis, Chandler B. *Banned Books, 387 B.C. to 1978 A.D.,* 4th ed. New York, N.Y.: Bowker Co., 1978.

4. *Index on Censorship.* London: Writers and Scholars International, Ltd., published bimonthly.

5. *Limiting What Students Shall Read: Books and Other Learning Materials in Our Public Schools: How They Are Selected and How They Are Removed.* Report on a survey sponsored by Association of American Publishers, American Library Association, Association for Supervision and Curriculum Development. Washington, D.C.: Association of American Publishers, 1981.

6. Nelson, Randy F. "Banned in Boston and Elsewhere." In *The Almanac of American Letters.* Los Altos, Calif.: William Kaufmann, Inc., 1981.

7. *Newsletter on Intellectual Freedom.* Judith F. Krug, ed. Chicago, Ill.: American Library Association, Intellectual Freedom Committee, published bimonthly.

8. O'Neil, Robert M. *Classrooms in the Crossfire: The Rights and Interests of Students, Parents, Teachers, Administrators, Librarians, and the Community.* Bloomington, Ind.: Indiana University Press, 1981.

9. Tebbel, John. *A History of Book Publishing in the United States.* New York, N.Y.: Bowker Co., 1981.

1
Abelard, Pierre. *The Letters of Abelard & Heloise.* Cooper Square. U.S. Customs lifted ban on Love Letters (1930). Source: 3, p. 6.

2
Abernathy, Rev. Ralph D. *And the Walls Came Tumbling Down.* Harper. Burned in protest in

Denver, Colo. (1989) because it alleges that Martin Luther King, Jr. was involved with three women. E. Napolean Walton, publisher of the *Denver Cosmopolitan Advertiser,* stated, "[Abernathy] has his freedom of speech, and we have our freedom to burn it." Source: 7, Jan. 1990, p. 19.

3
Abrahams, Roger D. *African Folktales: Traditional Stories of the Black World.* Pantheon. Dallas, Tex. school administrators (1991) told teachers to rip an offending page from the school textbooks because the story, which refers to male genitals and bodily functions, didn't fit the curriculum. Instructors were also asked to avoid teaching the first two chapters of another book that dealt in part with circumcision and puberty. Source: 7, Nov. 1991, p. 197.

4
Adler, C. S. *Down by the River.* Coward. Removed from the Evergreen School District of Vancouver, Wash. (1983) along with twenty-nine other titles. The American Civil Liberties Union of Washington filed suit contending that the removals constituted censorship, a violation of plaintiff's rights to free speech and due process, and the acts were a violation of the state Open Meetings Act because the removal decisions were made behind closed doors. Source: 7, Nov. 1983, pp. 185-86.

5
Adoff, Arnold. *The Cabbages Are Chasing the Rabbits.* Harcourt. Challenged at the Deer Ridge, Ind. Elementary School (1992) because the book could breed intolerance for hunters in children's minds. Source: 7, May 1992, p. 94.

6
_____. *Poetry of Black America.* Harper Collins. Challenged at the Fort Walton Beach, Fla. school libraries (1996) because it "promotes violence" and contains "expletives and a reference to abortion." Source: 7, July 1996, p. 133.

7
Affabee, Eric. *Wizards, Warriors & You.* Corgi. Removed from the Fairfield, Ohio elementary school libraries (1992) because of "wizardry themes." The series of books were initially challenged because they "promote violence and acceptance and involvement in occult practices." Source: 7, Sept. 1992, p. 138; Nov. 1992, p. 185.

8
Agee, Philip. *Inside the Company: CIA Diary.* Bantam; Stonehill. U.S. Customs stopped delivery of imported copies of Agee's book (1974). Source: 3, p. 99.

9
Aho, Jennifer S., and Petras, John W. *Learning about Sex: A Guide for Children and Their Parents.* Holt. Challenged at the Hays, Kans., Public Library (1980) and the Great Bend, R.I. Public Library (1981), but retained in both libraries. Challenged, but retained, at the Washoe County Library System in Reno, Nev. (1994) because "Nobody in their right mind would give a book like that to children on their own, except the library." Source: 7, Nov. 1980, p. 138; Nov. 1981, p. 169; Sept. 1994, p. 147; Nov. 1994, pp. 200-201.

10
Alderson, Sue Ann, and Blades, Ann. *Ida and the Wool Smugglers.* Macmillan. Challenged in the Howard County, Md. school libraries (1991). The mother in the picture book was considered neglectful because she sent her daughter to the neighbors when she knew the smugglers were in the vicinity. Source: 7, Sept. 1991, p. 178.

11
Alexander, Lloyd. *The Prydain Chronicles.* Dell. Challenged as required reading at the Northbridge Mass. Middle School (1993). The complainants said that the series of fantasy novels contains religious themes that are pagan in nature and young minds would be drawn to the allure of witchcraft and black magic that runs through the books. Source: 7, Mar. 1994, p. 54.

12
_____. *The Wizard in the Tree.* Dell. After hearing impassioned pleas from parents against book banning, a Duneland School Committee in Chesterton, Ind. (1995) voted to keep the elementary school library book on the shelves. The book came under attack by a parent because a character in the story uses the words "slut" and "damn." Source: 7, Sept. 1995, p. 157.

13
Alexander, Rae Pace. *Young and Black in America.* Random. After the Minnesota Civil Liberties Union sued the Elk River, Minn. School Board (1983), the Board reversed its decision to restrict this title to students who have written permission from their parents. Source: 7, Sept. 1982, pp. 155-56; May 1983, p. 71; Sept. 1983, p. 153.

14
Alinsky, Saul. *Rules for Radicals.* Random. Challenged at the Plymouth-Canton school system in Canton, Mich. (1987) because the book holds "Lucifer or the Devil up as a role model." Source: 7, May 1987, p. 109.

15
Allard, Harry. *Bumps in the Night.* Bantam. Challenged at the South Prairie Elementary School in Tillamook, Oreg. (1989) because a medium and seances are in the story. Source: 7, Jan. 1990, pp. 4-5.

16
Allard, Harry, and Marshall, James. *The Stupids Have a Ball.* Houghton. Challenged in the Iowa City, Iowa elementary school libraries (1993) because the book reinforces negative behavior and low self-esteem, since the Stupids rejoice in their children's behavior. Source: 7, Jan. 1994, p. 35.

17
_____. *The Stupids Step Out.* Houghton. Removed from the Silver Star Elementary School in Vancouver, Wash. (1985) because "it described families in a derogatory manner and might encourage children to disobey their parents." Challenged at the Cunningham Elementary School in Beloit, Wis. (1985) because it "encourages disrespectful language." Challenged, removed, and then returned to the shelves in the Horsham, Pa. schools (1993). The book was challenged because it "makes parents look like boobs and undermines authority." Source: 7, May 1985, p. 91; Nov. 1985, p. 204; July 1993, p. 101.

18
Allen, Donald, ed. *The New American Poetry, 1945-1960.* Grove. Banned for use in Aurora, Colo. High School English classes (1976) on the grounds of "immorality." Source: 7, May 1977, p. 79; 8, pp. 128-32, 238.

19
Allende, Isabel. *The House of the Spirits.* Knopf; Bantam. Retained in the Paso Robles, Calif. High School (1994) despite objections to accounts of sexual encounters and violence. Source: 7, Sept. 1994, p. 167; Nov. 1994, p. 201.

20
Allison, Dorothy. *Bastard Out of Carolina.* NAL. Removed from the Mt. Abram High School English classes in Salem, Maine (1996) because the language and subject matter (incest and rape) were inappropriate for fifteen-year-olds. Source: 7, Mar. 1996, p. 49; Nov. 1996, p. 196; Mar. 1997, p. 39.

21
Alyson, Sasha, ed. *Young, Gay and Proud.* Alyson Pubns. Challenged at the public libraries of Saginaw, Mich. (1989) because the book promoted acts in violation of Michigan law and "appears to qualify as obscene material." Source: 7, May 1989, p. 78.

22
American Heritage Dictionary. Dell; Houghton. Removed in school libraries in Anchorage, Alaska (1976); Cedar Lake, Ind. (1976); Eldon, Mo. (1977); and Folsom, Calif. (1982) due to "objectionable language." Challenged, but retained, in the Churchill County, Nev. school libraries (1993). The controversy began after another dictionary was removed due to "objectionable language." It was removed from, and later returned to, classrooms in Washoe County, Nev. Source: 7, Sept. 1976, p. 115; Nov. 1976, p. 145; Jan. 1977, p. 7; July 1977, p. 101; Mar. 1983, p. 39; Mar. 1994, p. 71.

23
American Jewish Yearbook. Jewish Pubn. Banned from the 1983 Moscow International Book Fair along with more than fifty other books because it is "anti-Soviet." Source: 7, Nov. 1983, p. 201.

24
Ames, Lee J. *Draw 50 Monsters, Creeps, Superheroes, Demons, Dragons, Nerds, Dirts, Ghouls, Giants, Vampires, Zombies and Other Curiosa.* Doubleday. Challenged, but retained at the Battle Creek, Mich. Elementary School library (1994) despite protests from a parent who said the book is satanic. Source: 7, Nov. 1994, p. 200.

25
Anaya, Rudolfo A. *Bless Me, Ultima.* TQS Pubns. Challenged at the Porterville, Calif. high schools (1992) because the book contains "many profane and obscene references, vulgar Spanish words and glorifies witchcraft and death." Retained on the Round Rock, Tex. Independent High School reading list (1996) after a challenge that the book was too violent. Source: 7, Jan. 1993, p. 29; May 1996, p. 99.

26
Andersen, Hans Christian. *The Little Mermaid.* Harcourt. An edition with illustrations of bare-breasted mermaids was challenged in the Bedford, Tex. School District (1994) because it was "pornographic" and contained "satanic pictures." Source: 7, Nov. 1994, pp. 188-89.

27

_____. *Wonder Stories*. Houghton. Banned in Russia by Nicholas I during the "censorship terror" (1835). Ban removed in 1849. Stamped in Illinois "For Adult Readers" to make it "impossible for children to obtain smut." Source: 3, pp. 41-42.

28

Anderson, Christopher. *Madonna—Unauthorized*. Dell; Simon. Challenged at the Loveland, Colo. High School library (1993) because the book has obscenities and sexual references, and one photo with Madonna posing topless. Source: 7, July 1993, p. 97.

"I fear more harm from everybody thinking alike than from some people thinking otherwise."

~ Charles G. Bolte

29

Anderson, Jean. *The Haunting of America*. Houghton. Challenged at the Sikes Elementary School media center in Lakeland, Fla. (1985) because the collection of historical ghost stories, "would lead children to believe in demons without realizing it." Source: 7, July 1985, p. 133.

30

Anderson, Jill. *Pumsy*. Timberline Press. The Putnam City, Okla. Elementary School counselors (1989) are forbidden to use this story of a fictional dragon because it propagates the principles of "secular humanism" and "new age religion" and that its use would "drive a wedge between children and parents." Source: 7, July 1989, p. 129.

31

Anderson, Lee, et al. *Windows on Our World Series*. Houghton. Removed from Alabama's list of approved texts — and from the state's classrooms — because the book promotes the "religion of secular humanism." U.S. District Court Judge W. Brevard Hand ruled on March 4, 1987, that thirty-nine history and social studies texts used in Alabama's 129 school systems "discriminate against the very concept of religion and theistic religions in particular, by omissions so serious that a student learning history from them would not be apprised of relevant facts about America's history.... References to religion are isolated and the

integration of religion in the history of American society is ignored." The series includes: *At Home, At School; In Our Community; Ourselves and Others; Our Home; The Earth; America: Past and Present;* and *Around Our World.* On August 26, 1987, the U.S. Court of Appeals for the Eleventh Circuit unanimously overturned Judge Hand's decision by ruling that the information in the book was "essentially neutral in its religious content." The fact that the texts omitted references to religion was not "an advancement of secular humanism or an active hostility toward theistic religion." Source: 7, Jan. 1987, p. 6; May 1987, pp. 75, 104-7; Sept. 1987, pp. 166-67; Nov. 1987, pp. 217-18; Jan. 1988, p. 17; Mar. 1988, p. 40.

32

Anderson, Robert, et al. *Elements of Literature*. Holt. Retained in the Fairfax County, Va. schools (1994) despite complaints that it might "plant seeds" of violence or disobedience in students. The anthology contains stories such as Edgar Allen Poe's "The Tell-Tale Heart" and John Steinbeck's "The Pearl." Source: 7, Nov. 1994, pp. 201-02.

33

Anderson, Sherwood. *Dark Laughter*. Dynamic Learning Corp.; Liveright. Blacklisted in Boston, Mass. (1930). Source: 1, p. 137; 3, p. 62.

34

Andrews, V. C. *Dark Angel*. Pocket Bks. Removed from Oconee County, Ga. school libraries (1994) "due to the filthiness of the material." The school board voted unanimously at a later date to rescind its controversial book-banning order, but then rescinded that action and ordered the removal of the book. Source: 7, Sept. 1994, pp. 145-46; Nov. 1994, pp. 187-88, 200; Jan. 1995, p. 6.

35

_____. *Darkest Hour*. Pocket Bks. Removed from Oconee County, Ga. school libraries (1994) "due to the filthiness of the material." The school board voted unanimously at a later date to rescind its controversial book-banning order but then rescinded that action and ordered the removal of the book. Source: 7, Sept. 1994, pp. 145-46; Nov. 1994, pp. 187-88, 200; Jan. 1995, p. 6.

36

_____. *Dawn*. Pocket Bks. Removed from Oconee County, Ga. school libraries (1994) "due to the filthiness of the material." The school board voted unanimously at a later date to rescind its controversial book-banning order but then rescinded that action and ordered the removal of the book. Source: 7, Sept. 1994, pp. 145-46; Nov. 1994, pp. 187-88, 200; Jan. 1995, p. 6.

37

_____. *Flowers in the Attic.* Pocket Bks. Challenged at the Richmond, R.I. High School (1983) because the book contains offensive passages concerning incest and sexual intercourse. Removed from Oconee County, Ga. school libraries (1994) "due to the filthiness of the material." The school board voted unanimously at a later date to rescind its controversial book-banning order but then rescinded that action and ordered the removal of the book. Source: 7, Sept. 1983, p. 153; Jan. 1984, pp. 9-10; Sept. 1994, pp. 145-46; Nov. 1994, pp. 187-88, 200; Jan. 1995, p. 6.

38

_____. *Garden of Shadows.* Pocket Bks. Removed from Oconee County, Ga. school libraries (1994) "because the book encouraged sexual activity and the result of reading or seeing it might be 'incestuous relationships' and 'aggressive sexual behavior.'" The book was removed despite a recommendation from a committee of parents and teachers to retain it. The action stemmed from a complaint filed in May 1994 when eight other V. C. Andrews books were removed. Source: 7, Nov. 1994, p. 188; Jan. 1995, p. 6; July 1996, p. 117.

39

_____. *If There Be Thorns.* Pocket Bks. Challenged at the Richmond, R.I. High School (1983) because the book contains offensive passages concerning incest and sexual intercourse. Source: 7, Sept. 1983, p. 153; Jan. 1984, pp. 9-10.

40

_____. *My Sweet Audrina.* Poseidon; Simon & Schuster; Pocket Bks. Rejected for purchase by the Hayward, Calif. school trustees (1985) because of "rough language" and "explicit sex scenes." Challenged at the Lincoln Middle School in Pullman, Wash. (1990) because it deals with themes related to sexual violence. Removed from Oconee County, Ga. school libraries (1994) "due to the filthiness of the material." The school board voted unanimously at a later date to rescind its controversial book-banning order but then rescinded that action and ordered the removal of the book. Source: 7, July 1985, p. 111; July 1990, p. 145; Sept. 1994, pp. 145-46; Nov. 1994, pp. 187-88, 200; Jan. 1995, p. 6.

41

_____. *Petals on the Wind.* Pocket Bks. Challenged at the Richmond, R.I. High School (1983) because the book contains offensive passages concerning incest and sexual intercourse. Removed from Oconee County, Ga. school libraries (1994) "due to the filthiness of the material." The school board voted unanimously at a later date to rescind its controversial book-banning order but then rescinded that action and ordered the removal of the book. Source: 7, Sept. 1983, p. 153; Jan. 1984, pp. 9-10; Mar. 1984, p. 53; Sept. 1994, pp. 145-46; Nov. 1994, pp. 187-88, 200; Jan. 1995, p. 6.

42

_____. *Seeds of Yesterday.* Simon & Schuster; Pocket Bks.; NAL. Removed from Oconee County, Ga. school libraries (1994) "due to the filthiness of the material." The school board voted unanimously at a later date to rescind its controversial book-banning order but then rescinded that action and ordered the removal of the book. Source: 7, Sept. 1994, pp. 145-46; Nov. 1994, pp. 187-88, 200; Jan. 1995, p. 6.

43

_____. *Twilight's Child.* Pocket Bks. Removed from Oconee County, Ga. school libraries (1994) "due to the filthiness of the material." The school board voted unanimously at a later date to rescind its controversial book-banning order but then rescinded that action and ordered the removal of the book. Source: 7, Sept. 1994, pp. 145-46; Nov. 1994, pp. 187-88, 200; Jan. 1995, p. 6.

44

Andry, Andrew C., and Schepp, Steven. *How Babies Are Made.* Time-Life. Moved from the children's section to the adult section of the Tampa-Hillsborough, Fla. County Public Library (1981) by order of the Tampa City Council. Placed on restricted shelves at the Evergreen School District elementary school libraries in Vancouver, Wash. (1987) in accordance with the school board policy to restrict student access to sex education books in elementary school libraries. Source: 7, Jan. 1982, p. 4; May 1987, p. 87.

45

Angelou, Maya. *And Still I Rise.* Random. Challenged at the Northside High School library in Lafayette, La. (1982). Removed from the required reading list for Wake County High School juniors in Raleigh, N.C. (1987) because of complaints about a scene in which eight-year-old Maya is raped. Challenged at the Longview, Wash. school system (1987) because some "students could be harmed by its graphic language." Source: 7, May 1982, p. 83; May 1987, p 91; Sept. 1987, p. 195.

46

_____. *I Know Why the Caged Bird Sings.* Bantam. Four

members of the Alabama State Textbook Committee (1983) called for its rejection because Angelou's work preaches "bitterness and hatred against whites." Challenged at Mount Abram Regional High School in Strong, Maine (1988) because parents objected to a rape scene. Rejected as required reading for a gifted ninth grade English class in Bremerton, Wash. (1990) because of the book's "graphic" description of molestation. Removed from a Banning, Calif. eighth grade class (1991) after several parents complained about explicit passages involving child molestation and rape. Challenged at the Amador Valley High School in Pleasanton, Calif. (1992) because of sexually explicit language. Temporarily banned from the Caledonia Middle School in Columbus, Miss. (1993) on the grounds that it is too sexually explicit to be read by children. Challenged in the Haines City, Fla. High School library and English curriculum (1993) because of objections to a passage that describes the author's rape when she was seven years old. Challenged in the Hooks, Tex. High School in a freshman honors history class (1993). Retained as required reading for all of Dowling High School's sophomores in Des Moines, Iowa (1994). The book became an issue after a parent objected to what he said were inappropriately explicit sexual scenes. Challenged as part of the Ponderosa High School curriculum in Castle Rock, Colo. (1994) because it is "a lurid tale of sexual perversion." Challenged at the Westwood High School in Austin, Tex. (1994) because the book is pornographic, contains profanity, and encourages premarital sex and homosexuality. The superintendent later ruled that parents must first give their children permission to be taught potentially controversial literature. Challenged at the Carroll School in Southlake, Tex. (1995) because it was deemed "pornographic" and full of "gross evils ." Challenged, but retained on the Beech High School reading list in Hendersonville, Tenn. (195). Challenged at the Danforth High School in Wimberley, Tex. (1995). Removed from the Southwood High School Library in Caddo Parish, La. (1995) because the book's language and content were objectionable. Eventually, the book was returned after students petitioned and demonstrated against the action. Challenged, but retained in the Volusia County, Fla. County Schools (1995). The complainants wanted the book removed because "it is sexually explicit and promotes cohabitation and rape." Challenged, but retained on an optional reading list at the East Lawrence High School in Moulton, Ala. (1996). The book was challenged because the School Superintendent decided "the poet's descriptions of being raped as a little girl were pornographic." Removed from the curriculum pending a review of its content at the Gilbert, Ariz. Unified School (1995). Complaining parents said the book did not represent "traditional values." Retained on the Round Rock, Tex. Independent High School reading list (1996) after a challenge that the book was too violent. Pulled from the reading list at

Lakota High School in Cincinnati, Ohio (1996) because of parents' claims that its is too graphic. Source: 7, Mar. 1983, p. 39; Jan. 1989, p. 8; Mar. 1989, p. 38; Nov. 1990, p. 211; Mar. 1992, p. 42; July 1992, p. 109; July 1993, p. 107; Jan. 1994, p. 34; July 1994, p. 130; Jan. 1995, pp. 11, 14; Mar. 1995, p. 56; May 1995, pp. 67, 72; Sept. 1995, pp. 158-59; Nov. 1995, pp. 183, 186-87; Jan. 1996, pp. 14, 30; Mar. 1996, pp. 47, 63; May 1996, pp. 84, 99; July 1996, p. 120; Sept. 1996, pp. 152-53; Nov. 1996, pp. 197-98; Jan. 1997, p. 26.

47

Annas, Pamela, and Rosen, Robert. *Literature in Society: Introduction to Fiction, Poetry and Drama.* Prentice-Hall. Pulled from the senior literature class at the Hempfield, Pa. Area School District (1994) after it was determined that some passages were "vulgar." Source: 7, Jan. 1995, pp. 13-14; Mar. 1995, p. 44.

48

Anonymous. *Arabian Nights* or *The Thousand and One Nights.* U.S. Customs held up 500 sets of the translation by the French scholar Mardrus, which were imported from England (1927-31). Confiscated (1985) in Cairo, Egypt on the grounds that it contained obscene passages which posed a threat to the country's moral fabric. The public prosecutor demanded the book, which contains stories such as "Ali Baba and the 40 Thieves" and "Aladdin and His Magic Lamp," be "burned in a public place" and said that it was the cause of "a wave of incidents of rape which the country has recently experienced." Judged inappropriate for Jewish pupils by the Israeli director of the British Consul Library in Jerusalem, Israel (1985). Source: 3, p. 28;4, June 1985, p. 50; Aug. 1985, p. 51; Oct. 1985, p. 65;7, July 1985, p. 120.

49

Anonymous. *Caroline.* Blue Moon Bks. Removed from the Multnomah, Oreg. County Library (1991) because the novel contains graphic descriptions of sexual acts. Source: 7, Jan. 1992, p. 6.

50

Anonymous. *Go Ask Alice.* Avon; Prentice-Hall. Removed from school libraries in Kalamazoo, Mich. (1974); Levittown, N.Y. (1975); Saginaw, Mich. (1975); Eagle Pass, Tex. (1977); Trenton, N.J. (1977); North Bergen, N.J. (1980) due to "objectionable" language and explicit sexual scenes. Challenged at the Marcellus, N.Y. School District (1975); Ogden, Utah School District (1979); Safety Harbor, St. Petersburg, Fla. Middle School Library (1982) where written parental permission was required to check out the title; Osseo School District in Brooklyn Park, Minn. (1983) where a school board member found the book's language "personally offensive"; Pagosa Springs, Colo. schools (1983) because a parent objected to the "graphic language, subject matter, immoral tone, and lack of literary quality found in the book." Challenged at the Rankin County, Miss. School District (1984) because it is "profane and sexually objectionable." Challenged at the Central Gwinnett, Ga. High School library (1986) because "it encourages students to steal and take drugs." Removed from the school library shelves in Kalkaska, Mich. (1986) because the book contains "objectionable language." The Gainesville, Ga. Public Library (1986) prohibits young readers from checking out this book along with forty other books. The books, on subjects ranging from hypnosis to drug abuse to breast-feeding and sexual dysfunction, are kept in a locked room. Challenged at the King Middle School in Portland, Maine (1988). Removed from the Wall Township, N.J. Intermediate School library (1993) by the Superintendent of Schools because the book contains "inappropriate" language and "borders on pornography." Responding to an anonymous letter in 1987, the superintendent ordered the book removed from all reading lists and classroom book collections. "I thought we'd got rid of them all about five years ago," he said. Removed from an English class at Buckhannon-Upshur, W.Va. High School (1993) because of graphic language in the book. Challenged as a required reading assignment at the Johnstown, N.Y. High School (1993) because of numerous obscenities. Banned from a ninth grade reading list at Shepherd Hill High School in Dudley, Mass. (1994) because of "gross and vulgar language and graphic description of drug use and sexual conduct." Banned from the Jonathan Alder School District in Plain City, Ohio (1995). Challenged at the Houston Junior and Senior High School in Wasilla, Alaska (1995). Removed from a supplemental reading list for sophomore English students in Warm Springs, Va. (1995) because of its "profanity and indecent situations." Source: 7, Jan. 1975, p. 6; Mar. 1975, p. 41; May 1975, p. 76; July 1977, p. 100; May 1977, p. 73; May 1979, p. 49; Mar. 1980, p. 32; July 1982, p. 142; Mar. 1983, p. 52; Mar. 1984, p. 53; May 1984, p. 69; July 1986, p. 117; Sept. 1986, pp. 151-52; Nov. 1986, p. 207; Jan. 1987, p. 32; Mar. 1989, p.

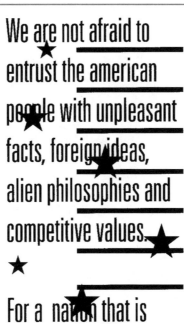

We are not afraid to ★ entrust the american people with unpleasant facts, foreign ideas, alien philosophies and competitive values. ★

★

For a nation that is afraid to let its people judge the truth and ★ falsehood in an open market is a nation that is afraid of its people.

John F Kennedy - Remarks made on the 20th anniversary of the Voice of America at H.E.W. Auditorium on February 26, 1962.

39; May 1993, p. 71; July 1993, pp. 109-10; Mar. 1994, p. 54; Sept. 1994, p. 150; July 1995, p. 94; Jan. 1996, p. 12; Mar. 1996, p. 50.

51
Anonymous. *Life: How Did It Get Here.* Jehovah's Witnesses. Challenged at the Jones Library in Amherst, Mass. (1992) because it is religious propaganda. "The book lists no authors or editors; there is no accountability for its statements." Source: 7, Sept. 1992, p. 162.

52
Anonymous. *Marisha II.* Blue Moon Bks. Removed from the Multnomah, Oreg. County Library (1991) because the novel contains graphic descriptions of sexual acts. Source: 7, Jan. 1992, p. 6.

53
Archer, Jerome W., and Schwartz, A. *A Reader for Writers.* McGraw-Hill. Removed from the Island Trees, N.Y. Union Free School District High School library in 1976 along with nine other titles because they were considered "immoral, anti-American, anti-Christian, or just plain filthy." Returned to the library after the U.S. Supreme Court ruling on June 25, 1982 in *Board of Education, Island Trees Union Free School District No. 26 et al. v. Pico et al.,* 457 U.S. 853 (1982). Source: 7, Nov. 1982, p. 197.

54
Aristophanes. *Lysistrata.* NAL; Penguin; Univ. Pr. of Virginia. U.S. Customs lifts ban (1930). In successful challenge to the Comstock Act of 1873, which empowered the Postmaster General to rule on obscenity of literature sent through the mail, Lysistrata was declared mailable. Source: 3, p. 2.

55
Arms, Karen, and Camp, Pamela S. *Biology.* Holt. Text was rejected by the superintendent of the city-county school system on the basis that it might violate a school policy forbidding the teaching of specific methods of birth control in Winston-Salem, N.C. (1980). Bowing to pressure from opponents of the textbook planned for use in a high school honors course, the Garland, Tex. Independent

School District's central textbook selection committee (1985) withdrew its recommendation because the text includes "overly explicit diagrams of sexual organs, intricate discussion of sexual stimulation, and the implication of abortion as a means of birth control." Source: 7, Nov. 1980, p. 128; July 1985, p. 114.

56
Armstrong, William Howard. *Sounder*. Harper. Challenged, but retained in the Rockingham County, N.C. schools (1996). A parent had problems with the use of the word "nigger" on page 21 and a reference to the main character, a black sharecropper, as "boy." Source: 7, Sept. 1996, p. 169; Nov. 1996, p. 212.

57
Asher, Don. *Blood Summer*. Putnam. Returned to publisher because it failed to meet literary standards in Little Rock, Ark. (1979). Source: 7, Sept. 1979, p. 104.

58
Asimov, Isaac. *In the Beginning: Science Faces God in the Book of Genesis*. Crown. Officials of the Christian Research Center requested San Diego, Calif. (1981) school administrators to keep this title out of all high school libraries because Asimov "subjects the Bible to merciless and unremitting destructive attack." Source: 7, Jan. 1982, p. 8.

59
Atwood, Margaret. *The Handmaid's Tale*. Fawcett; Houghton; Simon; G. K. Hall. Challenged as a book assignment at the Rancho Cotati High School in Rohnert Park, Calif. (1990) because it is too explicit for students. Challenged in the Waterloo, Iowa schools (1992) because of profanity, lurid passages about sex, and statements defamatory to minorities, God, women, and the disabled. Removed from the Chicopee, Mass. High School English class reading list (1993) because it contains profanity and sex. Source: 7, Jan. 1991, p. 15; July 1992, p. 126; May 1993, p. 73.

60
Auel, Jean. *Clan of the Cave Bear*. Coronet. Challenged at the Berrien Springs, Mich. High School for use in classrooms and libraries (1988) because the novel is "vulgar, profane, and sexually explicit." Banned from the Cascade Middle School library in Eugene, Oreg. (1992) after a parent complained about a rape scene. Challenged, but retained on the Moorpark High School recommended reading list in Simi Valley, Calif. (1993) despite objections that it contains "hard-core graphic sexual content." Source: 7, Jan. 1989, p. 28; July 1992, p. 107; Jan. 1994, p. 14; Mar. 1994, p. 70; May 1994, p. 99.

61
_____. *The Mammoth Hunters*. Bantam; Crown; Thorndike Pr. Challenged, but retained from the Moorpark High School recommended reading list in Simi Valley, Calif. (1993) despite objections that it contains "hard-core graphic sexual content." Source: 7, Mar. 1994, p. 70; May 1994, p. 99.

62
_____. *Plains of Passage*. Bantam; Thorndike Pr. Challenged, but retained from the Moorpark High School recommended reading list in Simi Valley, Calif. (1993) despite objections that it contains "hard-core graphic sexual content." Source: 7, Mar. 1994, p. 70; May 1994, p. 99.

63
_____. *Valley of the Horses*. Bantam; Crown. Challenged at the Bastrop, Tex. Public Library (1985) because "the book violates Texas obscenity laws." Banned from the Stroudsburg, Pa. High School library (1985) because it was "blatantly graphic, pornographic, and wholly unacceptable for a high school library." Challenged, but retained on the Moorpark High School recommended reading list in Simi Valley, Calif. (1993) despite objections that it contains "hard-core graphic sexual content." Source: 7, May 1985, pp. 75, 79; Mar. 1986, pp. 33, 64; Jan. 1994, p. 145; Mar. 1994, p. 70; May 1994, p. 99.

64
Avent, Sue. *Spells, Chants and Potions*. Contemporary Perspectives. Pulled, but later placed on reserve to children with parental permission at the Forrest Elementary School library in Newport News, Va. (1992). Source: 7, July 1992, p. 108; Sept. 1992, p. 139.

65
Aylesworth, Thomas G. *Servants of the Devil: A History of Witchcraft*. Addison-Wesley. Removed from the Cleveland, Okla. middle school libraries (1989) because witchcraft is a "religion" and that the First Amendment bars the teaching of religion in schools. Source: 7, July 1989, p. 128.

66
Babbitt, Natalie. *The Devil's Storybook*. Farrar. Returned to the Clayton, Tenn. Elementary School library (1986) shelves. The complaint against the book objected to "the total theme of the book," which makes "hell and the devil innocent and alluring." Source: 7, Mar. 1987, p. 50.

67
_____. *The Imp in the Basket*. Chatto. Challenged as required reading in the Annville-Cleona, Pa. School District

(1991) because of the story's references to demon possession. Source: 7, July 1991, p. 130.

68
Babinski, Edward T. *Leaving the Fold: Testimonials of Former Fundamentalists.* Prometheus Books. Challenged, but retained at the Anderson, S.C. County Library (1995) because the book presented fundamentalism in a negative light. Source: 7, Jan. 1996, p. 30.

69
Bach, Alice. *When the Sky Began to Roar.* Houghton. Removed from the East Junior-Senior High School library in Lincoln, Nebr. (1987) because the book "creates despair, disrespect for parents, and a sense of hopelessness." Challenged at the Seward, Nebr. Public Library (1988) because it is "obscene." Source: 7, May 1987, p. 87; May 1988, p. 85.

70
Bacon, Francis. *Advancement of Learning.* Humanities; Rowman & Littlefield. All works by Bacon were banned by the Inquisition in Spain and placed on the Sotomayor's Index (1640). Book IX of Bacon's work, dedicated to the king, was placed on the *Index Librorum Prohibitorum* in Rome, where it remained in the 1948 edition of the list. Source: 3, p. 17.

71
Bailey, Thomas A., and Kennedy, David M. *The American Pageant: A History of the Republic.* Heath. Removed (1981) from the Mississippi state-approved textbook list. Returned to the Racine, Wis. Unified School District (1984) curriculum just one week after the school board voted to ban it. Opponents of the books on the board charged that the social studies volumes contained "judgmental writing" and, in the words of one board member, "a lot more funny pictures of Republicans and nicer pictures of Democrats." Opponents also said that one text did not present an adequate analysis of the Vietnam War. Source: 7, May 1981, p. 67; July 1981, p. 93; Sept. 1984, p. 158.

72
Baker, Keith. *Who Is the Beast?* Harcourt. Temporarily removed from the Marple, Pa. schools (1994) following a verbal request from a parent who said its message offended his family's religious beliefs. Source: 7, July 1994, p. 116.

73
Baldwin, James. *Another Country.* Dial; Dell. Considered obscene, the book was banned from the New Orleans, La. Public Library (1963). After a year of litigation, it was restored. Source: 3, p. 97.

74
_____. *Blues for Mr. Charlie.* Doubleday. Challenged in Sioux Falls, S.Dak. (1980) because it's "pornographic" and it "tears down Christian principles." Source: 7, May 1980, p. 61.

75
_____. *Go Tell It on the Mountain.* Dell. Challenged as required reading in the Hudson Falls, N.Y. schools (1994) because the book has recurring themes of rape, masturbation, violence, and degrading treatment of women. Source: 7, Nov. 1994, p. 190; Jan. 1995, p. 13; Mar. 1995, p. 55.

James Baldwin (1974)

76
_____. *If Beale Street Could Talk.* Dial; NAL. Removed from the St. Paul, Oreg. High School library (1989) because the book contains obscene language and explicit descriptions of sexual activity. Source: 7, July 1989, p. 128.

77
_____. *Tell Me How Long the Train's Been Gone.* Dial; Dell. Four members of the Alabama State Textbook Committee (1983) called for its rejection because Baldwin's work preaches "bitterness and hatred against whites." Source: 7, Mar. 1983, p. 39.

78
Balian, Lorna. *Humbug Potion: An A-B-Cipher.* Abingdon. Challenged for promoting satanism and witchcraft, but retained at the Multnomah, Oreg. County Library (1991). Source: 7, Jan. 1992, p. 6.

79
Balzac, Honore de. *Droll Stories.* French & European. All works banned in Russia (1850). Droll Stories banned by Canadian Customs (1914). U.S. Customs lifts ban (1930). U.S. declares the Concord Book Catalog as obscene because it features *Droll Stories.* Source: 3, p. 39; 7, p. 140.

80
Banks, Lynne Reid. *The Indian in the Cupboard.* Avon; Doubleday. The school librarian at the Suwannee County,

Fla. Elementary School (1993) routinely erased words from books deemed objectionable. In this instance, the words "heck" and "hell" were removed. Removed from the Bemidji, Minn. school district voluntary reading list and from the school library shelves (1995) because it contains subtle stereotypes inconsistent with district diversity goals. Source: 7, May 1993, pp. 69-70; Nov. 1995, p. 183.

81

_____. *Return of the Indian.* Avon; Doubleday. Removed from the Bemidji, Minn. school district voluntary reading list and from the school library shelves (1995) because it contains subtle stereotypes inconsistent with district diversity goals. Source: 7, Nov. 1995, p. 183.

82

Bannerman, Helen. *Little Black Sambo.* Putnam; Buccaneer Bks.; Greenhouse Pubs. Removed from the open shelves of the Lincoln, Nebr. school system (1964) on the orders of the School Superintendent because of the inherent racism of the book. The superintendent relocated the book on the "Reserved" shelves, with a note explaining that while it was not "a part of the instructional program, it will be available to those who want to read it as optional material." Source: 2, p. 173.

83

Baraka, Imamu Amiri. *The Toilet.* Grove. Expurgated at Eastern High School (1969) to eliminate all "four-letter words or vernacular." Source: 7, May 1969, p. 51.

84

Bargar, Gary W. *What Happened to Mr. Foster?* Clarion. Challenged at the Greenville County, S.C. Library (1982) because the novel's principal character is a homosexual. Source: 7, Jan. 1983, p. 9.

85

Barker, Clive. *Tapping the Vein, Book 2.* Eclipse. Removed from the Multnomah, Oreg. County Library (1991) because of its graphic violence, language, and sexual content. Source: 7, Jan. 1992, p. 6.

86

Barnes, Djuna. *Ryder.* St. Martin. Seized (1984) by the British Customs Office as "indecent and obscene." Source: 7, Jan. 1985, p. 16.

87

Barth, Edna. *Witches, Pumpkins and Grinning Ghosts.* Houghton. Challenged at the Neely Elementary School in Gilbert, Ariz. (1992) because the book "interests little minds into accepting the devil with all of his evil works." Challenged in the Salem-Keizer, Oreg. school libraries (1992) because it would encourage children to experiment with witchcraft. Source: 7, May 1992, p. 78; July 1992, pp. 124-25.

88

Bass, Herbert J. *Our American Heritage.* Silver Burdett. Removed from Alabama's list of approved texts—and from the state's classrooms—because the book promotes the "religion of secular humanism." U.S. District Court Judge W. Brevard Hand ruled on March 4, 1987, that 39 history and social studies texts used in Alabama's 129 school systems "discriminate against the very concept of religion and theistic religions in particular, by omissions so serious that a student learning history from them would not be apprised of relevant facts about America's history…. References to religion are isolated and the integration of religion in the history of American society is ignored." Other texts removed included: *History of a Free People* by Henry W. Bragdon; *Teen Guide* by Valerie Chamberlain; *America Is* by Frank Freidel; *Today's Teen* by Joan Kelly; *A History of Our American Republic* by Glenn M. Linden; *Caring, Deciding and Growing* by Helen McGinley; *Homemaking: Skills for Everyday Living* by Frances Baynor Parnell; *People and Our Country* by Norman K. Risjord; *Contemporary Living* by Verdene Ryder; *Exploring Our Nation's History* by Sidney Schwartz; *These United States* by James P. Shenton; *The American Dream* by Lew Smith; *Social Studies Series* published by Scott, Foresman; and *The Rise of the American Nation* by Lewis Paul Todd. On August 26, 1987, the U.S. Court of Appeals for the Eleventh Circuit unanimously overturned Judge Hand's decision by ruling that the information in the book was "essentially neutral in its religious content." The fact that the texts omitted references to religion was not "an advancement of secular humanism or an active hostility toward theistic religion." Source: 7, Jan. 1987, p. 6; May 1987, pp. 75, 104-7; Sept. 1987, pp. 166-67; Nov. 1987, pp. 217-18; Jan. 1988, p. 17; Mar. 1988, p. 40.

89

Baudelaire, Charles. *The Flowers of Evil.* New Directions; Norton. Ban lifted in France (1949). Source: 3, p. 46.

90

Bauer, Marion Dane. *On My Honor.* Dell; Ticknor. Retained at the Orchard Hill Elementary School in Cedar Falls, Iowa (1989) after being challenged because the 1986 Newbery Honor Book contained "two swear words and one vulgarity." Challenged at the Alamo Heights, Tex. School District Elementary School (1992) because the book uses the words "hell," "damn" and "frigging." Challenged in fourth to sixth grade reading classes in Grove City, Pa. (1995) because it was "depressing." The criteria used to select the Newbery Award winning book along with a list of other books that focus on "divorce, death, suicide and defeat," was contested. Source: 7, Mar. 1990, p. 47; May 1990, p. 107; Jan. 1993, p. 13.; Sept. 1995, p. 137.

91
Bauman, Robert. *The Gentleman from Maryland: The Conscience of a Gay Conservative.* Arbor House. Challenged at the Deschutes County Library in Bend, Oreg. (1993) because it "encourages and condones" homosexuality. Source: 7, Sept. 1993, pp. 158-59.

92
Beard, Charles. *Rise of American Civilization.* Macmillan. This Pulitzer Prize winner was seized and destroyed by New Orleans, La. (1937) police. Source: 8, Vol. III, p. 650.

93
Beaumarchais, Pierre Augustin Caron de. *Barber of Seville.* Penguin. Forbidden to be performed in France (1773-1775). Source: 3, p. 32.

94
_____. *Marriage of Figaro.* Penguin. Suppressed for six years by Louis XVI at court and in public performances on the ground of profound immorality. The author was imprisoned in St. Lazare (1778). Source: 3, p. 32.

95
Beck, Robert E., ed. *Literature of the Supernatural.* McDougal, Littell. Challenged at the Jefferson County school libraries in Lakewood, Colo. (1986) because parents objected to many of the stories because they "promoted the occult, sexual promiscuity, and anti-Americanism, and that they attacked other traditional American values." The textbook is a collection of stories written by such authors as Edgar Allen Poe, O. Henry, Ray Bradbury, Dante, and Shakespeare. The Jefferson County School Board refused to ban the book. Source: 7, May 1986, p. 82; Sept. 1986, p. 173; Nov. 1986, p. 224.

96
Beisner, Monika. *Secret Spells and Curious Charms.* Farrar. Retained by the Salem-Keizer, Oreg. School Board after complaints that the book was a how-to book for satanism. Source: 7, May 1992, p. 94.

97
Belair, Richard L. *Double Take.* Morrow. Challenged in Livingston, La. (1982) due to "objectionable" language. Source:

7, May 1982, p. 83.

98
Bell, Alan P., and Weinberg, Martin S. *Homosexualities: A Study of Diversity among Men and Women.* Macmillan; Simon. Challenged at the Deschutes County Library in Bend, Oreg. (1993) because it "encourages and condones" homosexuality. Source: 7, Sept. 1993, pp. 158-59.

99
Bell, Ruth, et al. *Changing Bodies, Changing Lives.* Random. Placed in a restrictive circulation category at the Muskego, Wis. High School library (1981). Challenged in Amherst, Wis. (1982) and the York, Maine (1982) school systems. Removed from the Sandy, Oreg. Union High School library (1984) due to "foul language and disregard for a wholesome balance about human sexuality." Challenged at the William Chrisman High School in Independence, Mo. (1984) because it is "filthy." Challenged at the Boone-Madison, W.Va. Public Library (1984). Challenged at the Gray-New Gloucester, Maine High School library (1986) because the book contains first person accounts of teenagers' sexual experiences. Challenged at the Eau Claire, Wis. Memorial High School library (1992) because of its graphic language and because the book condones abortion, homosexuality, and incest. Removed from the Kenai Peninsula Borough School District libraries in Homer, Alaska (1992) because the book was too explicit. Challenged at the Council Rock School District in Bucks County, Pa. (1994) because of passages that "undermine parental authority and depict sexual relations in explicit and vulgar language." Source: 7, July 1981, p. 92; May 1982, p. 100; July 1982, p. 124; July 1984, pp. 104, 106; Sept. 1984, p. 138; Nov. 1984, p. 186; Jan. 1985, pp. 27-28; July 1986, pp. 135-36; Sept. 1992, p. 140; Mar. 1993, p. 41; Mar. 1995, p. 44.

100
Bellairs, John. *The Figure in the Shadows.* Dell; Dial. Restricted at the Dysart Unified School District libraries in El Mirage, Ariz. (1990) because of two uses of profanity and because of its link to magic. Source: 7, Jan. 1991, p. 11.

101
Belpre, Pura. *Perez and Martina.* Warne. Challenged at the Multnomah County Library in Portland, Oreg. (1988) because the death of a mouse in the story could upset children. Source: 7, Jan. 1989, p. 3.

102
Benchley, Peter. *Jaws.* Bantam; Doubleday. Removed from all school libraries in Gardner, Kans. (1978) due to sexually explicit section. Challenged at the Ogden, Utah School Dis-

trict (1979) and placed in a restricted circulation category. Removed from all elementary and middle school libraries in Clinton, N.C. (1980) due to "objectionable" language. Challenged in the Gwinnett County, Ga. public schools (1986) because of "obscene language." Source: 7, May 1978, p. 56; May 1979, p. 49; Sept. 1980, p. 99; Mar. 1987, p. 65.

103
Bender, David L., and McCuen, Gary E. *The Sexual Revolution.* Greenhaven. All sex education books were removed from the Brighton, Mich. High School library (1977). Source: 7, Sept. 1977, p. 133.

104
Benjamin, Carol Lea. *The Wicked Stepdog.* Avon. Challenged by a parent at Newman Elementary School in Billings, Mont. (1994) because of objectionable language including the words "boobs," "ass," and "smoldering kisses." Despite an appeal from parents at a meeting where the offending words were emblazoned on pickets in the audience, two trustees (1994) upheld a decision not to remove the book from the district's library shelves. Source: 7, July 1994, p. 110; Sept. 1994, p. 166.

105
Berger, Melvin. *The Supernatural: From ESP to UFOs.* John Day. Challenged, but retained at the Cleveland, Tenn. Public Library (1993) along with seventeen other books, most of which are on sex education, AIDS awareness, and some titles on the supernatural. Source: 7, Sept. 1993, p. 146.

106
Berger, Thomas. *Little Big Man.* Delacorte; Fawcett; Dell. Retained on a list of supplementary texts for honor history classes at Juanita High School in Bellevue, Wash. (1986) despite claims that the book is "full of sexual material and questionable messages and should be banned." Source: 7, Sept. 1986, p. 173.

107
Betancourt, Jeanne. *Sweet Sixteen and Never...*Bantam. Challenged in the Howard County, Md. schools (1991) because of the book's graphic depiction of teenage romance. Source: 7, Mar. 1992, p. 40.

108
The Bible. Martin Luther's translation of 1534 was burned by Papal authority in Germany in 1624. Soviet officials stated in 1926, "The section [in libraries] on religion must contain solely anti-religious books," and the Bible was not published again in the USSR until 1956. In 1952 and 1953 Fundamentalists in the U.S. attacked the Revised Standard

Version because of changes in terminology. Banned in Ethiopia (1978) as "contradictory to the ongoing revolution." Translations of the Old and New Testament were banned in Turkey (1986). Challenged by an atheist "seeking to turn the tables on the religious right," but retained at the Brooklyn Center, Minn. Independent School District (1992). The challenger stated "the lewd, indecent, and violent contents of that book are hardly suitable for young students." Challenged as "obscene and pornographic," but retained at the Noel Wien Library in Fairbanks, Alaska (1993). Challenged, but retained in the West Shore schools near Harrisburg, Pa. (1993) despite objections that it "contains language and stories that are inappropriate for children of any age, including tales of incest and murder. There are more than three hundred examples of 'obscenities' in the book." Source: 3, pp. 3-5; 4, Sept. /Oct. 1978, p. 66; July/Aug. 1986, p. 46; 7, Jan. 1993, p. 8; Mar. 1993, p. 55; Mar. 1993, p. 55; July 1993, p. 123; Jan. 1994, p. 36.

109
Billington, Ray. *Limericks: Historical and Hysterical.* Norton. Removed, but later returned to the Tokay High School library in Lodi, Calif. (1988) because it was "really inappropriate and there ought to be better books on limericks available." Source: 7, May 1989, p. 75.

110
Bing, Leon. *Do or Die.* Harper. Challenged at the Sweetwater County Library in Green River, Wyo. (1993) because the book tells young people how to become involved in a gang. The book was retained. Source: 7, Jan. 1994, p. 14; Mar. 1994, p. 70.

111
Bird, Malcolm. *The Witch's Handbook.* Macmillan. Challenged for promoting witchcraft, but retained at the Multnomah, Oreg. County Library (1991). Source: 7, Jan. 1992, p. 6.

112
Bishop, Claire H. *The Five Chinese Brothers.* Putnam. Challenged at the Spokane, Wash. School District library (1994) because it is too violent. Source: 7, Jan. 1995, p. 9.

113
Blank, Joan. *A Kid's First Book about Sex.* Down There Pr. Challenged at the Hammond, Ind. Public Library (1986) because "the book promotes immorality and promiscuity. It promotes no moral values whatsoever." Source: 7, Jan. 1987, p. 30.

114

_____. *Laugh Lines*. Grapetree Prods.; Putnam. Removed from the McKinleyville, Calif. Elementary School library (1990) for its "demeaning manner" toward individuals who read the riddles and cannot figure out the answers, rather than for its political or sexual content. Source: 7, Mar. 1991, p. 42.

115

Blatty, William P. *The Exorcist*. Bantam; Harper. Challenged at the Grinnell-Newburg, Iowa school system as "vulgar and obscene by most religious standards." Banned for use in Aurora, Colo. High School English classes (1976) on the grounds of "immorality." Source: 7, Mar. 1975, p. 41; May 1975, p. 87; May 1976, p. 70; May 1977, p. 79.

116

Blumberg, Rhoda. *Devils and Demons*. Watts. Challenged at the Newberg, Oreg. Public Library (1988) because the book was too graphic and the topic was negative and degrading. Source: 7, Jan. 1990, pp. 4-5.

117

Blume, Judy. *Are You There God? It's Me, Margaret*. Bradbury Pr. Challenged in many libraries but removed from the Gilbert, Ariz. elementary school libraries (1980), and ordered that parental consent be required for students to check out this title from the junior high school library. Restricted in Zimmerman, Minn. (1982) to students who have written permission from their parents. Challenged in Tuscaloosa, Ala. (1982) and Fond du Lac, Wis. (1982) school systems because the book is "sexually offensive and amoral"; challenged at the Xenia, Ohio school libraries (1983) because the book "is built around just two themes: sex and anti-Christian behavior." After the Minnesota Civil Liberties Union sued the Elk River, Minn. School Board (1983), the Board reversed its decision to restrict this title to students who have written permission from their parents. Challenged as profane, immoral, and offensive, but retained in the Bozeman, Mont. school libraries (1985). Source: 5 & 7, Jan. 1981, p. 9; Sept. 1982, pp. 155-56; Mar. 1983, pp. 34, 39; May 1983, p. 71; Sept. 1983, pp. 139, 153; Nov. 1983, p. 197; July 1985, p. 112.

118

_____. *Blubber*. Bradbury Pr.; Dell; Dutton. Removed from all library shelves in the Montgomery County, Md.

Judy Blume (1983)

(1980) elementary schools. Temporarily banned in Sunizona, Ariz. (1981). Challenged in the Des Moines, Iowa schools (1983) due to "objectionable" subject matter; challenged at the Smith Elementary School in Del Valle, Tex. (1983) because it contained the words "damn" and "bitch" and showed children cruelly teasing a classmate; challenged at the Xenia, Ohio school libraries (1983) because the book "undermines authority since the word 'bitch' is used in connection with a teacher"; challenged at the Akron, Ohio School District libraries (1983). Restricted at the Lindenwold, N.J. elementary school libraries (1984) because of "a problem with language." Banned, but later restricted to students with parental permission at the Peoria, Ill. School District libraries (1984) because of its strong sexual content and language, and alleged lack of social or literary value. Removed from the Hanover, Pa. School District's elementary and secondary libraries (1984), but later placed on a "restricted shelf" at middle school libraries because the book was "indecent and inappropriate." Challenged at the Casper, Wyo. school libraries (1984). Challenged as profane, immoral, and offensive, but retained in the Bozeman, Mont. school libraries (1985). Challenged at the Muskego, Wis. Elementary School (1986) because "the characters curse and the leader of the taunting (of an overweight girl) is never punished for her cruelty." Challenged at the Perry Township, Ohio elementary school libraries (1991) because in the book, "bad is never punished. Good never comes to the fore. Evil is triumphant." Source: 5 & 7, May 1980, p. 51; Mar. 1982, p. 57; May 1982, p. 84; July 1982, pp. 124, 142; May 1983, pp. 73, 85-86; July 1983, p. 121; Sept. 1983, pp. 139, 153; Nov. 1983, p. 197; Nov. 1984, p. 185; Jan. 1985, pp. 8-9; Mar. 1985, pp. 33, 42, 58; July 1985, p. 112; Jan. 1987, p. 31; Mar. 1992, p. 41; July 1992, p. 124.

119

_____. *Deenie*. Bradbury Pr. Removed from the Utah State Library bookmobile (1980) because the book contains "the vilest sexual descriptions" and if given to "the wrong kid at the wrong time (would) ruin his life." Removed from the Gilbert, Ariz. elementary school libraries (1980), and ordered that parental consent be required for students to check out this title from the junior high school library. Challenged in Orlando, Fla. (1982); challenged in the Cotati-Rohnert Park, Calif. School District (1982) because the novel allegedly undermines parental moral values. After the Minnesota Civil Liberties Union sued the Elk River, Minn. School Board (1983), the Board reversed its decision to restrict this title to students who have written permission from their parents. Banned, but later restricted to students with parental permission at the Peoria, Ill. School District libraries (1984) because of its strong sexual content and language, and alleged lack of social or literary value. Removed from the Hanover, Pa. School District's elementary and secondary libraries (1984), but later placed on a "restricted shelf" at middle school libraries because the book was "indecent and inappropriate." Challenged at the Casper, Wyo. school libraries (1984). Challenged as profane, immoral, and offensive, but retained in the Bozeman, Mont. school libraries (1985). Banned from district elementary school libraries in Gwinnett County, Ga. (1985) as "inappropriate." Returned to the elementary and junior high school library shelves in Clayton County, Ga. (1985) after school officials determined that the book is appropriate for young readers. Challenged by a parent in the Cornelius Elementary School library in Charlotte, N.C. (1996) due to the novel's sexual content. Source: 5 & 7, Nov. 1980, p. 128; Jan. 1981, p. 9; July 1982, p. 125; Sept. 1982, pp. 155-56; Jan. 1983, p. 21; May 1983, p. 71; Sept. 1983, p. 153; Jan. 1985, pp. 8-9; Mar. 1985, pp. 33, 42, 58; July 1985, p. 112; Sept. 1985, p. 151; Nov. 1985, p. 193; Jan. 186, pp. 8-9, 21; May 1996, p. 83.

120

_____. *Forever.* Bradbury Pr. Challenged at the Midvalley Junior-Senior High School in Scranton, Pa. (1982) because it contains "four-letter words and talked about masturbation, birth control, and disobedience to parents"; challenged at the Park Hill, Mo. South Junior High School library (1982) where it was housed on restricted shelves because the book promotes "the stranglehold of humanism on life in America"; challenged at the Orlando, Fla. schools (1982); the Akron, Ohio School District libraries (1983); challenged at the Howard-Suamico, Wis. High School (1983) because "it demoralizes marital sex." Challenged and eventually moved from the Holdrege, Nebr. Public Library young adult section to the adult section (1984) because the "book is pornographic and does not promote the sanctity of life, family life." Challenged at the Cedar Rapids, Iowa Public Library (1984) because it is "pornography and explores areas God didn't intend to explore outside of marriage." Placed on a restricted shelf at Patrick County, Va. School Board (1986). Challenged at the Campbell County, Wyo. school libraries (1986) because it is "pornographic" and would encourage young readers "to experiment with sexual encounters." Challenged at the Moreno Valley, Calif. Unified School District libraries

(1987) because it "contains profanity, sexual situations, and themes that allegedly encourage disrespectful behavior." Challenged at the Marshwood Junior High School classroom library in Eliot, Maine (1987) because the "book does not paint a responsible role of parents"; its "cast of sex-minded teenagers is not typical of high schoolers today"; and the "pornographic sexual exploits (in the book) are unsuitable for junior high school role models." West Hernando, Fla. Middle School principal (1988) recommended that Blume's novel be removed from school library shelves because its is "inappropriate." Placed on reserve at the Herrin, Ill. Junior High School library (1992) and can be checked out only with a parent's written permission because the novel is "sexually provocative reading." Removed from the Frost Junior High School library in Schaumburg, Ill. (1993) because "it's basically a sexual 'how-to-do' book for junior high students. It glamorizes [sex] and puts ideas in their heads." Placed on the "parental permission shelf" at the Rib Lake, Wis. high school libraries (1993) after Superintendent Ray Parks filed a "request for reconsideration" because he found the book "sexually explicit." It was subsequently confiscated by the high school principal. A federal jury in Madison, Wis. awarded $394,560 to a former Rib Lake High School guidance counselor after finding that his contract was not renewed in retaliation for speaking out against the district's material selection policy. The counselor criticized the decision of the Rib Lake High School principal to restrict student access to the novel. Removed from Mediapolis, Iowa School District libraries (1994) because it "does not promote abstinence and monogamous relationships [and] lacks any aesthetic, literary, or social value." Returned to the shelves a month later but accessible only to high school students. Removed from the Fort Clarke Middle School library in Gainesville, Fla. (1995) after a science teacher objected to its sexually explicit content and a reference to marijuana. Restricted to a reserve section of the Delta High School Library in Muncie, Ind. (1995). Parents must give their permission in writing before their children can check out the book. Challenged at the Wilton, Iowa School District for junior and senior high school students (1996) because of its sexual content. Source: 5 & 7, July 1982, pp. 124, 142; May 1982, p. 84; May 1983, pp. 85-86; Mar. 1984, p. 39; May 1984, 69; Mar. 1985, p. 59; Sept. 1985, p. 167; Mar. 1986, p. 39; Mar. 1987, pp. 66-67; July 1987, p. 125; Nov. 1987, p. 239; Mar. 1988, p. 45;

May 1992, p. 80; May 1993, p. 70; July 1993, pp. 98, 104-5; Sept. 1993, pp. 146-47; May 1994, pp. 83, 86; July 1994, p. 109; Mar. 1995, p. 56; July 1995, p. 93; ov. 1995, p. 183; May 1996, p. 97.

121

_____. *Iggie's House.* Bradbury Pr. Challenged at the Casper, Wyo. school libraries (1984). Source: 7, Mar. 1985, p. 42.

122

_____. *It's Not the End of the World.* Bradbury Pr. Restricted at the Lindenwold, N.J. elementary school libraries (1984) because of "a problem with language." Removed from the Hanover, Pa. School District's elementary and secondary libraries (1984), but later placed on a "restricted shelf" at middle school libraries because the book was "indecent and inappropriate." Challenged at the Casper, Wyo. school libraries (1984). Challenged at the Orchard Lake Elementary School library in Burnsville, Minn. (1985). Source: 7, Nov. 1984, p. 185; Jan. 1985, p. 9; Mar. 1985, p. 42; Nov. 1985, p. 203.

123

_____. *The One in the Middle Is the Green Kangaroo.* Bradbury Pr. Challenged at the Casper, Wyo. school libraries (1984). Source: 7, Mar. 1985, p. 42.

124

_____. *Otherwise Known as Sheila the Great.* Bradbury Pr. Challenged at the Casper, Wyo. school libraries (1984). Source: 7, Mar. 1985, p. 42.

125

_____. *Starring Sally J. Freedman as Herself.* Bradbury Pr. Removed from the Hanover, Pa. School District's elementary and secondary libraries (1984), but later placed on a "restricted shelf" at middle school libraries because the book was "indecent and inappropriate." Challenged at the Casper, Wyo. school libraries (1984). Challenged as profane, immoral, and offensive, but retained in the Bozeman, Mont. school libraries (1985). Source: 7, Jan. 1985, p. 9; Mar. 1985, p. 42; July 1985, p. 112.

126

_____. *Superfudge.* Bradbury Pr. Challenged at the Casper, Wyo. school libraries (1984). Challenged as profane, immoral, and offensive, but retained in the Bozeman, Mont. school libraries (1985). Source: 7, Mar. 1985, p. 42; July 1985, p. 112.

127

_____. *Then Again, Maybe I Won't.* Bradbury Pr. Challenged in many libraries but removed from the Gilbert, Ariz. elementary school libraries (1980), and ordered that parental consent be required for students to check out this title from the junior high school library. Challenged in Orlando, Fla. (1982); challenged in Tuscaloosa, Ala. (1982) because the book is "sexually offensive and amoral"; and challenged in the Harford County, Md. school systems (1982). After the Minnesota Civil Liberties Union sued the Elk River, Minn. School Board (1983), the Board reversed its decision to restrict this title to students who have written permission from their parents. Removed from all school library collections in St. Tammany Parish, La. (1984) because its "treatment of immorality and voyeurism do not provide for the growth of desirable attitudes," but later reinstated. Banned, but later restricted to students with parental permission at the Peoria, Ill. School District libraries (1984) because of its strong sexual content and language, and alleged lack of social or literary value. Challenged at the Casper, Wyo. school libraries (1984). Challenged as profane, immoral, and offensive, but retained in the Bozeman, Mont. school libraries (1985). Challenged in the Des Moines, Iowa elementary schools (1988) because of sexual content. Challenged at the Salem-Keizer, Oreg. School District (1989) because it is a "dismal tale of a young boy's inability to cope and his very inappropriate responses to the changes taking place in his life." Challenged at the elementary library in Tyrone, Pa. (1990) because the book deals with masturbation and erections, and that it explains how to drink whiskey, vodka, and gin. Source: 5 & 7, July 1982, p. 124; Sept. 1982, pp. 155-56; May 1983, p. 71; Sept. 1983, p. 153; May 1984, p. 69; July 1984, p. 121; Jan. 1985, p. 8; Mar. 1985, pp. 33, 42, 58; July 1985, p. 112; Jan 1990, pp. 4-5; July 1990, p. 127; Mar. 1991, p. 62.

128

_____. *Tiger Eyes.* Bradbury Pr. Removed from the Hanover, Pa. School District's elementary and secondary libraries (1984), but later placed on a "restricted shelf" at middle school libraries because the book was "indecent and inappropriate." Challenged at the Daleville, Ind. Elementary School library (1984) due to alleged sexual innuendo in the book. Challenged at the Casper, Wyo. school libraries (1984). Source: 7, Jan. 1985, p. 9; Mar. 1985, pp. 42, 59.

129

Boccaccio, Giovanni. *The Decameron.* AMS Pr.; Johns Hopkins Univ. Pr.; Norton; Penguin. Burned and prohibited in Italy (1497, 1559). Seized by Detroit, Mich. police (1934), still banned in Boston, Mass. (1935). Banned in U.S. (1926-

1931). Source: 4, p. 7; 6, p. 140.

130
Bode, Janet and Mack, Stan. *Heartbreak and Roses: Real Life Stories of Troubled Love.* Delacorte. Pulled from the Ouachita Parish school library in Monroe, La. (1996) because of sexual content. The Louisiana chapter of the ACLU filed a lawsuit in the federal courts on October 3, 1996, claiming that the principal and the school superintendent violated First Amendment free speech rights and also failed to follow established procedure when they removed the book. Source: 7, Sept. 1996, pp. 151-52; Jan. 1997, p. 7.

131
Bode, Janet. *View from Another Closet.* Watts. Challenged at the Niles, Mich. Community Library (1982) because the book is "a devious attempt to recruit our young people into the homosexual lifestyle." Source: 7, Jan. 1983, p. 8.

132
Bogart, Bonnie. *Ewoks Join the Flight.* Random. Challenged at the La Costa, Calif. Public Library (1987) because "every page except for three has some sort of violence — somebody gets knocked down or the Death Star is destroyed." Source: 7, July 1987, p. 125

Toni Morrison

133
Bonner, Cindy. Lily. *Algonquin.* Removed temporarily from the Richland, Pa. Middle School Library (1994) while a "Parental Guidance" program that gives parents more control over what their children read in school is explored. A local parent complained that it was "sexually explicit" and had "no moral guidance." Source: 7, Jan. 1995, p. 8; Mar. 1995, p. 41.

134
Booth, Jack. *Impressions Series.* Holt. Challenged in the Oak Harbor, Wash. school system (1987) because it "undermines parental authority, is filled with morbid, frightening imagery and involves children in witchcraft and sorcery." In addition, opponents claimed, "the series promotes Eastern and other religions to the exclusion of Christianity." Challenged at the Talent Elementary School in Phoenix, Oreg. (1988) because it "promotes witchcraft and secular humanism and lacks Christian values." Temporarily banned at the Hacienda La Puente Unified School District in Hacienda Heights, Calif.

(1989) because of morbid imagery. Removed from the East Whittier, Calif. School District (1989) because parents complained that some stories were evil and morbid. Challenged in the Coeur d'Alene, Idaho elementary schools (1989); Stockton, Calif. (1990); Redondo Beach, Calif. (1990); Yucaipa, Calif. (1990); Nashville, Tenn. (1990); Winters, Calif. (1990); Shingletown, Calif. (1990); Fairbanks, Alaska (1990); Wheaton, Ill. (1990); Albuquerque, N.Mex. (1990); Santa Fe, N.Mex. (1990); Campbell, Calif. (1990); Saratoga, Calif. (1990); Boise, Idaho (1990); Palatine, Ill. (1990); Barrington, Ill. (1990); Arlington Heights, Ill. (1990); Box Elder, S.Dak. (1990); Lakewood, N.Y. (1990); Newport, Oreg. (1991); Grass Valley, Calif (1991); Gardiner, Maine (1991); Eureka, Calif. (1991); and Willard, Ohio (1991) because the series of readers "undermines absolute truth and value, teaches situational ethics and a lack of respect for authority, and curiosity in the occult." The first editions of the series were challenged because there was too much of a Canadian emphasis. Removed in the North Marion School District in Aurora, Oreg. (1991). Challenged in Frederick County, Md. schools (1992). U.S. District Court Judge William Shubb dismissed a lawsuit in California alleging that the series violated the state and federal constitutions by promoting the "religion of witchcraft and neo-paganism." U.S. District Court Judge James B. Moran dismissed a lawsuit filed against Wheaton-Warrenville, Ill. School District (1992) by parents who claimed school officials failed to implement rules allowing their children to be excluded from using the series. Source: 7, Jan. 1988, p. 13; Jan. 1989, p. 3; Jan. 1990, p. 11; Mar. 1990, p. 46; May 1990, p. 85; Sept. 1990, pp. 160-61; Nov. 1990, p. 210; Jan. 1991, pp. 14, 16, 17, 29; Mar. 1991, pp. 46-48; July 1991, pp. 107, 131-32; Sept. 1991, p. 178; Jan. 1992, p. 9; Mar. 1992, pp. 32, 45; July 1992, pp. 110-11, 117; Sept. 1992, p. 163; Jan. 1993, pp. 11, 18.

135
Bopp, Joseph B. *Herbie Capleenies.* Addison-Wesley. Removed from the Hermiston, Oreg. Elementary School library (1982) because of the main character's activities, which included machine-gunning his boring friends and making naked snowwomen. Source: 7, July 1982, p. 124.

136
Borland, Hal. *When the Legends Die.* Bantam. Removed from the Lincoln County, Wyo. High School curriculum (1995) because of "considerable obscenities." The parent complained that there were 57 swear words in 40 consecutive pages. Source: 7, July 1995, p. 100.

137
Borten, Helen. *Halloween.* Crowell. Challenged at the Neely Elementary School in Gilbert, Ariz. (1992) because the book shows the dark side of religion through the occult, the devil, and satanism. Source: 7, May 1992, p. 78; July 1992, p. 124.

138
Bossert, Jill. *Humor 2.* Madison Square Pr. Challenged at the Sno-Isle Regional Library System in Marysville, Wash. (1992) because the jokes in the book deal with adult subjects. Source: 7, Nov. 1992, p. 185.

139
Boston Women's Health Book Collective. *Our Bodies, Ourselves.* Simon & Schuster. Removed from high school libraries in Townshend, Vt. (1975); Pinellas County, Fla. (1975); Morgantown, W.Va. (1977), and Helena, Mont. (1978). Challenged in Amherst, Wis. (1982) due to its "pornographic" nature; Three Rivers, Mich. Public Library (1982) because it "promotes homosexuality and perversion." Challenged at the William Chrisman High School in Independence, Mo. (1984) because the book is "filthy." The controversial feminist health manual was on a bookshelf in the classroom and was the personal property of the teacher. Source: 5 & 7, July 1975, p. 105; Sept. 1975, p. 138; July 1977, p. 100; Mar. 1979, p. 27; May 1982, p. 100; Mar. 1983, p. 29; July 1984, p. 106; 8, Vol. IV, p. 714.

140
Boswell, Robert. *Mystery Ride.* Harper; Knopf; Thorndike Pr. Expurgated by an apparent self-appointed censor at the Coquille, Oreg. Public Library (1994) along with several other books. Most were mysteries and romances in which single words and sexually explicit passages were whited out by a vandal who left either dots or solid ink pen lines where the words had been. Source: 7, Sept. 1994, p. 148.

141
Bower, William C. *The Living Bible.* Arno. Burned in Gastonia, N.C. (1981) because it is "a perverted commentary of the King James Version." Source: 7, July 1981, p. 105.

142
Bradbury, Ray. *Fahrenheit 451.* Ballantine. Expurgated at the Venado Middle School in Irvine, Calif. (1992). Students received copies of the book with scores of words—mostly "hells" and "damns"—blacked out. The novel is about book-burning and censorship. After receiving complaints from parents and being contacted by reporters, school officials said the censored copies would no longer be used. Source: 7, July 1992, pp. 108-9.

143
_____. *The Martian Chronicles.* Bantam. Challenged at the Haines City, Fla. High School (1982) due to several instances of profanity and the use of God's name in vain in the work. Challenged at the Newton-Conover, N.C. High School (1987) as a supplemental reading due to profanity. Challenged as required reading at the Gatlinburg-Pittman, Tenn. High School (1993) due to profanity. Source: 7, Jan. 1983, p. 22; May 1987, p. 103; Sept. 1993, p. 149.

144
Bradford, Richard. *Red Sky at Morning.* Harper. Challenged in Omak, Wash. (1979) due to "profane language." Challenged at the Big Sky High School in Missoula, Mont. (1987) because the "language was inappropriate for freshman." Source: 7, July 1979, p. 75; July 1987, p. 150.

145
Brancato, Robin. *Winning.* Bantam. Challenged at the Greeley-Evans School District in Greeley, Colo. (1986) because the book contained "obscenities, allusions to sexual references, and promoted contempt for parents and acceptance of drug use." Source: 7, Sept. 1986, p. 171.

146
Brashler, Anne. *Getting Jesus in the Mood.* Cane Hill Pr. Challenged at the Carroll County Public Library in Westminster, Md. (1992) because the widely praised short story collection is "smutty" and contains pornography aimed at Jesus Christ. Source: 7, Sept. 1992, pp. 137-38.

147
Brautigan, Richard. *The Abortion: An Historical Romance.* Pocket Bks.; Simon & Schuster. Removed from high school library in Redding, Calif. (1978) due to "unsuitable obscene and sexual references." A California state appeals court has ruled (1989) in *Wexner v. Anderson Union High School District Board of Trustees* that the school board acted improperly when it banned this book. Source: 7, Jan. 1979, p. 11; Mar. 1989, p. 52.

148
_____. *A Confederate General from Big Sur.* Delta. Removed from high school library in Redding, Calif. (1978) due to "unsuitable obscene and sexual references." A Califor-

nia state appeals court has ruled (1989) in *Wexner v. Anderson Union High School District Board of Trustees* that the school board acted improperly when it banned this book. Source: 7, Jan. 1979, p. 11; Mar. 1989, p. 52.

149

_____. *The Pill vs. the Springhill Mine Disaster.* Dell. Removed from high school library in Redding, Calif. (1978) due to "unsuitable obscene and sexual references." A California state appeals court has ruled (1989) in *Wexner v. Anderson Union High School District Board of Trustees* that the school board acted improperly when it banned this book. Removed from the shelves of the Southeast Whitfield, Ga. High School library (1988) because it includes four poems that use "inappropriate" language or have sexual connotations. Source: 7, Jan. 1979, p. 11; Jan. 1989, p. 7; Mar. 1989, p. 52.

150

_____. *The Revenge of the Lawn.* Pocket Bks. Removed from high school library in Redding, Calif. (1978) due to "unsuitable obscene and sexual references." A California state appeals court has ruled (1989) in *Wexner v. Anderson Union High School District Board of Trustees* that the school board acted improperly when it banned this book. Source: 7, Jan. 1979, p. 11; Mar. 1989, p. 52.

151

_____. *Rommel Drives on Deep into Egypt.* Delacorte; Dell. Removed from high school library in Redding, Calif. (1978) due to "unsuitable obscene and sexual references." A California state appeals court has ruled (1989) in *Wexner v. Anderson Union High School District Board of Trustees* that the school board acted improperly when it banned this book. Source: 7, Jan. 1979, p. 11; Mar. 1989, p. 52.

152

_____. *Trout Fishing in America.* Delacorte. Removed from high school library in Redding, Calif. (1978) due to "unsuitable obscene and sexual references." A California state appeals court has ruled (1989) in *Wexner v. Anderson Union High School District Board of Trustees* that the school board acted improperly when it banned this book. Source: 7, Jan. 1979, p. 11; Mar. 1989, p. 52.

153

Bredes, Don. *Hard Feelings.* Atheneum; Bantam. Removed from the Montello, Wis. High School library (1981). Challenged in Flat Rock, Mich. (1982) because of "objectionable" language. Source: 7, Sept. 1981, p. 126; Sept. 1982, p. 156.

154

Briggs, Raymond. *Father Christmas.* Coward. Removed from all elementary classrooms in Holland, Mich. (1979) after several parents complained that the work portrays Santa Claus as having a negative attitude toward Christmas. Challenged at the Albany, Oreg. Public Library (1988) because it contains cursing, drinking, and a negative image of Santa Claus. Source: 5 & 7, Jan. 1980, p. 7; Jan. 1989, p. 3.

155

Brink, Andre. *A Dry White Season.* Morrow. Banned in South Africa in Sept. 1979. The ban was lifted in Nov. 1979, but Brink was branded a "malicious writer." Source: 4, Feb. 1980, p. 73.

156

Bronstein, Leo. *El Greco.* Abrams. Retained at Maldonado Elementary School in Tucson, Ariz. (1994) after being challenged by parents who objected to nudity and "pornographic," "perverted," and "morbid" themes. Source: 7, July 1994, p. 112.

157

Brooks, Bruce. *The Moves Make the Man.* Harper. Removed from a San Lorenzo, Calif. High School reading list (1992) after a parent complained that racist terms in the dialogue were offensive to black students. Source: 7, Sept. 1992, pp. 140-41.

158

Brown, Claude. *Manchild in the Promised Land.* Macmillan; NAL. Removed from high school libraries in Waukesha, Wis. (1974); Plant City, Fla. (1976); North Jackson, Ohio (1980) due to "filth and obscenity." Challenged at the Parkrose, Oreg. High School (1987) because the content is "violent, the language offensive, and women are degraded." The protesters also questioned its relevance, claiming that Parkrose students have no need to understand life in a black ghetto. Source: 5 & 7, May 1980, p. 51; Sept. 1987, p. 176; Nov. 1987, p. 240.

159

Brown, Dee. *Bury My Heart at Wounded Knee.* Holt. Removed in Wild Rose, Wis. (1974) by a district administrator because the book was "slanted" and "if there's a possibility that something might be controversial, then why not eliminate it." Source: 7, Nov. 1974, p. 145.

160

Brown, Laurene Krasny and Brown, Marc. *Dinosaurs Divorce.* Little. Challenged at the Rebecca Minor Elementary School in Gwinnett County, Ga. (1995) because the book could offend children whose parents are going through a divorce and create fears and anxiety in children from stable families. Source: 7, Sept. 1995, p. 157.

161
Browning, Elizabeth Barrett. *Aurora Leigh*. Academy. Condemned in Boston, Mass. (1857) as "the hysterical indecencies of an erotic mind." Source: 3, p. 42.

162
Bryant, Sara Cone. *Epaminondas and His Auntie*. Houghton. Retained, but moved from the children's section to the folk life section at the Spartanburg, S.C. County Library (1989) because "the book's drawings were stereotypical and demeaning to black people." Source: 7, Nov. 1989, pp. 236-37.

163
Budbill, David. *Bones on Black Spruce Mountain*. Bantam; Dial. Challenged at the Bennington, Vt. School District (1988) because of inappropriate language. Challenged in the Gettysburg, Pa. public schools (1993) because of offensive language. Source: 7, Mar. 1989, p. 61; Mar. 1994, p. 55.

164
Bunn, Scott. *Just Hold On*. Delacorte. Banned at the Covington Junior High School in Vancouver, Wash. (1988) because the book is devoid of hope and positive role models. Source: 7, Mar. 1989, p. 61; May 1989, p. 79.

165
Bunting, Eve. *Karen Kepplewhite Is the World's Best Kisser*. Houghton; Archway. Challenged at the Little Butte Intermediate School in Eagle Point, Oreg. (1989) because the book was too mature for the elementary class students. Source: 7, Jan 1990, pp. 4-5.

166
Burgess, Anthony. *A Clockwork Orange*. Ballantine; Norton. Removed from high school classrooms in Westport, Mass. (1977) and Aurora, Colo. (1976) due to "objectionable" language; removed from two Anniston, Ala. high school libraries (1982), but later reinstated on a restricted basis. Source: 7, May 1976, p. 70; Jan. 1977, p. 8; Mar. 1983, p. 37.

167
Burroughs, Edgar Rice. *Tarzan*. Ballantine. Removed from the Los Angeles, Calif. Public Library (1929) because Tarzan was allegedly living in sin with Jane. Source: 6, p. 130.

168
Burroughs, William. *Naked Lunch*. Grove. Found obscene in

Boston, Mass. Superior Court (1965). The finding was reversed by the State Supreme Court the following year. Source: 3, p. 89.

169
Burroughs, William, and Ginsberg, Allen. *The Yage Letters*. City Lights. Banned from use in Aurora, Colo. High School English classes (1976) on the grounds of "immorality." Source: 7, May 1976, p. 70; May 1977, p. 79.

170
Buss, Fran Leeper. *Journey of the Sparrows*. Dell; Dutton. Challenged at the Carmel, Ind. Junior High School (1994) because a parent objected to profanity and language dealing with urination, rape, violence, and sex. The parent also objected to the depiction of illegal immigration. The book was retained. Source: 7, Mar. 1995, p. 43; July 1995, p. 111.

171
Butler, William. *The Butterfly Revolution*. Ballantine. Challenged as a supplemental reading list at the Fort Scott, Kans. High School library (1987) because the book "suggested dislike of the Bible, belief in atheism, vile social habits, obscene language, and plots against adult authority." Source: 7, May 1987, p. 90.

172
Butz, Arthur R. *The Hoax of the Twentieth Century*. Inst. for Hist. Rev. Removed from the shelves of the University of Calgary library (1984) by the Royal Canadian Mounted Police. Import of the book was banned, after the university bought its copy, under a Canadian law barring import of materials considered seditious, treasonable, immoral, or indecent. Source: 7, Jan. 1985, p. 15.

173
Cabell, James Branch. *Jurgen*. Dover. Prosecuted by the New York Society for the Suppression of Vice (1920). Banned in Ireland (1953). Source: 3, p. 64; 8, Vol. III, pp. 412-13.

174
Calderone, Mary S., and Ramey, James W. *Talking with Your Child about Sex: Questions and Answers for Children from Birth to Puberty*. Morrow; Random. The Gainesville, Ga. Public Library (1986) prohibits young readers from checking out this book along with forty other books. The books, on subjects ranging from hypnosis to drug abuse to breast-feeding and sexual dysfunction, are kept in a locked room. Source: 7, July 1986, p. 117; Sept. 1986, pp. 151-52; Nov. 1986, p. 207.

175
Caldwell, Erskine. *God's Little Acre.* NAL. Sued (1933) for obscenity but acquitted. Banned in Ireland (1948), and Australia (1960), and Mass. (1950) as indecent, obscene, and impure. Source: 1, p. 148; 3, p. 83; 8, Vol. III, p. 643, Vol. IV, p. 701.

176
_____. *Tobacco Road.* NAL. Banned in Ireland (1953). Source: 3, pp. 83-84.

177
Califia, Pat. *Sapphistry: The Book of Lesbian Sexuality.* Naiad Pr. Challenged as an "inappropriate" recommended text for college students at Long Beach State University, Calif. (1982). Seized and shredded (1984) by the British customs office. Source: 7, Sept. 1982, p. 158; Jan. 1985, p. 16.

178
Callen, Larry. *Just-Right Family: Cabbage Patch Kid Series.* Parker Bro. Challenged at the Rutherford County, N.C. Elementary School library (1987) because the book used ungrammatical writing. Source: 7, Nov. 1987, p. 239.

179
Calvin, John. *Civil and Canonical Law.* Forbidden by the Sorbonne in Paris (1542). Banned in England (1555). Listed as heresy in the *Index Librorum Prohibitorum* in Rome (1559 and 1564). Source: 3, p. 14.

180
Cameron, Paul. *Exposing the AIDS Scandal.* Huntington Hse. Challenged at the Downers Grove, Ill. Public Library (1990) because it is factually inaccurate and promotes common fallacies related to the disease. Source: 7, Mar. 1991, p. 61.

181
Canaday, John. *The Artist as Visionary.* Metropolitan Museum of Art. Retained at Maldonado Elementary School in Tucson, Ariz. (1994) after being challenged by parents who objected to nudity and "pornographic," "perverted," and "morbid" themes. Source: 7, July 1994, p. 112.

182
_____. *Painting in Transition: Precursors of Modern Art.*

Metropolitan Museum of Modern Art. Retained at Maldonado Elementary School in Tucson, Ariz. (1994) after being challenged by parents who objected to nudity and "pornographic," "perverted," and "morbid" themes. Source: 7, July 1994, p. 112.

183
Carle, Eric. *Draw Me a Star.* Philomel Bks. Challenged in the elementary school libraries in the Edmonds, Wash. School District (1996). The book is illustrated with highly stylized representations of a naked woman and man. Source: 7, Nov. 1996, pp. 211-12.

184
Carpenter, Edward. *Iolaus: An Anthology of Friendship.* Gale; Pagan Pr. Seized (1984) by the British Customs Office as "indecent and obscene." When first published in London in 1902, the book was not suppressed. Source: 7, Jan. 1985, p. 16.

185
Carroll, Lewis. *Alice's Adventures in Wonderland.* Ace; Bantam; Crown; Delacorte; Dover; NAL; Norton; Penguin; Random; St. Martin. Banned in China (1931) on the ground that "Animals should not use human language, and that it was disastrous to put animals and human beings on the same level." Source: 3, p. 49.

186
Carter, Alden R. *Sheila's Dying.* Putnam; Scholastic. Restricted to those in the eighth grade or above at the Pitman, N.J. Middle School library (1992) because the book promotes teenage stealing, drinking, profanity, and premarital sex. Source: 7, July 1992, p. 106; Jan. 1993, p. 27.

187
Carter, Forrest. *The Education of Little Tree.* Univ. of New Mex. Pr. Challenged, but retained at the Astoria, Oreg. Elementary School (1995). The complainants wanted the book removed because it includes profanity, mentions sex and portrays Christians as "liars, cheats and child molesters." Source: 7, Jan. 1996, p. 17; Mar. 1996, p. 64.

188
Carter, Jimmy. *Keeping Faith: Memories of a President.* Bantam. Banned from the 1983 Moscow International Book

Fair along with more than fifty other books because it is "anti-Soviet." Source: 7, Nov. 1983, p. 201.

189
Carus, Marianne. *What Joy Awaits You.* Open Court Pub. Co. The Utah State Textbook Commission (1988) declined to remove this elementary school book from its list of approved texts. The book contains essays by Plymouth settler John Smith and early American writer Washington Irving which refer to Indians as "savages" and "bloodthirsty" and was branded as racist and demeaning to contemporary Indian people. Source: 7, May 1988, p. 104.

190
Casanova de Seingalt. *Memoires (History of My Life).* Harcourt. Original manuscript confined to the German publisher's safe (1820) and never published in unexpurgated form until the twentieth century. Placed on the *Index Librorum Prohibitorum* in Rome (1834). Condemned in France (1863). Banned in Ireland (1933). Seized by police in Detroit, Mich. (1934). Banned by Mussolini (1935). Source: 3, p. 31.

191
Casey, Bernie. *Look at the People.* Doubleday. Removed from the Southport, N.C. school libraries (1980) due to inappropriate words and ideas. Source: 7, Sept. 1980, p. 100.

192
Cashdan, Linda. *It's Only Love.* Thorndike Pr. Expurgated by an apparent self-appointed censor at the Coquille, Oreg. Public Library (1994) along with several other books. Most were mysteries and romances in which single words and sexually explicit passages were whited out by a vandal who left either dots or solid ink pen lines where the words had been. Source: 7, Sept. 1994, p. 148.

193
Cavendish, Richard, ed. *Man, Myth and Magic: Illustrated Encyclopedia of Mythology, Religion and the Unknown.* Marshall Cavendish. Challenged by the "God Squad," a group of three students and their parents, at the El Camino High School in Oceanside, Calif. (1986) because the book "glorified the devil and the occult." The debate evoked interest in witchcraft books in other Oceanside school libraries. Source: 7, Sept. 1986, p. 151; Nov. 1986, p. 224; Jan. 1987, p. 9.

194
Cervantes, Saavedra Miguel de. *Don Quixote.* Methuen; NAL; Norton; Random. Placed on the Index in Madrid for one sentence: "Works of charity negligently performed are of no worth." Source: 3, p. 16.

195
Chamberlain, Wilt. *Wilt.* Warner; Macmillan. Banned from the Gaylord, Mich. Middle School library (1975) because pupils "are more interested in learning how to dribble and shoot" than in his off-court activities. Source: 5 & 7, Sept. 1975, p. 138.

196
Chambers, Aidan. *Dance on My Grave: A Life and Death in Four Parts.* Bodley Head; Harper. Challenged at the Deschutes County Library in Bend, Oreg. (1993) because it "encourages and condones" homosexuality. Source: 7, Sept. 1993, pp. 158-59.

197
Chapman, Robert L. *New Dictionary of American Slang.* Harper. Labeled and restricted at the Walled Lake School District in Commerce Township, Mich. (1994) because "This book contains words which might be offensive to the reader." Source: 7, Sept. 1994, pp. 146-47.

198
Charyn, Jerome. *Billy Budd, KGB.* Catalan Communs. Challenged at the Noel Wien Library in Fairbanks, Alaska (1992) because it was too sexually explicit and violent. Source: 7, Sept. 1992, p. 161; Nov. 1992, p. 196.

199
Chaucer, Geoffrey. *Canterbury Tales.* Bantam; Bobbs-Merrill; Doubleday; Penguin; Raintree Pubs.; NAL; Univ. of Okla. Pr. "Expurgated almost from its first appearance in America, and was still being subjected to revisions as late as 1928. Even editions available today and considered otherwise acceptable avoid some four-letter words." Removed from a senior college preparatory literature course at the Eureka, Ill. High School (1995) because some parents thought the sexual content of some of the tales was not appropriate for the students. Source: 8, Vol. II, p. 617; 7, Nov. 1995, p. 185; Jan. 1996 p. 14.

200
Chelminski, Rudolph. *Paris.* Time-Life. Nine pages, depicting Parisian nightlife and showing pictures of nude dancers, were removed by the Indian River, Fla. County school superintendent (1981). Source: 5 & 7, Mar. 1982, p. 43.

201
Chick, Jack T. *The Big Betrayal.* Chick. Banned in Canada (1981) and challenged in New Jersey (1981) as immoral and indecent anti-Catholic literature. Source: 7, Jan. 1982, pp. 24-25.

202
Childress, Alice. *A Hero Ain't Nothin' but a Sandwich.* Avon; Coward; Putnam. Removed from Island Trees School, N.Y. Union Free District High School library in 1976 along with nine other titles because they were considered "immoral, anti-American, anti-Christian, or just plain filthy." Returned to the library after the U.S. Supreme Court ruling on June 25, 1982 in *Board of Education, Island Trees Union Free School District No. 26 et al. v. Pico et al.,* 457 U.S. 853 (1982). Removed from the San Antonio, Tex. high school libraries (1978) due to "objectionable" passages, but later reinstated after teachers filed a grievance in protest; removed from the Savannah, Ga. school libraries (1978) due to "objectionable" language. Challenged at the Lamar Elementary School library in Darlington, S.C. (1994) by a parent who stated that "offensive language in the book makes it unsuitable for any children." Challenged at the Aberdeen High School in Bel Air, Md. (1994) because the novel is "racist and vulgar." Source: 7, Sept. 1978, p. 123; Nov. 1982, p. 197; July 1978, p. 87; May 1994, p. 85; Jan. 1995, p. 12.

203
_____. *Rainbow Jordan.* Avon; Coward. Challenged at the Gwinnett County, Ga. public schools (1986) because of "foul language and sexual references." Source: 7, Mar. 1987, p. 65.

204
Chopin, Kate O'Flaherty. *The Awakening.* Avon; Bantam; Norton. Banned from the St. Louis, Mo. Public Library (1899) for bringing up an indelicate subject. Source: 3, p. 53.

205
Christelow, Eileen. *Jerome and the Witchcraft Kids.* Houghton. Challenged, but retained, in the Wichita, Kans. public schools (1991) because it promotes witchcraft. Source: 7, Jan. 1992, p. 26.

206
Christopher, John. *The Prince in Waiting.* Macmillan. Challenged at the Canby, Oreg. junior high school library (1988) because it promotes "positive attitudes toward the occult and ridicule toward Christianity." Source: 7, May 1989, p. 78.

207
Christopher, Matt. *The Kid Who Only Hit Homers.* Little. Challenged at the Beaverton, Oreg. (1989) School District because the book mentions the occult, witchcraft, and astrology. Source: 7, Jan. 1990, pp. 4-5.

208
Chute, Carolyn. *The Beans of Egypt.* Harcourt; Warner. Challenged at the Oxford Hills High School in Paris, Maine (1996). A parent stated that "teachers are not qualified to explore the issues of rape, incest, suicide and mental illness contained in Chute's novel." Source: 7, Nov. 1996, p. 212.

209
Clapp, Patricia C. *Witches' Children.* Penguin. Challenged at Cannon Road Elementary School library in Silver Spring, Md. (1990) because students who read it will be encouraged "to dabble with the occult." Challenged at the Howard County, Md. schools (1991) because the book was "not appropriate positive pleasurable reading for the young age group." Source: 7, Mar. 1991, p. 43; Mar. 1992, p. 40.

210
Clark, Mary Higgins. *I'll Be Seeing You.* Simon. Challenged at the Big Spring School in Carlisle, Pa. (1994). Source: 7, Mar. 1995, p. 56.

211
Clark, Walter Van Tilburg. *The Ox Bow Incident.* NAL. Challenged in Johnston City, Ill. (1980) "because of the profanity and the use of God's name in vain." Source: 7, Sept. 1980, p. 107.

212
Clauser, Suzanne. *A Girl Named Sooner.* Hamilton; Double-day; Avon. Removed from the Stott Elementary School library in Arvada, Colo. (1988) after a parent complained that its graphic sex scenes make it inappropriate for children. Removed by decision of the school board from the library at the Jefferson, Oreg. Middle School (1991) because of its explicit sexual content. Source: 7, July 1988, p. 119; July 1992, p. 103.

213
Cleaver, Eldridge. *Soul on Ice.* Dell; McGraw-Hill. Barred (1969) from elective courses on black studies by California Superintendent of Instruction. Challenged at the Greenwich, Conn. High School library (1975) because the book is "crime provoking and anti-American as well as obscene and pornographic;" challenged at Omak, Wash. (1979) due to "profane language." Removed from Island Trees N.Y. Union Free School District High School library in 1976 along with nine other titles because they were considered "immoral, anti-American, anti-Christian, or just plain filthy." Returned to the library after the U. S. Supreme Court ruling on June 25, 1982 in *Board of Education, Island Trees Union Free School District No. 26 et al. v. Pico et al.,* 457 U. S. 853 (1982). Source: 3, p. 100; 4; 7, May 1975, p. 87; July 1979, p. 75; Nov. 1982, p. 197.

214
Cleland, John. *Fanny Hill.* Dell; Grove. Banned in Massachusetts (1821) in the first known U.S. obscenity case. The highest court in New Jersey declared as obscene (1963). Seized in Berlin (1965), burned in Manchester, England, and Japan (1965). Source: 3, p. 29; 8, Vol. I, pp. 561-62, II, p. 610.

215
Cohen, Barbara. *Unicorns in the Rain.* Atheneum. Challenged at the Jefferson County, Colo. school library (1986) because the book "puts too much emphasis on drugs and sex." Source: 7, Jan. 1987, p. 10; Mar. 1987, p. 49.

216
Cohen, Daniel. *Curses, Hexes and Spells.* Lippincott. Placed on restricted status at the Claxton, Tenn. Elementary School library (1986) because the book "contains satanic themes." Removed from the Cleveland, Okla. middle school libraries (1989) because witchcraft is a "religion" and the First Amendment bars the teaching of religion in schools. Removed from elementary school libraries in Howard County, Md. (1990) because it is virtual "how-to" manual on demon worship. Source: 7, Mar. 1987, p. 50; July 1989, p. 128; Jan. 1991, pp. 11-12.

217
_____. *The Headless Roommate and Other Tales of Terror.* M. Evans. Restricted from fourth and fifth graders at the Old Turnpike School in Tewksbury Township, N.J. (1993) because of its violence. Source: 7, July 1993, p. 100.

218
_____. *The Restless Dead: Ghostly Tales from Around the World.* Archway. Challenged at the Ochoco Elementary School in Prineville, Oreg. (1989) because the book is "totally preoccupied with the macabre, occult, and demonic activity." Source: 7, Jan. 1990, pp. 4-5.

219
_____. *Southern Fried Rat and Other Gruesome Tales.* Avon. Challenged at the Matthew Henson Middle School in Waldorf, Md. (1991) because the collection of folktales contains stories involving unusual violence, relate humorous anecdotes of drug use in school and of ways for students to cheat on exams. Source: 7, July 1991, p. 129.

220
Cole, Brock. *The Goats.* Farrar. Removed from the Housel Middle School library in Prosser, Wash. (1992) because it contains a passage describing the rescue of a naked girl. Challenged at the Timberland Regional Middle School in

Plaistow, N.H. (1994) because parents said it contained "offensive and inappropriate" language for seventh graders. Source: 7, Mar. 1993, p. 43; Jan. 1995, p. 25.

221
Cole, Joanna. *Asking about Sex and Growing Up.* Morrow. Challenged, but retained in Anchorage, Alaska School District elementary school libraries (1994) after the school board voted to "retain the book despite complaints that it is inappropriate for elementary school children and teaches values opposed to those of the majority of parents." Source: 7, May 1994, p. 97.

222
_____. *Bony-Legs.* Macmillan; Scholastic. Challenged at the Jefferson County, Colo. school library (1986) because the book deals with subjects such as "witchcraft, cannibalism, and white magic." Source: 7, Mar. 1987, p. 49.

223
_____. *How You Were Born.* Morrow. Placed on restricted shelves at the Evergreen School District elementary school libraries in Vancouver, Wash. (1987) in accordance with the school board policy to restrict student access to sex education books in elementary school libraries. Source: 7, May 1987, p. 87.

224
_____. *I'm Mad at You.* Random; Collins. Placed on "restricted access" at the North Kansas City, Mo. elementary schools (1988) because "some children might not understand the book's use of humor and sarcasm." Source: 7, July 1988, p. 121; Sept. 1988, pp. 151-52.

225
_____. *A Snake's Body.* Morrow. Challenged at the Multnomah County Library in Portland, Oreg. (1988) because the photographs of a python crushing and eating a chick would upset and sadden children. Source: 7, Jan. 1990, pp. 4-5.

226
Cole, William. *Oh, That's Ridiculous!* Penguin. Challenged as inappropriate for children and kept off the Mansfield, Ohio school library shelves (1990) for over a year after a complaint against it got lost in the shuffle of a school system reorganization. It was returned to open access in January when the Board of Education voted to retain the title. Source: 7, May 1990, p. 106.

227
Collier, James Lincoln, and Collier, Christopher. *Jump Ship to Freedom.* Delacorte; Dell. Removed from the Fairfax County,

Va. elementary school libraries (1993) because its young black hero, a slave, questions his own intelligence, refers to himself as a "nigger," and is called that by other characters. Challenged at the Nathan Hale Middle School in Crestwood, Ill. (1996) because it "was damaging to the self-esteem of young black students." Source: 7, July 1993, p. 102-3; Sept. 1993, p. 146; Jan. 1994, p. 13; Mar. 1997, p. 39.

228

_____. *My Brother Sam Is Dead.* Scholastic. Challenged at the Gwinnett County, Ga. school libraries (1984) because some of its characters use profanity. An abridged version with the profanity deleted has been substituted in the elementary school libraries. Removed from the curriculum of fifth grade classes in New Richmond, Ohio (1989) because the 1974 Newbery Honor Book contained the words "bastard," "goddamn," and "hell" and did not represent "acceptable ethical standards for fifth graders." Challenged in the Greenville County, S.C. Schools (1991) because the book uses the name of God and Jesus in a "vain and profane manner along with inappropriate sexual references." Challenged at the Walnut Elementary School in Emporia, Kans. (1993) by parents who said that it contained profanity and graphic violence. Removed from fifth grade classes at Bryant Ranch Elementary School in the Placentia-Yorba Linda, Calif. Unified School District (1994) because "the book is not G-rated. Offensive language is offensive language. Graphic violence is graphic violence, no matter what the context." Challenged, but retained at the Palmyra, Pa. area schools (1994) due to profanity and violence. Challenged in the Jefferson County Public Schools in Lakewood, Colo. (1996) because of "the persistent usage of profanity" in the book, as well as references to rape, drinking, and battlefield violence. Retained in the Antioch, Calif. elementary school libraries (1996) after a parent complained about the novel's profanity and violence. Source: 7, Sept. 1983, p. 139; Mar. 1990, p. 48; July 1991, p. 129; July 1993, pp. 126-27; Sept. 1994, p. 149; Nov. 1994, p. 190; Jan. 1995, p. 26; July 1996, p. 121; Jan. 1997, p. 25.

229

_____. *War Comes to Willy Freeman.* Delacorte. Removed from the Nettleton Math and Science Magnet School in Duluth, Minn. (1994) because of objections to the book's portrayal of African American characters as demeaning, and claims that use of the word "nigger" in the text led students to use it outside the classroom. Pulled from two classes at

Western Avenue School in Flossmoor, Ill. (1996) after a parent complained that the book "represents totally poor judgment, a complete lack of racial sensitivity and is totally inappropriate for fifth-graders. This book is an education in racism, a primer for developing prejudice." Source: 7, Sept. 1994, pp. 150-51; Jan. 1997, p. 9.

230

Collins, Jackie. *Lovers and Gamblers.* Allen; Grosset; Warner. Destroyed in Beijing, China (1988) and legal authorities threatened to bring criminal charges against the publishers. Source: 7, Jan. 1989, p. 15.

231

Collins, Jim. *Unidentified Flying Objects.* Raintree. Challenged at the Escambia County, Fla. School District (1984) because the complainant claimed the book indicated that "Ezekiel had seen a UFO when he spoke in the Bible about seeing something that looked like a wheel in the sky." Source: 7, Sept. 1984, p. 156.

232

Comfort, Alex, and Comfort, Jane. *The Facts of Love.* Ballantine; Crown. Challenged in Great Bend, Kans. Public Library (1981). Challenged at the Boise, Idaho Public Library (1982). Source: 7, Nov. 1981, p. 169; Sept. 1982, p. 155.

233

Comfort, Alex. *Joy of Sex.* Crown; Simon & Schuster. Confiscated from three bookstores by police in Lexington, Ky. (1978). Removed from the Fairhope, Ala. (1979) Public Library. Banned in Ireland (1987) to protect the young. Challenged at the Guilford Free Library, Conn. (1994), but the Board of Directors voted to reaffirm the library's circulation and book selection policies which allow all patrons access to all library materials. Source: 3, p. 93; 7, July 1979, p. 93; May 1987, p. 110; Sept. 1994, p. 165.

234

_____. *The Joy of Sex: The Cordon Bleu Guide to Lovemaking.* Crown; Pocket Bks. Removed from the Clifton, N.J. Public Library (1996) and replaced with a dummy book made of styrofoam. The library's new policy restricts to adults any material containing "patently offensive graphic illustrations or photographs of sexual or excretory activities or contact as measured by contemporary community standards for minors." Source: 7, July 1996, pp. 118-19.

235

_____. *More Joy of Sex.* Crown. Confiscated from three bookstores by police in Lexington, Ky. (1978). Removed from the Fairhope, Ala. (1979) Public Library. Restricted to patrons over 18 years of age at the Main Memorial Library in Clifton, N.J. (1996). The book is hidden behind the checkout counter and on the shelves is a dummy book jacket. The book was described as hard-core pornography by the complainant. Source: 3, p. 93; 7, July 1979, p. 93; Mar. 1996, p. 63; May 1996, p. 83.

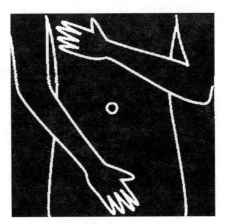

236

Confucius. *Analects.* Dover; Random. The first ruler of the Chin Dynasty, wishing to abolish the feudal system, consigned to the flames all books relating to the teaching of Confucius; he also buried alive hundreds of his disciples (250 B.C.). Source: 3, p. 1.

237

Conley, Jane Leslie. *Crazy Lady.* Harper. Challenged at the Prospect Heights, Ill. school libraries (1996) because of "swear words." Source: 7, Mar. 1996, p. 46.

238

Conner, Macet Al, and Contreras, Gerry. *You and Your Family.* Bowmar. Challenged and nearly banned from the Allentown, Pa. schools (1982) because the book asked questions about the students' families, e.g., "Every family has rules. Who makes rules in your family?" Source: 7, Mar. 1983, p. 52.

239

Conniff, Richard. *The Devil's Book of Verse.* Dodd. Publication canceled by Dodd, Mead & Company (1983) because of language in the book considered "objectionable" by Thomas Nelson, Inc. of Nashville, Tenn. — Dodd, Mead's parent company. Source: 7, Nov. 1983, p. 188.

240

Conrad, Joseph. *The Nigger of the Narcissus.* Norton. Challenged in the Waukegan, Ill. School District (1984) because Conrad's work uses the word "nigger." Source: 7, July 1984, p. 105.

241

Conrad, Pam. *Holding Me Here.* Bantam. Challenged at the Lynchburg, Va. school libraries (1991) because the book contains "cursing and profane language and uses God's name" in

a slanderous manner. Source: 7, Sept. 1991, p. 178.

242

Conran, Shirley. *Lace.* Simon & Schuster. Challenged at the Covington, La. Public Library (1984) as "pornographic." The complainant checked the book out after watching the TV series and found that while the TV program had been tastefully done, in the book "pornographic styling [was] unnecessary." Source: 7, July 1984, p. 103.

243

Conroy, Pat. *The Great Santini.* Bantam. Removed from the Eagan High School classroom in Burnsville, Minn. (1992). Challenged, but retained on the Guilderland, N.Y. High School's list of approved reading materials (1993). A student filed the complaint stating that it was offensive and inappropriate for students his age. Challenged as "obscene and pornographic," but retained in the Anaheim, Calif. Union High School District (1993). Source: 7, Mar. 1993, p.56; Mar. 1993, p. 56; Sept. 1993, p. 160; Nov. 1993, pp. 192-93; Jan. 1994, p. 14.

244

_____. *The Lords of Discipline.* Bantam. Challenged in the Cobb County, Ga. schools (1992) because of passages that include profane language and describe sadomasochistic acts. Removed from an elective English course by the Westonka, Minn. School Board (1992) after parents complained about bad language and sex in the story. Source: 7, July 1992, p. 110; Mar. 1993, p. 44.

245

_____. *The Prince of Tides.* Bantam; Houghton. Removed as a reading assignment for an advanced English class at the St. Andres Parish, S.C. Public School (1988) because it is "trashy pulp pornography." Following the challenge, the school board passed a resolution urging teachers to "use professional judgement and discretion in selecting works. . which… contain passages which most people would find abhorrent." Source: 7, May 1988, p. 89.

246

_____. *The Water Is Wide.* Bantam. Challenged in the Greenville County, S.C. schools (1991) because the book uses the name of God and Jesus in a "vain and profane manner along with inappropriate sexual references." Source: 7, July 1991, p. 130.

247
Cook, Robin. *Coma.* NAL. Removed from Big Spring High School English classes in Newville, Pa. (1992), but retained in the library. The decision came in response to complaints that the book is obscene and encourages the maltreatment of women and "radical feminism." Source: 7, Jan. 1993, p. 13; Mar. 1993, p. 44.

248
Cooke, John Peyton. *The Lake.* Avon. Challenged for having too much violence, but retained at the Multnomah, Oreg. County Library (1991). Source: 7, Jan. 1992, p. 6.

249
Cooney, Nancy H. *Sex, Sexuality and You: A Handbook for Growing Christians.* W. C. Brown. Because of its approach to abortion, the book was removed from the library shelves of the Roman Catholic chancery of Worcester, Mass. (1985), dropped from their sex education program, and is no longer used as a reference source. Source: 7, Mar. 1986, pp. 38-39.

250
Cormier, Robert. *After the First Death.* Pantheon. Challenged as an assigned ninth grade reading in the Troutdale, Oreg. schools (1989) because of the book's portrayal of teen suicide as well as the way the U.S. Army and the Palestine Liberation Organization were depicted. Source: 7, Mar. 1990, p. 63.

251
_____. *The Chocolate War.* Dell; Pantheon. Challenged and temporarily removed from the English curriculum in two Lapeer, Mich. high schools (1981) because of "offensive language and explicit descriptions of sexual situations in the book." Removed from the Liberty High School in Westminster, Md. (1982) due to the book's "foul language," portrayal of violence and degradation of schools and teachers. Challenged at the Richmond, R.I. High School (1983) because the book was deemed "pornographic" and "repulsive." Banned from the Richland Two School District middle school libraries in Columbia, S.C. (1984) due to "language problems," but later reinstated for eighth graders only. Removed from the Lake Havasu, Ariz. High School freshman reading list (1984). The school district board charged the Havasu teachers with failing to set good examples for students, fostering disrespect in the classroom, and failing to support the board. Challenged at the Cornwall, N.Y. High School (1985) because the novel is "humanistic and destructive of religious and moral beliefs and of national spirit." Banned from the Stroudsburg, Pa. High School library (1985) because it was "blatantly graphic, pornographic and wholly unacceptable for a high school library." Challenged at Barnstable High School in Hyannis, Mass. (1986) because of

the novel's profanity, "obscene references to masturbation and sexual fantasies," and "ultimately because of its pessimistic ending." The novel, complainants said, fostered negative impressions of authority, of school systems, and of religious schools. Removed from the Panama City, Fla. school classrooms and libraries (1986) because of "offensive" language. Challenged at the Moreno Valley, Calif. Unified School District libraries (1987) because it "contains profanity, sexual situations, and themes that allegedly encourage disrespectful behavior." West Hernando, Fla. Middle School principal (1988) recommended that Cormier's novel be removed from the school library shelves because it is "inappropriate." Suspended from classroom use, pending review, at the Woodsville High School in Haverhill, N.H. (1990) because the novel contains expletives, references to masturbation and sexual fantasies, and derogatory characterizations of a teacher and of religious ceremonies. Challenged as suitable curriculum material in the Harwinton and Burlington, Conn. schools (1990) because it contained profanity and subject matter that set bad examples and gave students negative views of life. Challenged at the New Milford, Conn. schools (1992) because the novel contains language, sexual references, violence, subjectivity, and negativism that are harmful to students. Challenged in the Kyrene, Ariz. elementary schools (1993) because of a masturbation scene. Returned to the Hephzibah High School tenth grade reading list in Augusta, Ga. (1994) after the complainant said, "I don't see anything educational about that book. If they ever send a book like that home with one of my daughters again I will personally burn it and throw the ashes on the principal's desk." Challenged as required reading in the Hudson Falls, N.Y. schools (1994) because the book has recurring themes of rape, masturbation, violence, and degrading treatment of women. Challenged at the Nauset Regional Middle School in Orleans, Mass. (1995) due to profanity and sexually explicit language. Removed from the Grosse Pointe, Mich. School District library shelves (1995) because it deals with "gangs, peer pressure, and learning to make your own decisions." Challenged in the Stroudsburg, Pa. high school (1995) because it fosters disobedience. Removed from the East Stroudsburg, Pa. ninth grade curriculum (1996) after complaints about the novel's language and content. Removed from the middle school libraries in the Riverside, Calif. Unified School District (1996) as inappropriate for seventh- and eighth- graders to read without class discussion due to mature themes, sexual situations, and smoking. Source: 5 & 7, Mar. 1981, p. 48; Sept. 1982, p. 156; Sept. 1983 p. 152; Sept. 1984, p. 138; Jan. 1985, p. 10; Mar. 1985, p. 45; May 1985, p. 79; May 1986, p. 79; Nov. 1986, p. 209; July 1987, pp. 125, 126-28; Sept. 1987, pp. 168-69, Mar. 1988, p. 45; May 1990, p. 87; Mar. 1991, p. 44; May 1991, p. 90; May 1992, pp. 96-97; Jan. 1994, p. 34; July 1994, p. 130;

Nov. 1994, p. 190; Jan. 1995, p. 13; Mar. 1995, p. 55; May 1995, p. 70; July 1995, p. 94; Nov. 1995, p. 184; May 1996, p. 99; July 1996, p. 82; Nov. 1996, p. 198.

252

————. *Fade.* Delacorte; Dell. Challenged in the Campbell County, Wyo. junior high schools (1990) because of sexual and violent themes. Source: 7, Jan. 1991, p. 13; Mar. 1991, p. 62.

253

————. *I Am the Cheese.* Pantheon. Challenged at the Cornwall, N.Y. High School (1985) because the novel is "humanistic and destructive of religious and moral beliefs and of national spirit." Banned from the Bay County's four middle schools and three high schools in Panama City, Fla. (1986) because of "offensive" language. The controversy snowballed further on May 7, 1987 when 64 works of literature were banned from classroom teaching at Bay and Mosley High Schools by the Bay County school superintendent. After 44 parents filed a suit against the district claiming that its instructional aids policy denies constitutional rights, the Bay County School Board reinstated the books. "Banned" from Bay High School: *A Farewell to Arms* by Ernest Hemingway; *The Great Gatsby* by F. Scott Fitzgerald; *Intruder in the Dust* by William Faulkner; *Lost Horizon* by James Hilton; *Oedipus Rex* by Sophocles; *The Red Badge of Courage* by Stephen Crane; *A Separate Peace* by John Knowles; *Shane* by Jack Shaefer; *Three Comedies of American Life,* edited by Joseph Mersand. "Banned" from Mosley High School: *Adventures in English Literature* by Patrick Murray; *After the First Death* by Robert Cormier; *Alas, Babylon* by Pat Frank; *Animal Farm* by George Orwell; *Arrangement in Literature* by Edmund J. Farrell; *The Autobiography of Benjamin Franklin; Best Short Stories* edited by Raymond Harris; *Brave New World* by Aldous Huxley; *The Call of the Wild* by Jack London; *The Canterbury Tales* by Geoffrey Chaucer; *The Crucible* by Arthur Miller; *Death Be Not Proud*

Last year, Borders created signage as a merchandising tool to draw attention to in-store displays which featured books that have been banned and/or challenged throughout the years. Borders believes that Banned Books Week offers a unique opportunity to educate ourselves and customers through demonstrating the harms of censorship.

Stores were provided with a full list of banned/challenged books; then given the freedom to create displays to best suit their store's individual character.

Even though Banned Books Week only covers one week we felt it appropriate to encourage stores to leave their display up for longer as an informational service to our customers.

Many of our stores held events such as reading discussion groups and author speaking engagements to highlight this important promotion. We encouraged all of our stores to "Celebrate the Freedom to Read" by focusing on the impact that censorship plays in our lives. A number of our stores devoted their window display space as well as several areas of the store to bring attention to this issue.

by John Gunther; *Deathwatch* by Robb White; *Desire under the Elms, The Emperor Jones,* and *Long Day's Journey into Night* by Eugene O'Neill; *Exploring Life through Literature* by Edmund J. Farrell; *Fahrenheit 451* by Ray Bradbury; *The Fixer* by Bernard Malamud; *Ghosts and Miss Julie,* by August Strindberg; *The Glass Menagerie* by Tennessee Williams; *Great Expectations* by Charles Dickens; *The Great Gatsby* by F. Scott Fitzgerald; *Growing Up* by Russell Baker; *Hamlet, King Lear, The Merchant of Venice* and *Twelfth Night* by William Shakespeare; *Hippolytus* by Euripides; *In Cold Blood* by Truman Capote; *The Inferno* by Dante; *The Little Foxes* by Lillian Hellman; *Lord of the Flies* by William Golding; *Major British Writers* by G. B. Harrison; *The Man Who Came to Dinner* by George S. Kaufman and Moss Hart; *The Mayor of Casterbridge* by Thomas Hardy; *McTeague* by Frank Norris; *Mister Roberts* by Thomas O. Heggen; *The Oedipus Plays of Sophocles; Of Mice and Men* and *The Pearl* by John Steinbeck; *The Old Man and the Sea* by Ernest Hemingway; *On Baile's Strand* by W. B. Yeats; *The Outsiders* by S. E. Hinton; *Player Piano* by Kurt Vonnegut; *The Prince and the Pauper* by Mark Twain; *Prometheus Unbound* by Percy Bysshe Shelley; *Tale Blazer Library* and *A Raisin in the Sun* by Lorraine Hansberry; *To Kill a Mockingbird* by Harper Lee; *Watership Down* by Richard Adams; *Winterset* by Maxwell Anderson; *Wuthering Heights* by Charlotte Bronte; *The Red Badge of Courage* by Stephen Crane; *A Separate Peace* by John Knowles. Source: 7, Mar. 1985, p. 45; Nov. 1986, p. 209; Mar. 1987, p. 52; July 1987, pp. 126-28; Sept. 1987, pp. 168-69; Nov. 1987, p. 224.

254

————. *We All Fall Down.* Dell. Pulled from elementary and junior high school libraries in Stockton, Calif. (1994) after parents complained that it glorifies alcoholism and violence, contains a violent rape scene, and its characters use too much profanity. Source: 7, Mar. 1995, p. 39.

255
Corsaro, Maria, and Korzeniowsky, Carole. *Woman's Guide to a Safe Abortion.* Holt. Challenged at the Walpole, Mass. Public Library (1984) because the book is "inaccurate factually, because it is deliberately misleading and deceitful, and because its avowed purpose is to promote a behavior — killing unborn babies… By maintaining and displaying this material at public expense, to the public, and in particular to pregnant women who are vulnerable and may be in need of real guidance, the Walpole Public Library is promoting and abetting abortion." Source: 7, Nov. 1984, p. 184.

256
Cory, Donald Webster. *Homosexuality in America.* Watts. Returned to shelves of the Horry County School District middle school libraries in Conway, S.C. (1989) after an attorney advised that the 1988 state health education law did not prohibit books on homosexuality and abortion. Other titles temporarily removed include: *The Abortion Controversy in America,* by Carol Emmens; *Kids Having Kids,* by Janet Bode; and *Who They Are: The Right-to-Lifers,* by C. Paige. Source: 7, July 1989, p. 143.

257
Cottrell, Randall. *Wellness: Stress Management.* Dushkin Pub. Rejected as a supplemental health book in the Eagle Point, Oreg. schools (1992) because three women complained that the book cited yoga and Transcendental Meditation as ways to reduce stress, but failed to mention Christian prayer. Source: 7, Jan. 1993, p. 12.

258
Courtney, Bryce. *The Power of One.* Ballantine. Retained on the Round Rock, Tex. Independent High School reading list (1996) after a challenge that the book was too violent. Source: 7, May 1996, p. 99.

259
Coville, Bruce. *The Dragonslayers.* Pocket Bks. Challenged in the Berkeley County, S.C. School District (1995) because of the "witchcraft" and "deception" and because a "main character openly disobeys his parents." Source: 7, Mar. 1996, p. 63.

260
_____. *Jeremy Thatcher, Dragon Hatcher.* Harcourt. Returned to the shelves of the Fairview Elementary and Carroll, Iowa Middle School libraries (1993) after an "avalanche" of appeals overturned a Reconsideration of Instructional Materials Committee decision that the book be removed from the libraries because it "was not forthright wit h the message it intended to present." Source: 7, Nov. 1993, p. 191.

261
_____. *My Teacher Glows in the Dark.* Pocket Bks. Contested in the classrooms and school libraries in Palmdale, Calif. (1995) because the book includes the words "armpit farts" and "farting." Source: 7, Mar. 1996, p. 45.

262
_____. *My Teacher Is an Alien.* Pocket Bks. Challenged in the Elizabethtown, Pa. schools (1994) because it demeans teachers and parents as dumb and portrays the main character as handling a problem on her own, rather than relying on the help of others. Source: 7, Mar. 1995, p. 44.

263
Coward, Noel. *Blithe Spirit.* Grove. Challenged in the Springfield, Oreg. schools (1989) because the play encourages occult activities. Source: 7, Mar. 1990, p. 63.

264
Cox, R. David. *Student Critic.* Winthrop Publishers. Expurgated in Warsaw, Ind. (1979) to remove four pages of a story entitled "A Chip off the Old Block" because the story contains the words "damn" and "hell." Source: 7, May 1979, p. 64.

265
Crichton, Michael. *Congo.* Ballantine. Challenged as an optional text in an Yerba Buena, Calif. High School interdisciplinary course (1995) by the father of two black students who said it is part of racially discriminatory practices. The parent has filed an $8 million civil rights suit against the school district. Source: 7, Jan. 1996, p. 13.

266
Crowley, Aleister. *Magick in Theory and Practice.* Routledge. Challenged at the Dalles-Wasco, Oreg. County Public Library (1988) because the book promotes criminal activity in its depiction of human and animal sacrifice. Source: 7, Jan. 1989, p. 15.

267
Crutcher, Chris. *Athletic Shorts.* Dell; Greenwillow; Thorndike Pr. Challenged at the Charleston County, S.C. School library (1995) because the books deals with divorce, violence, AIDS and homosexuality. Source: 7, July 1995, p. 94.

268
_____. *Running Loose.* Dell; Greenwillow. Challenged at the Gwinnett County, Ga. public schools (1986) because of its discussion of sex. Source: 7, Mar. 1987, p. 65.

269
Currie, Ian. *You Cannot Die.* Methuen. Challenged at the Plymouth-Canton school system in Canton, Mich. (1987) because the book is "not only offensive to our faith, but it is a dangerous teaching to children today when the suicide rate is so high." Source: 7, May 1987, p. 110.

270
Curry, Hayden, and Clifford, Denis. *A Legal Guide for Lesbian and Gay Couples.* Nolo Pr. Challenged at the Deschutes County Library in Bend, Oreg. (1993) because it "encourages and condones" homosexuality. Source: 7, Sept. 1993, pp. 158-59.

271
Curtis, Helena. *Biology.* Worth. San Diego, Calif. school system (1982) was threatened with a law suit unless the book was removed because "it treats the topic of evolution in a dogmatic manner." Source: 7, Mar. 1983, p. 40.

272
Cusack, Isabel. *Mr. Wheatfield's Loft.* Holt. Challenged at the Springfield, Oreg. (1988) Public Library because of profanity and the appearance of the subject of prostitution. Source: 7, Jan. 1990, pp. 4-5.

273
Dacey, John S. *Adolescents Today.* Scott, Foresman. The Norwin, Pa. School Board (1985) decided to retain the textbook used in the district's tenth grade health classes despite accusations that it is amoral, anti-family, and has a Marxist bent. A group of nineteen parents filed a federal lawsuit in March 1987. The suit charged that in the book abstaining from sex until marriage is portrayed unfavorably, birth control techniques are evaluated, and homosexuality is taught as a natural stage of sexual development. Source: 7, July 1985, p. 135; July 1987, p. 131.

274
Dahl, Roald. *The BFG.* Farrar. Challenged at the Amana, Iowa first grade curriculum (1987) because the book was "too sophisticated and did not teach moral values." Source: 7, Sept. 1987, pp. 194-95.

275
_____. *Charlie and the Chocolate Factory.* Bantam; Knopf; Penguin. Removed from a locked reference collection at the Boulder, Colo. Public Library (1988). The book was originally locked away because the librarian thought the book espouses a poor philosophy of life. Source: 7, Jan. 1989, p. 27.

276
_____. *The Enormous Crocodile.* Caedmon; Knopf. Challenged at the Multnomah County Library in Portland, Oreg. (1988) because of the book's sinister nature and the negative action of animals. Source: 7, Jan. 1989, p. 3.

277
_____. *George's Marvelous Medicine.* Bantam; Puffin. Challenged at the Stafford County, Va. Schools (1995) because the book "posed a safety threat because the boy in the story warms household items, such as paint thinner and soap, to make a potion." Source: 7, Sept. 1995, pp. 159-60.

278
_____. *James and the Giant Peach.* ABC-Clio; Knopf. Challenged at the Deep Creek Elementary School in Charlotte Harbor, Fla. (1991) because it is "not appropriate reading material for young children." Challenged at the Pederson Elementary School in Altoona, Wis. (1991) because the book uses the word "ass" and parts of the book deal with wine, tobacco, and snuff. Challenged at the Morton Elementary School library in Brooksville, Fla. (1992) because the book contains a foul word and promotes drugs and whiskey. Challenged at the Stafford County, Va. Schools (1995) because the tale contains crude language and encourages children to disobey their parents and other adults. The book was removed from the classrooms and placed in the library, where access was restricted. Source: 7, July 1991, p. 108; Mar. 1992, p. 65 ; Jan. 1993, p. 27; Sept. 1995, p. 160.

279
_____. *Matilda.* Harper; Puffin; Viking. Retained on the shelves in the Grand Rapids, Mich. school libraries (1993), but not allowed to be read in the elementary classrooms. Ten parents complained about the book, calling it offensive and "appalling in its disrespect for adult figures and children." Challenged, but retained in the Margaret Chase Smith School library in Skowhegan, Maine (1994) after the complainant came to understand that attaching a warning label would also amount to censorship. Challenged at the Stafford County, Va. Schools (1995) because the tale contains crude language and encourages children to disobey their parents and other adults. The book was removed from the classrooms and placed in the library, where access was restricted. Source: 7, Nov. 1993, p. 179; May 1994, p. 98; Sept. 1995, p. 160.

280
_____. *The Minipins.* Viking. Challenged at the Stafford County, Va. Schools (1995) because the tale contains crude language and encourages children to disobey their parents and other adults. The book was removed from the class-

rooms and placed in the library, where access was restricted. Source: 7, Sept. 1995, p. 160.

281

_____. *Revolting Rhymes.* Bantam. Challenged at the Northeast High School in Goose Lake, Iowa (1990) because of its alleged violence, the use of the word "slut," and the subject of witches. Banned in the Rockland, Mass. elementary schools (1992) after a parent complained that the book of fractured fairy tales was offensive and inappropriate for children. Challenged at the Stafford County, Va. Schools (1995) because the book spoofs nursery rhymes. Source: 7, May 1990, p. 105; Jan. 1993, p. 8; Sept. 1995, pp. 159-60.

282

_____. *Rhyme Stew.* Viking. Moved from the children's section to the adult section at the Dover, Del. Public Library (1990). The complainant called for the establishment of a national rating system similar to that of the motion picture industry that would classify books according to local community standards. Source: 7, Mar. 1991, p. 42.

283

_____. *The Witches.* Farrar; Penguin. Challenged at the Amana, Iowa first grade curriculum because the book was "too sophisticated and did not teach moral values." Challenged at the Goose Lake, Iowa Elementary School (1990) because of its alleged violence, the use of the word "slut," the subject of witches, and the fact that "the boy who is turned into a mouse by the witches will have to stay a mouse for the rest of his life." Challenged at the Dallas, Oreg. Elementary School library (1991) because the book entices impressionable or emotionally disturbed children into becoming involved in witchcraft or the occult. Placed on a library restricted list by the Escondido, Calif. Union Elementary School District (1992) after four parents filed complaints that it promoted the occult and was too frightening. Challenged at the La Mesa-Spring Valley, Calif. School District (1992) because it includes horrifying depictions of witches as ordinary-looking women, against whom there is no defense. Other opponents added that it promotes the religion of Wicca, or witchcraft. Challenged in the Spencer, Wis. schools (1993) because it desensitizes children to crimes related to witchcraft. Returned to the shelves of the Escondido, Calif. Union School District school libraries (1993) after the school board lifted a partial ban. A complaint was filed by four parents who stated the book promoted satanism. The district still retains bans on four books, including *Halloween ABC*, which some parents charged with promoting the occult. Challenged at Pine Forge Elementary School in the Boyertown, Pa. area (1993). Challenged, but retained at the Battle Creek, Mich. Elementary School library (1994)

despite the protests from a parent who said the book is satanic. Challenged at the Stafford County, Va. Schools (1995) because the tale contains crude language and encourages children to disobey their parents and other adults. The book was to be removed from the classrooms and placed in the library, where access could be restricted. Source: 7, Sept. 1987, pp. 194-95; May 1990, p. 105; Jan. 1992, p. 26; May 1992, pp. 78-79; Nov. 1992, pp. 196-97; July 1993, p. 127; Sept. 1993, p. 157; May 1994, p. 85; Nov. 1994, p. 200; Sept. 1995, p. 160.

284

Dahrendorf, Ralf. *Class and Class Conflict in Industrial Society.* Stanford Univ. Pr. Banned in South Korea (1985). Source: 4, April 1986, pp. 30-33.

285

Dakin, Edwin. *Mrs. Eddy.* Scribner. The Christian Science Church attempted to suppress this biography of Mary Baker Eddy, the Church's founder, by demanding its withdrawal from sale. Source: 9, Vol. III, p. 418.

286

Dalrymple, Douglas J., and Parsons, Leonard J. *Marketing Management: Text and Cases.* Wiley. Seven pages of this book were expurgated at the University of Nebraska-Omaha (1981) because they contain a case study dealing with a firm that sells contraceptive devices. Source: 7, Jan. 1982, p. 19.

287

Dalrymple, Willard. *Sex Is for Real.* McGraw-Hill. Banned from the Brighton, Mich. (1977) High School library along with all the other sex education materials. Source: 7, Sept. 1977, p. 133.

288

Dante Alighieri. *The Divine Comedy.* Norton; Pocket Bks.; Random; Regnery. Burned in Florence, Italy (1497). Prohibited by Church authorities in 1581 in Lisbon, Portugal until all copies were delivered to the Inquisition for correction. Banned in Ethiopia (1978). Source: 3, p. 6; 4, Sept./Oct. 1978, p. 66.

289

Darwin, Charles B. *On the Origin of Species.* Harvard Univ. Pr.; Macmillan; Modern Library; NAL; Norton; Penguin; Rowman; Ungar. Banned from Trinity College in Cambridge, UK (1859); Yugoslavia (1935); Greece (1937). The teaching of evolution was prohibited in Tennessee from 1925-1967. Source: 3, p. 42.

290
Davis, Jenny. *Sex Education.* Dell. Challenged at Hughes Junior High School in Bismarck, N.Dak. (1993) because it is "offensive." Source: 7, Sept. 1993, p. 145.

291
Davis, Jim. *Garfield: His Nine Lives.* Ballantine. Moved to the adult section of the Public Libraries of Saginaw, Mich. (1989) after patrons requested that children be denied access. Source: 7, May 1989, p. 77.

292
Davis, Kathryn. *The Dakotas: At the Wind's Edge.* Pinnacle Bks. Banned from sale in all Medora, N.Dak. bookstores (1983) because some Medora residents did not approve of some of Davis' fictional embellishments to the history of their town. Source: 7, July 1983, p. 123.

293
Davis, Terry. *Vision Quest.* Viking. Challenged at the Mead, Wash. School District (1984), the New Berlin, Wis. High School library (1984), and the West Milwaukee, Wis. High School library (1984) because it is "obscene." Placed on a restricted reading list by the New Berlin, Wis. School Board (1985) because it is "vulgar and not educational." Banned from the West Allis-West Milwaukee, Wis. school libraries (1986) because of its profanities. Moved from the Hughes Junior High School in Bismarck, N.Dak. (1993) to the high school because a parent considered some passages obscene, pornographic, or inappropriate for junior high students. Source: 7, July 1984, p. 101; Sept. 1984, pp. 139-40; Nov. 1984, pp. 186, 196; Jan. 1985, p. 10; Mar. 1986, p. 39; Mar. 1987, p. 51; Sept. 1993, p. 145; Nov. 1993, pp. 178-79; Jan. 1994, p. 38.

294
Day, Doris. *Doris Day: Her Own Story.* Morrow. Removed from two Anniston, Ala. high school libraries (1982) due to the book's "shocking" contents particularly "in light of Miss Day's All-American image" but later reinstated on a restricted basis. Source: 7, Mar. 1983, p. 37.

295
Day, Susan, and McMahan, Elizabeth. *The Writer's Resource: Readings for Composition.* McGraw. Banned from the Jasper, Mo. schools (1991) because a character in a story used profanity and slang. Source: 7, Jan. 1992, p. 8.

296
De Clements, Barthes. *No Place for Me.* Viking. Challenged in the Douglas County school libraries in Castle Rock, Colo. (1991) because it introduces children to witchcraft. Source:

7, May 1991, p. 89.

297
de Jenkins, Lyll Becerra. *The Honorable Prison.* Dutton. Challenged at the Commodore Middle School in Bainbridge Island, Wash. (1992) as inappropriate by three parents because of violence, sexual scenes, and "lack of family values." Source: 7, May 1992, p. 84.

298
de Schweinitz, Karl. *Growing Up: How We Become Alive, Are Born and Grow.* Macmillan; Collier. Placed on restricted shelves at the Evergreen School District elementary school libraries in Vancouver, Wash. (1987) in accordance with the school board policy to restrict student access to sex education books in elementary school libraries. Source: 7, May 1987, p. 87.

299
De Veaux, Alexis. *Na-ni.* Harper. Removed from open shelves to students in grades K-2 at South Accomack Elementary Schools, Va. (1988) after the county school board agreed that it contains vulgar words ("dog turd") and improper punctuation. Source: 7, May 1988, p. 87.

300
Dean, Roger. *Album Cover Album.* St. Martin. Challenged at the Evergreen School District Junior High School library in Vancouver, Wash. (1987) because "of the way some of the covers represented women" citing one album cover depicting the "Statue of Liberty with bare breasts as exemplary of several photos that were pretty raw toward women." Source: 7, May 1987, p. 102.

301
Defoe, Daniel. *Adventures of Robinson Crusoe.* Bantam; Grosset; NAL; Norton. Placed on the Spanish Index in 1720. Source: 3, p. 25.

302
_____. *Moll Flanders.* Houghton; Modern Library; NAL; Penguin. U.S. Customs raised its ban in 1930. Source: 3, p. 25.

303
_____. *Political History of the Devil.* AMS Pr.; Rowman & Littlefield. Listed on the *Index Librorum Prohibitorum* in Rome (1743). Source: 3, p. 25.

304
_____. *Roxana.* Oxford Univ. Pr.; Viking. U.S. Customs raised its ban in 1930. Source: 3, p. 25.

305

_____. *The Shortest Way with the Dissenters.* Crowell. Burned and the author fined, imprisoned, and pilloried in London, England, in 1703. Source: 3, p. 25.

306

Del Vecchio, John M. *The Thirteenth Valley.* Bantam. Banned from the Amundsen High School classrooms in Chicago, Ill. (1993) because of "explicit sexual content." Source: 7, Sept. 1993, pp. 147-48.

307

DeLillo, Don. *Americana.* Houghton. Removed from the Davis County, Utah Library (1980). Source: 7, Nov. 1980, p. 127.

308

Dengler, Marianna. *A Pebble in Newcomb's Pond.* Holt. Judged unacceptable at the Thompson Junior High School in Bakersfield, Calif. (1984). Source: 7, July 1984, p. 105.

309

Denneny, Michelle; Ortlieb, Charles; and Steele, Thomas. *First Love/Last Love: New Fiction from Christopher Street.* Perigee Bks; Putnam. Challenged at the Deschutes County Library in Bend, Oreg. (1993) because it "encourages and condones" homosexuality. Source: 7, Sept. 1993, pp. 158-59.

310

DeSaint, Niki. *AIDS: You Can't Catch It Holding Hands.* Lapis Pr. Challenged at the Derby, Kans. Library (1993) because "the book didn't say abstinence is the answer and just teach it." Source: 7, July 1993, p. 124.

311

Deveraux, Jude. *A Knight in Shining Armor.* Simon. Retained at the Lassen Union High School in Quincy, Calif. (1993). The book was checked out from a recreational reading library provided by the English instructor. Parents called the romance novel "obscene." Source: 7, Nov. 1993, p. 193.

312

Diagram Group. *Man's Body: An Owner's Manual.* Bantam; Paddington. Banned from the Monroe, Oreg. High School (1979) when parents complained that the reference book's portrayals of male and female anatomies were too explicit. Source: 5 & 7, May 1979, p. 51.

313

_____. *Woman's Body: An Owner's Manual.* Bantam; Paddington; Pocket Bks. Banned from the Monroe, Oreg. High School (1979) when parents complained that the reference book's portrayals of male and female anatomies were too explicit. Challenged at the Evansville, Wis. High School library (1987) because the book is "filth" and it is "sick" even though it is on a restricted shelf behind the librarian's desk. Source: 5 & 7, May 1979, p. 51; May 1987, p. 102.

314

Dickens, Charles. *Oliver Twist.* Airmont; Bantam; Dodd; NAL; Oxford Univ. Pr.; Penguin. A group of Jewish parents in Brooklyn, N.Y. (1949) went to court claiming that the assignment of Dickens's novel to senior high school literature classes violated the rights of their children to receive an education free of religious bias in *Rosenberg v. Board of Education of the City of New York,* 196 Misc. 542, 92 N.Y. Supp. 2d 344. Source: 8, pp. 23, 230.

315

Dickens, Frank. *Albert Herbert Hawkins and the Space Rocket.* Scroll Pr. Relegated to an adult shelf at the Castle Rock, Colo. elementary school libraries (1985) because it "advocates defiance of adult authority by showing misbehavior for which the protagonist goes unpunished," the Douglas County Board of Education reversed its ruling seven months later and decided the book could go back into general circulation. Source: 7, May 1985, p. 76; Sept. 1985, p. 151; Nov. 1985, p. 203.

316

_____. *Albert Herbert Hawkins—The Naughtiest Boy in the World.* Scroll Pr. Relegated to an adult shelf at the Castle Rock, Colo. elementary school libraries (1985) because it "advocates defiance of adult authority by showing misbehavior for which the protagonist goes unpunished." The Douglas County Board of Education reversed its ruling seven months later and decided the book could go back into general circulation. Source: 7, May 1985, p. 76; Sept. 1985, p. 151; Nov. 1985, p. 203.

317

Dickey, James. *Deliverance.* Dell. Challenged in Montgomery County, Md. (1974) on the grounds that it employs "gutter language" and depicts "perverted acts." Burned in Drake, N.Dak. (1973), but U. S. District Court ruled that teachers should be allowed to use this title in eleventh and twelfth grade English classes. Moved from the Hughes Junior High School in Bismarck, N.Dak. (1993) to the High School because a parent considered some passages obscene, pornographic, or inappropriate for junior high students. Source: 7, July 1975, p. 118; Nov. 1975, p. 174; Sept. 1993, p. 145; Nov. 1993, pp. 178-79; Jan. 1994, p. 38.

318
Dieckman, Ed, Jr. *The Secret of Jonestown: The Reason Why.* Noontide. Challenged at the La Grange, Ill. Public Library (1990) because it promotes "hate" for the Jewish people. "It is a Nazi book and it doesn't belong in La Grange." Source: 7, May 1990, p. 84.

319
Diehl, William. *Sharky's Machine.* Dell. Challenged at the Northside High School Library in Lafayette, La. (1982) due to "the book's treatment of drugs, prostitution, and race." Source: 7, May 1982, p. 83.

320
Donleavy, John P. *The Ginger Man.* Delacorte; Dell. Originally published by Girodias in Paris. Author expurgated that text himself to permit publication in England (1955). Source: 3, p. 97.

321
Dorner, Marjorie. *Nightmare.* Warner. Pulled from the Winona, Minn. Middle School media center and classroom libraries (1995) because of language and violence in the book. Source: 7, Jan. 1996, p. 11.

322
Dorson, Richard M. *America in Legend: Folklore from the Colonial Period to the Present.* Pantheon. Removed from a library in Cobb County, Ga. (1977) because the book "condones draft dodging" and contains the song "Casey Jones," which includes several stanzas describing the fabled railroad engineer's sexual prowess. Source: 7, Sept. 1977, p. 133.

323
Double Cross. *Chick.* Banned in Canada (1981) and challenged in New Jersey (1981) as immoral and indecent anti-Catholic literature. Source: 7, Nov. 1981, pp. 162-63.

324
Doyle, Sir Arthur Conan. *The Adventures of Sherlock Holmes.* Avon; Berkley; Harper. Banned in the USSR (1929) because of its references to occultism and spiritualism. Source: 3, p. 56.

325
Dozois, Gardner, ed. *Isaac Asimov's Skin Deep.* Berkley Pub. Challenged in the Fairfield County, Ohio District Library (1995) because it includes profanity and explicit sex scenes.

Source: 7, Nov. 1995, p. 184; Jan. 1996, p. 29.

326
Dragnich, Alex N. *Serbs and Croats: The Struggle in Yugoslavia.* Harcourt. Challenged at the Lincolnwood, Ill. Public Library (1994) because the book is pro-Serbian and anti-Croatian. Source: 7, Mar. 1995, p. 53.

327
Dragonwagon, Crescent, and Zindel, Paul. *To Take a Dare.* Bantam; Harper. Challenged at the Crook County, Oreg. Middle School library (1989) because of "excessive use of profanity." Source: 7, May 1989, p. 93.

328
Dramer, Dan. *Monsters.* Jamestown Pub. Challenged at the Jefferson County school libraries in Lakewood, Colo. (1986). The book is a junior high text of monster stories

> ## "Did you ever hear anyone say: 'That work had better be banned because I might read it and it might be very damaging to me'?"
> ~ Joseph Henry Jackson

including several Greek myths on the Cyclops, the Minotaur, and Medusa, as well as stories of several modern monsters such as King Kong, Dracula, and Frankenstein's monster. The Jefferson County School Board refused to ban the book. Source: 7, May 1986, p. 82; Sept. 1986, p. 173; Nov. 1986, p. 224.

329
Dreiser, Theodore. *An American Tragedy.* NAL. Banned in Boston, Mass. (1927) and burned by the Nazis in Germany (1933) because it "deals with low love affairs." Source: 1, p. 133; 3, p. 61; 9, Vol. III, pp. 404, 407.

330
_____. *Dawn.* Liveright. Banned in Ireland (1932). Source: 3, p. 61.

331
_____. *Genius.* Liveright. Suppressed by the New York Society for the Suppression of Vice (1916) and burned by the Nazis in Germany (1933) because it "deals with low love

affairs." Source: 1, p. 100; 3, p. 61; 9, Vol. II, pp. 631-32.

332

_____. *Sister Carrie.* Airmont; Bantam; Bobbs-Merrill; Holt; Houghton; Penguin. Suppressed in New York City (1900). Banned in Vermont (1958). Source: 3, p. 61; 5, p. 141.

333

Driggs, John, and Finn, Stephen. *Intimacy between Men.* NAL. Challenged, but retained, at the Rogers-Hough, Ark. Memorial Library (1991) because "we're headed down the road to another San Francisco community." Source: 7, Sept. 1991, pp. 151, 177.

334

Dumas, Alexandre. *Camille.* French & European. Banned in England (1850), France (1852), Italy (1863); ban lifted in USSR (1958). Source: 3, p. 48.

335

Duncan, Lois. *Don't Look Behind You.* Delacorte; Dell. Challenged at the Charlestown, Ind. Middle School library (1993) because of graphic passages, sexual references, and alleged immorality in the book. Source: 7, July 1993, p. 124.

336

_____. *Killing Mr. Griffin.* Little; Dell; Scholastic. Challenged at the Sinnott Elementary School in Milpitas, Calif. (1988) because the book contained "needlessly foul" language and had no "redeeming qualities." Pulled from a Bonsall, Calif. Middle School eighth grade reading list (1992) because of disgusting violence and profanity. Challenged in the Shenandoah Valley, Pa. Junior-Senior High School curriculum (1995) because of violence, strong language and unflattering references to God. Source: 7, July 1988, pp. 122-23; Sept. 1988, p. 179; Mar. 1993, p. 43; July 1995, p. 99.

337

Durack, Mary, and Durack, Elizabeth. *Kookanoo and the Kangaroo.* Lerner. Removed from Howard County, Md. (1978) because "it would be hard for primary youngsters to make the distinction between the aborigines in Australia and black children in the U.S." Source: 7, Mar. 1978, p. 30.

338

Durant, Penny. *When Heroes Die.* Macmillan. Challenged at the Seaside, Oreg. Public Library (1993) for promoting homosexuality. Source: 7, Jan. 1994, p. 36.

339

Durrell, Lawrence. *The Black Book.* Dutton. Seized by the U.S. Customs Bureau (1961). Source: 3, p. 88.

340

Earth Science. American Book. Challenged at the Plymouth-Canton school system in Canton, Mich. (1987) because this book "teaches the theory of evolution exclusively. It completely avoids any mention of Creationism… The evolutionary propaganda also underminds {sic} the parental guidance and teaching the children are receiving at home and from the pulpits." Source: 7, Nov. 1981, pp. 162-63; May 1987, p. 109.

341

Eban, Abba. *My People: The History of the Jews.* Random. Banned from the 1983 Moscow International Book Fair along with more than fifty other books because it is "anti-Soviet." Source: 7, Nov. 1983, p. 201.

342

Ebert, Alan. *The Homosexual.* Macmillan. Challenged at the Niles, Mich. Community Library (1982) because "it belongs on the shelves of a porno-shop." Source: 7, Jan. 1983, p. 8.

343

Edgerton, Clyde. *The Floatplane Notebooks.* Algonquin Bks; Ballantine. Challenged at the Carroll County High School in Hillsville, Va. (1992) because "it was wishy-washy" and "could warp a child's mind." The complainants circulated a petition demanding the firing of an English teacher and the dismissal of all school officials connected with the decision to use the novel. Source: 7, May 1992, p. 84; Sept. 1992, p. 143.

344

Ehrlich, Max. *The Reincarnation of Peter Proud.* Bobbs-Merrill. Banned from use in Aurora, Colo. High School English classes (1976) on the grounds of "immorality." Source: 7, May 1976, p. 70; May 1977, p. 79.

345

Eliot, George. *Adam Bede.* Houghton; NAL; Penguin. Attacked as "the vile outpourings of a lewd woman's mind" and withdrawn from the British circulating libraries (1859). Source: 3, p. 45.

346

_____. *Silas Marner.* Bantam; NAL; Zodiac Pr. Banned from the Anaheim, Calif. Union High School District English classrooms (1978) according to the Anaheim Secondary Teachers Association. Source: 7, Jan. 1979, p. 6.

347
Ellis, Bret Easton. *American Psycho.* Random; Simon. The Carthage, Mo. public librarian (1991) was directed first "to take the book off the shelf and keep it under the circulation desk" and then "lose it." The incident involving the novel "snowballed" and was one of the reasons why, under protest, the librarian submitted her resignation. Source: 7, Nov. 1991, p. 195.

348
Ellis, Havelock. *Studies in the Psychology of Sex.* Random. Condemned and burned in England (1898), banned from the mail by the U.S. Post Office Department unless addressed to a doctor (1941), and banned in Ireland (1953). Source: 3, pp. 56-57.

349
Ellison, Ralph. *Invisible Man.* Random; Vintage. Excerpts banned in Butler, Pa. (1975); removed from the high school English reading list in St. Francis, Wis. (1975). Retained in the Yakima, Wash. schools (1994) after a five-month dispute over what advanced high school students should read in the classroom. Two parents raised concerns about profanity and images of violence and sexuality in the book and requested that it be removed from the reading list. Source: 7, July 1975, p. 105; Nov. 1994, pp. 202-3.

350
Elson, Robert T. *Prelude to World War II.* Time-Life. Challenged at the Douglas County Library in Roseburg, Oreg. (1989) because the book contains nudity and violent photos harmful to children researching the war. Source: 7, Jan. 1990, pp. 4-5.

351
Elwell, Walter A., ed. *Evangelical Commentary on the Bible.* Baker. Bk. Challenged, but retained, at the Multnomah, Oreg. County Library (1991) by a patron who believed public funds should not be expended on religious books. Source: 7, Jan. 1992, p. 6.

352
Emerson, Zack. *Echo Company.* Scholastic. Restricted access at the Marana, Ariz. Unified School District (1993) because of complaints about profanity. Source: 7, Sept. 1993, p. 143.

353
Encyclopaedia Britannica. Ency. Brit. Ed. Banned and then pulped in Turkey (1986) because it was a "means of separatist propaganda." Source: 2, p. 319.

354
The Endless Quest. TSR Hobbies. Challenged in Newton, Iowa (1985) because the books in the series contain excessive violence, destruction, witchcraft, and the occult. The titles in the series include: *The Hero of Washington Square, The King's Quest, Light on Quest Mountain, Spell of the Winter Wizard,* and *Under the Dragon's Wing.* Source: 7, Mar. 1986, p. 38.

355
Enger, Eldon D., et al. *Concepts in Biology.* W. C. Brown. Two pages removed from the Waltham, Mass. High School text (1980) due to their explicit nature. Source: 7, Jan. 1981, p. 10.

356
Escher, M. C. *The Graphic Work of M. C. Escher.* Pan/Ballantine. Retained at Maldonado Elementary School in Tucson, Ariz. (1994) after being challenged by parents who objected to nudity and "pornographic," "perverted," and "morbid" themes. Source: 7, July 1994, p. 112.

357
Etchison, Dennis. *Cutting Edge.* Doubleday. Challenged at the Eugene, Oreg. Public Library (1988) for its language, sexual nature, and "perversity." Source: 7, Jan. 1989, p. 3.

358
Evans, Tabor. *Longarm in Virginia City.* Jove. Challenged at the Allen County Public Library in Fort Wayne, Ind. (1985) as "pornographic and objectionable." Removed from the Jordan Valley, Oreg. Union High School (1988) because it was "too sexually graphic." Source: 7, July 1985, pp. 111-12; Jan. 1989, p. 3.

359
Everetts, E. *Holt Basic Readings.* Holt. Challenged at the Hawkins County school system in Church Hill, Tenn. (1983) by the Citizens Organized for Better Schools because they claim the reading series indoctrinates students in "secular humanist" beliefs. Over 400 specific objections were filed against the reading series including specific complaints against the following works included in the series: *Rumpelstiltskin; Cinderella; The Wizard of Oz,* by L. Frank Baum; Shakespeare's *Macbeth; Anne Frank: The Diary of a Young Girl;* readings from anthropologist Margaret Mead; science fiction writer Isaac Asimov; and fairy tale creator Hans Christian Andersen. On October 24, 1986, U.S. District Court Judge Thomas G. Hull ruled in favor of the citizens' group and that the school's use of the textbook series "burdened" the plaintiffs' First Amendment rights to exercise freedom of religion. He ordered the Hawkins County public schools to excuse fundamentalist children from reading class.

On August 24, 1987, a three-judge panel of the U.S. Court of Appeals for the Sixth Circuit reversed Judge Hull's decision by ruling unanimously that public school students can be required to read and discuss the disputed books, even though parts of those books might conflict with their beliefs. The court further ruled that there was no evidence that "the conduct required of the students was forbidden by their religion." On February 22, 1988, the U.S. Supreme Court declined to consider the appeal. The denial of certiorari in the case of *Mozert v. Hawkins County* left standing the August decision by the U. S. Court of Appeals for the Sixth Circuit. Source: 7, Jan. 1984, p. 11; Mar. 1984, p. 40; May 1984, p. 79; July 1984, pp. 112-13; Jan. 1987, pp. 1, 36-38; May 1987, pp. 75, 104-7; Sept. 1987, pp. 166-67; Nov. 1987, pp. 217-18; Mar. 1988, pp. 40-41, 58; May 1988, pp. 94-95.

360
Evslin, Bernard. *Cerberus.* Chelsea Hse. Removed from the elementary school library shelves, but retained in the junior and senior high school libraries in the Francis Howell School District in St. Peters, Mo. (1990). Allegedly, the book's story line is too graphic, its titles too gruesome, and its illustrations "pornographic." (The illustrations are drawings by Michelangelo and other Masters.) The book was said to "encourage satanism." Source: 7, May 1990, p. 84; July 1990, pp. 126-27; Sept. 1990, p. 159.

361
Families. Challenged in Mosinee, Wis. (1982) because it teaches family living. Source: 5 & 7, May 1982, p. 87.

362
Fanon, Frantz. *The Wretched of the Earth.* Grove. Banned in South Korea (1985). Source: 4, April 1986, pp. 30-33.

363
Farmer, Philip J. *Image of the Beast.* Essex House. Challenged at the Chapmanville, W.Va. Public Library (1981) because the book puts "mental pictures in the mind [that] have no place in the library." Source: 7, Mar. 1981, p. 41.

364
Farrell, James. *Studs Lonigan: A Trilogy.* Avon; Vanguard. Young Lonigan (1932) was published with the notice that it was "limited to physicians, social workers, teachers, and other persons having a professional interest in the psychology of adolescence." Banned in Canada (1942); seized in Philadelphia, Pa. (1948); banned in St. Cloud, Minn. (1953) and Ireland (1953); banned in overseas libraries controlled by the U. S. Information Agency. Source: 1, p. 148; 3, p. 85.

365
_____. *A World I Never Made.* Vanguard; Constable; World; Popular Living. Tried for obscenity in the U.S. (1935) and acquitted. Source: 1, p. 159; 9, Vol. III, pp. 648, 650.

366
Fassbender, William. *You and Your Health.* Wiley. Challenged in the Seattle, Wash. school system (1987) because of its views on substance abuse and morality, as well as promiscuity. Source: 7, July 1987, p. 131.

367
Fast, Howard. *Citizen Tom Paine.* Bantam; Duell; World. Banned from high school libraries in New York City (1947) because it was allegedly written by a spokesman of a totalitarian movement and because it contains incidents and expressions not desirable for children, and was improper and indecent. Book was withdrawn (1953) from U. S. Information Agency libraries overseas. Source: 3, p. 89; 9, Vol. IV, p. 700.

368
_____. *The Immigrants.* Hall. Restricted to high school students with parental permission at the Governor Morehead School in Raleigh, N.C. (1982) due to the explicit sexual scenes and vulgarities. Source: 7, Nov. 1982, p. 205.

369
_____. *Second Generation.* Hall. Restricted to high school students with parental permission at the Governor Morehead School in Raleigh, N.C. (1982) due to the explicit sexual scenes and vulgarities. Source: 7, Nov. 1982, p. 205.

370
Faulkner, William. *As I Lay Dying.* Random. Banned in the Graves County School District in Mayfield, Ky. (1986) because it contained "offensive and obscene passages referring to abortion and used God's name in vain." The decision was reversed a week later after intense pressure from the ACLU and considerable negative publicity. Challenged as a required reading assignment in an advanced English class of Pulaski County High School in Somerset, Ky. (1987) because the book contains "profanity and a segment about masturbation." Challenged, but retained, in the Carroll County, Md. schools (1991). Two school board members were concerned about the book's coarse language and dialect. Banned at Central High School in Louisville, Ky. (1994) on a temporary basis because the book uses profanity and questions the existence of God. Source: 7, Nov. 1986, p. 208; May 1987, p. 90; Mar. 1992, p. 64; Nov. 1994, p. 189.

371
_____. *The Hamlet.* Random. Banned in Ireland (1954). Source: 3, p. 77.

372
_____. *Mosquitoes.* Liveright. Seized in raid in Philadelphia, Pa. (1948); banned in Ireland (1954). Source: 3, p. 78.

373
_____. *Pylon.* Random. Blacklisted by the National Organization of Decent Literature; condemned by local censorship groups; banned in Ireland (1954). Source: 3, p. 78.

374
_____. *Sanctuary.* Random; Vintage. Blacklisted by the National Organization of Decent Literature; condemned by local censorship groups; banned in Ireland (1954). Source: 3, p. 78.

375
_____. *Soldier's Pay.* Liveright. Blacklisted by the National Organization of Decent Literature; condemned by local censorship groups; banned in Ireland (1954). Source: 3, p. 78.

376
_____. *Wild Palms.* Random. Seized in raid in Philadelphia, Pa. (1948); banned in Ireland (1954). Source: 3, p. 77.

377
Federico, Ronald. *Sociology.* Addison-Wesley. Removed from the Florida list of approved textbooks because, as the Pro-Family Forum argued, the textbook attacked religion and promoted nudity and profanity. Source: 7, July 1982, p. 125.

378
Feelings, Muriel. *Jambo Means Hello: The Swahili Alphabet.* Dial; Puffin. Challenged by a school board member in the Queens, N.Y. school libraries (1994) because it "denigrate[s] white American culture, 'promotes racial separation, and discourages assimilation.'" The rest of the school board voted to retain the book. Source: 7, July 1994, pp. 110-11; Sept. 1994, p. 166.

379
Ferguson, Alane. *Show Me the Evidence.* Avon; Macmillan. Challenged at the Charlestown, Ind. Middle School library (1993) because of graphic passages, sexual references, and alleged immorality in the book. Source: 7, July 1993, p. 124.

380
Ferlinghetti, Lawrence. *Coney Island of the Mind.* New Directions. Banned for use in Aurora, Colo. High School English classes (1976) on the grounds of "immorality." Source: 7, May 1976, p. 70; May 1977, p. 79; 8, pp. 128-32, 238.

381
_____. *Starting from San Francisco.* New Directions. Banned for use in Aurora, Colo. High School English classes (1976) on the grounds of "immorality." Source: 7, May 1976, p. 70; May 1977, p. 79; 8, pp. 128-32, 238.

382
Fielding, Henry. *Tom Jones.* NAL; Norton; Penguin. Banned in France (1749). Source: 3, p. 29.

383
Fitzgerald, F. Scott. *The Great Gatsby.* Scribner. Challenged at the Baptist College in Charleston, S.C. (1987) because of "language and sexual references in the book." Source: 7, July 1987, p. 133.

384
Fitzgerald, Frances. *Cities on a Hill: A Journey through Contemporary American Cultures.* Simon. Challenged at the Deschutes County Library in Bend, Oreg. (1993) because it "encourages and condones" homosexuality. Source: 7, Sept. 1993, pp. 158-59.

385
Fitzgerald, John D. *The Great Brain.* Dial. Removed from a list of supplemental reading material for fourth graders at the Port Jervis, N.Y. schools (1992) because the novel contains a discussion of suicide. Source: 7, Nov. 1992, pp. 186-87.

386
Fitzhugh, Louise. *Harriet the Spy.* Harper. Challenged in the Xenia, Ohio school libraries (1983) because the book "teaches children to lie, spy, back-talk, and curse." Source: 5 & 7, Sept. 1983, p. 139; Nov. 1983, p. 197.

387
_____. *The Long Secret.* Harper. Challenged in the Eagle Cliffs Elementary School library in Billings, Mont. (1993) because the book is "demented" and pokes fun at religion. Source: 7, Jan. 1994, p. 36.

388
Flaubert, Gustave. *Madame Bovary.* Bantam; Houghton; Modern Library; NAL; Norton; Penguin. Placed on the *Index Librorum Prohibitorum* in Rome (1864). Banned by the National Organization of Decent Literature (1954). Source: 3, p. 47; 6, p. 142.

389
Flora, James. *Grandpa's Ghost Stories.* Macmillan. Challenged as inappropriate at the Broadwater Elementary School Library in Billings, Mont. (1994) because "[children] don't need to be allowed to read anything they want." Source: 7, May 1994, p. 84.

390
Follett, Ken. *Eye of the Needle.* Morrow; NAL. Banned from the Marysville, Kans. high school and junior high school libraries (1993) along with five other Follett novels — *The Key to Rebecca, Lie Down with Lions, Night Over Water, The Pillars of the Earth,* and *Triple* because the books were "pornographic." Later, however, the board decided to reconsider its vote, follow an established review procedure, and retain the six books. Source: 7, May 1993, pp. 70-71; Nov. 1993, p. 177; Jan. 1994, p. 35.

391
_____. *Night over Water.* Macmillan; Morrow; Penguin. Returned to the open shelves at the Medina, Ohio High School library (1993) despite some sexually explicit passages. The complainant then filed a police complaint against the Medina city schools, claiming the district is pandering obscenity to its students. Source: 7, May 1993, p. 86; July 1993, p. 101.

392
_____. *Pillars of the Earth.* Morrow; NAL. Moved to a new "reserve" section of the Chanute, Kans. school library (1994). The book came under fire because of some use of obscenity and graphic violence. Moved to a new "reserve" section of the Chanute, Kans. school library (1994). The book came under fire because of some use of obscenity and graphic violence. Source: 7, Sept. 1994, p. 146; Mar. 1995, p. 40.

393
Ford, Michael Thomas. *One Hundred Questions and Answers about AIDS.* Morrow. Challenged because it encourages sexual activity, but retained in the Eau Claire, Wis. public school libraries (1993). Source: 7, July 1993, p. 104; Sept. 1993, p. 159.

394
Forrest, Katherine. *Beverly Malibu.* Naiad Pr. Challenged, but retained, at the Oak Lawn, Ill. Public Library (1991) because the sleuth in the mystery is a lesbian. Source: 7, Nov. 1991, p. 209.

395
Forster, E. M. *Maurice.* Norton. Banned from the Mascenic

Regional High School in New Ipswich, N.H. (1995) because it is about gays and lesbians. An English teacher was fired for refusing to remove the book. An arbitrator ruled in April 1996 that she can return to work in September without a year's back pay. The Mascenic Regional School Board is appealing the ruling. The teacher was eventually reinstated after a decision by the state's Public Employee Labor Relations Board. Source: 7, Sept. 1995, p. 166; Jan. 1996, p. 15; July 1996, pp. 130-31; Jan. 1997, p. 27.

396
Forsyth, Frederick. *The Devil's Alternative.* Viking. Removed from the Evergreen School District of Vancouver, Wash. (1983) along with twenty-nine other titles. The American Civil Liberties Union of Washington filed suit contending that the removals constitute censorship, a violation of plaintiff's rights to free speech and due process, and the acts are a violation of the state Open Meetings Act because the removal decisions were made behind closed doors. Source: 7, Nov. 1983, pp. 185-86.

397
Fossey, Dian. *Gorillas in the Mist.* Houghton. Teachers at the Westlake Middle School in Erie, Pa. (1993), using felt-tip pens, blacked out passages pertaining to masturbation and mating. Source: 7, July 1993, p. 109.

398
Fox, Mem. *Guess What?* Harcourt. Challenged at the Cook Memorial Library in Libertyville, Ill. (1991) because it features witches, boiling cauldrons, names of punk rockers, and a reference that could be interpreted as meaning "God is dead." Source: 7, Sept. 1991, p. 153.

399
Fox, Paula. *The Slave Dancer.* Bradbury Pr. Challenged, but retained by the Fayette County, Ga. school system (1996). The 1974 Newbery Medal winner about a 13-year-old boy who is snatched from the docks of New Orleans and put on a slave ship bound for Africa. The book was considered objectionable because of language that is "insensitive and degrading." Source: 7, May 1996, p. 99.

400
Frank, Anne. *Anne Frank: The Diary of a Young Girl.* Modern Library. Challenged in Wise County, Va. (1982) due to protests of several parents who complained the book contains sexually offensive passages. Four members of the Alabama State Textbook Committee (1983) called for the rejection of this title because it is a "real downer." Source: 7, Mar. 1983, p. 39.

401

Frank, Pat. *Alas, Babylon*. Bantam. Challenged at the Taylorville, Ill. Junior High School (1987) because it "contains profane language." Source: 7, Sept. 1987, p. 194.

402

Franklin, Benjamin. *The Autobiography of Benjamin Franklin*. Airmont; Buccaneer Pr.; Macmillan; Norton; Random; Univ. of Tenn. Pr.; Yale Univ. Pr. "The expurgation of Benjamin Franklin seems to have increased over the years until he became in the early twentieth century one of the most censored and yet at the same time one of the most widely reprinted writers in American history. Two essays, in particular, are frequently expurgated, 'Advice on the Choice of a Mistress' and the 'Letters to the Royal Academy of Brussels.'" Source: 6, p. 134; 9, Vol. II, p. 616.

403

Friday, Nancy. *Men in Love*. Delacorte; Dial. Temporarily placed in storage on the second floor of the Alpha Park, Ill. Library (1981) and restricted to patrons over eighteen years old unless they have written parental consent because several area residents objected to its "vulgarity." Source: 7, Jan. 1982, p. 9; May 1982, p. 100.

404

_____. *Women on Top: How Real Life Has Changed Women's Fantasies*. Pocket Bks. Removed from the Chestatee Regional Library System in Gainesville, Ga. (1994) because the book on women's sexual fantasies is "pornographic and obscene" and lacks "literary merit." After months of protest and maneuvering, the library's only copy was destroyed when the child of a patron accidentally dropped it into a dishpan full of water. The book is out of print and the library does not plan to replace it. Challenged at the Chester County Library at Charlestown, Pa. (1996) because of graphic details about sex acts and fantasies. Source: 7, Nov. 1994, p. 187; Mar. 1995, p. 39; May 1995, p. 65; Nov. 1996, p. 194 ;Jan 1997, p. 8; Mar. 1997, p. 49.

405

Fritz, Jean. *Around the World in a Hundred Years: Henry the Navigator—Magellan*. Putnam. Removed from the Carroll County, Md. schools (1995) because a passage on the burning of the library in Alexandria during the fourth century said that "Christians did not believe in scholarship" and mentioned intellectual suppression by Christians. "It's a sweeping generalization and it's definitely anti-Christian." Source: 7, Nov. 1995, p. 186.

406

Fuentes, Carlos. *The Death of Artemio Cruz*. Farrar. Retained in the Yakima, Wash. schools (1994) after a five-month dispute over what advanced high school students should read in the classroom. Two parents had raised concerns about profanity and images of violence and sexuality in the book and requested that it be removed from the reading list. Source: 7, Nov. 1994, pp. 202-3.

407

_____. *The Old Gringo*. Farrar. Retained in the Guilford County, N.C. school media centers (1996) after a parent wanted the book removed because of its explicit language. Source: 7, Jan. 1997, p. 25.

408

Fugard, Athol. *Master Harold and the Boys*. Knopf; Oxford Univ. Pr. A South African banning order on printed copies of the play was imposed in Dec. 1982, but was temporarily lifted a week later. Source: 4, Mar. 1983, p. 47.

409

Gaines, Ernest. *The Autobiography of Miss Jane Pittman*. Bantam. Pulled from a seventh grade class in Conroe, Tex. (1995) after complaints about racial slurs in the book. It was later reinstated by school officials. Source: 7, Mar. 1995, p. 46; May 1995, p. 84.

410

Galdone, Joanna. *The Tailypo*. Houghton. Challenged at the Jefferson Terrace Elementary School library in East Baton Rouge, La. (1988) because "it is too scary" and gave the complainant's "child a nightmare." Source: 7, May 1988, p. 87.

411

Gale, Jay. *A Young Man's Guide to Sex*. Holt; Putnam. Challenged, but retained at the Cleveland, Tenn. Public Library (1993) along with seventeen other books, most of which are on sex education, AIDS awareness, and some titles on the supernatural. Removed from the Kenai Peninsula Borough School District libraries in Homer, Alaska (1993) because it was thought to have "outdated material that could be harmful to student health." Source: 7, Sept. 1993, p. 146; Jan. 1994, p. 33.

412

Galileo, Galilei. *Dialogue Concerning the Two Chief World Systems*. Univ. of California Pr. Banned by Pope Urban VIII for heresy and breach of good faith (1633). Source: 3, p. 17.

413

Gallagher, I. J. *The Case of the Ancient Astronauts*. Raintree. Challenged at the Escambia County, Fla. school district

(1984) because the complainant claimed the book indicated that "Ezekiel had seen a UFO when he spoke in the Bible about seeing something that looked like a wheel in the sky." Source: 7, Sept. 1984, p. 156.

414
Garcia-Marquez, Gabriel. *One Hundred Years of Solitude.* Avon; Harper. Purged from the book list for use at the Wasco, Calif. Union High School (1986) because the book, whose author won the 1982 Nobel Prize for literature, was "garbage being passed off as literature." Removed from the advanced English placement reading list at St. Johns High School in Darlington, S.C. (1990) because of profane language. Source: 7, July 1986, p. 119; May 1989, p. 78; Jan. 1991, p. 18.

415
Garden, Nancy. *Annie on My Mind.* Farrar. Challenged at the Cedar Mill Community Library in Portland, Oreg. (1988) because the book portrays lesbian love and sex as normal. Challenged in the Colony, Tex. Public Library (1992) because "it promotes and encourages the gay lifestyle." Challenged because it "encourages and condones" homosexuality, but retained at the Bend, Oreg. High School (1993). Challenged, but retained at the Lapeer, Mich. West High School library (1993). Challenged, but retained at the Lapeer, Mich. West High School library (1993). Challenged at several Kansas City area schools (1993) after the books were donated by a national group that seeks to give young adults "fair, accurate, and inclusive images of lesbians and gay men"—at the Shawnee Mission School District the book was returned to general circulation; at the Olathe East High School the book was removed; protesters burned copies of the book but the Kansas City, Mo. School District kept Garden's novel on the high school shelves; in Kansas City, Kans., the school district donated the book to the city's public library; and in Lee's Summit, Mo., the superintendent removed the book. The federal district court in Kansas, later found the removal of the book unconstitutional and ordered it restored to the school district's libraries. Challenged, but retained at the Liberty, Mo. High School library (1994). Removed from shelves of the Chanute, Kans. (1994) High School Library and access to them limited to only those students with written parental permission because of concerns about its content. Source: 7, Jan. 1990, pp. 4-5; July 1992, pp. 125-26; Sept. 1993, pp. 158-59; Nov. 1993, pp. 191-92; Jan. 1994, p. 13; Mar. 1994, pp. 51-52; May 1994 p. 84; July 1994, p. 129; Sept. 1994, pp. 140-41; Mar. 1995, p. 40; Mar. 1996, p. 54.

416
_____. *Witches.* Lippincott. Challenged by the "God Squad," a group of three students and their parents, at the El Camino High School in Oceanside, Calif. (1986) because the book "contains a lot of information on witch covens. This information can be easily used to form a coven." Source: 7, Sept. 1986, p. 151; Nov. 1986, p. 224; Jan. 1987, p. 9.

417
Gardner, Benjamin Franklin. *Black.* Books for Libraries Pr. Removed from the Dayton, Ohio schools (1976) after complaints that the work contained "hard-core pornography." Source: 7, Jan. 1977, p. 7.

418
Gardner, John C. *Grendel.* Knopf. Challenged at the Frederick County, Md. school system (1978) because the novel is "anti-Christian, anti-moral, full of vulgarity." Placed on a restricted list at the Wasco, Calif. High School (1986) which prohibits the novel's use in the classroom until every student in the class receives parental permission. The novel is the only book on the restricted list and an objection by the high school principal to the "profane" nature of the novel was the catalyst that generated the restricted list policy. Challenged in the Indianapolis, Ind. schools (1986) as an accelerated English class assignment. Challenged at the Viewmont High School in Farmington, Utah (1991) because the book "was obscene and should not be required reading." Challenged, but retained, as part of the Pinelands Regional High School's English curriculum in Bass River Township, N.J. (1992) because of obscenities. Challenged in the Clayton County School District's supplemental reading list for advanced English students in Jonesboro, Ga. (1993) because the book was too violent and graphic. Source: 7, Mar. 1978, p. 39; May 1978, p. 58; May 1986, pp. 81-82; July 1986, p. 119; Jan. 1987, p. 32; May 1989, p. 87; May 1991, p. 92; Jan. 1993, p. 11; Mar. 1993, p. 56; May 1993, p. 87.

419
Garrigue, Sheila. *Between Friends.* Bradbury Pr. Challenged in the Des Moines, Iowa schools (1983) due to the use of the word "damn." Source: 7, May 1983, p. 73.

420
Gassner, John, and Barnes, Clive, eds. *Best American Plays: Sixth Series, 1963—1967.* Crown. Challenged at the Miami, Okla. High School library (1984) because the anthology contains "The Toilet" by Leroi Jones [Imamu Amiri Baraka]. Source: 7, May 1984, p. 87.

421
Gates, Doris. *Two Queens of Heaven.* Viking. Placed on restricted shelves in the libraries of Prescott, Ariz. elementary schools (1979) because it contains two illustrations of a barebreasted goddess. Source: 7, Jan. 1980, p. 6.

422
Gautier, Theophile. *Mademoiselle de Maupin*. French & European; Penguin. Challenged in New York City (1917) and finally cleared in 1921 after a long court fight. Banned by Nicholas I in Russia (1831-1853). Source: 3, p. 43; 9, Vol. III, p. 413.

423
Genet, Jean. *Our Lady of the Flowers*. Grove. Seized from the Birmingham, England Public Library (1957) and banned in France (1958). Source: 3, p. 88.

424
George, Jean Craighead. *Julie of the Wolves*. Harper. Challenged in Mexico, Mo. (1982) because of the book's "socialist, communist, evolutionary, and anti-family themes." Challenged in Littleton, Colo. (1989) school libraries because "the subject matter was better suited to older students, not sixth graders." Challenged at the Erie Elementary School in Chandler, Ariz. (1994) because the book includes a passage that some parents found inappropriate in which a man forcibly kisses his wife. The Newbery Award—winning book, depicting the experiences of an Eskimo girl, was chosen by the teacher of a third, fourth, and fifth grade class for the Antarctic unit she was teaching. Challenged in the classrooms and school libraries in Palmdale, Calif. (1995) because the book describes a rape. Removed from the sixth-grade curriculum of the New Brighton Area School District in Pulaski Township, Pa. (1996) because of a graphic marital rape scene. Challenged at the Hanson Lane Elementary School in Ramona, Calif. (1996) because the award-winning book includes an attempted rape of a 13-year-old girl. Source: 7, Nov. 1982, p. 215; Sept. 1989, p. 186; Jan. 1995, p. 9; Mar. 1996, p. 45; May 1996, p. 88; Jan. 1997, p. 9.

425
Gibbon, Edward. *History of the Decline and Fall of the Roman Empire*. Modern Library. Placed on the *Index Librorum Prohibitorum* in Rome (1783) because it contradicted official church history. Source: 3, p. 33.

> ## "If there is a bedrock principle underlying the First Amendment, it is that the Government may not prohibit the expression of an idea simply because society finds the idea itself offensive or disagreeable."
>
> ~ United States Supreme Court Justice William Brennan, Texas v. Johnson

426
Gibson, Walter Brown. *Complete Illustrated Book of Divination and Prophecy*. Doubleday; NAL. Challenged at the Plymouth-Canton school system in Canton, Mich. (1987) because the book deals with witchcraft. Source: 7, May 1987, p. 110; Jan. 1988, p. 11.

427
Gide, Andre. *If It Die*. Seized in New York City (1935). Banned in Soviet Union (1938) and Ireland (1953). Placed on the *Index Librorum Prohibitorum* in Rome (1952). Source: 3, p. 59; 9, Vol. III, p. 648.

428
Ginsberg, Allen. *Collected Poetry, 1947-1980*. Harper; Viking. Removed from the Murray County High School library in Chatsworth, Ga. (1989) because "it was really gutter stuff." Challenged at the North Central High School library in Indianapolis, Ind. (1989) because explicit descriptions of homosexual acts were deemed inappropriate subject matter for high school students. Source: 7, July 1989, p. 128; Jan. 1990, p. 9; Mar. 1990, pp. 61-62.

429
_____. *Howl and Other Poems*. City Lights. Seized by U.S. Customs officials in San Francisco (1957). Source: 3, p. 97.

430
_____. *Kaddish and Other Poems*. City Lights. Banned for use in Aurora, Colo. High School English classes (1976) on the grounds of "immorality." Source: 7, May 1976, p. 70; May 1977, p. 79; 8, pp. 128-32, 238.

431
Giovanni, Nikki. *My House*. Morrow. Banned from the Waukesha, Wis. public school libraries (1975). Challenged at the West Gennessee High School in Syracuse, N.Y. (1990) because the book contains obscenities. Challenged at the Duval County, Fla. public school libraries (1992) because it

contains the word "nigger" and was accused of vulgarity, racism, and sex. Source: 7, July 1975, p. 104; July 1990, p. 127; July 1992, p. 105.

432
Glasser, Ronald J. *365 Days*. Braziller. Banned, but later reinstated by a U.S. District Court ruling in Baileyville, Maine (1982). Source: 7, Mar. 1982, p. 33.

433
Godchaux, Elma. *Stubborn Roots*. Macmillan. Seized and destroyed by New Orleans, La. (1937) police. Source: 9, Vol. III, p. 650.

434
Goethe, Johann Wolfgang von. *Faust*. Doubleday; Macmillan; Norton; Oxford Univ. Pr.; Penguin. Production suppressed in Berlin (1808) until certain dangerous passages concerning freedom were deleted. Franco purged Spanish libraries of all of Goethe's writings (1939). Source: 3, p. 35.

435
_____. *The Sorrows of Werther*. Ungar. Prohibited in Denmark (1776). Source: 3, p. 35.

436
Gold, Robert S., ed. *Point of Departure*. Dell. Removed from the required reading list at the North Thurston, Wash. High School (1983) because of the book's "alleged strong language and allusions to sexual conduct." The decision was later reversed. Source: 7, July 1983, p. 109; Nov. 1983, p. 187.

437
Goldfarb, Mace. *Fighters, Refugees, Immigrants: A Tale of the Hmong*. Carolrhoda Bks. Restricted to teachers only at the Des Moines, Iowa elementary schools (1988) because the book "could lead students to form a derogatory image of Southeast Asians if they are not mature enough." Source: 7, Mar. 1988, p. 46

438
Golding, William. *Lord of the Flies*. Coward. Challenged at the Dallas, Tex. Independent School District high School libraries (1974); challenged at the Sully Buttes, S.Dak. High school (1981); challenged at Owen, N.C. High School (1981) because the book is "demoralizing inasmuch as it implies that man is little more than an animal"; challenged at the Marana, Ariz. High School (1983) as an inappropriate reading assignment. Challenged at the Olney, Tex. Independent School District (1984) because of "excessive violence and bad language." A committee of the Toronto,

Canada Board of Education ruled on June 23, 1988 that the novel is "racist and recommended that it be removed from all schools." Parents and members of the black community complained about a reference to "niggers" in the book and said it denigrates blacks. Challenged in the Waterloo, Iowa schools (1992) because of profanity, lurid passages about sex, and statements defamatory to minorities, God, women, and the disabled. Source: 7, Jan. 1975, p. 6; July 1981, p. 103; Jan. 1982 p. 17; Jan. 1984, pp. 25-26; July 1984, p. 122; Sept. 1988, p. 152; July 1992, p. 126.

439
Goode, Erich, and Troiden, Richards, eds. *Sexual Deviance and Sexual Deviants*. Morrow. Destroyed by the St. Mary's, Pa. Public Library Board (1977). Source: 7, Sept. 1977, p. 100.

440
Goodwin, June. *Cry Amandla!: South African Women and the Question of Power*. Holmes & Meier. Banned by the Directorate of Publications in Cape Town, South Africa (1984). Without giving a reason, the Directorate declared "it will be an offense to import or distribute" the work. Source: 7, Nov. 1984, p. 197.

441
Gordimer, Nadine. *Burger's Daughter*. Penguin; Viking. Banned on July 5, 1979 in South Africa. The decision was lifted in Oct. 1979 when the government's Publication Appeal Board overruled the earlier decision of a censorship committee. Two previous novels by Gordimer were also banned but later reinstated. Source: 4, Nov. /Dec. 1979, p. 69; Apr. 1980, p. 73.

442
_____. *July's People*. Viking. Challenged in the honors and academic English classes in the Carlisle, Pa. schools (1993). Teachers must send parents a letter warning about the work's content and explaining that their children may read alternate selections. Retained in the Yakima, Wash. schools (1994) after a five-month dispute over what advanced high school students should read in the classroom. Two parents raised concerns about profanity and images of violence and sexuality in the book and requested that it be removed from the reading list. Source: 7, July 1993, p. 127; Nov. 1994, pp. 202-3.

443
Gordon, Sol. *Facts about Sex: A Basic Guide*. Educational Univ. Pr. Challenged and recommended for a "parents only" section at the Concord, Ark. school library (1984) because the book "has in it terms that would be considered vulgar by

any thoughtful person." Source: 7, Jan. 1985, p. 7; May 1985, p. 75; Jan. 1986, pp. 7-8.

444

_____. *You: The Teenage Survival Book.* Times Books. Removed from the Hurst-Euless-Bedford, Tex. School District libraries (1982). Source: 5 & 7, May 1982, p. 84.

445

Gould, Lois. *Necessary Objects.* Random; Dell. Removed from the Hutchinson, Kans. High School library (1976) due to its explicit sexual content. Source: 7, Jan. 1977, p. 7.

446

_____. *Such Good Friends.* Random; Dell. Removed from the Hutchinson, Kans. High School library (1976) due to its explicit sexual content. Source: 7, Jan. 1977, p. 7.

447

Gould, Steven C. *Jumper.* Tor Bks. Challenged at the West Linn-Wilsonville, Oreg. School District (1995) because according to the complainant "it was inappropriate for school children to read" because of a violent scene when the book's main character escapes from a sexual attack by a group of male truck drivers. Challenged at the Plattsburgh, N.Y. schools (1995) because of vulgarity, sex and excessive violence. Source: 7, July 1995, p. 110; Jan. 1996, p. 16.

448

Gramick, Jeannine, and Furey, Pat. *The Vatican and Homosexuality: Reactions to the "Letter to the Bishops of the Catholic Church on the Pastoral Care of Homosexual Persons."* Crossroad NY. Challenged at the Deschutes County Library in Bend, Oreg. (1993) because it "encourages and condones" homosexuality. Source: 7, Sept. 1993, pp. 158-59.

449

Graves, Robert. *I, Claudius.* Random. Banned in South Africa under the Customs Act of 1955. Source: 3, p. 76.

450

Grawunder, Ralph, and Steinmann, Marion. *Life and Health.* Random. Banned from the Boulder, Colo. Valley Board of Education's health and sex education classes (1980) attended only by students with parental permission. Challenged in the Parma, Ohio (1985) classrooms because "it preaches a religion of moral indifference." Source: 7, Jan. 1981, p. 9; Mar. 1986, p. 42.

451

Green, G. Dorsey, and Clunis, D. Merilee. *Lesbian Couple.* Seal Pr. Challenged at the Muscatine, Iowa Public Library

(1990) because it is "wrong to promote immorality." Source: 7, Nov. 1990, p. 225.

452

Greenberg, Jerrold S., and Gold, Robert. *Holt Health.* Holt. Challenged in the Garrettsville, Ohio school system (1993) because it "condones" homosexuality. Source: 7, Nov. 1993, pp. 179-80.

453

Greenburg, David. *Slugs.* Atlantic Monthly Pr. Challenged at the Evergreen, Wash. School District libraries (1984) because of its graphic descriptions of "slugs being dissected with scissors" and its verses describing the roasting, toasting, stewing, and chewing of the creatures were potentially frightening to young children. Banned from the Escondido, Calif. Elementary School District libraries (1985) as "unsuitable and should not have been allowed in the libraries in the first place." Source: 7, Sept. 1984, p. 155; July 1985, p. 111.

454

Greene, Bette. *The Drowning of Stephan Jones.* Bantam. Removed from the curriculum and school library shelves in Boling, Tex. (1993) because the book "teaches anti-Christian beliefs and condones illegal activity." The story is about two gay men who are the objects of prejudice and violence, resulting in the drowning death of one of them. Banned from the Mascenic Regional High School in New Ipswich, N.H. (1995) because it is about gays and lesbians. An English teacher was fired for refusing to remove the book. Source: 7, Mar. 1994, p. 53; Sept. 1996, p. 166; Jan. 1996, p. 15.

455

_____. *Summer of My German Soldier.* Bantam; Dial. Challenged as suitable curriculum material in the Harwinton and Burlington, Conn. schools (1990) because it contains profanity and subject matter that set bad examples and gives students negative views of life. Temporarily removed from an eighth-grade supplemental reading list in Cinnaminson, N.J. (1996) because it contains offensive racial stereotypes. Source: 7, Mar. 1991, p. 44; May 1991, p. 90; Jan. 1997, p. 10.

456

Greene, Constance. *Al(Exandra) the Great.* Dell; Viking. Restricted at the Lindenwold, N.J. elementary school libraries (1984) because of "a problem with language." Source: 7, Nov. 1984, p. 185.

457

_____. *Beat the Turtle Drum.* Dell; Viking. Challenged at

the Orchard Lake Elementary School library in Burnsville, Minn. (1985). Source: 7, Nov. 1985, p. 203.

458

_____. *I Know You, Al.* Viking. Removed from the Hockinson, Wash. Middle School library (1984) because the book did not uphold the principles of the United States which were "established on the moral principles of the Bible." Challenged at the Multnomah County Library in Portland, Oreg. (1989) because of sexual references, the presentation of divorce as a fact of life, and derogatory remarks about friends. Source: 7, Sept. 1984, p. 139; Jan. 1990, pp. 4-5.

459

Greene, Gael. *Dr. Love.* St. Martin. Challenged at the White County Public Library in Searcy, Ark. (1983) because "it's the filthiest thing I've ever seen." Source: 7, Nov. 1983, p. 185; Jan. 1984, p. 25.

460

Greene, Graham. *J'Accuse: Nice, the Dark Side.* Merrimack Pub. Cir. A French court ordered (1982) the seizure of all copies of this expose of alleged corruption in Nice. The author was also ordered to pay 100 francs for each copy seized to a building developer, Daniel Guy, who is the main figure in the book. Greene told the press that the court had made no attempt to give him or his publishers advance warning about the seizure. Source: 4, Oct. 1982, p. 34.

461

Greene, Sheppard M. *The Boy Who Drank Too Much.* Dell. Removed from an eighth grade literature class in the Underwood, Minn. schools (1991) because of the book's alleged sexism, and its seeming toleration of alcohol consumption by minors. Source: 7, Mar. 1992, p. 44.

462

Grimm, Jacob, and Grimm, Wilhelm K. Translated by Jack Zipes. *The Complete Fairy Tales of the Brothers Grimm.* Bantam. Restricted to sixth through eighth grade classrooms at the Kyrene, Ariz. elementary schools (1994) due to its excessive violence, negative portrayals of female characters, and anti-Semitic references. Source: 7, Jan. 1994, p. 34; Sept. 1994, p. 149.

463

Grimm, Jacob. *Hansel and Gretel.* Dial; Putnam. Challenged at the Mount Diablo, Calif. School District (1992) because it teaches children that it is acceptable to kill witches and paints witches as child-eating monsters. Source: 7, July 1992, p. 108.

464

_____. *Little Red Riding Hood.* Houghton. Banned by two California school districts—Culver City and Empire (1990)—because an illustration shows Little Red Riding Hood's basket with a bottle of wine as well as fresh bread and butter. The wine could be seen as condoning the use of alcohol. Source: 7, July 1990, p. 128.

465

_____. *Snow White.* Knopf; Little. Restricted to students with parental permission at the Duval, Fla. County public school libraries (1992) because of its graphic violence: a hunter kills a wild boar, and a wicked witch orders Snow White's heart torn out. Source: 7, July 1992, pp. 105-6.

466

Grisham, John. *The Client.* Doubleday. Challenged in a sixth-grade high-level reading class in Hillsborough, N.J. (1996) because of its violence and use of "curse words." Source: 7, July 1996, p. 122; Sept. 1996, p. 155.

467

Groening, Matt. *The Big Book of Hell.* Random House. Challenged at the Hershey, Pa. Public Library (1995) because "the entire book teaches conduct contrary to wishes of parents" and is "trash" with "no morals." A request was made to "destroy all books of a similar nature." Source: 7, Sept. 1995, p. 158.

468

Gruenberg, Sidonie M. *The Wonderful Story of How You Were Born.* Doubleday. Moved from the children's room of the Tampa-Hillsborough County, Fla. Public Library (1982) to the adult section. Source: 7, Jan. 1982, pp. 4-5.

469

Grumbach, Jane and Emerson, Robert, eds. *Monologues: Women II.* Drama Bks. Removed from a suggested reading list at Adams City, Colo. High School (1990) after a parent complained about obscene language in the book. Source: 7, Jan. 1991, p. 15.

470

Guammen, David. *To Walk the Line.* Knopf. Banned from all libraries in the Enid, Okla. public school system libraries (1974). Source: 7, Mar. 1975, p. 41.

471

Guest, Judith. *Ordinary People.* Ballantine; Hall; Viking. Temporarily banned in Enon, Ohio (1981) from junior and senior English classrooms. Challenged at the Merrimack, N.H. High School (1982) after a parent found the novel obscene and depressing. Challenged in North Salem, N.Y. (1985) as an optional summer reading book because of profanity and graphic sex scenes and because its topic - teenage suicide - was too intense for tenth graders. Challenged because it is "degrading to Christians," but retained at the Anaheim, Calif. Union High School District (1993). No longer required reading at Delta High School in Delaware, Ind. (1994) due to profanity and descriptions of sexual situations in the novel. Removed from the Faulkton, S.Dak. (1994) district classrooms. Temporarily pulled from the Lancaster, N.Y. High School curriculum (1996) because two parents contended it contained foul language, graphic references to sex and inappropriate handling of the subject of suicide. A Lancaster student took the matter to the New York Civil Liberties Union which sent a letter to the school board saying that were "greatly dismayed" with the board's action. Source: 7, Jan. 1982, p. 77; Sept. 1982, p. 170; Sept. 1985, p. 168; May 1993, pp. 86-87; Nov. 1993, pp. 192-93; Jan. 1994, p. 14; Sept. 1994, pp. 150, 152; Sept. 1996, pp. 155-56; Nov. 1996, p. 197.

472

_____. *Second Heaven*. NAL. Challenged in the Greenville County, S.C. schools (1991) because the book uses the name of God and Jesus in a "vain and profane manner along with inappropriate sexual references." Source: 7, July 1991, p. 130.

473

Gunther, John. *Death Be Not Proud*. Harper. Retained by the Edgecombe County Board of Education in Tarboro, N.C. (1995) after complaints that the "book has words in it that even unsaved people would have spanked their children for saying." Source: 7, May 1995, p. 84.

474

Guthrie, Alfred B., Jr. *The Big Sky*. Bantam. Banned in Amarillo, Tex. (1962). Challenged in the Big Timber, Mont. schools (1991) because the book is filled with explicit, vulgar language. Source: 3, p. 82; 7, Mar. 1992, p. 44.

475

_____. *The Way West*. Houghton. Banned in Amarillo, Tex. (1962). Source: 3, p. 82.

476

Guy, Rosa. *Edith Jackson*. Viking. Removed from all school libraries collections in St. Tammany Parish, La. (1984) because its "treatment of immorality and voyeurism does not provide for the growth of desirable attitudes," but later reinstated. Source: 7, May 1984, p. 69; July 1984, p. 121.

477

_____. *The Music of Summer*. Delacorte. Removed from Adamson Middle School shelves, and Clayton, Ga.'s public libraries (1994) and placed in the young adult section for eighth graders and up because of a "really gross" sex scene. Source: 7, July 1994, p. 109.

478

Haas, Ben. *Daisy Canfield*. Pocket Bks.; Simon & Schuster. Challenged at the Covington, La. Public Library (1984) because it "had objectionable language throughout." Source: 7, July 1984, p. 103.

479

Hahn, Mary Downing. *Wait Till Helen Comes*. Clarion Bks. Challenged in the Lawrence, Kans. School District curriculum (1996) because the book presents suicide as a viable, "even attractive way of dealing with family problems. Ghosts, poltergeists and other supernatural phenomena are presented as documented reality and these are capable of deadly harm to children." Source: 7, May 1996, pp. 87-88.

480

Haislip, Barbara. *Stars, Spells, Secrets and Sorcery*. Dell. Challenged at Nashotah, Wis. school library (1993) because the book "promotes satanism." Source: 7, May 1993, p. 86.

481

Haldeman, Joe. *War Year*. Holt. Removed from the Soldotna, Alaska Junior High School library (1981) because of its raw language and graphic descriptions of battlefield violence. Source: 7, July 1981, p. 91.

482

Haley, Gail E. *Go Away, Stay Away*. Scribner. Challenged, but retained in the Echo Park Elementary School media center in Apple Valley, Minn. (1994). A parent filed the complaint because the story "was frightening subject matter and [I] didn't see a good lesson in [it]." Source: 7, July 1994, p. 129.

483

Hall, Elizabeth. *Possible Impossibilities*. Houghton. Challenged at the Sikes Elementary School media center in Lakeland, Fla. (1985) because the book "would lead children to believe ideas contrary to the teachings of the Bible." Source: 7, July 1985, p. 133.

484

Hall, Radclyffe. *The Well of Loneliness*. Avon. Suppressed in England (1928) as obscene. *The London Sunday Express* denounced it as "a challenge to every instinct of social sanity and moral decency which distinguishes Christian civilization from the corruptions of paganism." Publisher arrested in New York City (1929). Source: 3, p. 71; 9, Vol. III, pp. 416-17.

485
Halle, Louis J. *Men and Nations.* Princeton. Challenged in the Jefferson County, Ky. School District (1982) because the book is a "soft sell of communism." Source: 7, Mar. 1983, p. 41.

486
Hamlin, Liz. *I Remember Valentine.* Dutton; Pocket Bks. Challenged at the Commerce, Tex. High School library (1990) because of "pornographic" material in the book. The complainant asked that all "romance" books be removed. Source: 7, Mar. 1991, p. 43.

487
Hanckel, Frances, and Cunningham, John. *A Way of Love, A Way of Life.* Lothrop. Challenged in Atlantic, Iowa (1982) because it is a "morally corrupting force"; removed from two Anniston, Ala. high school libraries (1982) but later reinstated on a restrictive basis. Challenged at the Fairbanks, Alaska North Star Borough School District libraries (1984) because schools should teach the basics, "not how to become queer dope users." Source: 7, May 1982, p. 82; Mar. 1983, p. 37; Sept. 1984, pp. 137, 149-50.

488
Handford, Martin. *Where's Waldo?* Little. Challenged at the Public Libraries of Saginaw, Mich. (1989) because "on some of the pages there are dirty things." Removed from the Springs Public School library in East Hampton, N.Y. (1993) because there is a tiny drawing of a woman lying on the beach wearing a bikini bottom but no top. Source: 7, May 1989, p. 78; July 1993, p. 100.

489
Hanigan, James P. *Homosexuality: The Test Case for Christian Sexual Ethics.* Paulist Pr. Challenged at the Deschutes County Library in Bend, Oreg. (1993) because it "encourages and condones" homosexuality. Source: 7, Sept. 1993, pp. 158-59.

490
Haning, Peter. *The Satanists.* Taplinger. Challenged by the "God Squad," a group of three students and their parents, at the El Camino High School in Oceanside, Calif. (1986) because the book "glorified the devil and the occult." Source: 7, Sept. 1986, p. 151; Nov. 1986, p. 224; Jan. 1987, p. 9.

491
Hansberry, Lorraine. *Raisin in the Sun.* Random. Responding to criticisms from an anti-pornography organization, the Ogden, Utah School District (1979) restricted circulation of Hansberry's play. Source: 7, May 1979, p. 49.

492
Hardin, Garrett. *Population, Evolution and Birth Control.* Freeman. The Brighton, Mich. School Board (1977) voted to remove all sex education books from the high school library. Source: 7, Sept. 1977, p. 133.

493
Hardy, Thomas. *Jude the Obscure.* Airmont; Bantam; Bobbs-Merrill; Houghton; NAL; Norton; St. Martin. Banned by Bristol, England circulating libraries (1896). Source: 3, p. 51.

494
_____. *Tess of the D'Urbervilles.* Bantam; Houghton; NAL; Norton; Penguin; St. Martin. Banned by Bristol, England circulating libraries (1896). Source: 3, p. 51.

495
Harington, Donald. *Lightning Bug.* Harcourt. Challenged at the Rogers-Hough Ark. Memorial Library (1991) because the book uses language "very descriptive of... perverted sex." Source: 7, Sept. 1991, p. 151.

496
Harkness, John, and Helgren, David, eds. *Populations.* Globe Book Co. Removed from the Palmyra, N.J. School District's science curriculum (1994) after nearly three hours of passionate debate between parents who believed the book presented only one side of how world overpopulation should be addressed and teachers who found it an integral part of the class curriculum. Source: 7, Mar. 1995, p. 45.

497
Harlan, Elizabeth. *Footfalls.* Atheneum; Ballantine. Challenged at the Obsidian Junior High School in Redmond, Oreg. (1988) for its profanity and sexual content. Source: 7, Jan. 1989, p. 3.

498
Harris, Frank. *My Life and Loves.* Grove. Banned in England (1922); imports banned in the U.S. and frequently destroyed by U.S. Customs (1922-1956). Source: 3, p. 54; 9, Vol. III, p. 415.

499

Harris, Raymond, ed. *Best Selling Chapters.* Jamestown Pubns. Challenged, but retained in a sixth grade literature class at Hichborn Middle School in Howland, Nebr. (1993). The challenge was directed at the Ray Bradbury story, "A Sound of Thunder," which contained "offensive" language. Challenged in the Keene, N.H. Middle School (1993) because of some of the language and subject matter in the textbook, specifically in passages from John Steinbeck's *Of Mice and Men; To Kill a Mockingbird* by Harper Lee; and *A Day No Pigs Would Die* by Robert Newton Peck. The complainant objected to expressions such as "crazy bastard," "hell" and "damn," "Jesus Christ," and "God Almighty. " Source: 7, Sept. 1993, p. 160; Jan. 1994, p. 15.

500

_____. *Best Short Stories, Middle Level.* Jamestown Pubs Challenged, but retained in a sixth grade literature class at Hichborn Middle School in Howland, Nebr. (1993). The challenge was directed at the Ray Bradbury story, "A Sound of Thunder," which contained "offensive" language. Source: 7, Sept. 1993, p. 160.

501

Harris, Robie H. *It's Perfectly Normal: A Book about Changing Bodies, Growing Up, Sex, and Sexual Health.* Candlewick Pr. Challenged at the Provo, Utah Library (1996) because it contains discussions of intercourse, masturbation and homosexuality. Removed from the Clover Park, Wash. School District library shelves (1996) because parents charged that it was too graphic and could foster more questions than it answers. Challenged at the Chester County, Pa. Library (1996) because the "book is an act of encouragement for children to begin desiring sexual gratification…and is a clear example of child pornography." Source: 7, Sept. 1996, p. 152; Jan. 1997, p. 8; Mar. 1997, p. 49.

502

Hart, Jack. *Gay Sex: Manual for Men Who Love Men.* Alyson Pubns. Challenged at the Fort Vancouver, Wash. Regional Library (1993) when a group of citizens asked the Goldendale City Council to establish more restrictive criteria for sexually explicit material. Source: 7, July 1993, p. 103.

503

Hashak, Israel. *Jewish History, Jewish Religion.* Westview. Challenged at the Milford, Mass. Library (1995) because it is anti-Semitic. Source: 7, May 1995, p. 66.

504

Haskins, Jim. *Voodoo and Hoodoo.* Madison Bks.; Original Pubns. Banned at the Clearwood Junior High School library in Slidell, La. (1992) because the book included "recipes" for spells. U.S. District Court Judge Patrick Carr ruled on October 6, 1994, that the St. Tammany Parish School Board cannot ban the book solely because members do not approve of its content. A week later, the board voted 8-5 to appeal the judgment. The school board appealed the decision to the U.S. Court of Appeals for the Fifth Circuit. On April 1, 1996, the St. Tammany Parish School Board, however, ended the four-year-old attempt to ban the book by returning it to the library. Under the agreement, it will be available only with written parental permission to students in eighth grade or above. Momentum for a settlement occurred after two board members who fought to ban the book left the board in 1994. Additionally, the board's insurer indicated that it might not foot the bill if the board continued to fight the suit. Source: 7, July 1992, p. 106; Sept. 1992, p. 137; Jan. 1993, p. 23; Mar. 1993, p. 41; Jan. 1995, pp. 19-20; Sept. 1995, p. 153; July 1996, p. 134.

505

Hastings, Selina. *Sir Gawain and the Loathly Lady.* Lothrop; Macmillan. Challenged at the public libraries of Saginaw, Mich. (1989). The complainant requested the library to "white out the swearing" which appears on page 16 of the book. The objectionable words were "God Damn You." Challenged at the elementary school libraries in Antigo, Wis. (1992) because a parent objected to a reference to the Loathly Lady as a "hell-hag" and to another passage in which the Black Knight suggests that King Arthur "roast in hell." Source: 7, May 1989, p. 77; Jan. 1993, p. 28.

506

Haugaard, Erick C. *The Samurai's Tale.* Houghton. Challenged at the Wilsona School District in Lake Los Angeles, Calif. (1995) because of violence and references to Buddha and ritual suicide. Source: 7, Jan. 1996, p. 13.

507

Hautzig, Deborah. *Hey Dollface.* Greenwillow. Challenged at the Bend, Oreg. High School (1993) because it "encourages and condones" homosexuality. Source: 7, Sept. 1993, pp. 158-59.

508

Hawes, Hampton. *Raise Up off Me.* Coward. Challenged at the King High School in Corpus Christi, Tex. (1989) because the book contains "vulgar language and descriptions of abnormal sexual activity." Source: 7, Jan. 1990, p. 32.

509

Hawthorne, Nathaniel. *The Scarlet Letter.* Bantam; Dell; Dodd; Holt; Houghton; Modern Library; NAL; Norton.

Subject of savage attacks by moralists in 1852. The National Board of Censorship forced the producers of the film version to change a few things; for one, Hester has to get married. Banned from the Lindale, Tex. advanced placement English reading list (1996) because the book "conflicted with the values of the community." Source: 5 & 7, p. 142; Nov. 1996, p. 199; 9, Vol. I, p. 562.

510

_____. *Young Goodman Brown and Other Short Stories.* Dover. Challenged at the Copenhagen, N.Y. Central School (1992) because the story might give children the wrong message about witchcraft. Source: 7, Jan. 1993, p. 12.

511

Hayden, Penny. *Confidence.* Bantam; Doubleday. Expurgated by an apparent self-appointed censor at the Coquille, Oreg. Public Library (1994) along with several other books. Most were mysteries and romances in which single words and sexually explicit passages were whited out by a vandal who left either dots or solid ink pen lines where the words had been. Source: 7, Sept. 1994, p. 148.

512

Hedderwick, Mairi. *Katie Morag and the Tiresome Ted.* Little. Challenged at the public libraries of Saginaw, Mich. (1989) because on the last page of the story "the mother's sweater is open to fully expose her breast." The library was asked to cover the drawing with a marker. Source: 7, May 1989, p. 77.

Joseph Heller (1974)

513

Heidish, Marcy. *Woman Called Moses.* Bantam; Houghton. Removed by a patron at the Wilmington, N.C. school library (1992) because of strong language. Source: 7, July 1992, p. 107.

514

Heller, Joseph. *Catch-22.* Modern Library; Simon & Schuster. Banned in Strongsville, Ohio (1972), but school board's action was overturned in 1976 by a U.S. District Court in *Minarcini v. Strongsville City School District,* 541 F 2d 577 (6th Cir. 1976). Challenged at the Dallas, Tex. Independent School District high school libraries (1974); in Snoqualmie, Wash. (1979) because of its several references to women as "whores." Source: 3, p. 96; 7, Jan. 1975, p. 6; July 1979, p. 85; 8, pp. 145-48.

515

_____. *Good as Gold.* Pocket Bks. Banned on June 28, 1979 in South Africa. The government's censorship authorities gave no reason. Source: 4, Nov. /Dec. 1979, p. 69.

516

_____. *Something Happened.* Ballantine; Knopf. Banned in South Africa (1974). The government's censorship authorities gave no reason. Source: 4, Nov. /Dec. 1979, p. 69.

517

Helms, Tom. *Against All Odds.* Crowell. Removed from the Evergreen School District of Vancouver, Wash. (1983) along with twenty-nine other titles. The American Civil Liberties Union of Washington filed suit contending that the removals constitute censorship, a violation of plaintiff's rights to free speech and due process, and the acts are a violation of the state Open Meetings Act because the removal decisions were made behind closed doors. Source: 7, Nov. 1983, pp. 185-86.

518

Helper, Hinton Rowan. *The Impending Crisis.* Burdick Brothers. The Reverend Daniel Worth had to stand trial for owning the text, and in Arkansas three men were hanged for owning the book. Source: 5, p. 131.

519

Hemingway, Ernest. *Across the River and into the Trees.* Scribner. Banned in Ireland (1953) and South Africa (1956) as "objectionable and obscene." Source: 3, p. 80.

520

_____. *A Farewell to Arms.* Scribner. The June 1929 issue of Scribner's Magazine, which ran Hemingway's novel, was banned in Boston, Mass. (1929). Banned in Italy (1929) because of its painfully accurate account of the Italian retreat from Caporetto, Italy; banned in Ireland (1939); challenged at the Dallas, Tex. Independent School District high school libraries (1974); challenged at the Vernon-Verona-Sherill, N.Y. School District (1980) as a "sex novel"; burned by the Nazis in Germany (1933). Source: 1, p. 137; 3, pp. 79-80; 7, Jan. 1975, pp. 6-7; May 1980, p. 62.

521

_____. *For Whom the Bell Tolls.* Scribner. Declared nonmailable by the U.S. Post Office (1940). On Feb. 21, 1973 eleven Turkish book publishers went on trial before an Istanbul martial law tribunal on charges of publishing, possessing, and selling books in violation of an order of the Istanbul martial law command. They faced possible sentences of between one month's and six month's imprisonment "for spreading propaganda unfavorable to the state" and the confiscation of their books. Eight booksellers were also on trial with the publishers on the same charge involving *For Whom the Bell Tolls*. Source: 3, p. 80; 4, Summer 1973, xii.

522

_____. *The Killers.* Macmillan. Challenged, but retained in the Bridgeport, Conn. public schools (1995). The short story, published in 1927, repeatedly uses the word "nigger." It was not part of the curriculum, but was chosen by a teacher as part of a unit on violence in literature. Source: 7, Jan. 1996, p. 30.

523

_____. *The Sun Also Rises.* Scribner. Banned in Boston, Mass. (1930), Ireland (1953), Riverside, Calif. (1960), and San Jose, Calif. (1960). Burned in Nazi bonfires (1933). Source: 3, pp. 79-80.

524

_____. *To Have and Have Not.* Scribner. Banned in Detroit, Mich. (1938) and distribution forbidden in Queens, N.Y. (1938). Source: 3, pp. 79-80; 9, Vol. III, p. 652.

525

Hendrix, Harvelle. *Keeping the Love You Find.* Pocket Bks. Pulled from the Staples-Motley, Minn. High School health classes (1995) because its sexual subject matter was deemed inappropriate for freshmen and sophomores. The book was not a textbook or required reading, but a resource. Source: 7, May 1995, p. 70.

526

Henege, Thomas. *Skim.* Dodd. Publication canceled by Dodd, Mead & Company (1983) because of language in the book considered "objectionable" by Thomas Nelson, Inc. of Nashville, Tenn. –Dodd, Mead's parent company. Source: 7, Nov. 1983, p. 188.

527

Hentoff, Nat. *The Day They Came to Arrest the Book.* Dell. Challenged in the Albemarle County schools in Charlottesville, Va. (1990) because it offers an inflammatory challenge to authoritarian roles. Source: 7, Jan. 1991, p. 18.

528

Herbert, Frank. *Soul Catcher.* Ace Bks. Challenged, but retained at the Lake Washington School District in Kirkland, Wash. (1993) despite objections there is "a very explicit sex scene," it is "a mockery of Christianity," and "very much anti-God." Source: 7, Jan. 1994, p. 16; Mar. 1994, p. 71.

529

Herge. *Tintin in America.* Little. Removed from the Spokane, Wash. School District libraries (1995) as racially demeaning and insulting. Source: 7, Jan. 1996, p. 12.

530

Hermes, Patricia. *Solitary Secret.* Harcourt. Moved from the library at Parker, Colo. Junior High School (1988) to the senior high school because of its graphic detail of sex. Source: 7, Mar. 1988, p. 45.

531

Heron, Ann. *How Would You Feel If Your Dad Was Gay?* Alyson Pubns. Challenged at the Mesa, Ariz. Public Library (1993) because it "is vile, sick and goes against every law and constitution." Retained at the Dayton and Montgomery County, Ohio Public Library (1993). Challenged, but retained in the Oak Bluffs, Mass. school library (1994). Though the parent leading the protest stated that "The subject matter … is obscene and vulgar and the message is that homosexuality is okay," the selection review committee voted unanimously to keep the book. Source: 7, Jan. 1994, p. 34; Mar. 1994, p. 69; May 1994, p. 98.

532

_____. *One Teenager in Ten: Testimony by Gay and Lesbian Youth.* Alyson Pubns. Challenged at the Deschutes County Library in Bend, Oreg. (1993) because it "encourages and condones" homosexuality. Retained at the Estes Park, Colo. Public Library (1994) after challenges to the book for its graphic content. Source: 7, Sept. 1993, pp. 158-59; Sept. 1994, p. 165.

533

Herzberg, Max J. *Myths and Their Meanings.* Allyn & Bacon. Challenged in the Woodland Park, Colo. High School (1992) because the stories about mythological figures like Zeus and Apollo threaten Western civilization's foundations. Source: 7, May 1992, p. 82.

534

Hesse, Hermann. *Steppenwolf.* Holt. Challenged at the Glenwood Springs, Colo. High School library (1982) due to book's references to lesbianism, hermaphroditism, sexual perversion, drug use, murder, and insanity. Source: 5 & 7, Sept. 1982, p. 169.

535

Hewitt, Kathryn. *Two by Two: The Untold Story.* Harcourt.

Challenged at the Hubbard, Ohio Public Library (1991) because the book alters the story of Noah's Ark making it secular and confusing to children. Source: 7, Sept. 1991, p. 153.

536

Heyman, Abigail. *Growing Up Female in America*. Holt. Prohibited for use in the Warsaw, Ind. schools (1979). Source: 7, Mar. 1980, p. 40.

537

Hinton, S. E. *The Outsiders*. Dell; Viking. Challenged on an eighth grade reading list in the South Milwaukee, Wis. schools (1986) because "drug and alcohol abuse was common" in the novel and "virtually all the characters were from broken homes." Challenged at the Boone, Iowa School District (1992) because the book glamorizes smoking and drinking and uses excessive violence and obscenities. Source: 7, Jan. 1987, p. 13; Nov. 1992, p. 199.

538

_____. *Rumble Fish*. Delacorte; Dell. Challenged at the Poca Middle School in Charleston, W.Va. (1991) because the book is "too frank." Source: 7, Jan. 1992, p. 9.

539

_____. *Tex*. Dell. Challenged due to foul language and violence, but retained at Campbell Middle School in Daytona Beach, Fla. (1995). Source: 7, May 1995, pp. 69-70; July 1995, pp. 110-11.

540

_____. *That Was Then, This Is Now*. Dell; Viking. Challenged at the Pagosa Springs, Colo. schools (1983) because a parent objected to the "graphic language, subject matter, 'immoral tone,' and lack of literary quality." Challenged on an eighth grade reading list in the South Milwaukee, Wis. schools (1986) because "drug and alcohol abuse was common" and "virtually all the characters were from broken homes." Challenged at the Poca Middle School in Charleston, W.Va. (1991) because the book is "too frank." Source: 5 & 7, Mar. 1984, p. 53; Jan. 1987, p. 13; Jan. 1992, p. 9.

541

Hitchcock, Alfred. *Alfred Hitchcock's Witches Brew*. Random. Challenged at the Fond du Lac, Wis. school system (1982) because the anthology contains stories about magic, witchcraft, and the supernatural. Source: 7, Mar. 1983, p. 39.

542

Hite, Shere. *The Hite Report on Male Sexuality*. Knopf. Chal-

lenged at the Southern Pine, N.C. Public Library (1983) because it is inappropriate "for the development of moral character in children or anyone for that matter." Source: 7, May 1983, p. 85.

543

Hitler, Adolf. *Mein Kampf*. Houghton. Banned in Palestine (1937), Czechoslovakia (1932) for its fierce militaristic doctrines. Banned from the 158 Stars and Stripes bookstores in West Germany. Since all Nazi literature has been banned in West Germany for decades, the circulation manager for the U.S. government chain stated, "we're guests in Germany, and I think we should show certain respect to our hosts." Source: 3, p. 72; 7, Jan. 1989, p. 14.

544

Hodges, Hollis. *Don't Tell Me Your Name*. Avon; Crown. Relegated to the restricted shelf at the Covington Junior High School Library in Vancouver, Wash. (1985), the Evergreen School Board reversed its earlier ruling and decided to keep the novel despite parents' contention it is sexually explicit and inappropriate for junior high readers. Source: 7, July 1985, p. 133; Nov. 1985, pp. 203-4; July 1986, p. 118.

545

Hogan, William. *The Quartzsite Trip*. Avon. Challenged at Vancouver, Wash. Pacific Junior High School library (1985) because "the subject matter was too adult for junior high school students." Placed in a collection for teacher use only in the Lincoln, Nebr. East High School library (1987) after a complaint was filed by a teacher. Source: 7, May 1985, p. 91; July 1985, p. 134; Nov. 1987, p. 225.

546

Hoke, Helen. *Witches, Witches, Witches*. Watts. Challenged at the Smith Valley, Nev. school libraries (1988) because the book "is replete with scenes of intrusion, oppression, cannibalism, abduction, transformation, incantations, deceptions, threats, and sexism." Source: 7, July 1988, pp. 121-22; Sept. 1988, p. 178.

547

Holland, Margaret, and McKee, Craig. *The Unicorn Who Had No Horn*. Willowsip Pr. Challenged at the Cornell, Wis. Elementary School library (1991) because it allegedly promotes "New Age religion" and includes content related to witchcraft and the occult. Source: 7, Jan. 1992, p. 6; Mar. 1992, p. 63.

548

Homer. *The Odyssey*. Airmont; Doubleday; Harper; Macmillan; NAL; Oxford Univ. Pr.; Penguin. Plato suggested expurgating Homer for immature readers (387 B.C.) and Caligula tried to suppress it because it expressed Greek ideals of freedom (35). Source: 3, p. 1.

549
Homes, A. M. *Jack*. Vintage. Placed on the Spindale, N.C. school library's (1996) reserve shelf. This meant parental permission was required for a student to check it out. A parent did not find the novel "proper to be in the library due to the language." Source: 7, Nov. 1996, pp. 193-94.

550
Hoobler, Dorothy, and Hoobler, Thomas. *Nelson and Winnie Mandela*. Watts. Challenged at the Hillsboro, Oreg. Public Library (1988) by a patron who charged that the Mandelas and the African National Congress are Communist-backed and advocate violence. Source: 7, Jan. 1989, p. 3.

551
Hotze, Sollace. *A Circle Unbroken*. Houghton. Challenged at Cary, Ill. Junior High School (1994) because references in the book to sex are too explicit for seventh and eighth graders; retained by school board vote. Source: 7, May 1994, p. 83; July 1994, pp. 128-29.

552
Howe, Norma. *God, the Universe and Hot Fudge Sundaes*. Houghton. Challenged at the Canby, Oreg. Junior High School library (1988) because the book "pushes several items of the humanist agenda: death education, anti-God, pro-evolution, anti-Bible, anti-Christian, and logic over faith." Source: 7, May 1989, p. 78.

553
Hoyt, Olga. *Demons, Devils and Djinn*. Abelard-Schuman. Challenged at Elkhorn Middle School in Frankfort, Ky. (1990) because "it describes devil worship." Source: 7, May 1990, p. 84; July 1990, p. 145.

554
Hubbard, L. Ron. *Mission Earth*. Bridge Pubns. Inc. Challenged at the Dalton, Ga. Regional Library System (1990) because of "repeated passages involving chronic masochism, child abuse, homosexuality, necromancy, bloody murder, and other things that are anti-social, perverted, and anti-everything." Source: 7, July 1990, p. 125.

555
Hughes, Langston. *The Best Short Stories by Negro Writers*. Little. Removed from the Island Trees, N.Y. Union Free District High School library in 1976 along with nine other titles because they were considered "immoral, anti-American, anti-

Christian, or just plain filthy"; returned to the library after the U.S. Supreme Court ruling on June 25, 1982 in *Board of Education, Island Trees Union Free School District No. 26 et al. v. Pico et al.*, 457 U.S. 853 (1982). Source: 7, Nov. 1982, p. 197.

556
Hughes, Tracy, ed. *Everything You Need to Know about Teen Pregnancy*. Rosen. Challenged, but retained at the Cleveland, Tenn. Public Library (1993) along with seventeen other books, most of which are on sex education, AIDS awareness, and some titles on the supernatural. Source: 7, Sept. 1993, p. 146.

557
Hugo, Victor. *Hernani*. French & European; Larousse. Banned by Nicholas I in Russia (1850). Source: 3, p. 41.

558
_____. *Les Miserables*. Dodd; Fawcett; Penguin. Listed in the *Index Librorum Prohibitorum* in Rome from 1864-1959; voted out of a library by a Philadelphia, Pa. (1904) because it mentioned a grisette. Source: 1, p. 92; 3, p. 41.

559
_____. *Notre Dame de Paris*. Penguin. Banned by Nicholas I in Russia (1850). Listed in the *Index Librorum Prohibitorum* from 1864-1959. Source: 3, p. 41.

560
Hull, Eleanor. *Alice with the Golden Hair*. Atheneum. Removed, but later reinstated at the Pine Middle School library in Gibsonia, Pa. (1990) because of its adult language. Source: 7, Nov. 1990, pp. 209-10; Jan. 1991, pp. 28-29.

561
Hume, David. *On Religion*. Collins; World Pub. Co. Banned in Turkey (1986). Source: 4, July/Aug. 1986, p. 46.

562
Humphrey, Derek. *Final Exit*. Hemlock Soc. Challenged at the Cook Memorial Library in Libertyville, Ill. (1991) because the book diminishes the value of the elderly and encourages breaking the law by assisting homicide and drug abuse. Banned in Australia (1992). Source: 7, Jan. 1992, p. 25.

563
Hunter, Evan. *The Chisholms*. Harper. A Livermore Valley, Calif. Unified School District book selection committee (1981) voted to remove this title from the Granada High School library due to poor literary quality, gratuitous vio-

lence, as well as explicitly sexual passages. Source: 7, Jan. 1982, p. 8.

564
Hutchins, Maude. *A Diary of Love.* Greenwood. Banned by the Chicago, Ill. Police Bureau of Censorship in 1950 because the book was "so candidly filthy in spots as to constitute a menace to public morals." Source: 9, Vol. IV, p. 710.

565
Huxley, Aldous. *Antic Hay.* Harper; Bantam; Modern Library. Banned on grounds of obscenity in Boston, Mass. (1930). A Baltimore, Md. (1952) teacher was dismissed for assigning Huxley's novel to his senior literature class. The teacher's unsuccessful quest for vindication is reported in *Parker v. Board of Education,* 237 F. Supp. 222 (D. Md.). Source: 3, p. 75; 8, pp. 23, 230.

566
_____. *Brave New World.* Harper. Banned in Ireland (1932). Removed from classroom in Miller, Mo. (1980) and challenged frequently throughout the U.S. Challenged as required reading at the Yukon, Okla. High School (1988) because of "the book's language and moral content." Challenged as required reading in the Corona-Norco, Calif. Unified School District (1993) because it is "centered around negative activity." The book was retained and teachers selected alternatives if students object to Huxley's novel. Source: 3, p. 75; 4; 7, May 1980, p. 52; July 1988, p. 140; Jan. 1994, p. 14; Mar. 1994, p. 70.

567
_____. *The Doors of Perception.* Harper. Challenged at the Oconto, Wis. Unified School District (1980) because it "glorifies the use of drugs." Source: 7, Mar. 1981, p. 41.

568
_____. *Eyeless in Gaza.* Harper. Banned in Ireland (1926-1953). Source: 3, p. 75.

569
_____. *Point Counter Point.* Harper. Banned in Ireland (1930) on the grounds of offending public morals. Source: 3, p. 75.

570
Hyde, Margaret O., and Forsyth, Elizabeth. *Know about AIDS.* Walker. Challenged, but retained at the Cleveland, Tenn. Public Library (1993) along with seventeen other books, most of which are on sex education, AIDS awareness, and some titles on the supernatural. Source: 7, Sept. 1993, p. 146.

571
Ibsen, Henrik. *A Doll's House.* Penguin. Four members of the Alabama State Textbook Committee (1983) called for the rejection of Ibsen's work because it propagates feminist views. Source: 7, Mar. 1983, p. 39.

572
_____. *An Enemy of the People.* Penguin. Works purged by Franco government (1939); works formerly banned reported to be extremely popular in USSR (1938). Source: 3, p. 48.

573
_____. *Four Great Plays by Ibsen.* NAL. Challenged, but retained, in the Carroll County, Md. schools (1991). Two school board members were concerned about the play, Ghosts, which deals with venereal disease, incest, and suicide. Source: 7, Mar. 1992, p. 64.

574
_____. *Ghosts.* Beekman; Dutton. Banned in England (1892); purged by the Franco government (1939). Ban lifted in USSR (1958). Source: 3, p. 48.

575
Illustrated Encyclopedia of Family Health. Marshall Cavendish. Removed from the library at Sage Valley Junior High School in Gillette, Wy. (1986) after a resident said the book contained photographs that were "very nude and very explicit." Challenged in an intermediate school library in Beaverton, Oreg. (1991) because of explicit line drawings of sexual intercourse positions and removed from the library, but maintained for staff use only. Source: 7, July 1986, p. 118; July 1992, p. 103.

576
Irving, John. *A Prayer for Owen Meany.* Ballantine; Morrow. Pulled from the Boiling Springs High School senior literature class in Carlisle, Pa. (1992) after several complaints from parents about its content and language. Source: 7, July 1992, p. 112; Sept. 1992, p. 142.

577
Isay, Richard. *Being Homosexual: Gay Men and Their Development.* Avon; Farrar. Challenged at the Deschutes County Library in Bend, Oreg. (1993) because it "encourages and condones" homosexuality. Source: 7, Sept. 1993, pp. 158-59.

578
Isensee, Rick. *Love Between Men.* Prentice-Hall; Alyson Pubns. Challenged at the Chester County Library at Charlestown, Pa. (1996) because it was "pornographic and

smutty." Source: 7, Nov. 1996, p. 194.

579
Izzi, John. *Metrication, American Style*. Phi Delta Kappa Ed. Banned at the Toll Gate High School in Warwick, R.I. (1985) because it is "discriminatory toward women." Source: 7, July 1985, p. 114.

580
Jackson, Jesse. *Call Me Charley*. Harper. Parents of a black fourth grade student filed suit against Grand Blanc, Mich. school officials (1979) after a teacher read this title to their son's class. The work includes a white character who calls a black youth "Sambo," "nigger," and "coon." Source: 7, Mar. 1979, p. 38.

581
Jackson, Shirley. *The Lottery*. Ency. Brit.; Farrar; Popular Library. The film version of Jackson's short story was banned in Forest Lake, Minn. but reinstated by U.S. District Court judge (1981). Source: 5 & 7, July 1981, p. 88.

582
Jacobs, Anita. *Where Has Deedie Wooster Been All These Years?* Delacorte. Removed from the Hockinson, Wash. Middle School library (1984) because it is "garbage" and the novel's discussion of a young girl's first menstrual cycle is particularly objectionable. Source: 7, Sept. 1984, p. 138.

583
Jagendorf, Moritz A. *Tales of Mystery:* Folk Tales from Around the World. Silver Burdett. Removed to a locked closet in the superintendent's office in Banner County, Nebr. (1992) because the book "has to do with a lot of negative things and might not be good for someone with low self-esteem or suicide tendencies." Source: 7, May 1992, p. 80.

584
Jakes, John. *Bastard*. Jove. Removed from the Montour, Pa. High School library (1976). Source: 7, Nov. 1976, pp. 143-44.

585
James, Henry. *Turn of the Screw*. Tor Bks. Challenged at the St. Johns County Schools in St. Augustine, Fla. (1995). Source: 7, Jan. 1996, p. 14.

586
Jay, Carla, and Young, Allen. *The Gay Report*. Summit. Challenged at the Niles, Mich. Community Library (1982). Source: 7, Jan. 1983, p. 8.

587
Jenness, Aylette. *Families: A Celebration of Diversity, Commitment and Love*. Houghton. Temporarily removed, but later reinstated, at the Winfield, Ill. Public Library (1990) because of objections to two of the stories. One involves a gay couple who adopted a baby at birth and the other involved a lesbian couple who raise one of the couple's children. Source: 7, Mar. 1991, p. 61.

588
Jennings, Gary. *Black Magic, White Magic*. Dell; Dial; Hart-Davis. Retained at the Ector County, Tex. school library (1989) after being challenged because the book might lure children into the occult. Source: 7, Jan. 1990, p. 9; May 1990, p. 107.

589
Jennings, Kevin, ed. *Becoming Visible: A Reader in Gay and Lesbian History for High School and College Students*. Alyson Pubns. Banned from the two high school libraries in Mehlville, Mo. (1996) by order of the superintendent. The donated book was removed because it "does not meet the needs of the curriculum." Source: 7, May 1996, pp. 82-83.

590
Jeschke, Susan. *The Devil Did It*. Holt. Challenged at the elementary school libraries in Howard County, Md. (1990) because it shows the devil as "a benign or friendly force." Source: 7, Jan. 1991, p. 12.

591
Jewkes, Wilfred Thomas. *The Perilous Journey*. Harcourt. Pulled from the curriculum of the Baltimore County, Md. school system (1989) because a three-page retelling of an African American folk legend was considered racially insensitive. The offensive story was "All God's Chillen Had Wings." Source: 7, Jan. 1990, p. 11.

592
Jimenez, Carlos M. *The Mexican-American Heritage*. TQS Pubs. Challenged in the Santa Barbara, Calif. schools (1996) because the book promotes "Mexican nationalism." Source: 7, May 1996, p. 98.

593
Johnson, Earvin (Magic). *What You Can Do to Avoid AIDS*. Times Books. Removed from the Horace Greeley High School in Chappaqua, N.Y. (1996) because a group of parents complained that the basketball player's written description of oral and anal sex were inappropriate for 14- and 15-year-olds. Johnson's book is endorsed by the American Medical Association and the Children's Defense Fund.

Source: 7, May 1996, p. 88; July 1996, p. 119.

594
Johnson, Eric W. *Love and Sex and Growing Up.* Bantam. Challenged, but retained at the Cleveland, Tenn. Public Library (1993) along with seventeen other books, most of which are on sex education, AIDS awareness, and some titles on the supernatural. Source: 7, Sept. 1993, p. 146.

595
_____. *Love and Sex in Plain Language.* Lippincott/Harper; Bantam. Moved from the children's room of the Tampa-Hillsborough County, Fla. Public Library (1982). Challenged in the Williamsport, Pa. schools (1988) because of allegedly inaccurate and misleading information in the book. Source: 7, Jan. 1982, pp. 4-5; May 1988, p. 104.

596
_____. *Sex: Telling It Straight.* Bantam; Lippincott. Placed on restricted shelves at the Evergreen School District elementary school libraries in Vancouver, Wash. (1987) in accordance with the school board policy to restrict student access to sex education books in elementary school libraries. Source: 7, May 1987, p. 87.

597
Johnson, Sam, et al. *Beavis and Butt-Head Ensucklopedia.* MTV Books; Pocket Bks. Challenged at the Salt Lake County, Utah Public Library (1995) by a parent because it has "no literary value whatsoever. It was totally perverse garbage, trash. I consider it pornography." The complainant requested the removal of all Beavis and Butt-Head materials, including seven cassettes, seven CDs and two copies of MTV's Beavis and Butt-Head Experience. Source: 7, May 1995, pp. 67-68.

598
Jonas, Ann. *Aardvarks Disembark.* Greenwillow. Challenged at the Hubbard, Ohio Public Library (1991) because the book alters the story of Noah's Ark making it secular and confusing children. Source: 7, Sept. 1991, p. 153.

599
Jones, Clinton R. *Understanding Gay Relatives and Friends.* Seabury Pr. Challenged at the Elkhart, Ind. Public Library (1982) because it attempts to "get people to accept the homosexual lifestyle, like there is nothing wrong with it."

Source: 7, Mar. 1983, p. 56.

600
Jones, James. *From Here to Eternity.* Dell; Dial. Banned in Holyoke and Springfield, Mass. and in Denver, Colo. (1951). Source: 3, p. 94.

601
Jong, Erica. *Fear of Flying.* Holt. Challenged in Terre Haute, Ind. (1982) as optional reading in an elective course for junior and senior high school students. Source: 7, May 1982, p. 86.

602
Jordan, June. *Living Room.* Thunder's Mouth. Banned from the Baldwin, Mich. High School library (1990) because it contains profanity and racial slurs. Source: 7, Jan. 1991, p. 12.

> ## "The books that the world calls immoral are the books that show the world its own shame."
> ~ Oscar Wilde

603
Josephs, Rebecca. *Early Disorders.* Fawcett; Farrar. Challenged at the Mukwonago, Wis. High School (1988) because the book's "portrayal of anorexia nervosa was not factual and the account of a girl's life, thoughts, and emotions used pornographic language and made fun of religion." Source: 7, May 1988, p. 104.

604
Joyce, James. *Dubliners.* Modern Library; Penguin. Destroyed by printer because he found passages objectionable (1912). Source: 3, p. 65.

605
_____. *Exiles.* Penguin. Banned in Turkey (1986). Source: 4, July/Aug. 1986, p. 46.

606
_____. *Ulysses.* Farrar; Modern Library; Random/Vintage. Burned in U.S. (1918), Ireland (1922), Canada (1922), England (1923) and banned in England (1929). Source: 3, p. 66; 9, Vol. III, pp. 411-12, 557-58, 645.

607
Julian, Cloyd J., and Simon, Nancy S. *Family Life and Human Sexuality.* Holt. Challenged as a supplemental text in an elective course in the Omaha, Nebr. School District

(1987) because the book promotes "Planned Parenthood, abortion, and artificial methods of birth control." The book was adopted after the course's previous text, *Finding My Way* by Andrew Riker, was replaced because it was considered too controversial. Source: 7, Nov. 1987, p. 225.

608
Juster, Norton. *The Phantom Tollbooth.* Collins; Knopf; Penguin; Random; Scholastic. Removed from a locked reference collection at the Boulder, Colo. Public Library (1988). The book was originally locked away because the librarian considered it a poor fantasy. Source: 7, Jan. 1989, p. 27.

609
Kallen, Stuart A. *Ghastly Ghost Stories.* Abdo & Dghtrs. Challenged, but retained in the Warrensburg-Latham, Ill. school library (1992) because the series of seven books are "possibly harmful to a child's psychological development." Source: 7, Jan. 1993, p. 7; Mar. 1993, p. 41.

610
_____. *Vampires, Werewolves and Zombies.* Abdo & Dghtrs. Challenged, but retained at the Cleveland, Tenn. Public Library (1993) along with seventeen other books, most of which are on sex education, AIDS awareness, and some titles on the supernatural. Source: 7, Sept. 1993, p. 146.

611
Kane, William; Blake, Peggy; and Frye, Robert. *Understanding Health.* Random. Banned from the curriculum at the Oak Hills, Ohio High School (1983) because the book discusses abortion, premarital sex, and euthanasia. Source: 7, Sept. 1983, p. 142; July 1984, p. 107; Sept. 1984, p. 157.

612
Kane, William M., and Merki, Mary Bronson. *Human Sexuality: Relationships and Responsibilities.* Glencoe. Challenged at the Bremerton, Wash. schools (1992) because it allegedly is "based on fraudulent research, stresses homosexuality, and is inappropriate for teenagers." Source: 7, July 1992, p. 112.

613
Kant, Immanuel. *The Critique of Pure Reason.* St. Martin. Placed on the Roman Index until the 20th century; both the Soviet Union (1928) and Spain (1939) purged Kant's works from their libraries. Source: 2, p. 163; 3, p. 31.

614
_____. *Religion within the Boundaries of Pure Reason.* Continuum. Banned by the Lutheran church because, "Our sacred person you have with your so-called philosophy attempted to bring into contempt...and you have at the same time assailed the truth of the Scriptures and the foundations of Creed beliefs...We order that henceforth you shall employ your talents to better purpose and that you shall keep silence on matters which are outside of your proper functions." Source: 2, p. 163.

615
Kantor, MacKinlay. *Andersonville.* NAL. Banned in Amarillo, Tex. (1962). Source: 3, p. 85.

616
Kaufman, Joe. *How We Are Born, How We Grow, How Our Bodies Work, and How We Learn.* Golden Pr. Removed from circulation collection, and now available only as a ref-erence book at the Old Kings Elementary School in Bunnell, Fla. (1991) because two pages on the reproductive process were found objectionable. Source: 7, Mar. 1992, p. 40.

617
Kaufman, Sue. *Falling Bodies.* Doubleday. Challenged in Terre Haute, Ind. (1982) as optional reading in an elective course for junior and senior high school students. Source: 7, May 1982, p. 86.

618
Kazan, Elia. *Acts of Love.* Knopf; Warner. Removed from the Utah State Library bookmobile (1980). Source: 7, Nov. 1980, p. 128.

619
Kazantzakis, Nikos. *The Last Temptation of Christ.* Simon & Schuster. Challenged in Long Beach, Calif. (1962-1965). Source: 3, p. 68.

620
Keehn, Sally. *I Am Regina.* Philomel Bks. Challenged as optional fifth-grade reading at the Orland Park, Ill. School District 135 (1996) because the book uses unflattering stereotypes to depict Native Americans and uses the word "squaw" which was offensive. Source: Jan. 1997, p. 10.

621
Keeping, Charles. *Through the Window.* Oxford Univ. Pr.; Watts; Weston Woods. Challenged at the Cedar Rapids, Iowa Public Library (1985) because "the harsh realities of life it depicts are not suitable for young readers." Source: 7, Sept. 1985, p. 167.

622
Kellerman, Faye. *Milk and Honey.* Morrow. Challenged at the Rogers-Hough, Ark. Memorial Library (1991) because of "sacrilegious language." Source: 7, Sept. 1991, p. 151.

623

Kelley, Leo P. *Night of Fire and Blood*. Childrens Pr. Found unsuitable for younger children in Aurora, Colo. (1984) because it deals with "violence and self-mutilation." Source: 7, May 1984, p. 69.

624

Kellogg, Marjorie. *Tell Me That You Love Me, Junie Moon*. Farrar. Challenged at the Frederick County, Md. school system (1978) because it teaches that "it's all right to do things against society's rules." Source: 7, Mar. 1978, p. 39; May 1978, p. 58.

625

Kennedy, X. J. *Literature: Introduction to Fiction, Poetry and Drama*. Harper. Challenged in the Ojai, Calif. schools (1993) because selections contained foul language and blasphemy, and that they glamorize sexual misconduct. Source: 7, Jan. 1994, p. 37.

626

Kerr, M. E. *Dinky Hocker Shoots Smack*. Dell; Harper. Removed from Kent, Wash. elementary school libraries (1977) because of complaints about "vulgarity" and "defamation of the word of God in the work." Source: 5 & 7, Mar. 1977, p. 36.

627

_____. *Gentle Hands*. Bantam; Harper. Challenged at the Lake Braddock, Va. Secondary School (1983) because the book is "anti-Semitic" and "glamorizes drug abuse and makes drugs 'tempting' to teenagers." Source: 7, July 1983, p. 109; Nov. 1983, p. 187; Mar. 1984, p. 53.

628

Kesey, Ken. *One Flew over the Cuckoo's Nest*. NAL; Penguin; Viking. Removed from the required reading list in Westport, Mass. (1977). Banned from the St. Anthony, Idaho Freemont High School classrooms (1978) and the instructor fired — *Fogarty v. Atchley*. Challenged at the Merrimack, N.H. High School (1982). Challenged as part of the curriculum in an Aberdeen, Wash. High School honors English class (1986) because the book promotes "secular humanism." The school board voted to retain the title. Source: 7, Jan. 1977, p. 8; May 1978, p. 57; July 1978, pp. 96, 100; Sept. 1982, p. 170; 8, pp. 104-11, 229; Nov. 1986, p. 225; 9, Vol. IV, p. 714.

629

Kessel, Joyce K. *Halloween*. Carolrhoda Bks; Lerner. Challenged at the Neely Elementary School in Gilbert, Ariz. (1992) because the book shows the dark side of religion through the occult, the devil, and satanism. Source: 7, May 1992, p. 78; July 1992, p. 124.

630

Keyes, Daniel. *Flowers for Algernon*. Bantam; Harcourt. Banned from the Plant City, Fla. (1976) and Emporium, Pa. (1977) public schools because of references to sex; banned from the Glen Rose, Ark. High School library (1981); challenged at the Oberlin, Ohio High School (1983) because several pages of the novel detail a sexual encounter of the protagonist. Challenged as a required reading at the Glenrock, Wyo. High School (1984) because several "explicit love scenes were distasteful." Challenged at the Charlotte-Mecklenburg, N.C. schools (1986) as a tenth grade supplemental reading because it is "pornographic." Challenged, but retained in the Yorktown, Va. schools (1996). A parent complained about the profanity and references to sex and drinking in the novel. Source: 7, July 1976, p. 85; May 1977, p. 73; July 1981, p. 91; Jan. 1984, p. 26; July 1984, p. 122; Jan. 1987, p. 12; Mar. 1987, p. 54; May 1987, p. 103; July 1987, p. 150; May 1996, p. 100.

631

Kidd, Flora. *Between Pride and Passion*. Harlequin. More than fifty Harlequin romances donated by Glide, Oreg. residents were threatened with removal from the high school library (1984) because "teenagers already have trouble with their emotions without being stimulated by poorly written books." Source: 7, July 1984, p. 104.

632

Kilgore, Kathleen. *The Wolfman of Beacon Hill*. Little. Challenged at the Pilot Butte Junior High School in Bend, Oreg. (1989) because the material does not enlighten, uplift, or encourage character building traits. Source: 7, Jan. 1990, pp. 4-5.

633

Killingsworth, Monte. *Eli's Songs*. Macmillan. Challenged in the Rural Dell School District in Molalla, Oreg. (1992) because the book is "anti-local," has "logger-bashing" sentiments and an "ecological slant." Source: 7, July 1992, pp. 124-25.

634

Kincaid, Jamaica. *Lucy*. Farrar; NAL; G.K. Hall. Challenged at the West Chester, Pa. schools (1994) as "most pornographic." The book was changed from required to optional reading. Source: 7, Jan. 1995, p. 25; Mar. 1995, p. 45; May 1995, p. 71.

635

King, Frederick; Rudman, Herbert; and Leavell, Doris. *Understanding the Social Sciences.* Laidlaw. Removed from Alabama's list of approved texts — and from the state's class-rooms — because the book promotes the "religion of secular humanism." U.S. District Court Judge W. Brevard Hand ruled on March 4, 1987, that thirty-nine history and social studies texts used in Alabama's 129 school systems "discriminate against the very concept of religion and theistic religions in particular, by omissions so serious that a student learning history from them would not be apprised of relevant facts about America's history.... References to religion are isolated and the integration of religion in the history of American society is ignored." The series includes: *Understanding People; Understanding Families; Understanding Communities; Understanding Religions of the World; Understanding Our Country;* and *Understanding the World.* On August 26, 1987, the U.S. Court of Appeals for the Eleventh Circuit unanimously overturned Judge Hand's decision by ruling that the information in the book was "essentially neutral in its religious content." The fact that the texts omitted references to religion was not "an advancement of secular humanism or an active hostility toward theistic religion." Source: 7, Jan. 1987, p. 6; May 1987, pp. 75, 104-7; Sept. 1987, pp. 166-67; Nov. 1987, pp. 217-18; Jan. 1988, p. 17; Mar. 1988, p. 40.

636

King, Larry. *Tell It to the King.* Putnam; Thorndike Pr. Challenged at the Public Libraries of Saginaw, Mich. (1989) because it is "an insult to one's intelligence" and contains foul language. Source: 7, May 1989, p. 77.

637

King, Stephen. *The Bachman Books.* NAL. Removed from the West Lyon Community School library in Larchwood, Iowa (1987) because "it does not meet the standards of the community." Source: 7, May 1987, p. 86; July 1987, p. 125.

638

_____. *Carrie.* Doubleday. Challenged at the Clark High School library in Las Vegas, Nev. (1975) because it is "trash." Placed in special closed shelf at the Vergennes, Vt. Union High School library (1978) because it could "harm" students, particularly "younger girls." Removed from the West Lyon Community School library in Larchwood, Iowa (1987) because "it does not meet the standards of the community." Banned from the Altmar-Parish-Williamstown, N.Y. district libraries (1991). Challenged, along with eight other Stephen King novels in Bismarck, N.Dak. (1994) by a local minister and a school board member, because of "age appropriateness." Challenged by a parent, and currently under review, at the Boyertown, Pa. Junior High East library (1994). The parent

"objected to the book's language, its violence, and its sexual descriptions, as well as what she described as a 'Satanic killing' sequence." Source: 7, Jan. 1979, p. 6; May 1987, p. 86; July 1987, p. 125; Mar. 1992, p. 40; May 1994, pp. 84-85.

639

_____. *Christine.* NAL; Viking. The Washington County, Ala. Board of Education (1985) voted unanimously to ban the novel from all county school libraries because the book contains "unacceptable language" and is "pornographic." Removed from the West Lyon Community School library in Larchwood, Iowa (1987) because "it does not meet the standards of the community." Removed from the Washington Middle School library in Meriden, Conn. (1989) after a parent complained about offensive passages. Removed from the Livingston, Mont. Middle School library (1990) because it was deemed not "suitable for intended audience," owing to violence, explicit sex, and inappropriate language. Challenged at the Webber Township High School library in Bluford, Ill. (1993) along with all other King novels. Challenged, along with eight other Stephen King novels in Bismarck, N.Dak. (1994) by a local minister and a school board member, because of "age appropriateness." Source: 7, Jan. 1986, p. 7; May 1987, p. 86; July 1987, p. 125; May 1989, p. 75; Jan. 1991, p. 12; July 1993, p. 124; May 1994, pp. 84-85.

640

_____. *Cujo.* NAL; Viking. Challenged at the Rankin County, Miss. School District (1984) because it is "profane and sexually objectionable." Removed from the shelves of the Bradford, N.Y. school library (1985) "because it was a bunch of garbage." Rejected for purchase by the Hayward, Calif. school trustees (1985) because of "rough language" and "explicit sex scenes." The Washington County, Ala. Board of Education (1985) voted unanimously to ban the novel from all county school libraries because the book contains "unacceptable language" and is "pornographic." Removed from a high school library in Durand, Wis. (1987) pending review by a nine-member panel of school personnel and community members. Challenged, along with eight other Stephen King novels in Bismarck, N.Dak. (1994) by a local minister and a school board member, because of "age appropriateness." Source: 7, May 1984, p. 69; Jan. 1985, p. 8; May 1985, pp. 75, 77; July 1985, p. 111; Jan. 1986, p. 7; Nov. 1987, p. 226; May 1994, pp. 84-85.

641

_____. *The Dark Half.* NAL; Viking. Retained in the Roseburg, Oreg. High School library (1994) despite a parent's complaint that the book contains "extreme, bloodthirsty violence." Source: 7, Sept. 1994, pp. 166-67.

642

_____. *The Dead Zone*. Doubleday. Removed from the West Lyon Community School library in Larchwood, Iowa (1987) because "it does not meet the standards of the community." Restricted to high school students with parental permission at the Duval County, Fla. school system (1992) because of "filthy language" in the book. Banned in the Peru, Ind. school system (1992) along with *Cujo* and *Christine* because the books are "filthy." Challenged, along with eight other Stephen King novels in Bismarck, N.Dak. (1994) by a local minister and a school board member, because of "age appropriateness." Source: 7, May 1987, p. 86; July 1987, p. 125; May 1992, pp. 79, 80; July 1992, pp. 105, 106; May 1994, pp. 84-85;

643

_____. *Different Seasons*. Doubleday. Removed from the West Lyon Community School library in Larchwood, Iowa (1987) because "it does not meet the standards of the community." Removed from the Washington Middle School library in Meriden, Conn. (1989) after a parent complained about offensive passages. Challenged at the Eagan High School in Burnsville, Minn. (1992). Source: 7, May 1987, p. 86; July 1987, p. 125; May 1989, p. 75; Mar. 1993, p. 56.

644

_____. *The Drawing of the Three*. NAL. Challenged, along with eight other Stephen King novels in Bismarck, N.Dak. (1994) by a local minister and a school board member, because of "age appropriateness." Source: 7, May 1994, pp. 84-85.

645

_____. *The Eyes of the Dragon*. NAL. Challenged, along with eight other Stephen King novels in Bismarck, N.Dak. (1994) by a local minister and a school board member, because of "age appropriateness." Source: 7, May 1994, pp. 84-85

646

_____. *Firestarter*. Viking. Challenged at the Campbell County, Wyo. School System (1983-1984) because of its alleged "graphic descriptions of sexual acts, vulgar language, and violence." Removed from the Washington Middle School library in Meriden, Conn. (1989) after a parent complained about offensive passages. Source: 7, Mar. 1984, p. 39; May 1989, p. 75.

647

_____. *Four Past Midnight*. NAL. Challenged at the Sparta, Ill. High School library (1992) along with all other King

novels due to violence, sex, and explicit language. Source: 7, July 1992, p. 106.

648

_____. *It*. Viking. Challenged in the Lincoln, Nebr. school libraries (1987) because of the novel's "corruptive, obscene nature." Placed on a "closed shelf" at the Franklinville, N.Y. Central High School library (1992) because of explicit sexual acts, violence, and profane language. Students will need parental permission to check it out. Source: 7, Nov. 1987, p. 225; Mar. 1993, p. 41.

649

_____. *Night Shift*. Doubleday. Removed from the West Lyon Community School library in Larchwood, Iowa (1987) because "it does not meet the standards of the community." Removed from the Green Bay, Wis. School District classrooms (1988) because the book contains a short story entitled "Children of the Corn" which "teaches about the occult and rebellion by children and makes a mockery of Christianity." The book was returned, however, after questions were raised by school board members about the administrative decision to ban the book. Source: 7, May 1987, p. 86; July 1987, p. 125; Jan. 1989, p. 11; Mar. 1989, p. 44.

650

_____. *Pet Sematary*. NAL. Challenged, along with eight other Stephen King novels in Bismarck, N.Dak. (1994) by a local minister and a school board member, because of "age appropriateness." Source: 7, May 1994, pp. 84-85

651

_____. *Salem's Lot*. Doubleday; NAL. Banned from the Cleveland, Tex. Independent High School English classes (1986) overruling a review committee's recommendation, even after teachers had already inked out objectionable words with a felt-tip marker. A single copy is available in the restricted section of the high school library to students who have a permission slip signed by their parents. Banned from the Goochard, Vt. High School library (1988) because of sexually explicit language. Source: 7, Jan. 1987, p. 12; Mar. 1987, pp. 54-55; Sept. 1988, p. 152.

652

_____. *The Shining*. Doubleday. Challenged at the Campbell County, Wyo. School System (1983) because "the story contains violence, demonic possession and ridicules the Christian religion." The novel is now available to all students in grades seven through twelve, at the discretion of district librarians. Removed from the Evergreen School District's four junior high school libraries in Vancouver, Wash. (1986) because the book's "descriptive foul language" made it unsuitable for teenagers. Removed from the Livingston, Mont. Middle School library (1990) because it was deemed not "suitable for intended audience," owing to violence, explicit sex, and inappropriate language. Challenged, along with eight other Stephen King novels in Bismarck, N.Dak. (1994) by a local minister and a school board member, because of "age appropriateness." Source: 7, Jan. 1984, p. 10; Mar. 1984, p. 39; May 1986, p. 81; July 1987, p. 125; Jan. 1991, p. 12; May 1994, pp. 84-85.

653

_____. *The Skeleton Crew.* NAL. Challenged at the Salmon, Idaho High School library (1993) because of graphic street language about homosexuality, among other things. Source: 7, July 1993, p. 124.

654

_____. *The Stand.* Doubleday; NAL. Restricted to ninth grade students with parental consent at the Whitford Intermediate School in Beaverton, Oreg. (1989) because of "sexual language, casual sex, and violence." Source: 7, Jan. 1990, pp. 4-5.

655

_____. *The Talisman.* Viking. Challenged at the Salmon, Idaho High School library (1993) because of graphic street language about homosexuality, among other things. Source: 7, July 1993, p. 124.

656

_____. *Thinner.* NAL. Challenged, along with eight other Stephen King novels in Bismarck, N.Dak. (1994) by a local minister and a school board member, because of "age appropriateness." Source: 7, May 1994, pp. 84-85

657

_____. *The Tommyknockers.* NAL. Restricted to high school students with parental permission at the Duval County, Fla. school system (1992) because of "filthy language" in the book and "it's extremely graphic." Source: 7, May 1992, p. 79; July 1992, p. 105.

658

Kingston, Jeremy. *Witches and Witchcraft.* Aldus Bks. Removed from the Duerson-Oldham County Public Library in LaGrange, Ky. (1987) because "young or immature minds may become intrigued by Satan as a result of reading the book." Source: 7, Sept. 1987, p. 174.

659

Kinsey, Alfred. *Sexual Behavior in the Human Female.* Saunders. Banned in South Africa (1953), Ireland (1953), and in

U.S. Army post exchanges in Europe as having "no worthwhile interest for soldiers." Source: 3, p. 75.

660

_____. *Sexual Behavior in the Human Male.* Saunders. Banned in South Africa (1953), Ireland (1953), and in U.S. Army post exchanges in Europe as having "no worthwhile interest for soldiers." Source: 3, p. 75.

661

Kipling, Rudyard. *Drums of the Fore and Aft.* Doubleday. Removed from the Sunday school library of the Crawfordsville, Ind. (1899) First Methodist Episcopal Church because a parishioner complained that it was "fairly reeking with profanity, and the most outrageous slang." Source: 9, Vol. II, p. 624.

662

_____. *The Elephant's Child.* Checkboard; Dutton; Harcourt; Interlink; Knopf; Prentice-Hall; Warne. Challenged in the Davenport, Iowa Community School District (1993) because the book is "99 percent" violent. Throughout the book, when the main character, an elephant child, asks a question, he receives a spanking instead of answers. Source: 7, July 1993, p. 99.

663

_____. *Just So Stories.* Macmillan; Penguin; Viking. Challenged at the Hardin Park Elementary School library in Watauga County, N.C. (1990) because the word "nigger" appears in the story "How the Leopard Got Its Spots." Source: 7, July 1990, p. 145.

664

Kirk, Marshall, and Madison, Hunter. *After the Ball: How America Will Conquer Its Hatred and Fear of Homosexuals in the '90s.* NAL. Challenged at the Deschutes County Library in Bend, Oreg. (1993) because it "encourages and condones" homosexuality. Source: 7, Sept. 1993, pp. 158-59.

665

Kirkwood, James. *There Must Be a Pony.* Avon. Seized (1984) by the British customs office as "indecent and obscene." Source: 7, Jan. 1985, p. 16.

666

Kittredge, Mary. *Teens with AIDS Speak Out.* Simon. Challenged, but retained at the Cleveland, Tenn. Public Library (1993) along with seventeen other books, most of which are on sex education, AIDS awareness, and some titles on the supernatural. Source: 7, Sept. 1993, p. 146.

667
Kitzinger, Sheila. *Being Born.* Putnam. Challenged at the Lakeview, Oreg. school libraries (1991) because the complainant's son asked "rather pointed questions" about childbirth. Challenged, but retained at the Washoe County Library System in Reno, Nev. (1994) because "Nobody in their right mind would give a book like that to children on their own, except the library." Source: 7, Nov. 1991, p. 209; Sept. 1994, p. 147; Nov. 1994, pp. 200-201.

668
Klein, Aaron. *Science and the Supernatural.* Doubleday. Challenged, but retained at the Cleveland, Tenn. Public Library (1993) along with seventeen other books, most of which are on sex education, AIDS awareness, and some titles on the supernatural. Source: 7, Sept. 1993, p. 146.

669
Klein, Norma. *Angel Face.* Fawcett; Viking. Challenged at the Commerce, Tex. High School library (1990) because of "pornographic" material in the book. The complainant asked that all "romance" books be removed. Source: 7, Mar. 1991, p. 43.

670
_____. *Confessions of an Only Child.* Bradbury Pr. Challenged, but retained in a Gwinnett County, Ga. Elementary School library (1985) because "the use of a profanity by the lead character's father during a single episode destroyed the entire book." Source: 7, Mar. 1986, p. 57; Mar. 1986, p. 57; July 1986, p. 135.

671
_____. *Family Secrets.* Fawcett. Removed from the Howard County, Md. middle school media centers (1991) because the book's "constant reference to the sex act" and "inappropriate foul language." Source: 7, Mar. 1992, p. 40.

672
_____. *Give Me One Good Reason.* Avon. Challenged at the Widefield, Colo. School District (1984) because the book is "filled with promiscuity, homosexuality, abortion, and profanity." Source: 7, May 1984, p. 69.

673
_____. *Honey of a Chimp.* Pantheon. Removed from the Hanover, Pa. School District's elementary and secondary libraries (1984), but later placed on a "restricted shelf" at middle school libraries because the book contained "strong sexual content, bias to liberal values and morals, and indecent language. The material condones certain values, attitudes, and behaviors." Source: 7, Jan. 1985, p. 9.

674
_____. *It's Not What You Expect.* Avon. Removed from all the Montgomery County, Md. elementary school libraries (1980). Source: 7, May 1980, p. 51.

675
_____. *It's OK If You Don't Love Me.* Dial; Fawcett. Banned in Hayward County, Calif. (1981) because of the book's sexually explicit passages and "rough language." Removed from the shelves of the Widefield, Colo. High School library (1983) because it portrays "sex as the only thing on young people's minds." Removed from the Vancouver, Wash. School District (1984) due to its sexual passages, but later reinstated at the high school level libraries. Source: 7, Mar. 1982, p. 44; May 1983, p. 71; July 1984, p. 104.

676
_____. *Just Good Friends.* Fawcett. Challenged at the Hamden, Conn. Middle School (1994) because it is "nothing more than pornographic smut." Source: 7, Nov. 1994, p. 189.

677
_____. *Love Is One of the Choices.* Dial. Removed from the Evergreen School District of Vancouver, Wash. (1983) along with twenty-nine other titles. The American Civil Liberties Union of Washington filed suit contending that the removals constitute censorship, a violation of plaintiff's rights to free speech and due process, and the acts are a violation of the state Open Meetings Act because the removal decisions were made behind closed doors. Source: 7, Nov. 1983, pp. 185-86.

678
_____. *Mom, the Wolf Man and Me.* Pantheon. Challenged at the Orlando, Fla. (1980) due to its "objectionable" subject matter. Source: 7, Mar. 1981, p. 47.

679
_____. *My Life as a Body.* Fawcett; Knopf. Challenged at the Douglas County Library in Roseburg, Oreg. (1989) because the book condones homosexuality and premarital sex. Challenged for being too explicit, but retained at the Multnomah, Oreg. County Library (1991). Source: 7, Jan. 1990, pp. 4-5; Jan. 1992, p. 6.

680
_____. *Naomi in the Middle.* Dial; Pocket/Archway. Restricted in Brockport, N.Y. (1977) to students with parental permission. Banned in Monroe, La. (1980) because "it is certainly not our intention to have objectionable materials on library shelves." Challenged at the Orlando, Fla.

Public Library (1980). Challenged at the Charlotte, N.C. public library system (1986) because the book "is a perfect picture of secular humanism." Challenged at the Napa, Calif. City-County Library (1992) because of sexually explicit language. Challenged at the Mesa, Ariz. Public Libraries (1995) because of four pages of inappropriate material describing human sexual anatomy and how babies are conceived. Source: 7, Nov. 1977, p. 155; July 1980, p. 76; Mar. 1981, p. 47; Jan. 1987, p. 31; July 1992, p. 105; July 1995, p. 109.

681

_____. *The Queen of the What Ifs*. Fawcett; Knopf. Pulled from the Monte Vista Middle School library in Tracy, Calif. (1989) after two parents complained that its sexual content made the book inappropriate for middle school students. About a half dozen other titles were also removed and the parents have indicated a desire to review all books ordered for the library. Source: 7, May 1989, p. 75.

682

_____. *Sunshine*. Avon; Holt. Removed from the East Baton Rouge Parish, La. (1975) after the parents of a student said they found the language and content of the book offensive. Source: 7, July 1975, p. 104.

683

_____. *What It's All About*. Dial. Challenged at the Dubuque, Iowa Community School District (1984) because "it condones and even endorses immoral behavior because it contains profanity, nudity, sexual relationships outside of marriage and an excessive number of people who are divorced." Source: 7, Sept. 1984, p. 155.

684

Klein, Stanley. *Steck Vaugh Social Studies*. Steck. Removed from Alabama's list of approved texts—and from the state's classrooms—because the book promotes the "religion of secular humanism." U.S. District Court Judge W. Brevard Hand ruled on March 4, 1987, that thirty-nine history and social studies texts used in Alabama's 129 school systems "discriminate against the very concept of religion and theistic religions in particular, by omissions so serious that a student learning history from them would not be apprised of relevant facts about America's history…References to religion are isolated and the integration of religion in the history of American society is ignored." The series includes: *Our Family; Our Neighbors; Our Communities; Our Country Today; Our Country's History;* and *Our World Today*. On August 26, 1987, the U.S. Court of Appeals for the Eleventh Circuit unanimously overturned Judge Hand's decision by ruling that the information in the book was "essentially neutral in

its religious content." The fact that the texts omitted references to religion was not "an advancement of secular humanism or an active hostility toward theistic religion." Source: 7, Jan. 1987, p. 6; May 1987, pp. 75, 104-7; Sept. 1987, pp. 166-67; Nov. 1987, pp. 217-18; Jan. 1988, p. 17; Mar. 1988, p. 40.

685

Knott, Blanche. *Truly Tasteless Jokes*. Ballantine. Removed from open display at the Casa Grande, Ariz. Public Library (1988) and restricted to adult use only with proof of age before checking the book out or even looking at it. Source: 7, Jan. 1989, p. 7.

686

Knowles, John. *A Separate Peace*. Bantam; Dell; Macmillan. Challenged in Vernon-Verona-Sherill, N.Y. School District (1980) as a "filthy, trashy sex novel." Challenged at the Fannett-Metal High School in Shippensburg, Pa. (1985) because of its allegedly offensive language. Challenged as appropriate for high school reading lists in the Shelby County, Tenn. school system (1989) because the novel contained "offensive language." Challenged at the McDowell County, N.C. schools (1996) because of "graphic language." Source: 7, May 1980, p. 62; Nov. 1985, p. 204; Jan. 1990, pp. 11-12; Jan. 1997, p. 11.

687

Knudsen, Eric. *Teller of Tales*. Mutual Pub. Co. Challenged in the Columbia County, Ga. school libraries (1992) because the biography of Hans Christian Andersen contains the phrase "go to hell." Source: 7, Nov. 1992, p. 197.

688

Koertge, Ronald. *The Arizona Kid*. Avon; Little. Challenged because it "encourages and condones" homosexuality, but retained at the Bend, Oreg. High School (1993). Pulled from and later restored to the seventh grade English classroom at Minnetonka, Minn. Middle School West (1994) after a parent found the content inappropriate for twelve- and thirteen-year-olds. Source: 7, Sept. 1993, pp. 158-59; Nov. 1993, p. 192; July 1994, p. 114; Sept. 1994, p. 166.

689

Koontz, Dean R. *Funhouse*. Berkley Pub. Removed from the South Brunswick Middle School Library in Boiling Spring Lakes, N.C. (1995) by a patron because the book "contains material on orgies, rape, and lesbianism. There is also blasphemy and the book promotes domestic violence and alcohol abuse." The book was donated by the Lions Club in a book drive. Source: 7, Nov. 1995, pp. 183-84; Jan. 1996, p. 11.

690
_____. *Night Chills.* Atheneum. Challenged at the Mountain View High School in Bend, Oreg. (1992) because it contains "explicit" sexual incidents. Source: 7, Jan. 1993, p. 9.

691
_____. *Watchers.* Putnam. Removed from the Hickory High School curriculum in Sharon, Pa. (1996) by the superintendent because the language was offensive. Source: 7, Mar. 1997, p. 50.

692
Kopay, David, and Young, Perry D. *The David Kopay Story: An Extraordinary Self-Revelation.* Fine. Challenged because it "encourages and condones" homosexuality, but retained at the Bend, Oreg. High School (1993). Source: 7, Sept. 1993, pp. 158-59; Nov. 1993, p. 192.

693
The Koran. Penguin; Tahrike Tarsile; Quran. Ban lifted by the Spanish Index (1790). Restricted to students of history in USSR (1926). Source: 3, p. 5.

694
Kornblum, William, and Julian, Joseph. *Social Problems.* Prentice-Hall. Reinstated at the Anadarko, Okla. Public Schools (1993) after a textbook review committee recommendation. The text was challenged by a minister who complained about the book's references to homosexuality, lesbians, and child molesters. Source: 7, Sept. 1993, p. 160.

695
Kosinski, Jerzy. *Being There.* Bantam. Challenged as a reading assignment for an eleventh grade English class at Crete, Nebr. High School (1989). Reinstated after being removed from the Mifflinburg, Pa. High School (1989) because the book's main character has a homosexual experience. Challenged as required reading in a senior advanced English course in Davenport, Iowa (1993) because of a description of masturbation. Challenged on the curricular reading list at Pomperaug High School in Southbury, Conn. (1995) because sexually explicit passages are not appropriate high school reading. Source: 7, May 1989, pp. 79, 93; July 1993, p. 105; July 1995, p. 98.

696
Kotzwinkle, William. *Nightbook.* Avon. Challenged at the Huron, S.Dak. Public Library (1980) because "there's not a page in [the book] fit to be read by anyone." Source: 7, July 1980, p. 84.

697
Krantz, Judith. *Mistral's Daughter.* Bantam. Banned from the Stroudsburg, Pa. High School library (1985) because it was "blatantly graphic, pornographic, and wholly unacceptable for a high school library." Source: 7, May 1985, p. 79.

698
Kroll, Ken. *Enabling Romance: A Guide to Love, Sex and Relationships for the Disabled.* First Woodline House. Removed from the Clifton, N.J. Public Library (1996) and replaced with a dummy book made of styrofoam. The library's new policy restricts to adults any material containing "patently offensive graphic illustrations or photographs of sexual or excretory activities or contact as measured by contemporary community standards for minors." Source: 7, July 1996, pp. 118-19.

699
Kropp, Paul. *Wilted.* Coward. Banned from the Evergreen School District libraries in Vancouver, Oreg. (1983) because the "sexual scenes were a bit much for elementary schools." Source: 7, Sept. 1983, p. 139.

700
Kushner, Ellen. *Mystery of the Secret Room.* Bantam. Challenged at the Berkeley County, S.C. school libraries (1992) because the book teaches witchcraft. Source: 7, July 1992, p. 108.

701
Kuskin, Karla. *The Dallas Titans Get Ready for Bed.* Harper. Challenged at the Douglas County Library in Roseburg, Oreg. (1989) because children are not ready for illustrations and conversation about jockstraps. Source: 7, Jan. 1990, pp. 4-5.

702
Lader, Lawrence. *Foolproof Birth Control.* Beacon Pr. Banned from the Brighton, Mich. High School library (1977) along with all other sex education materials. Source: 7, Sept. 1977, p. 133.

703
Laing, Frederick. *Tales from Scandinavia.* Silver Burdett. Removed to a locked closet in the superintendent's office in Banner County, Nebr. (1992) because the book "has to do with a lot of negative things and might not be good for someone with low self-esteem or suicide tendencies." Source: 7, May 1992, p. 80.

704
Landis, James David. *The Sisters Impossible.* Knopf.

Removed from the Sallisaw, Okla. school libraries (1985) due to offensive language. Later, returned to the shelves of the Eastside Elementary School library in Sallisaw, Okla. (1986) after the school board agreed to an out-of-court settlement with a group of parents who filed a suit to reverse the board's 1985 decision to ban the book. The book was originally banned because it uses "hell" seven times and the words "fart" and "bullshit" once each in its 169 pages. Challenged in the Fairbanks, Alaska school libraries (1988) because off "the language in the book and to a scene in which aspiring young ballerinas danced naked in a dressing room before class." Source: 7, July 1985, p. 112; Mar. 1986, pp. 60, 65-66; July 1985, p. 112; Mar. 1986, pp. 60, 65-66; July 1986, p. 136; Mar. 1988, p. 71.

705
Langton, Jane. *The Fragile Flag.* Harper. Challenged at the Jefferson County, Colo. school library (1986) because the book portrays the U.S. government as "shallow" and "manipulative," and "lacking in intelligence and responsibility." Source: 7, Jan. 1987, p. 29; Mar. 1987, p. 49.

706
LaPlace, John. *Health.* Prentice-Hall. Banned from senior high school classrooms in the Diocese of Buffalo, N.Y. (1981). Challenged at the Randolph, N.J. High School (1984) by a group of parents and clergy who say "the textbook is too liberal and should be replaced or supplemented by a more traditional book." Source: 7, Jan. 1981, p. 10; July 1984, p. 106.

707
Larrick, Nancy, and Merriam, Eve. *Male and Female under 18.* Prentice-Hall. Banned by the Chelsea, Mass. School Board (1977) from the high school library because of objections to one poem by a teenage girl. The banning was reversed by a U. S. District Court ruling in *Right to Read Defense Committee v. School Committee of the City of Chelsea,* 454 F. Supp. 703 (D. Mass. 1978). Source: 3, p. 104; 8, pp. 12-14, 148-53, 229, 239.

708
Laurence, Margaret. *Christmas Birthday Story.* Knopf. Challenged at the York, Maine school system (1982). Source: 7, July 1982, p. 124.

709
_____. *The Diviners.* Bantam. Challenged at the Peterborough, Ontario County schools (1984) after a resolution from the nearby Burleigh-Anstruther municipal council asked that the books be reviewed for their moral content. Source: 7, Mar. 1985, p. 45.

710
_____. *A Jest of God.* Knopf. Challenged at the Peterborough, Ontario County schools (1984) after a resolution from the nearby Burleigh-Anstruther municipal council asked that the books be reviewed for their moral content. Source: 7, Mar. 1985, p. 45.

711
_____. *The Stone Angel.* Bantam. Challenged at the Peterborough, Ontario County schools (1984) after a resolution from the nearby Burleigh-Anstruther municipal council asked that the books be reviewed for their moral content. Source: 7, Mar. 1985, p. 45.

712
Lawrence, D. H. *Collected Paintings.* Banned by U.S. Customs (1929). Source: 6, p. 142; 9, Vol. III, p. 414.

713
_____. *Lady Chatterley's Lover.* Bantam; Grove; NAL; Random. Banned by U. S. Customs (1929), banned in Ireland (1932), Poland (1932), Australia (1959), Japan (1959), India (1959), and Canada (1960-1962). Dissemination of Lawrence's novel has been stopped in China (1987) because the book "will corrupt the minds of young people and is also against the Chinese tradition." Source: 1, p. 137; 3, pp. 69-70; 9, Vol. III, pp. 407, 414; 7, July 1987, pp. 135-36.

714
_____. *Paintings of D. H. Lawrence.* Cory, Adams & McKay. Barred by U.S. Customs (1929). Source: 3, p. 69.

715

_____. *Pansies*. Penguin. Seized by postal authorities (1928) in England and was substantially altered prior to its republication in 1929. Source: 2, p. 170.

716

_____. *The Rainbow*. Penguin; Modern Library/Random; Viking. Ordered destroyed by the British magistrate's court (1915). Source: 1, p. 100; 3, p. 69.

717

_____. *Sons and Lovers*. Penguin; Modern Library/Random; Viking. In 1961 an Oklahoma City group called Mothers United for Decency hired a trailer, dubbed it "smutmobile" and displayed books deemed objectionable including Lawrence's novel. Source: 3, p. 119.

718

_____. *Women in Love*. Penguin/Viking. Seized by John Summers of the New York Society for the Suppression of Vice and declared obscene (1922). Source: 6, p. 142; 9, Vol. III, p. 415.

719

Lawson, Robert. *They Were Strong and Good*. Viking. Challenged because the novel "glorifies slavery and racism," but retained at the Multnomah, Oreg. County Library (1991). Source: 7, Jan. 1992, p. 6.

720

Leach, Maria. *Whistle in the Graveyard: Folktales to Chill Your Bones*. Puffin Bks. Challenged at the Neely Elementary School in Gilbert, Ariz. (1992) because the book shows the dark side of religion through the occult, the devil, and satanism. Source: 7, May 1992, p. 78; July 1992, p. 124.

721

Lee, Harper. *To Kill a Mockingbird*. Lippincott/Harper; Popular Library. Challenged in Eden Valley, Minn. (1977) and temporarily banned due to words "damn" and "whore lady" used in the novel. Challenged in the Vernon-Verona-Sherill, N.Y. School District (1980) as a "filthy, trashy novel." Challenged at the Warren, Ind. Township schools (1981) because the book does "psychological damage to the positive integration process" and "represents institutionalized racism under the guise of 'good literature.'" After unsuccessfully banning Lee's novel, three black parents resigned from the township human relations advisory council. Challenged in the Waukegan, Ill. School District (1984) because the novel uses the word "nigger." Challenged in the Kansas City, Mo. junior high schools (1985). Challenged at the Park Hill, Mo. Junior High School (1985) because the novel "contains pro-

fanity and racial slurs." Retained on a supplemental eighth grade reading list in the Casa Grande, Ariz. Elementary School District (1985), despite the protests by black parents and the National Association for the Advancement of Colored People who charged the book was unfit for junior high use. Challenged at the Santa Cruz, Calif. Schools (1995) because of its racial themes. Removed from the Southwood High School Library in Caddo Parish, La. (1995) because the book's language and content were objectionable. Challenged at the Moss Point, Miss. School District (1996) because the novel contains a racial epithet. Banned from the Lindale, Tex. advanced placement English reading list (1996) because the book "conflicted with the values of the community." Source: 7, Mar. 1978, p. 31; May 1980, p. 62; Mar. 1982, p. 47; July 1984, p. 105; May 1985, p. 80; July 1985, p. 134; Mar. 1986, pp. 57-58; May 1995, p. 68; Nov. 1995, p. 183; Nov. 1996, pp.196-97, 199.

722

Lee, Joanna. *I Want to Keep My Baby*. NAL. Removed from the Morehead High School library in Rockingham County, N.C. (1994) because of "antireligious sentiments—the girl's comment that her boyfriend was 'her God'—and sexual situations." After a three-hour public debate, the Rockingham County School Board later reversed its previous ban against the book. Source: 7, Sept. 1994, p. 148; Nov. 1994, p. 201.

723

Legman, Gershon, ed. *The Limerick: 1,700 Examples with Notes, Variants and Index*. Carol Pub. Group. Challenged at the Oak Lawn, Ill. Public Library (1991) because the book contains bawdy limericks with explicit sexual references. Source: 7, Nov. 1991, p. 209; Jan. 1992, p. 26.

724

LeGuin, Ursula K. *Lathe of Heaven*. Avon. Challenged on a Washougal, Wash. High School reading list (1984) because it contained "profuse profanity." Source: 7, Sept. 1984, p. 157.

725

Lehrman, Robert. *Juggling*. Harper. Challenged at Woodbury, Minn. Library (1990). The book is about the life and sexual encounters of a teenage soccer player. Source: 7, July 1990, p. 145.

726

L'Engle, Madeleine C. *Many Waters*. Farrar; Dell. Challenged at the Hubbard, Ohio Library (1991) because the book alters the story of Noah's Ark making it secular and confusing children. Source: 7, Sept. 1991, p. 153.

727

_____. *A Wrinkle in Time*. Dell. Challenged, but retained on the media center shelves of the Polk City, Fla. Elementary School (1985). A student's parent filed the complaint, contending the story promoted witchcraft, crystal balls, and demons. Challenged in the Anniston, Ala. schools (1990) because the book sends a mixed signal to children about good and evil. The complainant also objected to listing the name of Jesus Christ together with the names of great artists, philosophers, scientists, and religious leaders when referring to defenders of Earth against evil. Challenged, but retained by the Catawba County School Board in Newton, N.C. (1996). A parent requested the book be pulled from the school libraries because it allegedly undermines religious beliefs. Source: 7, July 1985, p. 133; Mar. 1991, p. 62; May 1996, pp. 97-98.

728

Lenin, Vladimir I. *Declaration of Independence*. Banned in Oklahoma City, Okla. (1940). Bookstore owners were sentenced to ten years in prison and fined $5,000.00 for selling Lenin's work (1940). Source: 3, p. 60; 6, p. 142.

729

_____. *The State and Revolution*. China Books; International Publishing. Seized as obscene in Boston, Mass. (1927); seized as subversive in Hungary (1927); in Providence, R.I. (1954) postal authorities attempted to withhold from delivery to Brown University 75 copies of this "subversive" title. Source: 3, p. 60.

730

_____. *United States Constitution*. Banned in Oklahoma City, Okla. (1940). Source: 3, p. 60.

731

Levin, Ira. *Rosemary's Baby*. Dell; Random. Removed from the required reading list in Westport, Mass. (1977); banned from use in Aurora, Colo. High School English classes (1976) on the grounds of "immorality." Source: 7, Jan. 1977, p. 8; May 1977, p. 79.

732

_____. *Stepford Wives*. Random. Prohibited for use in the Warsaw, Ind. schools (1979) because of its "questionable nature" and because it might offend someone in the community. Source: 7, Mar. 1980, p. 40.

733

Levine, Ellen. *I Hate English*. Scholastic. Challenged by a school board member in the Queens, N.Y. school libraries (1994) because "The book says what a burden it is they have

to learn English. They should just learn English and don't complain about it." The rest of the school board voted to retain the book. Source: 7, July 1994, pp. 110-11; Sept. 1994, p. 166.

734

Levoy, Myron. *Alan and Naomi*. Dell; Harper. Challenged in Gwinnett County, Ga. (1981) because of objections to the book's language ("hell" and "damn") and mature subject matter. Challenged, but retained, in the Carroll County, Md. schools (1991). Two school board members were concerned about the "sad ending" and "poor" portrayal of Jews. Source: 7, Nov. 1981, p. 168; Mar. 1992, p. 64.

735

Levy, Edward. *Came a Spider*. Arbor House. Removed and later returned to the shelves of the Freeman High School library in Spokane, Wash. (1986) because it contained a two-page description of teenagers engaged in sexual intercourse. Source: 7, May 1986, pp. 80-81.

736

Lewin, Esther. *Random House Thesaurus of Slang*. Random. Placed on a limited access shelf at the Floyd Light Middle School library in Portland, Oreg. (1992). Source: 7, May 1992, p. 81.

737

Lewis, C. S. *The Lion, the Witch and the Wardrobe*. Macmillan. Challenged in the Howard County, Md. school system (1990) because it depicts "graphic violence, mysticism, and gore." Source: 7, Jan. 1991, p. 28.

738

Lewis, Sinclair. *Cass Timberlane*. Woodhill. Banned in Ireland (1953), in East Berlin (1954). Source: 3, p. 70

739

_____. *Elmer Gantry*. NAL. Banned in Boston, Mass. (1927); Camden, N.J. (1927); Glasgow, Scotland (1927); Ireland (1931). U.S. Post Office banned any catalog listing of this title (1931). Source: 1, p. 133; 3, pp. 70-71; 9, Vol. III, pp. 404-5.

740

_____. *Kingsblood Royal*. Grosset; Random; Popular Library. Removed from Illinois libraries (1953) on a mother's complaint that her daughter had borrowed a book that was offensive. Banned in Ireland (1953). Source: 3, p. 71.

741

Leyland, Winston, ed. *My Deep Dark Pain Is Love: A Collec-*

tion of Latin American Gay Fiction. Gay Sunshine. Seized and shredded (1984) by the British Customs Office. Source: 7, Jan. 1985, p. 16.

742
_____. *Now the Volcano: An Anthology of Latin American Gay Literature.* Gay Sunshine. Seized and shredded (1984) by the British Customs Office. Source: 7, Jan. 1985, p. 16.

743
Lieberman, Gail. *Sex and Birth Control: A Guide for the Young.* Crowell; Harper. Challenged at the Cleveland, Tenn. Public Library (1993) along with seventeen other books, most of which are on sex education, AIDS awareness, and some titles on the supernatural. Source: 7, Sept. 1993, p. 146.

744
Lightner, A. M. *Gods or Demons?* Fourwinds Pr. Challenged at the Canby, Oreg. Junior High School library (1988) because the book "promotes a secular-humanistic belief in evolution and portrays the 'Bible as myth.'" Source: 7, May 1989, p. 78.

745
Lindgren, Astrid. *The Children on Troublemaker Street.* Macmillan. Challenged at the Sweetwater County Library in Green River, Wyo. (1992) because of concerns about how it depicts the "almost swearing of a 4-year-old child." Source: 7, July 1992, p. 126.

746
Lingeman, Richard R. *Drugs from A to Z: A Dictionary.* McGraw-Hill. Challenged, but retained in the Des Moines, Iowa school libraries (1986) because the book "not only gives definitions of drugs but also tells how and what to use to get a cheap high—which could be lethal." Source: 7, July 1986, p. 135.

747
Lion, Elizabeth M. *Human Sexuality in Nursing Process.* Wiley. President of the National Black Nurses Association called (1982) on nursing schools to boycott this text because it contains material that is "offensive and insensitive" to blacks. Source: 7, Jan. 1983, p. 23.

748
Lionni, Leo. *In the Rabbit's Garden.* Pantheon. Challenged at the Naas Elementary School library in Boring, Oreg. (1986) because the story about two rabbits living in a lush garden paradise made a mockery of the Bible's tale of Adam and Eve. Unlike the story of Adam and Eve, Lionni rewards his bunnies for eating the forbidden fruit by allowing them to

live happily ever after. Source: 7, Mar. 1987, p. 66.

749
Lipke, Jean C. *Conception and Contraception.* Lerner Pubs. The Brighton, Mich. School Board (1977) voted to remove all sex education books from the high school library. Source: 7, Sept. 1977, p. 133.

750
Lipsyte, Robert. *The Contender.* Bantam; Harper. Challenged as a summer youth program reading assignment in Chattanooga, Tenn. (1989) because "it sounds like pretty explicit stuff." Source: 7, Nov. 1989, p. 162.

751
Locke, John. *An Essay Concerning Human Understanding.* Dover; Oxford Univ. Pr.; NAL. Placed on the *Index Librorum Prohibitorum* in Rome (1700); prohibited reading at Oxford (1701). A Latin version was permitted only on the proviso that "no tutors were to read with their students this essential investigation into the basis of knowledge." Source: 2, p. 174; 3, p. 24.

752
Lockridge, Ross, Jr. *Raintree Country.* Attacked in New York City (1953) as "1066 pages of rank obscenity, blasphemy and sacrilege…inimical to faith and morals [and] within the prohibition of the Catholic Index." Source: 9, Vol. IV, p. 709.

753
Loewen, James W., and Sallis, Charles, eds. *Mississippi: Conflict and Change.* Pantheon. Rejected from use in the Mississippi public schools because the textbook stressed black history too much. A U.S. District Court ruled that the criteria used for rejecting this text were not justifiable in *Loewen v. Turnipsend,* 488 F. Supp. 1138 (N. D. Miss. 1980). Source: 7, July 1980, p. 86; 8, pp. 167-71, 239.

754
Logan, Daniel. *America Bewitched: The Rise of Black Magic and Spiritism.* Morrow. Challenged by the "God Squad," a group of three students and their parents, at the El Camino High School in Oceanside, Calif. (1986) because the book "glorified the devil and the occult." Source: 7, Sept. 1986, p. 151; Nov. 1986, p. 224; Jan. 1987, p. 9.

755
London, Jack. *The Call of the Wild.* Ace; Bantam; Grosset; Macmillan; NAL; Penguin; Pocket Bks.; Raintree; Tempo. Banned in Italy (1929), Yugoslavia (1929), and burned in Nazi bonfires (1932). Source: 3, p. 63.

756
Longstreet, Stephen, ed. *The Drawings of Renoir*. Borden. Retained at Maldonado Elementary School in Tucson, Ariz. (1994) after being challenged by parents who objected to nudity and "pornographic," "perverted," and "morbid" themes. Source: 7, July 1994, p. 112.

757
Louys, Pierre. *Aphrodite*. AMS Pr. Banned by U.S. Customs Department (1929) as lascivious, corrupting, and obscene. In 1930 a New York book dealer, E. B. Marks, was fined $250 for possessing a copy of Aphrodite in contravention of the state laws on obscene publications. In 1935 an attempt was made to import the publication into America. This was banned, although the authorities overlooked a 49-cent edition, openly advertised in the *New York Times Book Review* and apparently, despite postal regulations, available through the mail. Source: 2, p. 176; 3, p. 60.

758
Louys, Pierre. *The Songs of Bilitis*. William Godwin; Capricorn Bks. Banned by U.S. Customs Department (1929) as lascivious, corrupting, and obscene. Source: 3, p. 60.

759
_____. *The Twilight of the Nymphs*. Fortune Pr. Banned by U.S. Customs Department (1929) as lascivious, corrupting, and obscene. Source: 3, p. 60.

760
Lowen, Paul. *Butterfly*. Blue Moon Bks.; St. Martin. Challenged at the Tigard, Oreg. Public Library (1988) because of explicit sex and extreme physical and psychological cruelty. Source: 7, Jan. 1990, pp. 4-5.

761
Lowry, Lois. *Anastasia at Your Service*. Houghton; Dell. Challenged at the Casper, Wyo. school libraries (1984). Source: 7, Mar. 1985, p. 42.

762
_____. *Anastasia Krupnik*. Bantam; Houghton. Removed by the school's principal, and later returned to the Roosevelt Elementary School library in Tulare, Calif. (1986) with the word "shit" whited out. Challenged, but retained, in the Wichita, Kans. public schools (1991) because it was offensive. Removed, but later returned to the Stevens Point, Wis. Area School elementary recommended reading list (1992) due to the book's profanity and occasional references to underage drinking. Source: 7, Mar. 1987, p. 49; Jan. 1992, p. 26; Mar. 1993, p. 45; May 1993, p. 87.

763
_____. *Autumn Street*. Houghton. Challenged at the Casper, Wyo. school libraries (1984). Source: 7, Mar. 1985, p. 42.

764
_____. *Find a Stranger, Say Good-bye*. Houghton. Challenged at the Casper, Wyo. school libraries (1984). Source: 7, Mar. 1985, p. 42.

765
_____. *The Giver*. Dell; Houghton. Temporarily banned from classes by the Bonita Unified School District in La Verne and San Dimas, Calif. (1994) after four parents complained that violent and sexual passages were inappropriate for children. Restricted to students with parental permission at the Columbia Falls, Mont. school system (1995) because of the book's treatment of themes of infanticide and euthanasia. Challenged at the Lakota High School in Cincinnati, Ohio (1996). Source: 7, Mar. 1995, p. 42; Jan. 1996, p. 11; Nov. 1996, p. 198.

766
_____. *The One Hundredth Thing about Caroline*. Houghton. Challenged at the Casper, Wyo. school libraries (1984). Source: 7, Mar. 1985, p. 42.

767
_____. *A Summer to Die*. Houghton. Challenged at the Casper, Wyo. school libraries (1984). Source: 7, Mar. 1985, p. 42.

768
_____. *Taking Care of Terrific*. Houghton. Challenged at the Casper, Wyo. school libraries (1984). Source: 7, Mar. 1985, p. 42.

769
Ludlum, Robert. *The Matarese Circle*. R. Marek. Restricted at the Pierce, Nebr. High School (1983) to students with parental consent because the book contains unnecessarily rough language and sexual descriptions. Source: 7, May 1983, p. 72.

770
Ludwig, Coy L. *Maxfield Parrish*. Watson-Guptill. Retained at Maldonado Elementary School in Tucson, Ariz. (1994) after being challenged by parents who objected to nudity and "pornographic," "perverted," and "morbid" themes. Source: 7, July 1994, p. 112.

771
Lund, Doris. *Eric*. Dell; Harper. Pulled from Lexington, N.C. Middle School (1994) classrooms because of the

intense way in which it addresses death. Source: 7, July 1994, p. 115.

772
Lundgren, Astrid. *The Runaway Sleigh Ride*. Viking. Challenged in the Kokomo-Howard County, Ind. Public Library (1995) because it makes "light of a drinking situation." The book is by the author of the Pippi Longstocking series. Source: 7, Mar. 1996, p. 46.

773
Luther, Martin. *Address to the German Nobility*. Concordia; Doubleday. Prohibited by edicts of the Emperor and the Pope (1521). Source: 3, pp. 11-12.

774
_____. *Works*. Concordia; Doubleday. Prohibited by edicts of the Emperor and the Pope (1521). Source: 3, pp. 11-12.

775
Lynch, Chris. *The Iceman*. Harper. Removed from the Carroll Middle School Library in Southlake, Tex. (1995) because of "profanity" and it "was not highly recommended for its literary value." Challenged at the Haysville, Kans. Middle School library (1996) when a parent counted 36 places where profanity was used in the book. Source: 7, May 1995, p. 67; Mar. 1997, p. 49.

776
Maas, Peter. *Serpico*. Viking. Challenged in the Zimmerman, Minn. School District high school libraries (1982). Maas's book was available to students under 18 only with parental permission. Source: 7, Sept. 1982, p. 156.

777
_____. *The Valachi Papers*. Putnam; Bantam. U.S. Department of Justice sued author to restrain the book's publication (1966). Source: 3, p. 99.

778
Machiavelli, Niccolo. *Discourses*. Bantam; Penguin; Routledge & Paul. Placed in the *Index Librorum Prohibitorum* in Rome (1555). Source: 3, p. 9.

779
_____. *The Prince*. Bantam; NAL; Penguin. Placed in the *Index Librorum Prohibitorum* in Rome (1555). Source: 3, pp. 9-10.

CAUTION!
SOME PEOPLE CONSIDER THESE BOOKS DANGEROUS

AMERICAN HERITAGE DICTIONARY • THE BIBLE • ARE YOU THERE, GOD? IT'S ME, MARGARET • OUR BODIES, OURSELVES • TARZAN ALICE'S ADVENTURES IN WONDERLAND • THE EXORCIST • THE CHOCOLATE WAR • CATCH-22 • LORD OF THE FLIES • ORDINARY PEOPLE • SOUL ON ICE • RAISIN IN THE SUN • OLIVER TWIST • A FAREWELL TO ARMS • THE BEST SHORT STORIES OF NEGRO WRITERS • FLOWERS FOR ALGERNON • ULYSSES • TO KILL A MOCKINGBIRD • ROSEMARY'S BABY • THE FIXER • DEATH OF A SALESMAN • MOTHER GOOSE • CATCHER IN THE RYE • THE MERCHANT OF VENICE • ONE DAY IN THE LIFE OF IVAN DENISOVICH • GRAPES OF WRATH • THE ADVENTURES OF HUCKLEBERRY FINN • SLAUGHTERHOUSE-FIVE • GO ASK ALICE

BANNED BOOKS WEEK—CELEBRATING THE FREEDOM TO READ

780
Madaras, Lynda. *Lynda Madaras Talks to Teens about AIDS: An Essential Guide for Parents, Teachers & Young People*. Newmarket. Challenged, but retained at the Cleveland, Tenn. Public Library (1993) along with seventeen other books, most of which are on sex education, AIDS awareness, and some titles on the supernatural. Source: 7, Sept. 1993, p. 146.

781
_____. *What's Happening to My Body? Book for Boys: A Growing-up Guide for Parents & Sons*. Newmarket. Challenged at the Mt. Morris, Ill. School District seventh grade class (1986) because it is written from a "permissive point of view." Challenged, but retained at the Cleveland, Tenn. Public Library (1993) along with seventeen other books, most of which are on sex education, AIDS awareness, and some titles on the supernatural. Challenged in the Kenai Peninsula Borough schools in Homer, Alaska (1993) because of objections to the way masturbation and homosexuality were presented and to slang words used to describe sexual methods as well as the male anatomy. Missing from the Northside Intermediate School library in Milton, Wis. (1994) after a parent complained "I don't think my ten-year-old son, or anyone's, needs to know that stuff." Challenged, but retained at the Washoe County Library System in Reno, Nev. (1994) because "nobody in their right mind would give a book like that to children on their own, except the library." Source: 7, Mar. 1987, p. 53; July 1987, pp. 149-50; Sept. 1993, p. 146; Jan. 1994, p. 33; July 1994, pp. 111-12; Sept. 1994, p. 147; Nov. 1994, pp. 200-01.

782
_____. *What's Happening to My Body? Book for Girls: A Growing-up Guide for Parents & Daughters*. Newmarket. Challenged at the Mt. Morris, Ill. School District seventh grade class (1986) because it is written from a "permissive point of view." Challenged, but retained at the Cleveland, Tenn. Public Library (1993) along with seventeen other books, most of which are on sex education, AIDS awareness, and some titles on the supernatural. Source: 7, Mar. 1987, p. 53; July 1987, pp. 149-50; Sept. 1993, p. 146.

783
Madden, David. *The Suicide's Wife*. Avon; Bobbs-Merrill. Challenged at the Covington, La. Public Library (1984)

because it was "just too immorally written all the way through." Source: 7, July 1984, p. 103.

784
Madonna. *Sex*. Warner. The mylar-wrapped, spiral-bound book of photographs of the exhibitionist pop star Madonna in revealing and erotic poses raised challenges across the country soon after its release in Oct. 1992. In several cities political leaders exerted pressure on libraries not to acquire or to restrict circulation of the book. In Houston, Tex. (1992) a group called Citizens Against Pornography (CAP) mobilized efforts to have the book removed. The public library agreed to keep the book, but not allow it to circulate and to restrict in-library access to adults only. In Mesa, Ariz. (1992), the mayor ordered the library not to shelve the book. In Austin, Tex. (1992), the county attorney told the library that to make the book available to minors in any way was illegal. The Pikes Peak Library in Colorado Springs, Colo. (1992) and the St. Louis, Mo. Public Library (1992) cancelled the library's order after citizen protest. In Nebraska, the Omaha Public Library (1992) did not plan to buy the book, but six of seven City Council members asked the library to remove it from any potential acquisitions list. The book was challenged at the Champaign, Ill. Public Library (1992) and in Ingham County, Mich. the library board (1992) declined to ban the controversial book. In the public libraries of Manchester, Conn., South Bend, Ind. and Topeka and Shawnee, Kans. (1992), and Spokane, Wash. (1993) the book was challenged. The Downers Grove, Ill. Public Library (1993) retained the book, but at the Naperville, Ill. Public Library (1993) it is excluded. Challenged at the Beloit, Wis. Public Library (1993), along with other adult literature, after complaints that minors were perusing the book's photographs of erotic poses and skimpy outfits. Source: 7, Jan. 1993, pp. 1, 31-33; Mar. 1993, pp. 37-38; May 1993, pp. 65-66; July 1993, p. 104; Nov. 1993, p. 179.

785
Magnus, Erica. *The Boy and the Devil*. Carolrhoda. Challenged at the Science Hill, Ky. Elementary School library (1987) because the book "hints of a satanic cult" since "there's no way a person can outwit the devil without God's help and nowhere is God mentioned in the book." Source: 7, May 1987, p. 86; July1987, pp. 147-48.

786
Mailer, Norman. *Ancient Evenings*. Little. Rejected for purchase by the Hayward, Calif. school trustees (1985) because of "rough language" and "explicit sex scenes." Source: 7, July 1985, p. 111.

787
_____. *The Naked and the Dead*. Holt; NAL. Banned in Canada (1949) and Australia (1949). Source: 3, p. 96.

788
Maimonides. *The Guide of the Perplexed*. Univ. of Chicago Pr.; Dover; Peter Smith; Shalom. Condemned by his orthodox opponents as heresy. Copies of the publication were burned (1200) when discovered, it was barred from Jewish homes, and anyone reading it was excommunicated; the work was still facing bans in the 19th century. Maimonides was probably the first Jewish author to have his works burned. Source: 2, p. 29.

789
Malamud, Bernard. *The Fixer*. Dell; Farrar; Pocket Bks. Banned from use in Aurora, Colo. High School English classes (1976); removed from the Island Trees, N.Y. Union Free School District High School library in 1976 along with nine other titles because they were considered "immoral, anti-American, anti-Christian, or just plain filthy." Returned to the library after the U.S. Supreme Court ruling on June 25, 1982 in *Board of Education, Island Trees Union Free School District No. 26 et al. v. Pico et al.*, 457 U.S. 853 (1982). Source: 7, May 1977, p. 79; Nov. 1982, p. 197.

790
Malcolm X and Haley, Alex. *The Autobiography of Malcolm X*. Ballantine. Challenged in the Duval County, Fla. public schools (1993) because the slain Black Muslim leader advocated anti-white racism and violence. Restricted at the Jacksonville, Fla. middle school libraries (1994) because it presents a racist view of white people and is a "how-to manual" for crime. Source: 7, Sept. 1993, p. 147; May 1994, p. 83.

791
Maloney, Ray. *The Impact Zone*. Delacorte; Dell. Challenged at the Multnomah County Library in Portland, Oreg. (1989) because of profanity and sexual references. Source: 7, Jan. 1990, pp. 4-5.

792
Malory, Sir Thomas. *Le Morte D'Arthur*. Scribner; Collier; Penguin. Challenged as a required reading assignment at the Pulaski County High School in Somerset, Ky. (1987) because it is "junk." Source: 7, May 1987, p. 90.

793
Manchester, William Raymond. *The Glory and the Dream*. Little. Challenged at the Conway, Ark. High School (1989) as having inappropriate sexual and racial content. Source: 7, July 1989, p. 129; Sept. 1989, p. 186.

794
Manes, Stephen. *Slim Down Camp.* Bantam; Houghton. Challenged at the Des Plaines, Ill. Public Library (1992) because it contains "repeated profanity and immoral situations." Source: 7, May 1992, p. 79.

795
Manet, Edouard. *Manet.* Abrams. Retained at Maldonado Elementary School in Tucson, Ariz. (1994) after being challenged by parents who objected to nudity and "pornographic," "perverted," and "morbid" themes. Source: 7, July 1994, p. 112.

796
Mann, Patrick. *Dog Day Afternoon.* Delacorte. Placed in a special closed shelf at the Vergennes, Vt. Union High School library (1978). Decision upheld in Bicknell v. Vergennes Union High School Board, 475 F. Supp. 615 (D. Vt. 1979), 638 F. 2d 438 (2d Cir. 1980). Source: 7, Jan. 1979, p. 6; 8, pp. 151, 239; 9, Vol IV, p. 715.

797
Maple, Eric. *Devils and Demons.* Pan; Kingfisher; Rouke. Challenged at the Essrig Elementary School in Carrollwood, Fla. (1988) because the book contains a pledge to Satan. Source: 7, Jan. 1989, p. 7.

798
Maraini, Fosco. *Tokyo.* Time-Life. Challenged at the Cherry River Elementary School library in Richwood, W.Va. (1983) because the book includes a photograph of the backsides of nude Japanese men in a public bath. Source: 7, July 1983, p. 122.

799
Marchetti, Victor, and Marks, John D. *The CIA and the Cult of Intelligence.* Dell; Knopf. The Central Intelligence Agency obtained a U. S. Court injunction against its publication (1972). Towards the close of its 1974-1975 term the U. S. Supreme Court declined for the second time to review an appeal by the authors thus upholding the CIA's right to enforce its secrecy agreement with Marchetti, a former employee, and required him to submit material before publication. Source: 3, p. 100; 4, Spring 1976, pp. 88-89.

800
Marcus, Eric. *Is It a Choice? Answers to Three Hundred of the Most Frequently Asked Questions about Gays and Lesbians.* Harper. Challenged at the Indianola, Iowa Public Library (1993) because it was not "of much concern to the Christian-believing people of this community." The book is about homosexuality. Source: 7, Jan. 1994, p. 35.

801
_____. *The Male Couple's Guide to Living Together: What Gay Men Should Know about Living with Each Other and Coping in a Straight World.* Harper. Challenged at the Muscatine, Iowa Public Library (1990) because it is "wrong to promote immorality." Source: 7, Nov. 1990, p. 225.

802
Marianna. *Miss Flora McFlimsey's Easter Bonnet.* Lothrop. Challenged at the Troy, Mich. Public Library (1991) because it contained an offensive and unflattering illustration of a black doll. Source: 7, Jan. 1992, p. 26.

803
Martin, Tony. *The Jewish Onslaught: Dispatches from the Wellesley Battlefront.* Majority Pr. Criticized at the Enoch Pratt Free Library in Baltimore, Md. (1994) because the book accuses Jews of masterminding the slave trade and blocking the advance of African Americans. "There's no reason for our public library to spend shrinking public funds to promote the circulation of such hatred." Source: 7, Sept. 1994, p. 146.

804
Marx, Karl. *Capital.* Imported Publishers; Random; Regnery. Prohibited reading in China (1929) and challenged at the Boston, Mass. Public Library (1950-1953) because of the book's communistic message. Source: 3, pp. 44-45.

805
_____. *The Communist Manifesto.* Intl. Pub. Co. Prohibited in Germany (1878), in China (1929), challenged at the Boston, Mass. Public Library (1950-1953) because of the book's communistic message. Source: 3, pp. 44-45.

806
Marx, Karl, and Engels, Friedrich. *German Ideology.* Intl. Pubs. Co. Banned in South Korea (1985). Source: 4, April 1986, pp. 30-33.

807
Masland, Robert P. Jr., ed., and Estridge, David, ex. ed. *What Teenagers Want to Know about Sex: Questions and Answers.* Little. Challenged in the Kenai Peninsula Borough schools in Homer, Alaska (1993) because it presents "sexual relations in an amoral light." Source: 7, Jan. 1994, pp. 33-34.

808
Mason, Bobbie Ann. *In Country.* Harper. Recalled as supplemental reading in two college preparatory English classes at the Charlton County High School in Folkston, Ga. (1994). All of the parents of the forty-eight students in the classes

had given permission for their children to read the book. But it was removed from their hands in May after one of those parents complained it included profanity. Challenged at the West Chester, Pa. schools (1994) as "most pornographic." Source: 7, Sept. 1994, p. 150; Jan. 1995, p. 25; Mar. 1995, p. 45; July 1995, p. 99.

809
Masters, Edgar Lee. *Spoon River Anthology.* Buccaneer Bks.; Macmillan. Several students brought suit against the Scioto-Darby School District in Willard, Ohio (1974) for removing two pages because the poems were "inappropriate" and their language might be offensive to some. The case was dismissed in *Kramer v. Scioto-Darby City School District,* Civil Action 72-406, Southern District of Ohio, Mar. 8, 1974. Source: 8, pp. 133-34, 238.

810
Mathabane, Mark. *Kaffir Boy.* NAL. Challenged at the Amador High School in Sutter Creek, Calif. (1993) and Manasquan, N.J. schools (1993) because of a brief but graphic passage involving homosexuality. Temporarily pulled from the Greensboro, N.C. high school libraries (1996) after a resident sent letters to school board members and some administrators charging that the book could encourage young people to sexually assault children. Challenged at the Lewis S. Mills High School (1996) in Burlington, Conn. because of brutal and graphic language. Source: 7, Jan. 1994, pp. 15, 38; July 1996, p. 119; Mar. 1997, p. 38.

811
Matthiessen, Peter. *In the Spirit of Crazy Horse.* Viking. South Dakota Governor William J. Janklow named three South Dakota bookstores in a $20-million libel suit because the bookstores refused to stop selling Matthiessen's book. A Sioux Falls judge ruled on June 18, 1984 that Matthiessen's work is not defamatory and threw out the case. Source: 7, July 1983, p. 112; Jan. 1984, p. 18; May 1984, p. 75; July 1984, p. 116; Sept. 1984, p. 148.

812
May, Julian. *A New Baby Comes.* Creative Ed. Soc. Placed on restricted shelves at the Evergreen School District elementary school libraries in Vancouver, Wash. (1987) in accordance with the school board policy to restrict student access to sex education books in elementary school libraries. Source: 7, May 1987, p. 87.

813
Mayer, Mercer. *Liza Lou & the Yellow Belly Swamp.* Macmillan. Challenged at the Douglas County Library in Roseburg, Oreg. (1988) because of scary pictures and references to boil-

ing children. Source: 7, Jan. 1990, pp. 4-5.

814
Mayer, Mercer. *A Special Trick.* Dial. Challenged at the Coburg Elementary School in Eugene, Oreg. (1992) for allegedly satanic art. The book was retained, but an accompanying audiotape that encourages children to look closely at the art work was removed by the school principal. Source: 7, July 1992, p. 103.

815
Mayle, Peter. *What's Happening to Me? The Answers to Some of the World's Most Embarrassing Questions.* Carol Pub. Group; Stuart. Challenged and eventually moved from the Henderson, Nev. Public Library (1983) children's section to the adult shelves because the book is "too sexually explicit and unsuitable for children." Challenged, but retained at the Cleveland, Tenn. Public Library (1993) along with seventeen other books, most of which are on sex education, AIDS awareness, and some titles on the supernatural. Source: 7, Mar. 1984, p. 39; May 1984, p. 71; Sept. 1993, p. 146.

816
_____. *Where Did I Come From?* Stuart. Banned from elementary classrooms in Hamden, Conn. (1980) because it was judged not appropriate. Challenged at the Washoe County Library System in Reno, Nev. (1994) because "Nobody in their right mind would give a book like that to children on their own, except a library." Source: 7, Mar. 1980, p. 32; Sept. 1994, p. 147.

817
Mazer, Harry. *I Love You, Stupid.* Crowell. Banned from Des Moines, Iowa junior high school libraries (1982) after a parent's complaint that the book was "morally inappropriate." Removed from the Evergreen School District of Vancouver, Wash. (1983) along with twenty-nine other titles. The American Civil Liberties Union of Washington has filed suit contending that the removals constitute censorship, a violation of plaintiff's rights to free speech and due process, and the acts are a violation of the state Open Meetings Act because the removal decisions were made behind closed doors. Source: 7, Sept. 1982, p. 155; Nov. 1983, pp. 185-86.

818
_____. *The Last Mission.* Dell. Challenged at the Pequannock Valley Middle School in Pompton Plains, N.J. (1984) because of its "language." Moved from the Alexander Middle School library to the Nekoosa, Wis. High School library (1986) because of "profanity" in the book. Banned, but later reinstated in the Carroll Middle School Library in South-

lake, Tex. (1995). In the original complaint, a parent requested its removal because of excessive profanity. Source: 7, Nov. 1984, p. 185; Mar. 1985, p. 59; Jan. 1987, p. 10; May 1995, p. 67; July 1995, p. 95; Sept. 1995, p. 159.

819

_____. *Snow Bound.* Dell; Peter Smith. Challenged at the Stoughton, Wis. middle school reading program (1987) because the book includes "several profane oaths invoking the deity, two four-letter words for bodily wastes, and the term 'crazy bitch' and 'stupid female.'" Source: 7, May 1987, p. 103.

820

Mazer, Norma Fox. *Out of Control.* Avon; Morrow; Thorndike Pr. Banned at the Cooper Middle School Library in Putnam City, Okla. (1995) because of language "inappropriate for that age level." Challenged also at the Oklahoma City, Okla. Metropolitan Library System (1995), but retained. Source: 7, July 1995, p. 94.

821

_____. *Saturday, the Twelfth of October.* Delacorte; Dell; Dial. Removed from the seventh grade classroom in Chester, Vt. (1977) after a parent described the book as "filthy." Source: 7, Mar. 1978, p. 31.

822

_____. *Up in Seth's Room.* Delacorte. Removed from the Campbell County, Wyo. School District libraries and classrooms (1982). After complaints of three district media specialists about the "illegitimately constituted" review committee, however, the book was reinstated. Source: 7, Mar. 1983, p. 51.

823

Mcalpine, Helen and Mcalpine, William. *Japanese Tales and Legends.* Oxford Univ. Pr. Challenged at the Wilsona School District in Lake Los Angeles, Calif. (1995) because of depictions of violence and references to Buddha and ritual suicide. Source: 7, Jan. 1996, p. 13.

824

McBride, Will, and Fleischhauer-Hardt, Helga. *Show Me!* St. Martin. Publisher prosecuted on obscenity charges in Massachusetts (1975), New Hampshire (1976), Oklahoma (1976), and Toronto, Canada (1976). In all four cases, the judges ruled as a matter of law that the title was not obscene. Frequently, challenged in libraries across the country, e.g., at the Stanislaus County, Calif. library (1984), and the San Jose, Calif. library (1984) because the book "condones child molestation or child pornography." Less than two weeks

later, the copy of the book was reported lost by the borrower, a member of the Turlock Action Committee, which organized the movement to ban the book. Challenged at the Seattle, Wash. Public Library (1985) because "it is inappropriate for the library collection." Challenged at the Alameda County, Calif. Library (1986) because "we are giving the pedophile a platform on which to stand" and placed on restrictive shelves in three branches. Challenged at the Steele Memorial Library in Elmira, N.Y. (1986) because it "promotes masturbation, sex between young people, and incest." Source: 7, Nov. 1984, pp. 183, 195; Jan. 1985, pp. 7, 27; May 1985, p. 79; July 1985, pp. 112-13; Mar. 1986, p. 37; May 1986, p. 97; Jan. 1987, pp. 29-31.

825

McCall, Don. *Jack the Bear.* Fawcett. Removed from the Monticello, Iowa school library (1978) due to "objectionable" language. Source: 7, May 1978, p. 56.

826

McCammon, Robert. *Boy's Life.* Pocket Bks.; Thorndike Pr. Challenged as required reading in the Hudson Falls, N.Y. schools (1994) because the book has recurring themes of rape, masturbation, violence, and degrading treatment of women. Source: 7, Nov. 1994, p. 190; Jan. 1995, p. 13; Mar. 1995, p. 55.

827

_____. *Mystery Walk.* Pocket Bks. Challenged in the Salem-Keizer, Oreg. school libraries (1992) because "it is full of violence and profanity." Source: 7, July 1992, p. 125.

828

McCarthy, Mary. *The Group.* Harcourt. Challenged in Terre Haute, Ind. (1982) as an optional reading in an elective English course for junior and senior high school students. Source: 7, May 1982, p. 86.

829

McCoy, Kathy, and Wibbelsman, Charles. *The New Teenage Body Book.* Body Pr. Withdrawn as a textbook, but retained as a "classroom resource," in the ninth grade health classes in Pembroke, Mass. (1990) because it is "obscene." Parents have asked that the abstinence-based sex education program Sex Respect be substituted. Complainant wants school officials indicted for distributing obscene materials to children. Source: 7, Jan. 1991, p. 17; Mar. 1991, p. 44; Jan. 1992, p. 8.

830

McCuen, Gary E., and Bender, David L. *The Sexual Revolution.* Greenhaven. Banned from the Brighton, Mich. High School library (1977) along with all other sex education materials. Source: 7, Sept. 1977, p. 133.

831
McCunn, Ruthanne Lum. *Thousand Pieces of Gold.* Design
Enterprises. Removed from elementary school library shelves
in Sonoma County, Calif. (1984) because certain passages
were too "sexually explicit." Challenged at the Commodore
Middle School in Bainbridge Island, Wash. (1992) as inappropriate by three parents because of violence, sexual scenes,
and "lack of family values." Rejected as an addition to a core
literature list by the Amador County, Calif. (1994) Unified
School District because "it makes America look bad."
Source: 7, Sept. 1984, p. 137; May 1992, p. 84; July 1994,
p. 109.

832
McDermott, Beverly Brodsky. *The Golem: A Jewish Legend.*
Lippincott. A first grade teacher asked the Newburgh, N.Y.
school officials (1993) to ban this Caldecott Award-winning
children's book about the persecution of Jews in sixteenth-
century Prague. The teacher objected to the strong language
and threatening artwork that children might not understand.
Source: 7, Nov. 1993, p. 178.

833
McFarland, Philip J., et al. *Themes in World Literature.*
Houghton. Challenged at the Tempe Union High School
District in Mesa, Ariz. (1995). The story, "A Rose for Emily,"
by William Faulkner was objectionable because it uses the
word "nigger" six times as well as other demeaning phrases.
Source: 7, Jan. 1996, p. 13; May 1996, p. 98.

834
McHargue, Georgess. *Meet the Werewolf.* Harper. Challenged
at the Evergreen School District in Vancouver, Oreg. (1983)
because the book was "full of comments about becoming a
werewolf, use of opium, and pacts with the devil." Challenged because the book would lead children to believe ideas
contrary to the teachings of the Bible, but retained by the
Sikes Elementary School media center in Lakeland, Fla.
(1985). Challenged at the Barringer Road Elementary
School in Ilion, N.Y. (1992) because the book's
passages on the occult were objectionable.
Source: 7, Sept. 1983, p. 139; July
1985, p. 133; Jan. 1993, p. 9.

835
McHugh, Vincent. *The Blue Hen's
Chicken.* Random. Confiscated in
New York City (1947) because the
poetry book contained a part
titled "Suite from Catullus," eight

short poems that were variations on a theme of the Roman
poet. Source: 9, Vol. IV, p. 699.

836
McKay, Susan. *Living Law.* Scholastic and Constitutional
Rights Foundation. Removed (1981) from the Mississippi
state-approved textbook list because of complaints that the
book "undermines" the values parents teach at home. Source:
7, May 1981, p. 67; July 1981, p. 93.

837
McKissack, Patricia. *Mirandy and Brother Wind.* Knopf.
Challenged at the Glen Springs Elementary School in
Gainesville, Fla. (1991) because of the book's use of black
dialect. Source: 7, July 1991, p. 129.

838
Meeks, Linda, and Heit, Philip. *Your Relationship.* Merill
Pub. Challenged in the Barrington, Ill. School District
(1990) because the book has a chapter on incest which creates "ugly imagery for innocent minds." Source: 7, Jan.
1991, p. 29.

839
Melville, Herman. *Moby Dick.* Modern Library. Banned
from the advanced placement English reading list at the Lindale, Tex. schools (1996) because it "conflicts with the values
of the community." Source: 7, Nov. 1996, p. 199.

840
Meretzky, Eric. *Zork: The Malifestro Quest.* Tor Bks. Chal-
lenged at the Jeffers Elementary School in Spring Lake,
Mich. (1990) because it "is a disgrace to the Lord and to the
Spring Lake school system." Source: 7, May 1990, p. 84;
July 1990, p. 145.

841
Meriwether, Louise. *Daddy Was a Numbers Runner.* Jove.
Removed from all Oakland, Calif. (1977) junior high school
libraries and its use restricted in senior high schools, following a complaint about the book's explicit depiction of
ghetto life. Source: 7, May 1977, p. 71.

842
Merriam, Eve. *Halloween ABC.* Macmillan. Challenged at the Douglas County Library in Roseburg,
Oreg. (1989) because the book encourages devil
worshipping. Challenged at the Howard County, Md. school libraries (1991) because "there
should be an effort to tone down Halloween
and there should not be books about it in the
schools." Challenged in the Wichita, Kans.

public schools (1991) because it is "satanic and disgusting." Challenged at the Acres Green Elementary School in Douglas County, Colo. (1992). Challenged and retained, but will be shelved with other works generally available only to older students and won't be used in future Halloween displays at the Federal Way School District in Seattle, Wash. (1992). The compromise was for a group of parents who objected to the book's satanic references. Challenged, but retained in the Othello, Wash. elementary school libraries (1993) because the book "promotes violent criminal and deviant behavior." Challenged, but retained at the Ennis, Texas Public Library (1993). Challenged in the Cameron Elementary School library in Rice Lake, Wis. (1993) because the "poems promote satanism, murder, and suicide." The book was retained. Challenged in the Spokane, Wash. School District library (1994) by a father who found the poems morbid and satanic. In particular, the parent disapproved of one poem which "appears to be a chant calling forth the Devil." Challenged in the Sandwich, Mass. Public Library (1995) because it is "too violent for young children." Source: 7, Jan. 1990, pp. 4-5; Sept. 1991, p. 178; Jan. 1992, p. 26; May 1992, p. 94; Mar. 1993, p. 43; July 1993, pp. 103-4; Sept. 1993, p. 159; Jan. 1994, pp. 13-14; Mar. 1994, pp. 69-70; Jan. 1995, p. 9; Mar. 1995, p. 41; Sept. 1995, p. 158.

843
_____. *The Inner City Mother Goose.* Simon & Schuster/Touchstone. An Erie County, N.Y. judge (1972) called for a grand jury investigation of this satirical book of adult nursery rhymes, alleging it taught crime; similar controversies were reported in Baltimore, Md.; Minneapolis, Minn.; San Francisco, Calif. Source: 3, p. 91.

844
Merriam-Webster Editorial Staff. *Merriam-Webster Collegiate Dictionary.* Merriam-Webster. Removed from classrooms in Carlsbad, N.Mex. schools (1982) because the dictionary defines "obscene" words. Challenged in the Upper Pittsgrove Township, N.J. schools (1989) because the definition of sexual intercourse was objectionable. Challenged, but the 1,100 copies of the dictionary were returned to the Sparks, Nev. Elementary School classrooms (1993). A sixth grade teacher objected to the book because it includes obscene words. Source: 7, Nov. 1982, p. 206; Jan. 1990, p. 11; Jan. 1994, p. 37.

845
Merrick, Gordon. *One for the Gods.* Avon. Seized (1984) by the British Customs Office. Source: 7, Jan. 1985, p. 26.

846
Metalious, Grace. *Peyton Place.* Simon & Schuster. Tempo-rary ban lifted in Canada (1958). Source: 3, p. 97.

847
Mill, John Stuart. *Social Philosophy.* Listed on the *Index Librorum Prohibitorum* in Rome (1856). Source: 3, p. 42.

848
_____. *System of Logic.* Univ. of Toronto Pr. Listed on the *Index Librorum Prohibitorum* in Rome (1856). Source: 3, p. 42.

849
Miller, Arthur. *The Crucible.* Penguin. Challenged at the Cumberland Valley High School, Harrisburg, Pa. (1982) because the play contains "sick words from the mouths of demon-possessed people. It should be wiped out of the schools or the school board should use them to fuel the fire of hell." Challenged as a required reading assignment at the Pulaski County High School in Somerset, Ky. (1987) because it is "junk." Source: 7, Mar. 1983, pp. 52-53; May 1987, p. 90.

850
_____. *Death of a Salesman.* Penguin; Viking. Challenged at the Dallas, Tex. Independent School District high school libraries (1974); banned from English classes at Spring Valley Community High School in French Lick, Ind. (1981) because the play contains the words "goddamn," "son of a bitch," and "bastard." Challenged as a required reading assignment at the Pulaski County High School in Sinking Valley, Ky. (1987) because it is "junk." Source: 7, July 1975, pp. 6-7; May 1981, p. 68; May 1987, p. 90.

851
Miller, Deborah A., and Waigandt, Alex. *Coping with Your Sexual Orientation.* Rosen. Moved from the Chestnut Ridge Middle School library in Washington Township, N.J. (1994) because school administrators have been accused of "indoctrinating children in the gay lifestyle." Source: 7, Sept. 1994, p. 148.

852
Miller, Henry. *Opus Pistorum.* Grove Pr. Removed from the Cumberland County, N.C. library system (1993) because it lacks "serious literary or artistic merit for this library's collection." Source: 7, Mar. 1993, p. 42.

853
_____. *Sexus.* Grove. Banned in France (1950); in Norway (1956). Source: 3, p. 74.

854

_____. *Tropic of Cancer.* Grove. Banned from U.S. Customs (1934). The U.S. Supreme Court found the novel not obscene (1964). Banned in Turkey (1986). Source: 3, p. 74; 4, July/Aug. 1986, p. 46.

855

_____. *Tropic of Capricorn.* Grove. Ban upheld by U.S. Court of Appeals in San Francisco (1953). An appeals court in Istanbul, Turkey authorized a public burning (1989) of Miller's 1939 novel as sexually exploitative. Source: 3, p. 74; 7, May 1989, p. 90.

856

Miller, Jim, ed. *The Rolling Stone Illustrated History of Rock and Roll.* Random. Challenged in Jefferson County, Ky. (1982) because it "will cause our children to become immoral and indecent." Source: 7, Mar. 1983, p. 41.

857

Milton, John. *Paradise Lost.* Airmont; Holt; Modern Library/Random; NAL; Norton. Listed on the *Index Librorum Prohibitorum* in Rome (1758). Source: 3, p. 22.

858

Mishima, Yukio. *The Sound of Waves.* Putnam. Challenged, but retained at the Lake Washington School District in Kirkland, Wash. (1993) despite objections that it is "crude, vulgar, degrading to women, seductive, enticing, and suggestive." Source: 7, Jan. 1994, p. 16; Mar. 1994, p. 71.

859

Mitchell, Margaret. *Gone with the Wind.* Avon; Macmillan. Banned from the Anaheim, Calif. Union High School District English classrooms (1978) according to the Anaheim Secondary Teachers Association. Challenged in the Waukegan, Ill. School District (1984) because the novel uses the word "nigger." Source: 7, Jan. 1979, p. 6; July 1984, p. 105.

860

Moe, Barbara A. *Everything You Need to Know About Sexual Abstinence.* Rosen. Pulled from the Ouachita Parish school library in Monroe, La. (1996) because of sexual content. The Louisiana chapter of the ACLU filed a lawsuit in the federal courts on October 3, 1996, claiming that the principal and the school superintendent violated First Amendment free speech rights and also failed to follow established procedure when they removed the book. Source: 7, Sept. 1996, pp. 151-52; Jan. 1997, p. 7.

861

Mohr, Richard D. *A More Perfect Union: Why Straight America Must Stand Up for Gay Rights.* Beacon Pr. Challenged, but retained at the Belfast, Maine Free Library (1996) because "homosexuality destroys marriages and families; it destroys the good health of the individual and the innocent are infected by it." Source: 7, May 1996, p. 97.

862

Momaday, N. Scott. *House Made of Dawn.* Harper; NAL; Penguin. Challenged at the Reynolds High School in Troutdale, Oreg. (1989) because two pages of the 1969 Pulitzer Prize winner were sexually explicit. Retained on the Round Rock, Tex. Independent High School reading list (1996) after a challenge that the book was too violent. Source: 7, Jan. 1990, p. 32; May 1996, p. 99.

863

Montaigne, Michel de. *Essays.* AMS Pr.; French & European; Gordon Pr.; Stanford Univ. Pr. Sections banned in France (1595), listed on the *Index Librorum Prohibitorum* in Rome (1676). Source: 3, p. 15.

864

Morris, Desmond. *The Naked Ape.* Dell; McGraw-Hill. Removed from the Island Trees, N.Y. Union Free School District High School library in 1976 along with nine other titles because they were considered "immoral, anti-American, anti-Christian, or just plain filthy." Returned to the library after the U. S. Supreme Court ruling on June 25, 1982 in *Board of Education, Island Trees Union Free School District No. 26 et al. v. Pico et al.,* 457 U. S. 853 (1982). Reinstated after being removed from the Mifflinburg, Pa. High School (1989) because the book includes material on human sexuality that is "explicit, almost manual description of what some would refer to as deviant sexual relations." Source: 7, Nov. 1982, p. 197; May 1989, p. 93.

865

Morrison, Lillian. *Remember Me When This You See.* Crowell; Scholastic. Challenged at the Gwinnett County, Ga. Elementary School library (1986) because a line from the poetry book – "Don't make love in a potato field/Potatoes have eyes" – was objectionable. Source: 7, Mar. 1987, p. 65.

866

Morrison, Toni. *Beloved.* Knopf; NAL. Challenged at the St. Johns County Schools in St. Augustine, Fla. (1995). Retained on the Round Rock, Tex. Independent High School reading list (1996) after a challenge that the book was too violent. Source: 7, Jan. 1996, p. 14; May 1996, p. 99.

867

_____. *The Bluest Eye.* NAL. Pulled from an eleventh grade classroom at Lathrop High School in Fairbanks, Alaska (1994) by school administrators because "It was a very controversial book; it contains lots of very graphic descriptions and lots of disturbing language." Challenged at the West Chester, Pa. schools (1994) as "most pornographic." Banned from the Morrisville, Pa. Borough High School English curriculum (1994) after complaints about its sexual content and objectionable language. Challenged at the St. Johns County Schools in St. Augustine, Fla. (1995). Challenged on the optional summer reading list at the Lynn, Mass. schools (1995) because of the book's sexual content. Source: 7, May 1994, p. 86; Jan. 1995, p. 25; Mar. 1995, pp. 44-45; May 1995, p. 71; July 1995, p. 98; Jan. 1996, p. 14.

868

_____. *Song of Solomon.* Knopf; NAL. Challenged, but retained in the Columbus, Ohio schools (1993). The complainant believed that the book contains language degrading to blacks, and is sexually explicit. Removed from required reading lists and library shelves in the Richmond County, Ga. School District (1994) after a parent complained that passages from the book were "filthy and inappropriate." Source: 7, July 1993, p. 108; Sept. 1993, p. 160; May 1994, p. 86; Jan. 1996, p. 14.

869

Mosca, Frank. *All-American Boy.* Alyson Pubns. Challenged at several Kansas City area schools (1993) after the books were donated by a national group that seeks to give young adults "fair, accurate and inclusive images of lesbians and gay men"—at the Shawnee Mission School District the book was returned to general circulation; at the Olathe East High School the book was removed; protesters burned copies of the book but the Kansas City, Mo. School District kept Mosca's novel on the high school shelves; in Kansas City, Kans., the school district donated the book to the city's public library; and in Lee's Summit, Mo. the superintendent removed the book. Source: 7, Mar. 1994, pp. 51-52; May 1994, p. 84.

870

Mother Goose: Old Nursery Rhymes. Arthur Rackham, illustrator. Durst. Challenged at the Dade County, Fla. Public Library (1983) by a Miami Metro Commissioner because the anthology of nursery rhymes contains the following anti-Semitic verse: "Jack sold his gold egg/to a rogue of a Jew/who cheated him out of/half of his due." Source: 7, July 1983, p. 107; Jan. 1984, p. 25.

871

Mowat, Farley. *And No Birds Sang.* Bantam. Challenged in the Northwestern Middle School library, Springfield, Ohio (1994) because of "improper language." Source: 7, July 1994, p. 111.

872

_____. *Never Cry Wolf.* Bantam; Little. Removed from the Panama City, Fla. school classrooms and libraries (1987) because of "offensive" language. Source: 7, July 1987, pp. 126-28; Sept. 1987, pp. 168-69.

873

_____. *Woman in the Mists: The Story of Dian Fossey & the Mountain Gorillas of Africa.* Warner. Removed from a required reading list in the Omaha, Nebr. public schools (1991) because the book has racial slurs, passages degrading to women, profanity, and a long discussion of the aftermath of Fossey's abortion. Source: 7, Mar. 1992, p. 44.

874

Muller, Gilbert H., and Wiener, Harvey S., comps. *The Short Prose Reader.* McGraw. Challenged at the Cecil County Board of Education in Elkton, Md. (1994). Many deemed the text controversial because it included essays dealing with issues of abortion, gay rights, alcohol, and sex education. Source: 7, Mar. 1995, p. 55.

875

Murdoch, Iris. *The Nice and the Good.* Penguin. Banned in South Africa (1977). Source: 4, Nov./Dec. 1977, p. 68.

876

Murphy, Barbara Beasley. *Home Free.* Delacorte; Dell. Retained at the Hillcrest School library in East Ramapo, N.J. (1988), but the book will not be lent to a fourth or fifth grader who is not deemed an "advanced reader or critical thinker" by a parent, teacher, or librarian. The book contains the word "nigger." Source: 7, May 1988, p. 86.

877

_____. *No Place to Run.* Archway. Removed from two Anniston, Ala. high school libraries (1982) due to "the curse words and using the Lord's name in vain," but later reinstated on a restricted basis. Source: 7, Mar. 1983, p. 37.

878

Murray, William. *Tip on a Dead Crab.* Dodd. Publication canceled by Dodd, Mead & Company (1983) because of language in the book considered "objectionable" by Thomas Nelson, Inc. of Nashville, Tenn. — Dodd, Mead's parent company. Source: 7, Nov. 1983, p. 188.

879
Myers, Lawrence W. *Improvised Radio Jamming Techniques.* Paladin Pr. Challenged for promoting illegal actions, but retained at the Multnomah, Oreg. County Library (1991). Source: 7, Jan. 1992, p. 6.

880
Myers, Walter Dean. *Fallen Angels.* Scholastic. Challenged in the Bluffton, Ohio schools (1990) because of its use of profane language. Restricted as supplemental classroom reading material at the Jackson County, Ga. High School (1992) because of undesirable language and sensitive material. Challenged at the West Chester, Pa. schools (1994). Removed from a twelfth-grade English class in Middleburg Heights, Ohio (1995) after a parent complained of its sexually explicit language. The novel won the Coretta Scott King Award and was named Best Book of 1988 by School Library Journal. Source: 7, Nov. 1990, p. 211; Sept. 1992, p. 142; Jan. 1995, p. 25; Mar. 1996, p. 49.

881
_____. *Fast Sam, Cool Clyde and Stuff.* Viking. Challenged by an elementary school administrator in Akron, Ohio (1983). Source: 5 & 7, May 1983, p. 86.

882
_____. *Hoops.* Dell. Challenged in Littleton, Colo. (1989) school libraries because the book "endorses" drinking, stealing, and homosexuality, uses offensive words, and contains a sex scene. Source: 7, Sept. 1989, p. 186.

883
_____. *Young Martin's Promise.* Raintree. Challenged by a school board member in the Queens, N.Y. school libraries (1994) because King "was a leftist hoodlum with significant Communist ties. King was a hypocritical adulterer." The rest of the school board voted to retain the book. Source: 7, July 1994, pp. 110-11; Sept. 1994, p. 166.

884
Myrer, Anton. *A Green Desire.* Avon. Banned from the Stroudsburg, Pa. High School library (1985) because it was "blatantly graphic, pornographic and wholly unacceptable for a high school library." Source: 7, May 1985, p. 79.

885
Nabokov, Vladimir. *Lolita.* Berkley; McGraw-Hill; Putnam. Banned as obscene in France (1956-1959), in Argentina (1959) and in New Zealand (1960). The South African Directorate of Publications announced on Nov. 27, 1982 that Lolita had been taken off the banned list, eight years after a request for permission to market the novel in paper-

back had been refused. Source: 3, p. 81; 4, Apr. 1983, p. 47.

886
National Register Publishing Co. Staff. *Official Catholic Directory.* National Register Publishing Co. Challenged by a patron who believed public funds should not be expended on religious books, but retained at the Multnomah, Oreg. County Library (1991). Source: 7, Jan. 1992, p. 6.

887
Naylor, Phyllis Reynolds. *Send No Blessings.* Puffin Bks.; Macmillan. Challenged at the Cedar Valley Elementary School in Kent, Wash. (1993) because parents claimed the book condones child molestation and promiscuity. Source: 7, Mar. 1993, p. 55.

888
_____. *Witch Herself.* Atheneum; Dell. Retained at the Ector County, Tex. school library (1989) after being challenged because the book might lure children into the occult. Source: 7, Jan. 1990, p. 9; May 1990, p. 107.

889
_____. *Witch Water.* Atheneum; Dell. Retained at the Ector County, Tex. school library (1989) after being challenged because the book might lure children into the occult. Source: 7, Jan. 1990, p. 9; May 1990, p. 107.

890
_____. *Witch's Sister.* Atheneum; Dell. Challenged at the Multnomah County Library in Portland, Oreg. (1988) because the occult topic could be frightening and traumatic for children. Retained at the Ector County, Tex. school library (1989) after being challenged because the book might lure children into the occult. Source: 7, Jan. 1989, p. 3; Jan. 1990, p. 9; May 1990, p. 107.

891
Nehring, James. *Why Do We Gotta Do This Stuff, Mr. Nehring?* M. Evans. Challenged, but retained by the Pocatello, Idaho Library Board (1994) who refused to remove or label books that contain obscene language. Source: 7, May 1994, pp. 97-98.

892
Neufeld, John. *Freddy's Book.* Ballantine; Random. Removed from the elementary school library in Spring Valley, Ill. (1977) after a parent complained about the book's theme. Challenged but retained, at the Lake Fenton, Mich. Elementary School library (1989) because of the book's descriptions of male and female genitalia, menstruation, erections, sexual intercourse, and wet dreams. The book was, however, placed

on a restricted shelf and requires parents to check the book out. Partly as a result of the controversy, all of the district's library books were slated to be reviewed by a four-member committee consisting of a parent, teacher, librarian, and district administrator. Source: 7, Jan. 1978, p. 6; Jan. 1990, p. 9.

893
Newman, Leslea. *Gloria Goes to Gay Pride.* Alyson Pubns. Removed from the Brooklyn, N.Y. School District's curriculum (1992) because the school board objected to words that were "age inappropriate." Retained at the Dayton and Montgomery County, Ohio Public Library (1993). Challenged at the Chandler, Ariz. Public Library (1994) because the book is a "skillful presentation to the young child about lesbianism/homosexuality." Source: 7, May 1992, p. 83; Mar. 1994, p. 69; July 1994, p. 128; Nov. 1994, p. 187.

894
_____. *Heather Has Two Mommies.* Alyson Pubns. Removed from the Brooklyn, N.Y. School District's curriculum (1992) because the school board objected to words that were "age inappropriate." Challenged in Fayetteville, N.C. (1992). Moved from the children's section to the adult section in Elizabethtown, N.C. library (1993) because it "promotes a dangerous and ungodly lifestyle from which children must be protected." Moved from the children's section to the young adult section at the Chestatee Regional Library System in Gainesville, Ga. (1993). Three area legislators wanted the book removed and said, "We could put together a resolution to amend the Georgia state constitution to say that tax dollars cannot be used to promote homosexuality, pedophilia, or sado-masochism." Moved from the children's section to the adult section at the Mercer County Library System in Lawrence, N.J. (1993). Challenged at the North Brunswick, N.J. Public Library (1993), the Cumberland County Public, N.C. Library (1993) and Wicomico County Free Library in Salisbury, Md. (1993). Challenged at the Mesa, Ariz. Public Library (1993) because it "is vile, sick, and goes against every law and constitution." Retained at the Dayton and Montgomery County, Ohio Public Library (1993). Challenged, but retained in the Oak Bluffs, Mass. school library (1994). Though the parent leading the protest stated that "The subject matter…is obscene and vulgar and the message is that homosexuality is okay," the selection review committee voted unanimously to keep the book. Removed by officials at the Cottage Grove, Oreg. (1994) Lane County Head Start Center. Challenged at the Chandler, Ariz. Public Library (1994) because the book is a "skillful presentation to the young child about lesbianism/ homosexuality." Source: 7, May 1992, p. 83; Jan. 1993, pp. 9, 28; May 1993, p. 71; July 1993, pp. 100-101, 126; Sept. 1993, pp. 143-44; Nov. 1993, pp. 177-78; Jan. 1994, pp. 13, 34-35; Mar. 1994, p. 69; May 1994,

p. 98; July 1994, pp. 110, 115; Spt. 1994, pp. 147-48, 166; Nov. 1994, p. 187.

895
Noel, Janet. *The Human Body.* Grosset. The York, Maine Middle School review committee (1982) voted unanimously to remove the book from the library "because of the inappropriateness of written and pictorial material." After a backlash from anti-censorship parents, the book was moved from the middle school library to the junior high library for use by seventh and eighth graders. Source: 7, July 1982, pp. 123-24.

896
Norstog, Knut J., and Meyerriecks, Andrew J. *Biology.* Merrill. A Sallisaw, Okla. Senior High School biology teacher (1986) removed pages 467-76 from the textbook because they were "irrelevant" to the school's curriculum requirements. The pages contained information on reproduction and birth control. The teacher said he was "trying to circumvent a problem, rather than create one, when students were forced to take the books parents might find objectionable into their homes." Source: 7, July 1986, p. 121.

897
Oates, Joyce Carol. *Where Are You Going, Where Have You Been?* Fawcett. Challenged in the Tyrone, Pa. schools (1990) because of its use of profane language. Source: 7, Mar. 1991, pp. 61-62.

898
Oates, Stephen. *Portrait of America, Vol II.* Houghton. Returned to the Racine, Wis. Unified School District (1984) curriculum just one week after the school board voted to ban it. Opponents of the books on the board charged that the social studies volumes contained "judgmental writing" and, in the words of one board member, "a lot more funny pictures of Republicans and nicer pictures of Democrats." Opponents also said that one text did not present an adequate analysis of the Vietnam War. Source: 7, Sept. 1984, p. 158.

899
O'Connor, Jane. *Just Good Friends.* Dell; Harper. Removed from the Jefferson Magnet Arts Library, and transferred to a middle school in Eugene, Oreg. (1988) because of the book's sexual references. Source: 7, Jan. 1989, p. 3.

900
_____. *Lu Lu and the Witch Baby.* Harper. Challenged at the Dakota, Ill. Primary School (1991) because it "promotes lying and witchcraft." Source: 7, May 1991, p. 89.

901
O'Donnell, E. P. *Green Margins.* Houghton. Seized and destroyed by New Orleans, La. (1937) police. Source: 9, Vol. III, p. 650.

902
O'Hara, Frank. *Lunch Poems.* City Lights. Banned for use in Aurora, Colo. High School English classes (1976) on the grounds of "immorality." Source: 7, May 1977, p. 79.

903
O'Hara, John. *Appointment in Samarra.* Random. Declared nonmailable by the U.S. Post Office Department (1941). Source: 3, p. 86.

904
_____. *Ten North Frederick.* Random. Banned by Police Commissioner in Detroit, Mich. (1957), a series of local bans and seizures spread over a two-year period (1957-1958). Source: 3, pp. 86-87.

905
O'Hara, Mary. *My Friend Flicka.* Harper; Lippincott. Pulled from fifth and sixth grade optional reading lists in Clay County, Fla. schools (1990) because the book uses the word "bitch" to refer to a female dog, as well as the word "damn." Source: 7, Jan. 1991, p. 16.

906
O'Huigin, Sean. *Scary Poems for Rotten Kids.* Black Moss Pr. Challenged in the Livonia, Mich. schools (1990) because the poems frightened first grade children. Source: 7, Mar. 1991, p. 62.

907
O'Keeffe, Georgia. *Georgia O'Keeffe.* Viking. Retained at Maldonado Elementary School in Tucson, Ariz. (1994) after being challenged by parents who objected to nudity and "pornographic," "perverted," and "morbid" themes. Source: 7, July 1994, p. 112.

908
O'Malley, Kevin, illus. *Froggy Went A-Courtin'.* Stewart, Tabori and Chang. Restricted at the Baltimore County, Md. school libraries (1996) because of Froggy's nefarious activities including burning money, and speeding away from the cat police, as well as robbery and smoking. The book is to be kept in restricted areas of the libraries where only parents and teachers will be allowed to check it out

and read it to children. Source: 7, Jan. 1997, p. 7; Mar. 1997, p. 35.

909
Oppenheim, Irene. *Living Today.* Bennett. Returned to the Racine, Wis. Unified School District (1984) curriculum just one week after the school board voted to ban it. The home economics text was criticized for encouraging premarital sex and advocating that unmarried couples live together. Source: 7, Sept. 1984, p. 158.

910
Orenstein, Peggy. *Schoolgirls: Young Women, Self-esteem and the Confidence Gap.* Doubleday. Challenged in Courtland, Ohio High School (1996) because of its "rotten, filthy language." The teacher offered the parents a black marker with which to delete offending passages, but the parents wanted it banned. The school board voted to continue the book. Source: 7, Mar. 1997, p. 50.

911
Orwell, George. *1984.* Harcourt. Challenged in the Jackson County, Fla. (1981) because Orwell's novel is "pro-communist and contained explicit sexual matter." Source: 5 & 7, May 1981, p. 73.

912
Ovid. *The Art of Love.* Harvard Univ. Pr.; Indiana Univ. Pr.; Oxford Univ. Pr. Emperor Augustus banished the author (8 A.D.); book burned in Florence (1497) and barred by U.S. Customs (1929). Proscribed in the Tridentine Index of 1564, and in England in 1599 a translation by the poet Christopher Marlowe was burned at Stationer's Hall on the orders of the archbishop of Canterbury, on account of its immorality. Source: 2, p. 224; 3, p. 2.

913
_____. *Elegies.* Liveright. Burned in Florence (1497) and in England (1599). Source: 3, p. 2.

914
Oxenbury, Helen. *Tiny Tim.* Delacorte. Challenged at the Cherry Hill, N.J. Elementary School (1987) because the book is too violent. One rhyme reads: "I had a little brother, his name is Tiny Tim. I put him in the bathtub to teach him how to swim. He drank up all the water. He ate up all the soap. He died last night with a bubble in his throat." In another rhyme, a man "who had a face made out of cake"

was baked in an oven and exploded. Source: 7, July 1987, p. 149.

915
Packer, Kenneth L., and Bower, Jeannine. *Let's Talk about Health.* Sebco. Challenged at the Salem-Keizer, Oreg. School District (1986) because of the book's handling of issues such as dating, premarital sex, homosexuality, and masturbation. Source: 7, May 1986, p. 84.

916
Paine, Thomas. *The Age of Reason.* Bobbs-Merrill; Citadel. Author and publisher imprisoned in England (1792, 1797, 1819). Source: 1, p. 7; 3, pp. 33-34.

917
_____. *The Rights of Man.* Citadel; Penguin. Author and publisher imprisoned in England (1792, 1797, 1819). Source: 3, pp. 33-34.

918
Parker, Stephen. *Life Before Birth: The Story of the First Nine Months.* Cambridge Univ. Pr. Placed on restricted shelves at the Evergreen School District elementary school libraries in Vancouver, Wash. (1987) in accordance with the school board policy to restrict student access to sex education books in elementary school libraries. Source: 7, May 1987, p. 87.

919
Parks, Gordon. *The Learning Tree.* Fawcett; Harper. Temporarily banned from the junior high school in Cheyenne, Wyo. (1976); Citizens United for Responsible Education demanded that Park's novel be removed from the Montgomery County, Md. school system (1978); challenged at the Westerly, R.I. High School (1979); subject of a court challenge by the Moral Majority of Washington State in Mead, Wash. (1982) because it includes "objectionable material, swearing, obscene language, explicit detail of premarital sexual intercourse, other lewd behavior, specific blasphemies against Jesus Christ and excessive violence and murder." The case was dismissed by U.S. District Court Judge Robert McNichols. Removed and then restored to a Suwannee, Fla. High School library (1991) because the book is "indecent." Challenged at the Eagan High School in Burnsville, Minn. (1992) on the grounds that it contains vulgar and sexually explicit language, and descriptions of violent acts. Source: 5 & 7, July 1976, p. 68; Sept. 1978, p. 123; May 1979, p. 59; Nov. 1982, p. 212; Jan. 1992, p. 25; Mar. 1993, p. 56.

920
Partridge, Eric. *Dictionary of Slang and Unconventional English.* Macmillan. Challenged in Pinellas County, Fla. (1973)

due to profanity. Source: 7, Mar. 1974, p. 32.

921
Pascal, Blaise. *Pensees.* Penguin. Placed on the *Index Librorum Prohibitorum* in Rome (1789). Source: 3, p. 24.

922
_____. *The Provincial Letters.* Penguin. Burned in France for its alleged anti-religiosity in 1657. Louis XIV ordered in 1660 that it "be torn up and burned... at the hands of the High Executioner, fulfillment of which is to be certified to His Majesty within the week; and that meanwhile all printers, booksellers, vendors and others, of whatever rank and station, are explicitly prohibited from printing selling, and distributing, and even from having in their possession the said book... under the pain of public, exemplary punishment." Pascal's work remained on the Roman Index until the 20th century. Source: 2, p. 229.

923
Pascal, Francine. *Hanging Out with Cici.* Archway; Dell; Viking. Challenged at the Greeley-Evans School District in Greeley, Colo. (1986) because the book contained "obscenities, allusions to sexual references, and promoted contempt for parents and acceptance of drug use." Source: 7, Sept. 1986, p. 171.

924
Pasternak, Boris Leonidovich. *Doctor Zhivago.* Ballantine; NAL; Pantheon. Moscow condemned the book (1958), refused to publish it, and vilified the author. Source: 3, p. 73.

925
Paterson, Katherine. *Bridge to Terabithia.* Crowell. The Newbery Award-winning book was challenged as sixth grade recommended reading in the Lincoln, Nebr. schools (1986) because it contains "profanity" including the phrase "Oh, Lord" and "Lord" used as an expletive. Challenged as suitable curriculum material in the Harwinton and Burlington, Conn. schools (1990) because it contains language and subject matter that set bad examples and give students negative views of life. Challenged at the Apple Valley, Calif. Unified School District (1992) because of vulgar language. Challenged at the Mechanicsburg, Pa. Area School District (1992) because of profanity and references to witchcraft. Challenged and retained in the libraries, but will not be required reading at the Cleburne, Tex. Independent School district (1992) because of profane language. A challenge to this Newbery Award-winning book in Oskaloosa, Kans. (1993) led to the enactment of a new policy that requires teachers to examine their required material for profanities. Teachers will list each profanity and the number of times it

was used in the book, and forward the list to parents, who will be asked to give written permission for their children to read the material. Challenged in the Gettysburg, Pa. public schools (1993) because of offensive language. Challenged at the Medway, Maine schools (1995) because the book uses "swear words." Removed from the fifth-grade classrooms of the New Brighton Area School District in Pulaski Township, Pa. (1996) due to "profanity, disrespect of adults, and an elaborate fantasy world they felt might lead to confusion." Source: 7, Mar. 1987, p. 67; Mar. 1991, p. 44; May 1992, p. 95; Sept. 1992, pp. 162-63; Nov. 1992, p. 198; Mar. 1993, p. 45; July 1993, pp. 105-6; Mar. 1994, p. 55; July 1995, p. 97; May 1996, p. 88.

926

_____. *The Great Gilly Hopkins.* Harper. Challenged at the Lowell Elementary School in Salina, Kans. (1983) because the book used the words "God," "damn" and "hell" offensively. Challenged at the Orchard Lake Elementary School library in Burnsville, Minn. (1985) because "the book took the Lord's name in vain" and had "over forty instances of profanity." Challenged at the Jefferson County, Colo. elementary schools (1988) because "Gilly's friends lie and steal, and there are no repercussions. Christians are portrayed as being dumb and stupid." Pulled, but later restored to the language arts curriculum at four Cheshire, Conn. elementary schools (1991) because the book is "filled with profanity, blasphemy and obscenities, and gutter language." Challenged at the Alamo Heights, Tex. School District elementary schools (1992) because it contains the words "hell" and "damn." Challenged at the Walnut Elementary School in Emporia, Kans. (1993) by parents who said that it contained profanity and graphic violence. Source: 7, July 1983, p. 121; Nov. 1985, p. 203; Mar. 1988, p. 45; Mar. 1992, p. 42; Mar. 1992, p. 42; May 1992, p. 96; July 1992, pp. 109-10; Jan. 1993, p. 13; July 1993, pp. 126-27.

927

_____. *Jacob Have I Loved.* Avon; Cromwell; Random. Challenged at the Bernardsville, N.J. schools (1989) as unsuitable for a sixth grade reading class. The Newbery award-winning book was offensive to several parents on moral and religious grounds. Challenged in the Gettysburg, Pa. public schools (1993) because of offensive language. Source: 7, Jan. 1990, p. 33; Mar. 1994, p. 55.

928

Paterson, Thomas. *American Foreign Policy, Vol. II.* Heath. Returned to the Racine, Wis. Unified School District (1984) curriculum just one week after the school board voted to ban it. Opponents of the books on the board charged that the social studies volumes contained "judgmental writing" and, in the words of one board member, "a lot more funny pictures of Republicans and nicer pictures of Democrats." Opponents also said that one text did not present an adequate analysis of the Vietnam War. Source: 7, Sept. 1984, p. 158.

929

Patrick, John and Berkin, Carol. *The History of the American Nation.* Macmillan; Collier. Challenged at the Amherst-Pelham, Mass. Regional Junior High School (1987) by a group of parents who charge that, among other things, it is sexist and distorts the history of minorities. Source: 7, Jan. 1988, p. 11.

930

Patterson, Lillie. *Halloween.* Garrard. Challenged at the Neely Elementary School in Gilbert, Ariz. (1992) because the book shows the dark side of religion through the occult, the devil, and satanism. Source: 7, May 1992, p. 78; July 1992, p. 124.

931

Paulsen, Gary. *The Foxman.* Viking; Puffin Bks. Challenged at Cary, Ill., Junior High School (1994) because references in the book to sex are too explicit for seventh and eighth graders; retained by a school board vote. Source: 7, May 1994, p. 83; July 1994, pp. 128-29.

932

Peck, Robert Newton. *A Day No Pigs Would Die.* ABC-Clio; Dell; Knopf. Challenged in Jefferson County, Colo. school libraries (1988) because "it is bigoted against Baptists and women and depicts violence, hatred, animal cruelty, and murder." Challenged as suitable curriculum material in the Harwinton and Burlington, Conn. schools (1990) because it contains language and subject matter that set bad examples and give students negative views of life. Challenged at the Sherwood Elementary School in Melbourne, Fla. (1993) because the book could give the "impression that rape and violence are acceptable." The comment was made in reference to a descriptive passage about a boar mating a sow in the barnyard. Challenged, but retained on the shelves of Waupaca, Wis. school libraries (1994) after a parent "objected to graphic passages dealing with sexuality in the book." Removed from seventh grade classes at Payson, Utah Middle School (1994) after several parents "had problems with language, with animal breeding, and with a scene that involves an infant grave exhumation." Challenged at the Pawhuska, Okla. middle school (1995) because the book uses bad language, gives "gory" details of mating, and lacks religious values. Pulled from an Anderson, S.C. middle school library (1995) because of the "gory" descriptions of two pigs mating, a pig being slaughtered, and a cow giving birth. Challenged at the Anderson, Mo. Junior High School (1996) because of its content. Source: 7, May 1988, p. 85; July 1988, pp. 119-20, 139; Sept. 1988, pp. 151, 177; Mar. 1991, p. 44; May 1991, p. 90; July 1993, pp. 97-98; May 1994, pp. 98-99; July 1994, pp. 117, 129; July 1995, p. 98; Mar. 1996, p. 46; Jan. 1997, p. 10.

933

_____. *Soup.* Dell; Knopf. Challenged as a fourth grade reading assignment at the Woodbridge, N.J. (1992) schools because of objectionable language and because "it teaches children how to lie, manipulate, steal, and cheat." Source: 7, Jan. 1993, p. 12.

934

_____. *Trig.* Little. Challenged at the Cunningham Elementary School in Beloit, Wis. (1985) because the book "encourages disrespectful language." Source: 7, July 1985, p. 134.

935

Pell, Derek. *Doktor Bey's Suicide Guidebook.* Avon. Placed "on reserve" at the Prairie High School library in Cedar Rapids, Iowa (1986) because the book "could push a classmate contemplating suicide over the edge." Source: 7, Sept. 1986, p. 152.

936

Penney, Alexandra. *How to Make Love to a Man...Safely.* Crown. Former Weslaco, Tex. (1995) librarian filed a federal lawsuit charging that she was fired for publicly discussing that city's efforts to ban Penney's work from the library. Source: 7, Sept. 1995, p. 155.

937

Perkins, Al. *Don and Donna Go to Bat.* Beginner Bks. Returned to Shaftsbury, Vt. Elementary School library (1987). The complainant stated that children should not be exposed to "sexist attitudes in the story." Source: 7, Sept. 1987, p. 194.

938

Perry, Shawn, ed. *Words of Conscience: Religious Statements of Conscientious Objectors.* National Interreligious Service Board for Conscientious Objectors. Access restricted in Coleman, Wis. (1982) due to the book's alleged political overtones. Source: 7, July 1982, p. 126.

939

Perry, Troy. *The Lord Is My Shepherd and He Knows I'm Gay.* Dell. Challenged at the Niles, Mich. Community Library (1982) because of the book's "pornographic" nature. Source:

7, Jan. 1983, p. 8.

940

Petronius, Gaius. *Satyricon.* NAL; Penguin. Ordered destroyed by the police court of the City of Westminster in London (1934). Source: 3, p. 3.

941

Pfeiffer, Susan. *About David.* Dell; Delacorte. Challenged at the Bay County's four middle schools and three high schools in Panama City, Fla. (1986) because it contains "profanity and sexual explicit passages." Source: 7, Nov. 1986, p. 209.

942

Pierce, Ruth I. *Single and Pregnant.* Beacon Pr. Challenged and recommended for a "parents only" section at the Concord, Ark. school library (1984) because the author had "little to say that would discourage premarital sex." Source: 7, Jan. 1985, p. 7; May 1985, p. 75; Jan. 1986, pp. 7-8.

943

Pierce, Tamara. *Alanna: Song of the Lioness, Book One.* Knopf. Removed by a library staff member, but later returned to the shelves of the David Hill Elementary School in Hillsboro, Oreg. (1989) because of sexual references and the use of amulet to prevent pregnancy. Source: 7, Jan. 1990, pp. 4-5.

944

_____. *In the Hand of the Goddess: Song of the Lioness, Book Two.* Macmillan. Removed by a library staff member, but later returned to the shelves of the David Hill Elementary School in Hillsboro, Oreg. (1989) because of sexual references and use of amulet to prevent pregnancy. Source: 7, Jan. 1990, pp. 4-5.

945

_____. *The Woman Who Rides Like a Man: Song of the Lioness, Book Three.* Macmillan. Removed by a library staff member, but later returned to the shelves of the David Hill Elementary School in Hillsboro, Oreg. (1989) because of sexual references and the use of amulet to prevent pregnancy. Source: 7, Jan. 1990, pp. 4-5.

946

Pike, Christopher. *The Graduation: Final Friends Book 3.* Pocket Bks. Challenged at the Weatherly, Pa. Area Middle School library (1992) because parents were upset by passages in the book dealing with depression, suicide, and contraception. Source: 7, May 1992, p. 81; July 1992, p. 125.

947
Pinkwater, Daniel. *The Devil in the Drain*. Dutton. Challenged in the Galesville-Ettrick, Wis. School District (1987). Source: 7, Nov. 1987, p. 226.

948
Plante, David. *The Catholic*. Atheneum; Chatto & Windus. Banned in South Africa (1986). Source: 4, June 1986, p. 41.

949
Plath, Sylvia. *The Bell Jar*. Bantam; Harper. Prohibited for use in the Warsaw, Ind. schools (1979). Challenged in Edwardsville, Ill. (1981) when three hundred residents signed a petition against Plath's novel because it contains sexual material and advocates an "objectionable" philosophy of life. Source: 7, Mar. 1980, p. 40; July 1981, p. 102.

950
Platt, Kin. *Head Man*. Greenwillow; Dell. The Anaconda, Mo. School Board (1982) handed school principal Patrick Meloy a list of thirty-four restricted titles including Platt's book and gave him authority to censor or destroy any book he believes is "pornographic." Challenged at the Elkader, Iowa Central High School library (1983) because the book's description of the Los Angeles ghetto by a youth gang leader contains "street talk and four-letter words offensive to Elkader residents." Challenged at the Rankin County, Miss. School District (1984) because it is "profane and sexually objectionable." Source: 7, Mar. 1983, p. 41; July 1983, p. 121; May 1984, p. 70; Jan. 1985, p. 8.

951
Pomeroy, Wardell B. *Boys and Sex*. Delacorte. Challenged at the Santa Fe, N.Mex. High School library (1983) by a school librarian because of its "sordid, suggestive, permissive type of approach." Removed from two middle school libraries in the Greece, N.Y. (1988) because the book "promotes prostitution, promiscuity, homosexuality, and bestiality." Pulled from the Black River Falls, Wis. Middle School library (1990) because the book "dealt with bestiality, masturbation and homosexuality, and endorsed pre-adolescent and premarital sex." Pulled from the Rangely, Colo. Middle School library shelves (1994). Source: 7, May 1983, p. 85; July 1988, p. 121; Sept. 1988, p. 178; May 1991, p. 75; May 1994, p. 83.

952
_____. *Girls and Sex*. Delacorte. Challenged at the Santa Fe, N.Mex. High School library (1983) by a school librarian because of its "sordid, suggestive, permissive type of approach." Pulled from the Black River Falls, Wis. Middle School library (1990) because the book "dealt with bestiality, masturbation and homosexuality, and endorsed pre-adolescent and premarital sex." Pulled from the Rangely, Colo. Middle School library shelves (1994). Source: 7, May 1983, p. 85; May 1991, p. 75; May 1994, p. 83.

953
Ponce, Charles. *The Game of Wizards*. Penguin. Challenged by the "God Squad," a group of three students and their parents, at the El Camino High School in Oceanside, Calif. (1986) because the Chinese yin and yang symbol is drawn on page 95. The complainant wrote "This is the symbol of Confucianism and represents reincarnation. This book also deals with transcendental meditation." Source: 7, Sept. 1986, p. 151; Nov. 1986, p. 224; Jan. 1987, p. 9.

954
Portal, Colette. *The Beauty of Birth*. Knopf. Moved from the children's room of the Tampa-Hillsborough County, Fla. Public Library (1982) to the adult section. Source: 7, Jan. 1982, pp. 4-5.

955
Porter, Jean Stratton. *Her Father's Daughter*. Am Repr-Rivercity Pr. Removed from the Clatskanie, Oreg. Library District (1991) because of alleged bigotry against the Japanese. Source: 7, July 1992, p. 103.

956
Potok, Chaim. *My Name Is Asher Lev*. Knopf. Banned from the 1983 Moscow International Book Fair along with more than fifty other books because it is "anti-Soviet." Source: 7, Nov. 1983, p. 201.

957
Prelutsky, Jack. *The Headless Horseman Rides Tonight and Other Poems to Trouble Your Sleep*. Greenwillow. Challenged at the Victor Elementary School media center in Rochester, N.Y. (1982) because it "was too frightening for young children to read." Source: 7, July 1982, p. 142.

958
_____. *Nightmares: Poems to Trouble Your Sleep*. Greenwillow. Placed in the professional reading section of the Kirkland, Wash. district libraries (1979) where it would be unavailable to students without a teacher's permission. Challenged at the Paul E. Culley Elementary School in Las Vegas, Nev. (1987) because the poems were too frightening for small children. Placed in a "reserved" section at Little Butte Intermediate School in Eagle Point, Oreg. (1988) because the book could "disturb a child's sleep and offered no learning experience." Removed from the Berkeley County, S.C. schools (1993) that include fourth graders and younger chil-

dren due to violent passages. Removed from the Eau Claire, Wis. elementary school libraries (1993) because the poems "graphically describe violent acts against children that would be criminal activity if acted out." Source: 7, Sept. 1979, p. 104; Jan. 1988, p. 32; Jan. 1989, p. 3; Sept. 1993, pp. 148-49; Mar. 1994, p. 53.

959

_____. *Rolling Harvey Down the Hill.* Greenwillow. Challenged at the Consolidated School library in New Fairfield, Conn. (1989) because the book of children's verses is "repulsive" and against the country's "moral fiber." Source: 7, July 1989, p. 127.

960

Price, Richard. *Bloodbrothers.* Houghton. Banned from the Stroudsburg, Pa. High School library (1985) because it was "blatantly graphic, pornographic, and wholly unacceptable for a high school library." Source: 7, May 1985, p. 79.

961

_____. *Wanderers.* Houghton. Banned from the Vergennes, Vt. Union High School library (1978). Decision upheld in *Bicknell v. Vergennes Union High School Board*, 475 F. Supp. 615 (D. Vt. 1979), 638 F. 2d 438 (2d Cir. 1980). Source: 7, Jan. 1979, p. 6; 8, pp. 151, 239; 9, Vol IV, p. 715.

962

Price, Susan. *The Devil's Piper.* Faber; Greenwillow. Challenged at the Canby, Oreg. Junior High School library (1988) because it "could encourage young minds to pursue occult, suicide, or adopt ill attitudes." Source: 7, May 1989, p. 78.

963

Purdy, Candace, and Kendziorski, Stan. *Understanding Your Sexuality.* Scott, Foresman. Challenged at the York, Maine school system (1982). Challenged at the Chambersburg, Pa. Area Senior High School health class (1984) because "the Christian child must go to school and be subjected to the immoral teachings of this book." Source: 7, July 1982, p. 124; Jan. 1985, pp. 11-12.

964

Puzo, Mario. *The Godfather.* NAL; Putnam. Challenged at the Grinnell-Newburg, Iowa school system (1975) because the book is "vulgar and obscene by most religious standards." Source: 5 & 7, Mar. 1975, p. 41; May 1975, p. 87.

965

Pyle, Howard. *King Stork.* Little. Challenged at the public libraries of Saginaw, Mich. (1989) because it "would encourage boys beating girls when the drummer beats the enchantress with a switch until she becomes a 'good' princess." Unavailable to children unless they have written permission from their parents to check out the book or to read it in the library at the Sandstone Elementary School library in Billings, Mont. (1993). The objections to the near hundred-year-old book included a scene in which a husband beat his witchy wife into submission and illustrations from the 1973 edition of a princess in revealing clothing. Source: 7, May 1989, p. 77; July 1993, p. 99.

966

Pynchon, William. *The Meritorius Price of Our Redemption.* First publicly burned in the United States, where it was destroyed by the Massachusetts Colony authorities in 1650. Although Pynchon was one of the founders of the colony, and a signatory to its charter, his book proved so contentious in its criticism of the puritan orthodoxy that dominated the theological attitudes of the colony, that after it had been read by the General Council it was condemned to be burned by the common executioner in the Market Place. Pynchon himself was publicly censured and escaped further punishment only by sailing back to England. Source: 2, pp. 247-48.

967

Rabelais, Francois. *Gargantua & Pantagruel.* Penguin. Blacklisted by French Parliament (1533); censored by the Sorbonne (1552); banned by Henry II (1554), listed on the *Index Librorum Prohibitorum* in Rome (1564); U.S. Customs Department lifted ban (1930) and banned in South Africa (1938). Source: 3, p. 14.

968

Radlauer, Ruth and Radlauer, Ed. *Chopper Cycle.* Watts. Challenged at the Morrish Elementary School in Swartz Creek, Mich. (1982) because of its negative approach to law enforcement. Source: 7, Nov. 1982, p. 215.

969

Rampling, Anne. Belinda. *Arbor House.* Challenged at the Multnomah County Library in Portland, Oreg. (1988) because of its sexual nature. Source: 7, Jan. 1989, p. 3.

970

Randall, Dudley. *Black Poets.* Bantam. Banned for use in English classrooms at the Tinley Park, Ill. High School (1982) because the book "extols murder, rape, theft, incest, sodomy, and other acts." Source: 7, Mar. 1983, p. 40.

971

Randolph, Vance, comp. *Pissing in the Snow and Other*

Ozark Folktales. Univ. of Ill. Pr.; Avon. Challenged at the Rogers-Hough, Ark. Memorial Library (1988) because the book is "vulgar and obscene." Source: 7, July 1988, p. 119.

972
Raucher, Herman. *Summer of '42.* Dell. Challenged at the Grinnell-Newburg, Iowa school system as "vulgar and obscene by most religious standards." Removed from the reading list of an elective English course at Pulaski County, Ky. (1978) High School after a parent complained about "four-letter language" in the work. Source: 5 & 7, Mar. 1975, p. 41; May 1975, p. 87; Mar. 1979, p. 27.

973
Ray, Ron. *Gays in or out of the Military.* Brassey's. Pulled from the Ouachita Parish school library in Monroe, La. (1996) because of sexual content. The Louisiana chapter of the ACLU filed a lawsuit in the federal courts on October 3, 1996, claiming that the principal and the school superintendent violated First Amendment free speech rights and also failed to follow established procedure when they removed the book. Source: 7, Sept. 1996, pp. 151-52; Jan. 1997, p. 7.

974
Reed, Rick. *Obsessed.* Dell. Permanently removed from the East Coweta County, Ga. High School library (1996) because of several sexually and violently graphic passages. Source: 7, Jan. 1997, p. 7; Mar. 1997, p. 35.

975
Reiss, Johanna. *The Upstairs Room.* Bantam; Harper. Removed from the required reading list for fourth graders at Liberty, Ind. Elementary School (1993). The Newbery Honor Book about a girl in Holland hiding from the Nazis during World War II was investigated because of profanity. Challenged as assigned reading for sixth grade students in Sanford, Maine (1996) because of profanity. Source: 7, July 1993, p. 105; July 1996, p. 118.

976
Remarque, Erich Maria. *All Quiet on the Western Front.* Fawcett; Little. Banned in Boston, Mass. (1929) on grounds of obscenity; seized by U. S. Customs in Chicago, Ill. (1929); Austrian soldiers forbidden to read it (1929); barred from Czech military libraries by the war department (1929); banned in Thuringia, Germany (1930); banned in Italy because of the book's anti-war propaganda (1933); and consigned to the Nazi bonfires (1933). Source: 1, pp. 137, 139; 3, p. 80; 9, Vol. III, pp. 417-18.

977
_____. *The Road Back.* Avon; Grosset; Little; Putnam.

Banned in Ireland (1931). Source: 3, p. 81.

978
Rench, Janice E. *Understanding Your Sexual Identity: A Book for Gay Teens & Their Friends.* Lerner Pubns. Pulled from the Rangely, Colo. Middle School library shelves (1994). Moved from the Chestnut Ridge Middle School library to the guidance center in Washington Township, N.J. (1994) because school administrators have been accused of "indoctrinating children in the gay lifestyle." Source: 7, May 1994, p. 83; Sept. 1994, p. 148.

979
Reuben, David. *Everything You Always Wanted to Know about Sex, but Were Afraid to Ask.* Bantam. Challenged at the William Chrisman High School in Independence, Mo. (1984) because the book is "filthy." The Reuben's work was on a bookshelf in the classroom and was the personal property of the teacher. Source: 7, July 1984, p. 106.

980
Revesz, Therese Ruth. *Witches.* Contemporary Perspective. Pulled, but later placed on reserve to children with parental permission at the Forrest Elementary School library in Hampton, Va. (1992). Source: 7, July 1992, p. 108; Sept. 1992, p. 139.

981
Rhyne, Nancy. *Murder in the Carolinas.* Blair. Removed from the Berkeley County, S.C. elementary and middle school libraries (1992) because the book—real-life stories of South Carolina murders based on newspaper accounts—contained descriptions of actual murders that were too graphic for young readers. Source: 7, July 1992, pp. 107-8.

982
Richards, Arlene K., and Willis, Irene. *What to Do If You or Someone You Know Is under 18 and Pregnant.* Lothrop. Challenged at the Racine, Wis. Unified School District libraries (1991) because the book uses street language to describe sexual intercourse and contraceptives, contains "sexually suggestive and provocative" language, and "promotes teenage sexual promiscuity." Source: 7, Jan. 1992, p. 27.

983
Richardson, Samuel. *Pamela.* Houghton; Penguin; Norton. Placed on the *Index Librorum Prohibitorum* in Rome (1740). Source: 2, p. 135

984
Riker, Andrew, et al. *Married Life.* Bennett. Challenged in Collinsville, Ill. (1981), in Jefferson County, Ky. (1982)

because it "pushes women's lib which is very degrading to women and will destroy the traditional family." Source: 7, May 1981, p. 68; Mar. 1983, p. 41.

985
Riker, Andrew. *Finding My Way.* Bennett. Challenged in Tell City, Ind. (1982). Challenged in Walker County, Ga. (1982) by the Eagle Forum because its "treatment of sexual matters was too explicit and its method of presentation faulty." Challenged at the Laramie, Wy. Junior High School (1987) because the book "doesn't stress saying 'No.'" Challenged at the Grove, Okla. High School (1991) because it was "too graphic for presentation in the classroom." Source: 7, May 1982, p. 85; July 1982, p. 142; Sept. 1987, p. 177; Sept. 1991, p. 179.

986
Riker, Audrey Palm, and Brisbane, Holly. *Married and Single Life.* Bennett. Returned to the Racine, Wis. Unified School District (1984) curriculum just one week after the school board voted to ban it. The home economics text was criticized for encouraging premarital sex and advocating that unmarried couples live together. Source: 7, Sept. 1984, p. 158; Jan. 1985, p. 10.

987
Ringgold, Faith. *Tar Beach.* Crown. Challenged in the Spokane, Wash. elementary school libraries (1994) because it stereotypes African Americans as eating fried chicken and watermelon and drinking beer at family picnics. The book is based on memories of its author's family rooftop picnics in 1930s Harlem. The book won the 1992 Coretta Scott King Illustrator Award for its portrayal of minorities. Source: 7, Jan. 1995, p. 9; Mar. 1995, p. 54.

988
Robbins, Harold. *The Carpetbaggers.* Trident; Pocket Bks. Sales restricted in Warwick, R.I.; Rochester, N.Y.; Mesquite, Tex.; Waterbury, Conn.; and Bridgeport, Conn. (1961). In Oct. 1982, Malaysian police confiscated the works of Robbins because they were considered "prejudicial to the public interest." Source: 3, p. 88; 4, Jan. 1983, p. 45.

989
_____. *The Lonely Lady.* Pocket Bks.; Simon & Schuster. Challenged in Abingdon, Va. (1980) because of the book's "pornographic" nature. Source: 7, Jan. 1981, p. 5.

990
Robbins, Russell H. *Encyclopedia of Witchcraft and Demonology.* Outlet Bk. Co. Removed from the Detroit, Mich. public school libraries (1994) after a complaint that

the book was "obscene, perverse, and immoral." Source: 7, Mar. 1994, p. 51.

991
Roberts, J. R. *Ambush Moon: Gunsmith Series 148.* Berkley Pub.; Jove. Challenged, but retained in the Fairfield County District Library in Lancaster, Ohio (1995) because it includes profanity and explicit sex scenes. Source: 7, Nov. 1995, p. 184; Jan. 1996, p. 29.

992
_____. *The Gunsmith: Hands of the Strangler.* Jove. Challenged but retained at the Selby, S.Dak. Library (1994) because of an inappropriate sex scene. Source: 7, July 1994, p. 129.

993
Roberts, Willo Davis. *The View from the Cherry Tree.* Macmillan. Retained in Elko County, Nev. classrooms (1995) despite the complaint of the elementary school student. School officials said the parents complained that the book contains language inappropriate for sixth-graders, including a cat named S.O.B. Source: 7, Sept. 1995, p. 160.

994
Robinson, David. *Herbert Armstrong's Tangled Web.* Interstate. A suit was filed in Tulsa, Okla. (1981) alleging that the book was based on privileged communications, whose secrecy is protected by law. A restraining order temporarily stopped the release of this book. Source: 7, Jan. 1982, p. 23.

995
Rock, Gail. *The House without a Christmas Tree.* Bantam. Challenged in the Des Moines, Iowa schools (1983) due to the use of the word "damn." Source: 7, May 1983, p. 73.

996
Rockwell, Thomas. *How to Eat Fried Worms.* ABC-Clio; Dell; Watts. Retained in the Middletown, N.J. elementary school libraries (1988) despite a parent's objection that the book contains violence and vulgar language. Removed from the LaVille Elementary School library in LaPaz, Ind. (1991) by a library user because the book contains the word "bastard." Source: 7, May 1988, p. 103; Sept. 1991, p. 153.

997
Rodriguez, Abraham, Jr. *The Boy without a Flag: Tales of the South Bronx.* Milkweed Ed. Retained in the Rosemount, Minn. High School (1994) after a complaint about "profane language and promiscuity in the stories." Source: 7, July 1994, p. 130.

998

Rodriguez, Luis J. *Always Running.* Curbstone Pr. Challenged as an optional reading at the Guilford High School in Rockford, Ill. (1996) because it is "blatant pornography." Source: 7, July 1996, p. 118.

999

Rojas, Don. *One People, One Destiny: The Caribbean and Central America Today.* Pathfinder Pr. Confiscated by custom officials in Grenada along with *Maurice Bishop Speaks; Thomas Sankara Speaks: The Burkina Faso Revolution, 1983-87,* and other books by Nelson Mandela, Karl Marx, Che Guevara, Fidel Castro, and Malcom X. The books were labeled as "subversive to the peace and security of the country." Source: 7, Mar. 1989, p. 49.

1000

Roman, Jo. *Exit House.* Bantam. Challenged at the Springdale, Ark. Public Library (1994) because it presented suicide as "a rational and sane alternative." Source: 7, July 1994, p. 128.

1001

Ronan, Margaret, and Ronan, Eve. *Astrology and Other Occult Games.* Scholastic. Challenged in the Akron, Ohio school system (1982) because the book promotes Satan. Source: 7, Mar. 1983, p. 38.

1002

Roquelaire, A. E. [Anne Rice]. *Beauty's Punishment.* NAL. Removed from the shelves of the Lake Lanier Regional Library system in Gwinnett County, Ga. (1992) following complaints that centered around sexuality. Removed from the Columbus, Ohio Metropolitan Library (1996) as hardcore pornography. Source: 7, Jan. 1993, p. 7; July 1996, pp. 119-20.

1003

_____. *Beauty's Release.* NAL. Removed from the shelves of the Lake Lanier Regional Library system in Gwinnett County, Ga. (1992) following complaints that centered around sexuality. Removed from the Columbus, Ohio Metropolitan Library (1996) as hard-core pornography. Source: 7, Jan. 1993, p. 7; July 1996, pp. 119-20.

1004

_____. *The Claiming of Sleeping Beauty.* NAL. Removed from the shelves of the Lake Lanier Regional Library system in Gwinnett County, Ga. (1992) following complaints that centered around sexuality. Removed from the Columbus, Ohio Metropolitan Library (1996) as hard-core pornography. Source: 7, Jan. 1993, p. 7; July 1996, pp. 119-20.

1005

Roth, Philip. *Goodbye, Columbus.* Bantam; Houghton. Challenged in Abingdon, Va. (1980) because of the book's "pornographic" nature. Source: 7, Jan. 1981, p. 5.

1006

_____. *Portnoy's Complaint.* Bantam; Random. Many libraries were attacked for carrying this novel, and some librarians' jobs were threatened. Source: 3, p. 99.

1007

Rounds, Glen. *Wash Day on Noah's Ark.* Holiday. Challenged at the Hubbard, Ohio Public Library (1991) because the book alters the story of Noah's Ark making it secular and confusing children. Source: 7, Sept. 1991, p. 153.

1008

Rousseau, Jean Jacques. *Confessions.* Penguin. Banned by the U.S. Customs Department for being injurious to public morals (1929); banned in the USSR (1935). Source: 3, p. 30.

1009

Royko, Mike. *Boss: Richard J. Daley of Chicago.* NAL. Barred from the Ridgefield, Conn. High School reading list (1972) because it "downgrades police departments." Challenged in the Hannibal, N.Y. High School (1983) because the book is "detrimental to students and contributed to social decay because it contains rough language." Source: 3, p. 99; 4; 7, May 1983, p. 74; July 1983, p. 123.

1010

Ruddell, Robert B., et al. *Person to Person.* Bennett. Challenged in the Jefferson County, Ky. School District (1982) because the book "confuses sex roles." The Evergreen School Board in Vancouver, Wash. (1985) banned the textbook because some members said it is too favorable to alternative lifestyles. The controversy centered on a chapter titled "Changing Life Styles," in which the book describes relationships other than the traditional family. Source: 7, Mar. 1983, p. 41; May 1985, p. 79; July 1985, p. 115.

1011

Rushdie, Salman. *The Satanic Verses.* Viking. Banned in Pakistan, Saudi Arabia, Egypt, Somalia, Sudan, Malaysia, Qatar, Indonesia, South Africa, and India because of its criticism of Islam. Burned in West Yorkshire, England (1989) and temporarily withdrawn from two bookstores on the advice of police who took threats to staff and property seriously. In Pakistan five people died in riots against the book. Another man died a day later in Kashmir. Ayatollah Khomeini issued a fatwa or religious edict, stating "I inform the proud Muslim people of the world that the author of the *Satanic Verses,* which is against Islam, the prophet, and the Koran, and all those involved in its publication who were aware of its content, have been sentenced to death." Challenged at the Wichita, Kans. Public Library (1989) because the book is "blasphemous to the prophet Mohammed." Source: 2, pp. 269-70; 7, Mar. 1989, p. 47; July 1989, p. 125; Sept. 1989, p. 185.

1012
Russell, Bertrand. *What I Believe.* Dutton. Banned in Boston, Mass. (1929). Source: 3, p. 62.

"The sound of tireless voices is the price we pay for the right to hear the music of our own opinions."

~ Adlai Stevenson

1013
Russo, Vito. *The Celluloid Closet: Homosexuality in the Movies.* Harper. Challenged at the Deschutes County Library in Bend, Oreg. (1993) because it "encourages and condones" homosexuality. Source: 7, Sept. 1993, pp. 158-59.

1014
Sachar, Louis. *The Boy Who Lost His Face.* Knopf. Challenged at the Thousand Oaks, Calif. Library (1991) because of inappropriate language. Removed from the Cuyler Elementary School library in Red Creek, N.Y. (1993) because "the age level and use of some swear words may make it inappropriate to younger children." Challenged at the Golden View Elementary school in San Ramon, Calif. (1993) because of its profanity, frequent use of obscene gestures, and other inappropriate subject matter. Removed from the Jackson Township Elementary School in Clay City, Ind. (1993) due to "unsuitable words." Source: 7, Mar. 1992, p. 39; May 1993, p. 71; July 1993, p. 97; Sept. 1993, p. 157; Mar. 1994, p. 51.

1015
_____. *Sideways Stories from Wayside Schools.* Avon; McKay. Challenged at the Neely Elementary School in Gilbert, Ariz. (1992) because the book shows the dark side of religion through the occult, the devil, and satanism. Source: 7, May 1992, p. 78; July 1992, p. 124.

1016
_____. *Wayside School is Falling Down.* Avon. Removed

from the list of suggested readings from the Antigo, Wis. elementary reading program (1995) because the book included passages condoning destruction of school property, disgraceful manners, disrespectful representation of professionals, improper English, and promotion of peer pressure. Source: 7, July 1995, p. 100.

1017
Sade, Marquis de. *Juliette.* Grove. Author imprisoned much of his life in France; still on the *Index Librorum Prohibitorum* in Rome (1948); seized by British Customs (1962). In Sept. 1982, Greek police confiscated thousands of books by Marquis de Sade. The publisher, Themis Banousis, was sentenced to two years' imprisonment for violating the laws on indecent literature by translating and publishing the works of de Sade. Forty-seven other publishers were reported arrested in mid-Sept. 1982 for denying the ban. In Oct. 1982 Malaysian police confiscated the works of de Sade because they were considered "prejudicial to the public interest." Source: 3, p. 34; 4, Jan. 1983, pp. 44-45.

1018
_____. *Justine or the Misfortunes of Virtue.* Grove. Author imprisoned much of his life in France; still on the *Index Librorum Prohibitorum* in Rome (1948); seized by British Customs (1962). Source: 3, p. 34.

1019
Salinger, J. D. *Catcher in the Rye.* Bantam; Little. Since its publication, this title has been a favorite target of censors. Recent examples include its removal from the Issaquah, Wash. Optional High School reading list (1978). Removed from the required reading list in Middleville, Mich. (1979). Removed from the Jackson-Milton school libraries in North Jackson, Ohio (1980). Removed from two Anniston, Ala. high school libraries (1982), but later reinstated on a restrictive basis. Removed from the school libraries in Morris, Manitoba (1982) along with two other books because they violated the committee's guidelines covering "excess vulgar language, sexual scenes, things concerning moral issues, excessive violence, and anything dealing with the occult." Challenged at the Libby, Mont. High School (1983) due to the "book's contents." Banned from English classes at the Freeport High School in De Funiak Springs, Fla. (1985) because it is "unacceptable" and "obscene." Removed from the required reading list of a Medicine Bow, Wyo. Senior High School English class (1986) because of

sexual references and profanity in the book. Banned from a required sophomore English reading list at the Napoleon, N.Dak. High School (1987) after parents and the local Knights of Columbus chapter complained about its profanity and sexual references. Challenged at the Linton-Stockton, Ind. High School (1988) because the book is "blasphemous and undermines morality." Banned from the classrooms in Boron, Calif. High School (1989) because the book contains profanity. Challenged at the Grayslake, Ill. Community High School (1991). Challenged at the Jamaica High School in Sidell, Ill. (1992) because the book contained profanities and depicted premarital sex, alcohol abuse, and prostitution. Challenged in the Waterloo, Iowa schools (1992) and Duval County, Fla. public school libraries (1992) because of profanity, lurid passages about sex, and statements defamatory to minorities, God, women, and the disabled. Challenged at the Cumerland Valley High School in Carlisle, Pa. (1992) because of a parent's objections that it contains profanity and is immoral. Challenged, but retained at the New Richmond, Wis. High School (1994) for use in some English classes. Challenged as required reading in the Corona-Norco, Calif. Unified School District (1993) because it is "centered around negative activity." The book was retained and teachers selected alternatives if students object to Salinger's novel. Challenged as mandatory reading in the Goffstown, N.H. schools (1994) because of the vulgar words used and the sexual exploits experienced in the book. Challenged at the St. Johns County Schools in St. Augustine, Fla. (1995). Challenged at the Oxford Hills High School in Paris, Maine (1996). A parent objected to the use of "the 'F' word." Source: 5 & 7, Nov. 1978, p. 138; Jan. 1980, pp. 6-7; May 1980, p. 51; Mar. 1983, pp. 37-38; July 1983, p. 122; July 1985, p. 113; Mar. 1987, p. 55; July 1988, p. 123; Jan. 1988, p. 10; Sept. 1988, p. 177; Nov. 1989, pp. 218-19; July 1991, pp. 129-30; May 1992, p. 83; July 1992, pp. 105, 126; Jan. 1993, p. 29; Jan. 1994, p. 14, Mar. 1994, pp. 56, 70; May 1994, p. 100; Jan. 1995, p. 12; Jan. 1996, p. 14; Nov. 1996, p. 212.

1020

_____. *Nine Stories*. Bantam; Little. Removed from the reading list of a writing class at Franklin, Va. High School (1987) after a parent of one student was offended by some of the language in a story. Source: 7, July 1987, p. 131.

1021

Salinger, Margaretta M. *Great Paintings of Children*. Abrams. Retained at Maldonado Elementary School in Tucson, Ariz. (1994) after being challenged by parents who objected to nudity and "pornographic," "perverted," and "morbid" themes. Source: 7, July 1994, p. 112.

1022

Salomon, George, and Feitelson, Rose. *The Many Faces of Anti-Semitism*. Am. Jewish Comm. Banned from the 1983 Moscow International Book Fair along with more than fifty other books because it is "anti-Soviet." Source: 7, Nov. 1983, p. 201.

1023

Sams, Ferrol. *Run with the Horsemen*. Viking; Penguin. Challenged in the Rockingham County, Va. schools (1995) because of sexual content. Source: 7, Nov. 1995, p. 188; Jan. 1996, p. 18.

1024

Samuels, Gertrude. *Run, Shelley, Run*. Harper; Crowell; NAL. Removed and destroyed from the Hot Springs, Ark. Central Junior High School library (1977) because of objectionable language; challenged at the Ogden, Utah School District (1979) and placed in a restricted circulation category; removed from the Onida and Blunt, S.Dak. High Schools (1981) due to "objectionable" language; removed from the Troutman, N.C. Middle School library (1982). Challenged at Alexander Central High School and East Junior High School libraries in Taylorsville, N.C. (1987) because of "foul language." Removed from the Palmyra, Pa. middle school classroom (1995) because of its language and the portrayal of incidents involving nudity, lesbianism and prostitution. Source: 5 & 7, Mar. 1977, p. 36; May 1979, p. 49; May 1981, pp. 65-66; Mar. 1982, p. 45; May 1987, p. 87; July 1987, p. 149; July 1995, pp. 98-99; Jan. 1996, p. 17.

1025

Sanders, Lawrence. *The Seduction of Peter S*. Putnam. Banned from the Stroudsburg, Pa. High School library (1985) because it was "blatantly graphic, pornographic, and wholly unacceptable for a high school library." Source: 7, May 1985, p. 78.

1026

Sanford, John. *Winter Prey*. Putnam. Expurgated by an apparent self-appointed censor at the Coquille, Oreg. Public Library (1994) along with several other books. Most were mysteries and romances in which single words and sexually explicit passages were whited out by a vandal who left either dots or solid ink pen lines where the words had been. Source: 7, Sept. 1994, p. 148.

1027

Sarton, May. *The Education of Harriet Hatfield*. Norton. Removed from the Mascenic Regional High School in New Ipswich, N.H. (1995) because it is about gays and lesbians.

An English teacher was fired for refusing to remove the book. Source: 7, Sept. 1995, p. 166; Jan. 1996, p. 15.

1028
Sartre, Jean-Paul. *Age of Reason.* Random. On Feb. 21, 1973 eleven Turkish book publishers went on trial before an Istanbul martial law tribunal on charges of publishing, possessing, and selling books in violation of an order of the Istanbul martial law command. They faced possible sentences of between one month's and six months' imprisonment "for spreading propaganda unfavorable to the state" and the confiscation of their books. Eight booksellers were also on trial with the publishers on the same charge involving the *Age of Reason.* Source: 4, Summer 1973, xii.

1029
_____. *Saint Genet.* French & European. Seized (1984) by the British Customs Office as "indecent and obscene." Source: 7, Jan. 1985, p. 26.

1030
Saunders, Richard, and Macne, Brian. *Horrorgami.* Sterling. Removed from the Glendale school libraries in Grants Pass, Oreg. (1993) for its alleged "satanic" content. The book is a craft book on origami, but incorporates stories about werewolves and vampires, and is allegedly illustrated with satanic symbols. Source: 7, July 1993, p. 101.

1031
Savonarola, Girolamo. *Writings.* After a ceremony of degradation, the author was hung on a cross and burned with all his writings, sermons, essays, and pamphlets (1498). Source: 3, p. 8.

1032
Schnitzler, Arthur. *Casanova's Homecoming.* AMS Pr. Simon & Schuster was brought to court for publishing this work (1930); banned by Mussolini (1939). Source: 3, p. 57; 9, Vol. III, p. 636.

1033
_____. *Reigen.* AMS Pr. A bookseller was convicted by the Court of Special Sessions for selling a copy of Reigen (1929). Source: 3, p. 57; 9, Vol. III, p. 420.

1034
Schusky, Ernest L. *Introduction to Social Science.* Prentice-Hall. Challenged in the South Umpqua, Oreg. School District (1985) because the book presents a variety of concepts that are "controversial and inappropriate for seventh graders. The book's sections on death education, extrasensory perception, genetic planning, group therapy, and religious values

had little to do with the teaching of basic social studies." Source: 7, Mar. 1986, p. 42.

1035
Schwartz, Alvin. *Cross Your Fingers, Spit in Your Eye.* Harper. Challenged at the Neely Elementary School in Gilbert, Ariz. (1992) because the book shows the dark side of religion through the occult, the devil, and satanism. Source: 7, May 1992, p. 78; July 1992, p. 124.

1036
_____. *In a Dark, Dark Room and Other Scary Stories.* Harper. Challenged at the Jefferson County school libraries in Lakewood, Colo. (1986) because the book is "too morbid for children." The Jefferson County School Board refused to ban the book. Source: 7, Sept. 1986, p. 173; Nov. 1986, p. 224.

1037
_____. *More Scary Stories to Tell in the Dark.* Harper; Lippincott. Challenged at the Dry Hollow Elementary School in The Dalles, Oreg. (1988) because it is too scary and violent. Challenged at the Neely Elementary School in Gilbert, Ariz. (1992) because the book shows the dark side of religion through the occult, the devil, and satanism. Challenged at the Lake Washington School District in Kirkland, Wash. (1992) as unacceptably violent for children. Restricted access at the Marana, Ariz. Unified School District (1993) because of complaints about violence and cannibalism. Removed from Vancouver, Wash. School District elementary school libraries (1994) after surviving two previous attempts (1991, 1993). Also challenged at neighboring Evergreen School District libraries in Vancouver, Wash. (1994) because "This book... is far beyond other scary books." Challenged, but retained at the Whittier Elementary School library in Bozeman, Mont. (1994). The book was challenged because it would cause children to fear the dark, have nightmares, and give them an unrealistic view of death. Challenged in the Tracy, Calif. school libraries (1995) because of the book's violent content and graphic nature. Challenged as "objectionable" and "disgusting", but retained on Harper Woods, Mich. school district reading lists (1995). Source: 7, Jan. 1989, p. 3; May 1992, pp. 78, 94-95; July 1992, p. 124; Sept. 1993, p. 143; July 1994, p. 111; Sept. 1994, pp. 148-49, 166; May 1995, p. 65; July 1995, p. 111.

1038
_____. *More Tales to Chill Your Bones.* Harper. Challenged at the Lake Washington School District in Kirkland, Wash. (1992) as unacceptably violent for children. Challenged at the West Hartford, Conn. elementary and middle school libraries (1992) because of violence and the subject matter. Removed from Vancouver, Wash. School District elementary

school libraries (1994) after surviving two previous attempts (1991, 1993). Challenged at neighboring Evergreen School District libraries in Vancouver, Wash. (1994) because "This book... is far beyond other scary books." Source: 7, May 1992, p. 94-95; Sept. 1992, p. 137; July 1994, p. 111; Sept. 1994, pp. 148-49.

1039

_____. *Scary Stories*. Harper. Challenged at the South-Western, Ohio elementary school libraries (1993) because children shouldn't be "scared by materials that they read in schools." Restricted to students in fourth grade or higher in the Enfield, Conn. elementary schools (1995). The school board was petitioned to remove all "horror" stories from the elementary schools. Source: 7, May 1993, pp. 85-86; May 1995, p. 69.

1040

_____. *Scary Stories to Tell in the Dark*. Harper. Challenged in the Livonia, Mich. schools (1990) because the poems frightened first grade children. Challenged at the Neely Elementary School in Gilbert, Ariz. (1992) because the book shows the dark side of religion through the occult, the devil and satanism. Challenged at the Lake Washington School District in Kirkland, Wash. (1992) as unacceptably violent for children. Challenged at the West Hartford, Conn. elementary and middle school libraries (1992) because of violence and the subject matter. Challenged at the elementary school library in Union County, Ind. (1992). Restricted access at the Marana, Ariz. Unified School District (1993) because of complaints about violence and cannibalism. Challenged by a parent of a student at Happy Valley Elementary School in Glasgow, Ky. (1993) who thought it was too scary. Removed from Vancouver, Wash. School District elementary school libraries (1994) after surviving two previous attempts (1991, 1993). Also challenged at neighboring Evergreen School District libraries in Vancouver, Wash. (1994) because "This book... is far beyond other scary books." Source: 7, Mar. 1991, p. 62; May 1992, pp. 78, 94-95; July 1992, p. 124; Sept. 1992, p. 137; Jan. 1993, p. 27; Sept. 1993, pp. 143, 158; July 1994, p. 111; Sept. 1994, pp. 148-49.

1041

Schwartz, Joel L.; Macfarlane, Aidan; and McPherson, Ann. *Will the Nurse Make Me Take My Underwear Off?* Laurel-Leaf Bks. Challenged at the Chestatee Regional Library in Gainesville, Ga. (1994). Source: 7, Nov. 1994, p. 187.

1042

_____. *Upchuck Summer*. Dell; Delacorte. Removed from the Winslow, N.J. Elementary School No. 4 (1988) because of "age inappropriateness." The specific problem was the explicitness of scenes in the protagonist recounts a fantasy about two "older kids" kissing while nude. Source: 7, Jan. 1989, p. 8.

1043

Scoppettone, Sandra. *Happy Endings Are All Alike*. Harper. Removed from the Evergreen School District of Vancouver, Wash. (1983) along with twenty-nine other titles. The American Civil Liberties Union of Washington filed suit contending that the removals constitute censorship, a violation of plaintiff's rights to free speech and due process, and the acts are a violation of the state Open Meetings Act because the removal decisions were made behind closed doors. Source: 7, Nov. 1983, pp. 185-86.

1044

Seeley, Robert A. *A Handbook for Conscientious Objectors*. Central Committee for Conscientious Objectors. Access restricted in Coleman, Wis. (1982) due to the book's alleged political overtones. Source: 7, July 1982, p. 126.

1045

Segel, Elizabeth. *Short Takes*. Dell; Lothrop. Challenged at the Cecil County Board of Education in Elkton, Md. (1994). Many deemed the text controversial because it included essays dealing with issues of abortion, gay rights, alcohol, and sex education. Source: 7, Mar. 1995, p. 55.

1046

Selby, Hubert, Jr. *Last Exit to Brooklyn*. Grove. A circuit court in Conn. (1966) issued a temporary injunction against the book, "as obscene and pornographic"; judged obscene by jury in England (1967). Source: 3, p. 98.

1047

Sendak, Maurice. *In the Night Kitchen*. Harper. Removed from the Norridge, Ill. school library (1977) due to "nudity for no purpose." Expurgated in Springfield, Mo. (1977) by drawing shorts on the nude boy. Challenged at the Cunningham Elementary School in Beloit, Wis. (1985) because the book desensitizes "children to nudity." Challenged at the Robeson Elementary School in Champaign, Ill. (1988) because of "gratuitous" nudity. Challenged at the Camden, N.J. elementary school libraries (1989) because of nudity. Challenged at the Elk River, Minn. schools (1992) because reading the book "could lay the foundation for future use of pornography." Challenged at the El Paso, Tex. Public Library (1994) because "the little boy pictured did not have any clothes on and it pictured his private area." Source: 5 & 7, May 1977, p. 71; Sept. 1977, p. 134; July 1985, p. 134; Mar. 1989, p. 43; Nov. 1989, p. 217; Mar. 1993, p. 41; Sept. 1994, p. 148.

1048

_____. *Some Swell Pup.* Farrar; Random. Challenged at the Multnomah County Library in Portland, Oreg. (1988) because in it a dog urinates on people, and children abuse animals. Source: 7, Jan. 1989, p. 3.

1049

Seth, Roland. *Witches and Their Craft.* Taplinger. Challenged at the Plymouth-Canton school system in Canton, Mich. (1987) because the book contains information about witches and the devil. Source: 7, May 1987, p. 110; Jan. 1988, p. 11.

1050

Seuss, Dr. *The Lorax.* Random. Challenged in the Laytonville, Calif. Unified School District (1989) because the book "criminalizes the foresting industry." Source: 7, Nov. 1989, p. 237; Jan. 1990, pp. 32-33.

1051

Shakespeare, William. *Hamlet.* Airmont; Cambridge Univ. Pr.; NAL; Norton; Penguin; Methuen. Banned in Ethiopia (1978). Source: 4, Sept./Oct. 1978, p. 66.

1052

_____. *King Lear.* Airmont; Methuen; NAL; Penguin; Pocket Bks. Prohibited on the English stage until 1820. Source: 3, p. 18.

1053

_____. *The Merchant of Venice.* Airmont; Cambridge Univ. Pr.; Methuen; NAL; Penguin; Pocket Bks.; Washington Square. Eliminated from the high school curricula of Buffalo and Manchester, N.Y. (1931). A group of Jewish parents in Brooklyn, N.Y. (1949) went to court claiming that the assignment of Shakespeare's play to senior high school literature classes violated the rights of their children to receive an education free of religious bias in *Rosenberg v. Board of Education of the City of New York,* 196 Misc. 542, 92 N.Y. Supp. 2d 344. Banned from classrooms in Midland, Mich. (1980). Banned from the ninth grade classrooms in Kitchener-Waterloo, Ont. until the Ontario Education Ministry or Human Rights Commission (1986) rules whether the play is anti-Semitic. Source: 3, p. 19; 4; 7, July 1980, p. 76; Sept. 1986, p. 154; 8, pp. 23, 230.

1054

_____. *Tragedy of King Richard II.* Airmont; Methuen; NAL; Penguin; Pocket Bks.; Washington Square. Contains a scene in which the King was deposed, and it so infuriated Queen Elizabeth that she ordered it eliminated from all copies (1597). Source: 3, p. 18.

1055

_____. *Twelfth Night.* Airmont; Cambridge Univ. Pr.; Methuen; NAL; Penguin; Pocket Bks.; Washington Square. Removed from a Merrimack, N.H. high school English class (1996) because of a policy that bans any instruction which has "the effect of encouraging or supporting homosexuality as a positive lifestyle alternative." Source: 7, May 1996, p. 96.

1056

Shannon, George. *Unlived Affections.* Harper. Removed from the library at the Lundahl Junior High School in Crystal Lake, Ill. (1993) because the book is unfit for sixth grade. Source: 7, July 1993, p. 98.

1057

Sharpio, Amy. *Sun Signs: The Stars in Your Life.* Contemporary Perspective. Pulled, but later placed on reserve to children with parental permission at the Forrest Elementary School library in Hampton, Va. (1992). Source: 7, July 1992, p. 108; Sept. 1992, p. 139.

1058

Shaw, George Bernard. *Man and Superman.* Airmont; Penguin. The New York Public Library withdrew it from public shelves (1905) because books "calculated to make light of dishonesty and criminality were worse than books merely indecent in statement"; banned from all public libraries in Yugoslavia (1929). Source: 1, p. 87; 3, p. 55; 9, Vol. II, p. 625.

1059

_____. *Mrs. Warren's Profession.* Garland. Suppressed in London (1905); banned from all public libraries in Yugoslavia (1929). Source: 3, p. 55.

1060

_____. *Beggarman Thief.* Dell. Banned from the Stroudsburg, Pa. High School library (1985) because it was "blatantly graphic, pornographic, and wholly unacceptable for a high school library." Source: 7, May 1985, p. 79.

1061

_____. *Nightwork.* Dell. Banned from the Stroudsburg, Pa. High School library (1985) because it was "blatantly graphic, pornographic and wholly unacceptable for a high school library." Source: 7, May 1985, p. 79.

1062

Sheehan, Kathryn, and Waidner, Mary. *Earth Child.* Coun. Oak Bks. Challenged at the Tulsa County, Okla. schools (1992) because the book promotes the Hindu religion and other religious rituals. Opponents also claimed the book is a manual for altering children's minds through psychological games and hypnotic techniques. Source: 7, Nov. 1992, p. 187.

1063

Sheffield, Margaret, and Bewley, Sheila. *Where Do Babies Come From?* Knopf; Stuart. Moved from the children's section to the adult section of the Tampa-Hillsborough, Fla. County Public Library (1981) by order of the Tampa City Council. Placed on restricted shelves at the Evergreen School District elementary school libraries in Vancouver, Wash. (1987) in accordance with the school board policy to restrict student access to sex education books in elementary school libraries. Source: 7, Jan. 1982, p. 4; July 1986, p. 118; Sept. 1986, p. 172; May 1987, p. 87.

1064

Sheldon, Sidney. *Bloodline.* Morrow; Warner. Challenged in Abingdon, Va. (1980) and Elizabethton, Tenn. (1981). Source: 2 & 7, Jan. 1981, p. 5; May 1981, p. 66.

1065

Shengold, Nina; Smith; and Kraus, eds. *The Actor's Book of Contemporary Stage Monologues.* Penguin. Challenged at the Salem Junior High School in Virginia Beach, Va. (1988) because it contains racial slurs, profanity, and lewd descriptions. Source: 7, Mar. 1989, p. 43.

1066

Showers, Paul. *A Baby Starts to Grow.* Crowell. Placed on restricted shelves at the Evergreen School District elementary school libraries in Vancouver, Wash. (1987) in accordance with the school board policy to restrict student access to sex education books in elementary school libraries. Source: 7, May 1987, p. 87.

1067

Showers, Paul, and Showers, Kay Sperry. *Before You Were a Baby.* Crowell. Placed on restricted shelves at the Evergreen School District elementary school libraries in Vancouver, Wash. (1987) in accordance with the school board policy to restrict student access to sex education books in elementary school libraries. Source: 7, May 1987, p. 87.

1068

Shreve, Susan. *Masquerade.* Knopf. Removed from the Grants Pass, Oreg. middle school libraries (1982) because of the profanity, violence, and sexual innuendos in the book. Source: 7, Mar. 1983, p. 39.

1069

Shulman, Irving. *The Amboy Dukes.* Bantam; Doubleday. Book under fire by local authorities in Milwaukee, Wis.; Detroit, Mich.; Newark, N.J. (1949-1951); and cleared of obscenity charges in Brantford, Ontario (1949). Source: 3, p. 89.

1070

Shyer, Marlene Fanta. *Welcome Home, Jellybean.* Macmillan. Challenged, but retained, in the Carroll County, Md. schools (1991). Two school board members considered the book depressing. Source: 7, Mar. 1992, p. 64.

1071

Silko, Leslie Marmon. *Ceremony.* Viking; Penguin. Removed at the Nease High School in St. Augustine, Fla. as a required summer reading book for honors English students (1995) because of its language, sexual descriptions and subject matter. The book was recommended for honor students by the National Council of Teachers of English. Retained on the Round Rock, Tex. Independent High School reading list (1996) after a challenge that the book was too violent. Source: 7, Nov. 1995, p. 184; Jan. 1996, p. 14; May 1996, p. 99.

1072

Silverstein, Alvin, and Silverstein, Virginia B. *The Reproductive System: How Living Creatures Multiply.* Prentice-Hall. Placed on restricted shelves at the Evergreen School District elementary school libraries in Vancouver, Wash. (1987) in accordance with the school board policy to restrict student access to sex education books in elementary school libraries. Source: 7, May 1987, p. 87.

1073

Silverstein, Charles, and White, Edmund. *The Joy of Gay Sex.* Crown; Simon & Schuster/Fireside. Confiscated from three Lexington, Ky. bookstores (1977) by the local police and challenged at the San Jose, Calif. Public Library (1981). Seized and shredded (1984) by the British Customs Office. Source: 7, Mar. 1978, p. 40; Jan. 1982, p. 9; Jan. 1985, p. 26.

1074

Silverstein, Charles. *Man to Man.* Morrow. Seized in London, United Kingdom (1986) as "indecent or obscene" and "contrary to the prohibition contained in Section 42 of the Customs Consolidation Act, 1876." Source: 4, May 1986, p. 38.

1075

Silverstein, Charles, and Picano, Felice. *The New Joy of Gay Sex.* Harper. Challenged, but retained at the Lewis and Clark Library in Helena, Mont. (1993). Challenged at the River Bluffs Regional Library in St. Joseph, Mo. (1994) as "pornography." The controversy began after a patron removed a copy of the book from the library and refused to return it, submitting instead a petition with 700 signatures calling for its permanent removal. Challenged at the Kansas City, Mo. Public Library (1995). The complainants asked the Jackson County prosecutor's office to ban the book under state's obscenity and sodomy laws. Restricted to patrons over 18 years of age at the Main Memorial Library in Clifton, N.J. (1996). The book is hidden behind the checkout counter and on the shelves is a dummy book jacket. The book was described as hard-core pornography by the complainant. Source: 7, July 1993, p. 100; Sept. 1993, p. 158; Nov. 1994, p. 188; Jan. 1995, p. 7; July 1995, p. 94; Mar. 1996, p. 63; May 1996, p. 83.

Shel Silverstein

1076

Silverstein, Shel. *The Giving Tree.* Harper. Removed from a locked reference collection at the Boulder, Colo. Public Library (1988). The book was originally locked away because the librarian considered it sexist. Source: 7, Jan. 1989, p. 27.

1077

_____. *A Light in the Attic.* Harper. Challenged at the Cunningham Elementary School in Beloit, Wis. (1985) because the book "encourages children to break dishes so they won't have to dry them." Removed from the shelves of the Minot, N.Dak. Public School libraries (1986) by the assistant superintendent "in anticipation of a parent's complaint." The superintendent found "suggestive illustrations" on several pages of Silverstein's work. Upon the recommendation of a review committee, the book was returned to the shelves. Challenged at the Big Bend Elementary School library in Mukwonago, Wis. (1986) because some of Silverstein's poems "glorified Satan, suicide and cannibalism, and also encouraged children to be disobedient." Challenged at the West Allis-West Milwaukee, Wis. school

libraries (1986) because the book "suggests drug use, the occult, suicide, death, violence, disrespect for truth, disrespect for legitimate authority, rebellion against parents," and because it inspires young people to commit "acts of violence, disbelief, and disrespect." Challenged at the elementary schools in the Papillion-LaVista School District in Omaha, Nebr. (1986) because the book promotes "behavior abusive to women and children, suicide as a way to manipulate parents, mockery of God, and selfish and disrespectful behavior." Challenged at the Appoquinimink schools in Middletown, Del. (1987) because the book "contains violence, idealizes death, and makes light of manipulative behavior." Challenged at the Moreno Valley, Calif. Unified School District libraries (1987) because it "contains profanity, sexual situations, and themes that allegedly encourage disrespectful behavior." The poem "Little Abigail and the Beautiful Pony" from this award-winning children's book was banned from second grade classes in Huffman, Tex. (1989) because a mother protested that it "exposes children to the horrors of suicide." Challenged at the Hot Springs, S.Dak. Elementary School (1989) as suitable classroom material because of its objectionable" nature. Challenged at the South Adams, Ind. school libraries (1989) because the book is "very vile" and "contained subliminal or underlying messages and anti-parent material." Restricted to students with parental permission at the Duval County, Fla. public school libraries (1992) because the book features a caricature of a person whose nude behind has been stung by a bee. Challenged at the West Mifflin, Pa. schools (1992) because the poem "Little Abigail and the Beautiful Pony" is morbid. Challenged at the Fruitland Park Elementary School library in Lake County, Fla. (1993) because the book "promotes disrespect, horror, and violence." Challenged, but retained on the Webb City, Mo. school library shelves (1996). A parent had protested that the book imparts a "dreary" and "negative" message. Source: 7, July 1985, p. 134; May 1986, p. 80; Sept. 1986, p. 172; Nov. 1986, p. 224; Jan. 1987, p. 12; Mar. 1987, pp. 51, 67-68; May 1987, p. 101; July 1987, p. 125; May 1989, p. 80; July 1989, p. 129; Jan. 1990, p. 32; July 1992, p. 105; Mar. 1993, p. 45; July 1993, p. 97; Sept. 1993, p. 157; May 1996, p. 97.

1078

_____. *Where the Sidewalk Ends.* Harper. Challenged at the Xenia, Ohio school libraries (1983) because the book is "anti-Christian, against parental and school authorities, and emphasized the use of drugs and sexual activity." Removed from the shelves of the Minot, N.Dak. public school libraries (1986) by the assistant superintendent "in anticipation of a parent's complaint." Upon the recommendation of a review committee, the book was returned to the shelves. Challenged at the Big Bend Elementary School library in Mukwonago,

Wis. (1986) because some of Silverstein's poems "glorified Satan, suicide and cannibalism, and also encouraged children to be disobedient." Challenged at the West Allis–West Milwaukee, Wis. school libraries (1986) because the book "suggests drug use, the occult, suicide, death, violence, disrespect for truth, disrespect for legitimate authority, rebellion against parents," and because it inspires young people to commit "acts of violence, disbelief, and disrespect." Challenged at the Moreno Valley, Calif. Unified School District libraries (1987) because it "contains profanity, sexual situations, and themes that allegedly encourage disrespectful behavior." Reversing an earlier decision to remove the poem "Dreadful" from the library's copy of this book in a Riverdale, Ill. elementary school (1989), the school board retained the book and poem which was challenged for bad taste. Retained in the Modesto, Calif. district libraries and classrooms (1990) after being challenged as inappropriate for young readers. Challenged at the Central Columbia School District in Bloomsburg, Pa. (1993) because a poem titled "Dreadful" talks about how "someone ate the baby." Challenged at the Fruitland Park Elementary School library in Lake County, Fla. (1993) because the book "promotes disrespect, horror, and violence." Source: 7, Sept. 1983, p. 139; Nov. 1983, p. 197; May 1986, p. 80; Sept. 1986, p. 172; Nov. 1986, p. 224; Mar. 1987, p. 51; May 1987, p. 101; July 1987, p. 125; Mar. 1990, p.61; May 1990, p. 105; May 1993, p. 86; July 1993, p. 97; Sept. 1993, p. 157.

1079
Simon, Neil. *Brighton Beach Memoirs*. NAL; Random. Challenged at the Grayslake, Ill. Community High School (1991). Removed from the required reading and optional reading lists from the Dallas, Tex. schools (1996) because of passages containing profanity and sexually explicit language. Source: 7, July 1991, p. 129-30; May 1996, p. 88.

1080
Simon, Sidney. *Values Clarification*. Hart. Burned in Warsaw, Ind. (1979). Source: 5 & 7, Mar. 1980, p. 40.

1081
Sinclair, April. *Coffee Will Make You Black*. Hyperion. Removed from the curriculum at the Julian High School in Chicago, Ill. (1996) because the book was not appropriate for freshman as required reading because of sexually explicit language. Source: 7, May 1996, p. 87.

1082
Sinclair, Upton. *The Jungle*. Airmont; Bantam; Bentley; NAL; Penguin. Banned from public libraries in Yugoslavia (1929). Burned in the Nazi bonfires because of Sinclair's socialist views (1933). Banned in East Germany (1956) as

inimical to Communism. Banned in South Korea (1985). Source: 3, p. 63; 4, April 1986, pp. 30-33.

1083
_____. *Oil!* Airmont; Bantam; Bentley; NAL; Penguin. Forbidden in Boston, Mass. (1927) because of its comments on the Harding Administration—although Harding had died in 1923 and his cronies were long dispersed. Sinclair defended the case himself, at a cost of $2,000, and addressed a crowd of some 2,000 people on Boston Commons, explaining at length the character and intent of his book. The court suppressed nine pages of the book, including a substantial portion of the Biblical "Song of Solomon." The bookseller from whose store the book had been seized was fined $100 and the offending pages were blacked out. Banned from public libraries in Yugoslavia (1929); burned by the Nazi bonfires because of Sinclair's socialist views (1933); banned in East Germany (1956) as inimical to Communism. Source: 1, p. 133; 2, pp. 282-83; 3, p. 63.

1084
_____. *Wide Is the Gate*. Airmont; Bantam; Bentley; NAL; Penguin. Banned from public libraries in Yugoslavia (1929); burned in the Nazi bonfires because of Sinclair's socialist views (1933); banned in East Germany (1956) as inimical to Communism; banned in Ireland (1953). Source: 3, p. 63.

1085
Sioux City Community School District. *Sioux City, Past and Present*. Sioux City Community School District. Banned from the Sioux City, Iowa schools (1984) because the textbook is "racist and offensive." Source: 7, Mar. 1985, p. 43.

1086
Sissley, Emily L. and Harris, Bertha. *The Joy of Lesbian Sex*. Crown; Simon & Schuster. Seized (1984) by the British Customs Office. Source: 7, Jan. 1985, p. 26.

1087
Skarmeta, Antonio. *Burning Patience*. Graywolf. Challenged as required reading in a freshman English class Orono, Maine High School (1995) because of the book's sexual content. The book was made into the successful film *The Postman*. Source: 7, Nov. 1995, p. 186.

1088
Slepian, Jan. *The Alfred Summer*. Macmillan. Challenged in Charlotte County, Va. (1983) due to "objectionable" words in the text. Pulled, but later restored to the language arts curriculum at four Cheshire, Conn. elementary schools (1991) because the book is "filled with profanity, blasphemy and

obscenities, and gutter language." Source: 7, Nov. 1983, p. 197; Mar. 1992, p. 42; May 1992, p. 96; July 1992, pp. 109-10.

1089
Slier, Deborah, ed. *Make a Joyful Sound*. Checkboard. Challenged at the Deer Park, Wash. elementary schools (1992) because the poetry collection contains the poem, "The Mask," by Dakari Kamaru Hru. A Deer Park parent complained that, "This is religious indoctrination. We in the Western World would refer to it as devil worship. It also smacks of New Age religion." Source: 7, May 1992, pp. 84-85.

1090
Small, Beatrice. *To Love Again: A Historical Romance*. Ballantine. Challenged at the Pocatello, Idaho Public Library (1993) because a patron considered the romance novel "pornographic." Source: 7, Mar. 1994, p. 69.

1091
Smiley, Jane. *A Thousand Acres*. Fawcett; Knopf; Thorndike Pr. Banned at the Lynden, Wash. High School (1994). Winner of the Pulitzer Prize for fiction in 1991, it was described as having "no literary value in our community right now." School officials note that the protesters have tried to block an anti-drug program, a multicultural program, and a Valentine's Day dance, saying that they did not reflect the values parents want taught. Retained on the Round Rock, Tex. Independent High School reading list (1996) after a challenge that the book was too violent. Source: 7, May 1994, p. 88; May 1996, p. 99.

1092
Smith, Lillian. *Strange Fruit*. Harcourt. Majority of bookstores in Boston, Mass. and Detroit, Mich. (1944) removed the book from sale. The book's distributor was charged in 1945 under the Massachusetts laws governing obscene material, in that he had distributed a publication that was "obscene, indecent, impure, or manifestly tends to corrupt the morals of youth." The court found the bookseller guilty and fined him $200, later reduced to $25. The fact that the novel might promote "lascivious thoughts and…arouse lustful desire" outweighed any artistic merit that the novel might possess. Banned in Ireland (1953). Source: 2, p. 305; 3, pp. 78-79; 9, Vol. IV, p. 698.

1093
Smith, Rebecca M. *Family Matters: Concepts in Marriage and Personal Relationships*. Butterick; Glencoe. Challenged as proposed ninth grade curriculum textbook in the Buffalo, N.Y. schools (1986) because it promotes "secular humanism." In particular, the complainant objected to references to the psychological theories of Erik Erikson, Sigmund Freud, Abraham Maslow, and Jean Piaget. Source: 7, Mar. 1987, p. 68.

1094
Smith, Robert Kimmell. *Chocolate Fever*. Dell. Challenged at the Gahanna-Jefferson, Ohio Public Schools (1992) because it contains the words "damn" and "sucks." Source: 7, Jan. 1993, p. 12.

1095
_____. *Jelly Belly*. Delacorte. Challenged at the Gahanna-Jefferson, Ohio Public Schools (1992) because it contains the words "damn" and "sucks." Source: 7, Jan. 1993, p. 12.

1096
_____. *Mostly Michael*. Delacorte. Challenged at the Gahanna-Jefferson, Ohio Public Schools (1992) because it contains the words "damn" and "sucks." Source: 7, Jan. 1993, p. 12.

1097
Smucker, Barbara. *Runaway to Freedom*. Harper. Challenged, but retained, in the Carroll County, Md. schools (1991). Two school board members were offended by its allegedly coarse language. Challenged at the West Dover, Del. Elementary School (1993) because it is offensive to African Americans. The objectionable passage reads, "Massa lay on the feather bed and nigger lay on the floor." Source: 7, Mar. 1992, p. 64; Jan. 1994, p. 15.

1098
Snepp, Frank. *A Decent Interval*. Random; Vintage. The U.S. Justice Department filed a civil complaint in 1978 against the author demanding a lifetime ban on his writing or speaking about the CIA. Source: 3, p. 100; 9, Vol IV, p. 717.

1099
Snow, Edgar. *Red Star over China*. Bantam; Grove. Banned in South Korea (1985). Source: 4, April 1986, pp. 30-33.

1100
Snyder, Zilpha Keatley. *The Egypt Game*. Dell; Macmillan. Challenged in the Richardson, Tex. schools (1995) because it

shows children in dangerous situations, condones trespassing and lying to parents, and teaches children about the occult. The school board declined to ban the award-winning novel but did decide that parents should be notified when it is used in class. Source: 7, Mar. 1995, p. 56.

1101
_____. *The Headless Cupid.* Atheneum; Random. Challenged at the Hays, Kans. Public Library (1989) because the book "could lead young readers to embrace satanism." Retained in the Grand Haven, Mich. school libraries (1990) after a parent objected to the book because it "introduces children to the occult and fantasy about immoral acts." The Newbery Award-winning book was retained on the approved reading list at Matthew Henson Middle School in Waldorf, Md. (1991) despite objections to its references to witchcraft. Challenged in the Escondido, Calif. school (1992) because it contains references to the occult. Source: 7, July 1989, p. 143; May 1990, p. 106; Sept. 1991, pp. 155-56; Sept. 1992, p. 161.

1102
_____. *The Witches of Worm.* Atheneum. Restricted in Escambia County, Fla. (1982) to sixth graders and above because "it contains 183 pages of rejection, fear, hatred, occult ritual, cruel pranks, lies and even an attempted murder by arson all perpetrated by a twelve-year-old girl." Challenged at the Kennedy High School in Mt. Angel, Oreg. (1988) for its witchcraft theme and scary illustrations. Retained in the Grand Haven, Mich. school libraries (1990) after a parent objected to the book because it "introduces children to the occult and fantasy about immoral acts." Source: 7, July 1982, p. 123; Jan. 1989, p. 3; May 1990, p. 106.

1103
Solotareff, Gregoire. *Don't Call Me Little Bunny.* Farrar. Challenged at the Douglas County Library in Roseburg, Oreg. (1989) because the character gets away with bad behavior. Challenged in the Cook Memorial Library in Libertyville, Ill. (1995) because the actions taken by the bunny character in the book were anti-social and inappropriate for children's reading. Source: 7, Jan. 1990, pp. 4-5; Jan. 1996, p. 29.

1104
Solzhenitsyn, Aleksandr Isayevich. *August 1914.* Bantam; Farrar. Barred from publication in the USSR, the author was stripped of Soviet citizenship and deported (1974). Source: 3, p. 91.

1105
_____. *Cancer Ward.* Bantam; Farrar. Barred from publi-cation in the USSR, the author was stripped of Soviet citizenship and deported (1974). Source: 3, p. 91.

1106
_____. *Candle in the Wind.* Univ. of Minn. Pr. Barred from publication in the USSR, the author was stripped of Soviet citizenship and deported (1974). Source: 3, p. 91.

1107
_____. *The First Circle.* Bantam. Barred from publication in the USSR, the author was stripped of Soviet citizenship and deported (1974). Source: 3, p. 91.

1108
_____. *The Gulag Archipelago.* Harper. Barred from publi-cation in the USSR, the author was stripped of Soviet citizenship and deported (1974). Source: 3, p. 91.

1109
_____. *The Love Girl and the Innocent.* Farrar. Barred from publication in the USSR, the author was stripped of Soviet citizenship and deported (1974). Source: 3, p. 91.

1110
_____. *One Day in the Life of Ivan Denisovich.* Dutton; Farrar; NAL. Barred from publication in the USSR, the author was stripped of Soviet citizenship and deported (1974). Removed from the Milton, N.H. High School library (1976) due to objectionable language. Challenged in Mahwah, N.J. (1976); Omak, Wash. (1979) and at the Mohawk Trail Regional High School in Buckland, Mass. (1981) because of profanity in the book. Removed from the Lincoln County, Wyo. high school curriculum (1995) because of "considerable obscenities." Source: 3, p. 91; 4; 7, May 1976, p. 61; Jan. 1977, p. 8; July 1979, pp. 10-11; July 1995, p. 100.

1111
_____. *Stories and Prose Poems.* Farrar. Barred from publi-cation in the USSR. The author was stripped of Soviet citizenship and deported (1974). Source: 3, p. 91.

1112
Spargo, Edward. *Topics for the Restless.* Jamestown Pub. Challenged at the Jefferson County school libraries in Lakewood, Colo. (1986). The textbook is a collection of stories and essays designed to promote critical thought among high school students. Parents found "most objectionable" selections from the *Feminine Mystique,* which they said was too favor-able to the Equal Rights Amendment; a story on Marilyn Monroe; "Death with Dignity," which addresses what chil-dren should be taught about death; and "Hiroshima – Death and Rebirth I and II," stories they claimed "make Americans

feel guilty about bombing Hiroshima." The Jefferson County School Board refused to ban the book. Source: 7, May 1986, p. 82; Sept. 1986, p. 173; Nov. 1986, p. 224.

1113
Spencer, Scott. *Endless Love*. Ballantine; Knopf. Banned from the Berkeley County, S.C. High School media center (1991) because of "explicit pornographic passages and adult material for teenage readers." Source: 7, Mar. 1992, p. 41.

1114
Spiegelman, Art, and Mouly, Francoise. *Raw*. Viking Penguin. Challenged at the Douglas County Library in Roseburg, Oreg. (1992) because "it's full of cartoon pornography." Source: 7, Jan. 1993, p. 9.

1115
Spies, Karen Bornemann. *Everything You Need to Know About Incest*. Rosen. Pulled from the Ouachita Parish school library in Monroe, La. (1996) because of sexual content. The Louisiana chapter of the ACLU filed a lawsuit in the federal courts on October 3, 1996, claiming that the principal and the school superintendent violated First Amendment free speech rights and also failed to follow established procedure when they removed the book. Source: 7, Sept. 1996, pp. 151-52; Jan. 1997, p. 7.

1116
Spinelli, Jerry. *Jason and Marceline*. Dell. Challenged at the Pitman, N.J. Middle School library (1992) because the book promotes stealing, drinking, profanity, and premarital sex. Challenged at the Pitman, N.J. school libraries (1992) because "it's not a positive book about life. Jason smokes and drinks and there are absolutely no repercussions." Challenged, but retained as part of the curriculum at Hughes Junior High School in Bismarck, N.Dak. (1993). The controversy centered around the use of profanity and sexually explicit language. Source: 7, July 1992, p. 106; Jan. 1993, p. 27; Sept. 1993, p. 145; Jan. 1994, p. 38.

1117
————. *Space Station, Seventh Grade*. Dell; Little. Challenged at the La Grande, Oreg. Middle School library (1988) because "profanity, sexual obscenity, immoral values are throughout the book." Source: 7, May 1989, p. 93.

1118
Spraggett, Allen. *Arthur Ford: The Man Who Talked with the*

Dead. NAL. Challenged at the Plymouth-Canton school system in Canton, Mich. (1987) because the book deals with witchcraft. Source: 7, May 1987, p. 110.

1119
Stadtmauer, Saul. *Visions of the Future: Magic Boards*. Raintree. Removed from the Philomath, Oreg. Middle School library (1984) because it was "badly written." Challenged at the Dallas, Oreg. school library (1991) because the book entices impressionable or emotionally disturbed children into becoming involved in witchcraft or the occult. Pulled, but later placed on reserve to children with parental permission at the Forrest Elementary School library in Hampton, Va. (1992). Source: 7, Sept. 1984, p. 138; Jan. 1992, p. 26; July 1992, p. 108; Sept. 1992, p. 139.

Alexander Solzhenitzyn (1974)

1120
Stamper, J. P. *More Tales for the Midnight Hour*. Scholastic. Challenged at the Neely Elementary School in Gilbert, Ariz. (1992) because the book shows the dark side of religion through the occult, the devil, and satanism. Source: 7, May 1992, p. 78; July 1992, p. 124.

1121
Stanislawski, Michael. *Tsar Nicholas I and the Jews: The Transformation of Jewish Society in Russia, 1825-1855*. Jewish Pubn. Banned from the 1983 Moscow International Book Fair along with more than fifty other books because it is "anti-Soviet." Source: 7, Nov. 1983, p. 201.

1122
Stanley, Lawrence A., ed. *Rap, The Lyrics*. Viking. Parent requested that all offensive materials be labeled at the Sno-Isle Regional Library in Marysville, Wash. (1993). Source: 7, July 1993, p. 103.

1123
Stanway, Andrew. *The Lovers' Guide*. St. Martin. Removed from the Clifton, N.J. Public Library (1996) and replaced with a dummy book made of styrofoam. The library's new policy restricts to adults any material containing "patently offensive graphic illustrations or photographs of sexual or excretory activities or contact as measured by contemporary community standards for minors." Source: 7, July 1996, pp. 118-19.

1124
Stark, Evan, ed. *Everything You Need to Know about Sexual Abuse.* Rosen. Challenged at the Arcadia, Wis. schools (1991) because the book presents sexual abuse situations too descriptively. Source: 7, Sept. 1991, p. 154.

1125
Starkey, Marion Lena. *The Tall Man from Boston.* Crown. Challenged at the Sikes Elementary School media center in Lakeland, Fla. (1985) because the book "would lead children to believe ideas contrary to the teachings of the Bible." Source: 7, July 1985, p. 133.

1126
Steel, Danielle. *Changes.* Delacorte; Dell. Banned from the Stroudsburg, Pa. High School library (1985) because it was "blatantly graphic, pornographic and wholly unacceptable for a high school library." Source: 7, May 1985, p. 79.

1127
_____. *Crossings.* Delacorte; Dell. Banned from the Stroudsburg, Pa. High School library (1985) because it was "blatantly graphic, pornographic and wholly unacceptable for a high school library." Source: 7, May 1985, p. 79.

1128
_____. *The Gift.* Delacorte. Challenged at a Coventry, Ohio school (1996) because "the schools had no business teaching his children about sex, that it was the job of the parents." Source: 7, Jan. 1997, p. 11.

1129
Steig, William. *Abel's Island.* Farrar. Pulled from the fifth and sixth grade optional reading lists in Clay County, Fla. schools (1990) because of references to drinking wine which administrators determined violated the district's substance abuse policy. The objectionable passage reads: "At home he had to drink some wine to dispel the chill in his bones. He drank large draughts of his wine and ran about everywhere like a wild animal, shouting and yodeling." Source: 7, Jan. 1991, p. 16.

1130
_____. *The Amazing Bone.* Farrar; Penguin. Challenged at the West Amwell school libraries in Lambertville, N.J. (1986) because a parent objected to "the use of tobacco by the animals." Challenged at the Discovery Elementary School library in Issaquah, Wash. (1993) because of the graphic and detailed violence. Source: 7, Mar. 1987, p. 65; Mar. 1994, p. 70.

1131
_____. *Caleb and Kate.* Farrar. Pulled from the Boyer-

town, Pa. elementary school library shelves (1992) because the book "depicts a dismal outlook on marriage and life." The book was eventually returned. Source: 7, Mar. 1993, p. 42; May 1993, p. 86.

1132
_____. *Sylvester and the Magic Pebble.* Simon & Schuster. The Illinois Police Association wrote (1977) to librarians asking them to remove the book because its characters, all shown as animals, present police as pigs—although in favorable portrayals. Similar problems reported in eleven other states. Source: 3, p. 87.

1133
Steiger, Brad. *Beyond Belief: True Mysteries of the Unknown.* Scholastic. Challenged at the Hemet, Calif. Elementary School (1995). The teacher was placed on paid administrative leave after a parent complained that the book deals with the supernatural and the occult. Source: 7, May 1995, p. 65.

1134
Stein, Sol. *The Magician.* Delacorte; Dell. Challenged in Montello, Wis. (1981). Source: 7, May 1981, p. 73.

1135
Steinbeck, John. *East of Eden.* Penguin. Removed from two Anniston, Ala. high school libraries (1982) because it is "ungodly and obscene" but later reinstated on a restrictive basis; removed from school libraries in Morris, Manitoba (1982). Challenged in the Greenville, S.C. schools (1991) because the book uses the name of God and Jesus in a "vain and profane manner along with inappropriate sexual references." Source: 7, Mar. 1983, p. 37; July 1991, p. 130.

1136
_____. *Grapes of Wrath.* Penguin; Viking. Burned by the St. Louis, Mo. Public Library (1939) and barred from the Buffalo, N.Y. Public Library (1939) on the grounds that "vulgar words" were used. Banned in Kansas City, Mo. (1939); Kern County, Calif., the scene of Steinbeck's novel, (1939); Ireland (1953); Kanawha, Iowa High School classes (1980); and Morris, Manitoba (1982). On Feb. 21, 1973 eleven Turkish book publishers went on trial before an Istanbul martial law tribunal on charges of publishing, possessing and selling books in violation of an order of the Istanbul martial law command. They faced possible sentences of between one month's and six months' imprisonment "for spreading propaganda unfavorable to the state" and the confiscation of their books. Eight booksellers were also on trial with the publishers on the same charge involving the *Grapes of Wrath.* Challenged in Vernon-Verona-Sherill, N.Y. School District (1980); challenged as required reading for Richford, Vt. (1981) High

School English students due to the book's language and portrayal of a former minister who recounts how he took advantage of a young woman. Removed from two Anniston, Ala. high school libraries (1982), but later reinstated on a restrictive basis. Challenged at the Cummings High School in Burlington, N.C. (1986) as an optional reading assignment because the "book is full of filth. My son is being raised in a Christian home and this book takes the Lord's name in vain and has all kinds of profanity in it." Although the parent spoke to the press, a formal complaint with the school demanding the book's removal was not filed. Challenged at the Moore County school system in Carthage, N.C. (1986) because the book contains the phase "God damn." Challenged in the Greenville, S.C. schools (1991) because the book uses the name of God and Jesus in a "vain and profane manner along with inappropriate sexual references." Challenged in the Union City, Tenn. High School classes (1993). Source: 3, p. 82; 4, Summer 1973, p.xii; 5, p. 142; 7, May 1980, pp. 52, 62; Jan. 1982, p. 18; Mar. 1983, p. 37; July 1986, p. 120; Nov. 1986, p. 210; Jan. 1987, p. 32; July 1991, p. 130; Mar. 1994, p. 55; 9, Vol. III, pp. 651-52.

1137

_____. *In Dubious Battle.* Penguin. Banned in Ireland (1953). Source: 3, p. 83.

1138

_____. *Of Mice and Men.* Bantam; Penguin; Viking. Banned in Ireland (1953); Syracuse, Ind. (1974); Oil City, Pa. (1977); Grand Blanc, Mich. (1979); Continental, Ohio (1980) and other communities. Challenged in Greenville, S.C. (1977) by the Fourth Province of the Knights of the Ku Klux Klan; Vernon-Verona-Sherill, N.Y. School District (1980); St. David, Ariz. (1981) and Tell City, Ind. (1982) due to "profanity and using God's name in vain." Banned from classroom use at the Scottsboro, Ala. Skyline High School (1983) due to "profanity." The Knoxville, Tenn. School Board chairman vowed to have "filthy books" removed from Knoxville's public schools (1984) and picked Steinbeck's novel as the first target due to "its vulgar language." Reinstated at the Christian County, Ky. school libraries and English classes (1987) after being challenged as vulgar and offensive. Challenged in the Marion County, W.Va. schools (1988), at the Wheaton-Warrenville, Ill. Middle School (1988), and at the Berrien Springs, Mich. High School (1988) because the book contains profanity. Removed from the Northside High School in Tuscaloosa, Ala. (1989) because the book "has profane use of God's name." Challenged as a summer youth program reading

assignment in Chattanooga, Tenn. (1989) because "Steinbeck is known to have had an anti-business attitude." In addition, "he was very questionable as to his patriotism." Removed from all reading lists and collected at the White Chapel High School in Pine Bluff, Ark. (1989) because of objections to language. Challenged as appropriate for high school reading lists in the Shelby County, Tenn. school system (1989) because the novel contained "offensive language." Challenged in the Riveria, Tex. schools (1990) because it contains profanity. Challenged as curriculum material at the Ringgold High School in Carroll Township, Pa. (1991) because the novel contains terminology offensive to blacks. Removed and later returned to the Suwannee, Fla. High School library (1991) because the book is "indecent."

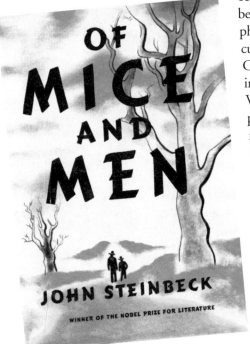

Challenged at the Jacksboro, Tenn. High School (1991) because the novel contains "blasphemous" language, excessive cursing, and sexual overtones. Challenged as required reading in the Buckingham County, Va. schools (1991) because of profanity. Temporarily removed from the Hamilton, Ohio High School reading list (1992) after a parent complained about its vulgarity and racial slurs. Challenged in the Waterloo, Iowa schools (1992) and the Duval County, Fla. public school libraries (1992) because of profanity, lurid passages about sex, and statements defamatory to minorities, God, women, and the disabled. Challenged at the Modesto, Calif. High School as recommended reading (1992) because of "offensive and racist language." The word "nigger" appears in the book. Challenged at the Oak Hill High School in Alexandria, La. (1992) because of profanity. Challenged as an appropriate English curriculum assignment at the Mingus, Ariz. Union High School (1993) because of "profane language, moral statement, treatment of the retarded, and the violent ending." Pulled from a classroom by Putnam County, Tenn. school superintendent (1994) "due to the language." Later, after discussions with the school district counsel, it was reinstated. Challenged at the Loganville, Ga. High School (1994) because of its "vulgar language throughout." Challenged in the Galena, Kans. school library (1995) because of the book's language and social implications. Retained in the Bemidji, Minn. schools (1995) after challenges to the book's "objectionable" language. Challenged at the Stephens County High School library in Toccoa, Ga. (1995) because of "curse words." The book was retained. Challenged, but retained in a Warm Springs, Va. High School (1995) English class. Source: 5 & 7, Mar. 1975, p. 41; Nov. 1977, p. 155; Jan. 1978, p. 7; Mar. 1979, p. 27; May 1980, p. 62; July 1980, p. 77; May 1982, pp. 84-85; July 1983, p. 198; July 1984, p. 104; May 1988, p. 90; July 1988, p. 140; Sept. 1988, pp. 154, 179; Nov. 1988, p. 201;Jan. 1989, p. 28; Nov 1989, p. 162; Jan. 1990, pp. 10-12; Mar. 1990, p. 45; Mar. 1991, p. 62; July 1991, p. 110; Jan. 1992, p. 25; Mar. 1992, p. 64; July 1992, pp. 111-12, 126; Sept. 1992, pp. 140, 163-64; Jan. 1993, p. 29; Mar. 1994, p. 53; Mar. 1995, pp. 46, 53; May 1995, p. 84; July 1995, pp. 93, 111-12; Sept. 1995, pp. 157-58; Jan. 1996, p. 29; Mar. 1996, pp. 50-63.

1139

_____. *Red Pony.* Viking. Challenged at the Vernon-Verona-Sherill, N.Y. School District (1980) as a "filthy, trashy, sex novel." Challenged in the Oconee County, Ga. school libraries (1994) because a parent complained the book contained profanity. The Oconee School Board voted to evaluate all 40,000 volumes in the system's library and remove any books and teaching materials from the public school that contain "explicit sex and pornography." Challenged, but retained on a recommended reading list at Holmes Middle School in Eden, N.C. (1996). A parent complained that there were curse words on ten different pages of the book. Source: 7, May 1980, p. 62; Sept. 1994, p. 145; Sept. 1996, p. 170.

1140

_____. *The Wayward Bus.* Penguin. Placed on list of books disapproved (1953) by the Gathings Committee (a House of Representatives select committee on indecent literature); banned in Ireland (1953). Source: 3, p. 83.

1141

Stern, Howard. *Miss America.* Regan. Challenged at the Prince William County, Va. Library (1996). Two newly appointed members of the library board want to limit young people's access to books by removing them from the collection or by creating an "adults-only" section of the library. Source: 7, Nov. 1996, p. 194.

1142

_____. *Private Parts.* Simon & Schuster; Pocket Bks. Challenged at the Weslaco, Tex. Public Library (1994). A petition, with more than 300 signatures, was presented to city officials asking them to more closely monitor what books the library purchases. The librarian labeled as "too lib-eral" subsequently resigned. Challenged, but retained at the Scott Public Library in Alabaster, Ala. (1994). The Shelby County District Attorney called the book "obscene" and threatened to prosecute the library for circulating it although no action was taken. Former Weslaco, Tex. (1995) librarian filed a federal lawsuit charging that she was fired for publicly discussing that city's efforts to ban Stern's work from the library. Source: 7, Nov. 1994, p. 189; Mar. 1995, p. 53; Sept. 1995, p. 153.

1143

Stillman, Peter R. *Introduction to Myth.* Hayden. Challenged as a text for an elective course for junior and senior high school students in Renton, Wash. (1982) because it was considered anti-Christian by some parents. Source: 7, Sept. 1982, p. 171.

1144

Stine, R. L. *Beach House.* Pocket Bks. Challenged at the Pulaski Heights Elementary School library in Little Rock, Ark. (1996) along with similar Stine titles. The book, part of the "Fear Street" series, includes graphic descriptions of boys intimidating and killing girls. Source: 7, Nov. 1996, p. 211.

1145

_____. *Goosebumps.* Scholastic. Challenged at the Bay County, Fla. elementary schools (1996) because of "satanic symbolism, disturbing scenes and dialogue." *The Barking Ghost,* for satanic symbolism and gestures, possession and descriptions of dogs as menacing and attacking; *Night of the Living Dummy II,* for spells or chants, violence and vandalism; *The Haunted Mask,* for graphic description of the ugly mask, demonic possession, violence, disturbing scenes and dialogue; *The Scarecrow Walks at Midnight,* for satanic acts and symbolism, and disturbing scenes; and *Say Cheese and Die!,* for promoting mischief, demonic possession, a reference to Satan and his goals, a disturbing scene describing a death, and a scene that tells of a child disappearing from a birthday party. Challenged at the Anoka-Hennepin, Minn. school system (1997) because "children under the age of twelve may not be able to handle the frightening content of the books." Source: 7, July 1996, p. 134; Mar. 1997, p. 35.

1146

_____. *The Haunted Mask.* Scholastic. Challenged, but retained at the Battle Creek, Mich. Elementary School library (1994) despite protests from a parent who said the book is satanic. Source: 7, Nov. 1994, p. 200.

1147

Stirling, Nora. *You Would If You Loved Me.* Avon.

Removed from the Utah State Library bookmobile (1980). Source: 7, Nov. 1980, p. 128.

1148
Stock, Gregory. *The Kid's Book of Questions.* Workman Pub. Challenged in the Albemarle County schools in Charlottesville, Va. (1990) because it is "inappropriate in an academic class." One parent cited a question from the book, which asked whether a child had ever farted and blamed someone else. Source: 7, Jan. 1991, p. 18.

1149
Stoker, Bram. *Dracula.* Airmont; Bantam; Delacorte; Dell; NAL; Puffin; Random; Scholastic; Viking. Eliminated from required reading lists for juniors and seniors in advanced English classes at the Colony High School in Lewisville, Tex. (1994) because "the book contains unacceptable descriptions in the introduction, such as 'Dracula is the symptom of a wish, largely sexual, that we wish we did not have.'" Source: 7, July 1994, p. 116.

1150
Stoppard, Miriam. *The Magic of Sex.* Newspaper Guild. Restricted to patrons over 18 years of age at the Main Memorial Library in Clifton, N.J. (1996). The book is hidden behind the checkout counter and on the shelves is a dummy book jacket. The book was described as hard-core pornography by the complainant. Source: 7, Mar. 1996, p. 63; May 1996, p. 83.

1151
_____. *Woman's Body.* Dorling Kindersley. Challenged at the Gwinnett-Forsyth, Ga. Regional Library (1995) because it is "too sexually explicit to be on regular library shelves." Source: 7, Jan. 1996, p. 29.

1152
Storm, Hyemeyohsts. *Seven Arrows.* Harper. Challenged at the Creswell, Oreg. High School (1985) because the book contains references to masturbation, rape, and incest. Source: 7, Mar. 1985, p. 45; May 1985, p. 81.

1153
Stowe, Harriet Beecher. *Uncle Tom's Cabin.* Airmont; Bantam; Harper; Houghton; Macmillan; NAL. Challenged in the Waukegan, Ill. School District (1984) because the novel contains the word "nigger." Source: 7, July 1984, p. 105.

1154
Strasser, Todd. *Angel Dust Blues.* Coward. Challenged as reading material for the Manhasset, N.Y. Public Library's young adult Popsicle series (1983) because of "explicit and

graphic sex scenes of a most crude and exploitative nature" and "blasphemy." Challenged at Alexander Central High School and East Junior High School libraries in Taylorsville, N.C. (1987) because of "sexually explicit passages." Challenged at the Crook County Middle School in Prineville, Oreg. (1989) because of explicit language. Source: 7, Nov. 1983, p. 185; May 1987, p. 87; July 1987, p. 149; Jan. 1990, pp. 4-5.

1155
_____. *Friends 'til the End.* Dell. Challenged at the Arlington, Tex. junior high school libraries (1985) because of "sexually descriptive words." Source: 7, Mar. 1985, p. 60.

1156
Street Law. *West Pub.* Challenged in Linthicum Heights, Md. (1983) because it is "biased and pressures teenagers to make moral judgments." Source: 7, Nov. 1983, p. 186; Mar. 1984, p. 53.

1157
Styron, William. *The Confessions of Nat Turner.* Bantam; Random. Removed from the Thompson High School library in Mason City, Iowa (1987) after a parent objected to some "sexual materials" in the book. Source: 7, July 1987, p. 126; Sept. 1987, p. 174.

1158
_____. *Sophie's Choice.* Bantam; Random. Banned in South Africa in Nov. 1979. Source: 4, Apr. 1980, p. 72.

1159
Sullivan, Tim, ed. *Cold Shocks.* Avon. Challenged at the Montclair, N.J. Public Library (1993) because the language in the collection of horror stories "was not conducive to a sixth grader." The complainant demanded that books with possibly offensive contents be labeled with warnings and kept in a limited access section. Source: 7, July 1993, p. 100.

1160
Sullivan, Tom, and Gill, Derek. *If You Could See What I Hear.* Harper. Removed from the Utah State Library bookmobile (1980). Source: 7, Nov. 1980, p. 128.

1161
Summers, Montague. *The Popular History of Witchcraft.* Causeway Bks. Challenged by the "God Squad," a group of three students and their parents, at the El Camino High School in Oceanside, Calif. (1986) because the book "glorified the devil and the occult." Source: 7, Sept. 1986, p. 151; Nov. 1986, p. 224; Jan. 1987, p. 9.

1162
Suzuki, D. T. *Zen Buddhism: Selected Writings.* Doubleday. Challenged at the Plymouth-Canton school system in Canton, Mich. (1987) because "this book details the teachings of the religion of Buddhism in such a way that the reader could very likely embrace its teachings and choose this as his religion." Source: 7, May 1987, p. 109.

1163
Swarthout, Glendon. *Bless the Beasts and the Children.* Pocket Bks. Banned in the Dupree, S.Dak. High School English classes (1987) because of what the school board called "offensive language and vulgarity." Source: 7, Jan. 1988, p. 12.

1164
Sweedloff, Peter. *Men and Women.* Time-Life. Banned from the Brighton, Mich. High School library (1977) along with all other sex education materials. Source: 7, Sept. 1977, p. 133.

1165
Swift, Jonathan. *Drapier's Letters.* Airmont; Bantam; Bobbs-Merrill; Dell; Grosset; Houghton; NAL; Norton; Oxford Univ. Pr.; Pocket Bks. All attempts to prosecute the printer or to identify the anonymous writer were frustrated by the aroused Irish nation (1724). Source: 3, p. 25.

1166
_____. *Gulliver's Travels.* Airmont; Bantam; Bobbs-Merrill; Dell; Grosset; Houghton; NAL; Norton; Oxford Univ. Pr.; Pocket Bks. Denounced as wicked and obscene in Ireland (1726). Source: 3, p. 25.

1167
_____. *Tale of a Tub.* AMS Pr.; Oxford Univ. Pr. Placed on the *Index Librorum Prohibitorum* in Rome (1704). Source: 2, p. 135.

1168
Talbert, Marc. *Dead Birds Singing.* Dell; Little. Challenged, but retained as part of the curriculum at Hughes Junior High School in Bismarck, N.Dak. (1993) because it is "offensive." Source: 7, Sept. 1993, p. 145; Jan. 1994, p. 38.

1169
The Talmud. Soncino Pr. Burned in Cairo, Egypt (1190); Paris, France (1244); and Salamanca, Spain (1490). Burned (1239) on the orders of Pope Gregory IX. Pope Innocent IV ordered Louis IX of France to burn all copies. This order, which met great opposition from the Jewish community, was repeated in 1248 and 1254. Pope Benedict XIII ordered all copies to be delivered to the bishops of the Italian diocese (1415) and held by them, subject to further instruction. Jews were forbidden to possess any material that was antagonistic to Christianity. On the instruction of the Inquisition of Rome (1555) the houses of the Jewish community were searched and all copies seized. Pope Julius III ordered that no Christian might own or read the Talmud, nor might they print such material, on pain of excommunication. After the publication of the Roman Index of 1559 which prohibited the Talmud and all other works of Jewish doctrine, some 12,000 volumes of Hebrew texts were burned after the Inquisitor Sixtus of Siena destroyed the library of the Hebrew school at Cremona. Pope Clement VIII forbade (1592) both "Christians and Jews from owning, reading, buying or circulating Talmudic or Cabbalistic books or other godless writing," either written or printed, in Hebrew or in the other languages, which contained heresies or attacks on the church, its persons or practices. Any such work, ostensibly expurgated or not, was to be destroyed. The prohibitions of Jewish doctrinal material as set out in 1559, 1564 and 1592 were all repeated by Pope Clement XIV. No Hebrew books were to be bought or sold until they had been submitted to the papal chaplain charged with administering the censorship system. Source: 2, pp. 55-56; 3, p. 5.

1170
Tamar, Erika. *Fair Game.* Harcourt. Challenged at the Springdale, Ark. Public Library (1995) because "ethics take a back seat to graphic sexual material. Perhaps there is a less prurient work that explores the issue of rape vs. consensual sex or date rape." Source: 7, Sept. 1995, p. 157.

1171
Tan, Amy. *The Joy Luck Club.* Putnam. Banned from the Lindale, Tex. advanced placement English reading list (1996) because the book "conflicted with the values of the community." Source: 7, Nov. 1996, p. 199.

1172
Tax, Meredith. *Families.* Little. Eliminated from the Fairfax County, Va. School's Family Life Education program (1994) after "parents complained that it glorifies divorce and shows two women living together." Source: 7, May 1994, p. 88; Sept. 1994, p. 153.

1173
Taylor, Mildred D. *Roll of Thunder, Hear My Cry.* Bantam; Dell. Removed from the ninth grade reading list at the Arcadia, La. High School (1993). The 1976 Newbery Medal-winning book was charged with racial bias. Source: 7, May 1993, p. 72.

1174
Taylor, Theodore. *The Cay.* Avon; Doubleday. Challenged as required reading at the Moorpark, Calif. schools (1992) because it allegedly maligns African Americans. Removed from the Oak Grove School District's core reading list for seventh-graders in San Jose, Calif. (1995) because of offensive, racist language. Placed on an "extended" list for use in the eighth grade. Source: 7, May 1992, p. 95; July 1995, p. 96.

1175
Taylor, William. *Agnes the Sheep.* Scholastic. Removed from the Nesbit Elementary School in Gwinnett County, Ga. (1995) because it overused the words "hell, damn, and God." After other parents wanted the book restored in the elementary school, the County Board of Education refused to reinstate the book. Source: 7, Jan. 1996, p. 11; Mar. 1996, p. 64.

1176
Tchudi, Stephen. *Probing the Unknown: From Myth to Science.* Scribner. Challenged in the West Branch-Rose City, Mich. school district (1995) because it discusses occult beliefs. Source: 7, Jan. 1996, p. 15.

1177
Telander, Rick. *Heaven Is a Playground.* Grosset. Removed from the Evergreen School District of Vancouver, Wash. (1983) along with twenty-nine other titles. The American Civil Liberties Union of Washington filed suit contending that the removals constitute censorship, a violation of plaintiff's rights to free speech and due process, and the acts are a violation of the state Open Meetings Act because the removal decisions were made behind closed doors. Source: 7, Nov. 1983, pp. 185-86.

1178
Teleny: A Novel Attributed to Oscar Wilde. Gay Sunshine; Warner. Seized (1984) by the British Customs Office as "indecent and obscene." Source: 7, Jan. 1985, p. 26.

1179
Terkel, Studs. *Working.* Pantheon. Challenged in Wales, Wis. (1978) due to the book's "obscene language." Challenged in the senior vocational-technical English class in Girard, Pa. (1982) because some parents and students considered the book obscene. Removed from an optional reading list at the South Kitsap, Wash. High School (1983) because the chapter "Hooker" demeaned marital status and degraded the sexual act. Deleted from the seventh and eighth grade curriculum in the Washington, Ariz. School District (1983) due to "profane language. When we require idealistic and sensitive youth to be burdened with despair, ugliness and

hopelessness, we shall be held accountable by the Almighty God." Source: 5 & 7, July 1978, p. 89; Sept. 1978, p. 123; July 1982, p. 143; Nov. 1983, p. 187; Jan. 1984, pp. 10-11.

1180
Terris, Susan. *Stage Brat.* Four Winds Pr. Removed, but later reinstated at the Pine Middle School library in Gibsonia, Pa. (1990) because "it talks of adults slithering around in hot tubs, abortions, palm reading and horoscopes as ways of making life decisions, anti-religious language, and four-letter words." Source: 7, Nov. 1990, pp. 209-10; Jan. 1991, pp. 28-29.

1181
Terry, Wallace. *Bloods: An Oral History of the Vietnam War by Black Veterans.* Ballantine; Random. Banned from the West Hernando Middle School library in Spring Hill, Fla. (1987) because of "harsh language and presents a moral danger to students." The librarian filed a grievance and the book was returned to the shelves following a ruling by the American Arbitration Association. Forty minutes after the book was returned, the book was removed again, pending a review by an advisory committee. Source: 7, May 1987, p. 85; Sept. 1987, pp. 173-74; Jan. 1988, p. 9.

1182
Thomas, Piri. *Down These Mean Streets.* Knopf; Random. Removed from the junior high school library Community School Board 1250, Queens, N.Y. (1972). Decision upheld by the court's ruling in *President's Council, District 25 v. Community School Board No. 25,* 457 F. 2d 289 (2d Cir. 1972), 409 U. S. 998 (1972). Removed from the Island Trees, N.Y. Union Free School District High School library in 1976 along with nine other titles because they were considered "immoral, anti-American, anti-Christian, or just plain filthy." Returned to the library after the U.S. Supreme Court ruling on June 25, 1982 in *Board of Education, Island Trees Union Free School District No. 26 et al. v. Pico et al.,* 457 U.S. 853 (1982). Source: 7, July 1973, p. 115; Nov. 1982, p. 197; 8, pp. 142-44, 239.

1183
Thompson, Charlotte E. *Single Solutions: An Essential Guide for the Career Woman.* Branden. Challenged for technical errors, but retained at the Multnomah, Oreg. County Library (1991). Source: 7, Jan. 1992, p. 6.

1184
The Three Billy Goats Gruff. Harcourt. Challenged at the Eagle Point, Oreg. Elementary School library (1984) because the story was too violent for children. Source: 7, Sept. 1984, p. 155.

1185

Tolstoy, Leo. *The Kreutzer Sonata*. AMS Pr. Forbidden publication in Russia (1880); banned by the U.S. Post Office Department (1890). Banned in Hungary (1926) and Italy (1929). Source: 3, p. 49; 6, p. 144; 9, Vol. II, pp. 621-22.

1186

The Treasury of American Poetry. Doubleday. Challenged at the Gretna, Va. High School library (1981) because it contained eight objectionable words. The review committee recommended to cut out pages or ink over the offending words. Source: 7, May 1981, p. 66.

1187

Tryon, Thomas. *The Other*. Knopf. Challenged at the Merrimack, N.H. High School (1982). Source: 7, Sept. 1982, p. 170.

1188

Turkle, Brinton. *Do Not Open*. Dutton. Challenged at the Jackson, Calif. Elementary School (1990) because of objections to its pictures of supernatural beings. Source: 7, May 1990, p. 105.

1189

Twain, Mark [Samuel L. Clemens]. *The Adventures of Huckleberry Finn*. Bantam; Bobbs-Merrill; Grosset; Harper; Holt; Houghton; Longman; Macmillan; NAL; Norton; Penguin; Pocket Bks. Banned in Concord, Mass. (1885) as "trash and suitable only for the slums"; excluded from the children's room of the Brooklyn, N.Y. Public Library (1905) on the grounds that "Huck not only itched but scratched, and that he said sweat when he should have said perspiration"; confiscated at the USSR border (1930); dropped from the New York City (1957) list of approved books for senior and junior high schools, partly because of objections to frequent use of the term "nigger." Removed from the Miami Dade, Fla. Junior College required reading list (1969) because the book "creates an emotional block for black students that inhibits learning." Challenged as a "racist" novel in Winnetka, Ill. (1976); Warrington, Pa. (1981); Davenport, Iowa (1981); Fairfax County, Va. (1982); Houston, Tex. (1982); State College, Pa. Area School District (1983); Springfield, Ill. (1984); Waukegan, Ill. (1984). Removed from the required reading in the Rockford, Ill. public schools (1988) because the book contains the word "nigger." Challenged at the Berrien Springs, Mich. High School (1988). Removed from a required reading list and school libraries in Caddo Parish, La. (1988) because of

Samuel Clemens, a.k.a. Mark Twain

racially offensive passages. Challenged at the Sevier County High School in Sevierville, Tenn. (1989) because of racial slurs and dialect. Challenged on an Erie, Pa. High School supplemental English reading list (1990) because of its derogatory references to African Americans. Challenged in Plano, Tex. Independent School District (1990) because the novel is "racist." Challenged in the Mesa, Ariz. Unified School District (1991) because the book repeatedly uses the word "nigger" and damages the self-esteem of black youth. Removed from the required reading list of the Terrebone Parish public schools in Houma, La. (1991) because of the repeated use of the word "nigger." Temporarily pulled from the Portage, Mich. classrooms (1991) after some black parents complained that their children were uncomfortable with the book's portrayal of blacks. Challenged in the Kinston, N.C. Middle School (1992) when the superintendent told the novel could not be assigned because the students were too young to read the book because of its use of the word "nigger." Challenged at the Modesto, Calif. High School as a required reading (1992) because of "offensive and racist language." The word "nigger" appears in the book. Challenged at the Carlisle, Pa. area schools (1993) because the book's racial slurs are offensive to both black and white students. Challenged, but retained on high school reading lists by the Lewisville, Tex. school board (1994). Challenged in English classes at Taylor County High School in Butler, Ga. (1994) because it contains racial slurs and bad grammar and does not reject slavery. The book will be taught in the tenth rather than the ninth grade. Challenged at the Santa Cruz, Calif. Schools (1995) because of its racial themes. Removed from the curriculum of the National Cathedral School in Washington, D.C. (1995) because of the novel's content and language. Removed from the eighth grade curriculum at a New Haven, Conn. middle school (1995) because parents complained it undermined the self-esteem of black youth. Removed from the required reading lists in East San Jose, Calif. high schools (1995) in response to objections raised by African-American parents. They said the book's use of racial epithets, including frequent use of the word "nigger," erodes their children's self-esteem and affects their performance in school. Challenged in the Kenosha, Wis. Unified School District (1995). The complaint was filed by the local NAACP which cited the book as offensive to African-American students. Challenged as required reading in an honors English class at the McClintock High School in Tempe, Ariz. (1996). Demonstrators called for the ouster of the principal. In May 1996, class-action lawsuit was filed in U.S. District Court in Phoenix, alleging that the district has deprived minority students of educational opportunities by requiring them to read racially offensive literature or allowing them to go the library if they objected. Dropped from the mandatory required reading list at the Upper Dublin, Pa. schools (1996) because of its allegedly insensitive and offensive language. Banned from the Lindale, Tex. advanced placement English reading list (1996) because the book "conflicted with the values of the community." Challenged for being on the approved reading list in the Federal Way, Wash. schools (1996) because it "perpetuates hate and racism." Challenged as required reading at the Cherry Hill, Pa. High Schools (1996) because of language. Source: 1, pp. 86-87; 3, pp. 49-50; 4; 7, May 1969, p. 52; July 1976, p. 87; Sept. 1976, p. 116; Nov. 1981, p. 162; Jan. 1982, pp. 11, 18; May 1982, p. 101; July 1982, p. 126; Sept. 1982, p. 171; Jan. 1984, p. 11; Jan. 1984, p. 11; May 1984, p. 72; July 1984, pp. 121-22; Nov. 1984, p. 187; 7, Sept. 1988, pp. 152-53; Nov. 1988, p. 201; Jan. 1989, p. 11; Mar. 1989, p. 43; May 1989, p. 94; Jan. 1991, pp. 17-18; Mar. 1991, pp. 44-45; May 1991, pp. 90-92; Mar. 1992 pp. 43, 64; July 1992, p. 126; Sept. 1992, p. 140; May 1993, p. 73; May 1994, pp. 99-100; Mar. 1995, p. 42; May 1995, pp. 68, 69, 83; July 1995, pp. 96-97; Jan. 1996, p. 13; Mar. 1996, pp. 64-65; May 1996, p. 98; July 1996, p. 120; Sept. 1996, p. 153; Nov. 1996, pp. 198-99; Jan. 1997, p. 12; 9, Vol. II, p. 617; Mar. 1997, p. 40.

1190

_____. *The Adventures of Tom Sawyer.* Airmont; And/Or Press; Bantam; Grosset; Longman; NAL; Pocket Bks. Excluded from the children's room in the Brooklyn, N.Y. Public Library (1876) and the Denver, Colo. Public Library (1876). Confiscated at the USSR border (1930). Removed from London, United Kingdom school libraries by education officials (1985) who found it "racist" and "sexist." Challenged in the Plano, Tex. Independent School District (1990) because the novel is racist. Retained in the O'Fallon, Ill. schools (1992), but parents will be able to request that their children not be required to read the book. A parent had sought the book's removal charging that its use of the word "nigger" is degrading and offensive to black students. Removed from the seventh grade curriculum in the West Chester, Pa. schools (1994) after parents complained that it is too full of racially charged language. Source: 3, pp. 49-50; 7, Sept. 1985, p. 156; Jan. 1991, p. 18; Mar. 1991, pp. 45-46; May 1991, p. 92; May 1992, p. 97; Sept. 1994, p. 152.

1191

_____. *Eve's Diary.* Arden Lib. Removed from circulation at the Charlton Library in Worcester, Mass. (1906) because the "Edenic costumes" worn by Eve in the book's fifty illustrations had created an inordinate demand for it among the library's patrons. Source: 9, Vol. II, p. 626.

1192

Understanding Health. Random. Challenged in Jefferson County, Ky. (1983) because it contains a chapter on sex education which includes slang sexual terminology. Source: 7, Nov. 1983, p. 186.

1193

Ungerer, Tomi. *Beast of Monsieur Racine.* Farrar. Challenged at the Rogers-Hough, Ark. Memorial Library (1989) because the book is violent. Source: 7, Sept. 1991, 151.

1194

_____. *Zeralda's Ogre.* Harper; Penguin. Removed from the Cascades Elementary School in Lebanon, Oreg. (1989) because the book had frightening illustrations. Source: 7, Jan. 1990, pp. 4-5.

1195

Updike, John. *Rabbit is Rich.* Knopf. Removed from the library at Sun Valley High School in Aston, Pa. (1996) because it contains "offensive language and explicit sexual scenes." The novel won the Pulitzer Prize for fiction in 1982. Source: 7, May 1996, pp. 83-84.

1196

_____. *Rabbit Run.* Fawcett. Restricted to high school students with parental permission in the six Aroostock County, Maine community high school libraries (1976) because of passages in the book dealing with sex and an extramarital affair. Removed from the required reading list for English class at the Medicine Bow, Wyo. Junior High School (1986) because of sexual references and profanity in the book. Source: 7, Mar. 1977, p. 36; Mar. 1987, p. 55.

1197

Valentine, Johnny. *The Daddy Machine.* Alyson Pubns. Challenged in the Wicomico County Free Library in Salisbury, Md. (1993) along with three other books on homosexuality intended for juvenile readers. Source: 7, Jan. 1994, p. 35.

1198

_____. *The Duke Who Outlawed Jelly Beans.* Alyson Pubns. Moved from the children's section to the adult section at the Elizabethtown, N.C. library (1993). Challenged in the Wicomico County Free Library in Salisbury, Md.

(1993) along with three other books on homosexuality intended for juvenile readers. Retained at the Dayton and Montgomery County, Ohio Public Library (1993). Source: 7, May 1993, p. 71; July 1993, pp. 100-101; Jan. 1994, p. 35; Mar. 1994, p. 69.

1199
Van Devanter, Lynda, and Morgan, Christopher. *Home before Morning.* Warner. Challenged at the Esperanza Middle School library in Lexington, Md. (1988) because the book's "liberal use of profanity and explicit portrayals of situations." Source: 7, Nov. 1988, p. 201.

1200
Van Lustbader, Eric. *White Ninja.* Fawcett. Challenged at the Prince William County, Va. Library (1995) because of passages that describe the vicious rape and flaying of a young woman. Source: 7, Jan. 1996, p. 12; Nov. 1996, pp. 194, 211; Jan. 1997, p. 26.

1201
Van Slyke, Helen. *Public Smiles, Private Tears.* Bantam; Thorndike. Challenged at the Public Libraries of Saginaw, Mich. (1989) because the book is "pornographic" with no redeeming value. Source: 7, May 1989, p. 77.

1202
Van Vooren, Monique. *Night Sanctuary.* Summit. Challenged at the White County Library in Searcy, Ark. (1983) by a local parent, a minister and a group called the Institute for American Ideals. Source: 7, Nov. 1983, p. 185; Jan. 1984, p. 25.

1203
Vasilissa the Beautiful: Russian Fairy Tales. Progress Pubns. Challenged at the Mena, Ark. schools (1990) because the book contains "violence, voodoo, and cannibalism." Source: 7, July 1990, p. 147.

1204
Vidal, Gore. *Live from Golgotha.* Random. Challenged at the Carrollton, Tex. Public Library (1992) because the book is "offensive and pornographic." Source: 7, Mar. 1993, p. 42.

1205
Vinge, Joan D. *Catspaw.* Warner. Restricted to Mediapolis, Iowa junior high students (1995) with parental consent because it was "unredeeming and destructive" as well as "morally decadent." Source: 7, May 1994, p. 83; July 1995, p. 109.

1206
Voigt, Cynthia. *Homecoming.* Fawcett; Macmillan. Challenged at the Lynchburg, Va. middle and high school Eng-

lish classes (1992) because it presents readers with negative role models and values. Source: 7, Sept. 1992, p. 164.

1207
Voltaire, Francois M. [Francois-Marie Arouet]. *Candide.* Bantam; Holt. Seized by U. S. Customs in Boston, Mass. (1929) and declared as obscene; suppressed in the USSR (1935). Voltaire's best-known work remained anathema to American authorities as late as 1944 when Concord Books, issuing a sale catalog that included the book, was informed by the Post Office that such a listing violated U.S. postal regulations on sending obscene matter through the mails. Source: 1, p. 137; 2, p. 354; 3, p. 27; 9, Vol. III, pp. 418-19.

1208
Vonnegut, Kurt, Jr. *Breakfast of Champions.* Dell. Challenged in the Monmouth, Ill. School District Library (1995) because it is "pornographic trash." Source: 7, Mar. 1996, p. 45.

1209
_____. *Cat's Cradle.* Delacorte; Dell. The Strongsville, Ohio School Board (1972) voted to withdraw this title from the school library; this action was overturned in 1976 by a U.S. District Court in *Minarcini v. Strongsville City School District,* 541 F. 2d 577 (6th Cir. 1976). Challenged at the Merrimack, N.H. High School (1982). Source: 3, p. 95; 7, Sept. 1982, p. 170; 8, pp. 145-48.

1210
_____. *God Bless You, Mr. Rosewater.* Delacorte; Dell. The Strongsville, Ohio School Board (1972) voted to withdraw this title from the school library; this action was overturned in 1976 by a U.S. District Court. Source: 3, p. 95; 4.

1211
_____. *Slaughterhouse-Five.* Dell; Dial. Challenged in many communities, but burned in Drake, N.Dak. (1973). Banned in Rochester, Mich. because the novel "contains and makes references to religious matters" and thus fell within the ban of the establishment clause. An appellate court upheld its usage in the school in *Todd v. Rochester Community Schools,* 41 Mich. App. 320, 200 N. W. 2d 90 (1972). Banned in Levittown, N.Y. (1975), North Jackson, Ohio (1979), and Lakeland, Fla. (1982) because of the "book's explicit sexual scenes, violence, and obscene language." Barred from purchase at the Washington Park High School in Racine, Wis. (1984) by the district administrative assistant for instructional services. Challenged at the Owensboro, Ky. High School library (1985) because of "foul language, a section depicting a picture of an act of bestiality, a reference to 'Magic Fingers' attached to the protagonist's bed to help him

sleep, and the sentence: 'The gun made a ripping sound like the opening of the fly of God Almighty.'" Restricted to students who have parental permission at the four Racine, Wis. Unified District high school libraries (1986) because of "language used in the book, depictions of torture, ethnic slurs, and negative portrayals of women." Challenged at the LaRue County, Ky. High School library (1987) because "the book contains foul language and promotes deviant sexual behavior." Banned from the Fitzgerald, Ga. schools (1987) because it was "filled with profanity and full of explicit sexual references." Challenged in the Baton Rouge, La. public high school libraries (1988) because the book is "vulgar and offensive." Challenged in the Monroe, Mich. public schools (1989) as required reading in a modern novel course for high school juniors and senior because of the book's language and to the way women are portrayed. Retained on the Round Rock, Tex. Independent High School reading list (1996) after a challenge that the book was too violent. Source: 7, Jan. 1974, p. 4; May 1980,p. 51; Sept. 1982, p. 155; Nov. 1982, p. 197; Sept. 1984, p. 158; Jan. 1986, pp. 9-10; Mar. 1986, p. 57; Mar. 1987, p. 51; July 1987, p. 147; Sept. 1987, pp. 174-75; Nov. 1987, p. 224; May 1988, p. 86; July 1988, pp. 139-40; July 1989, p. 144, May 1996, p. 99; 8, pp. 78-79.

1212

_____. *Welcome to the Monkey House.* Delacorte; Dell. A teacher was dismissed for assigning this title to her eleventh grade English class because the book promoted "the killing off of elderly people and free sex." The teacher brought suit and won in *Parducci v. Rutland,* 316 F. Supp. 352, (M. D. Ala 1970). Pulled from the high school classes in Bloomington, Minn. (1977). Source: 8, pp. 126-27, 238; 5, July 1977, p. 101.

1213

Wagner, Jane. *J. T.* Dell. Removed from classroom use in Raleigh, N.C. (1981) due to book's racial stereotyping, but later reinstated by an ad hoc review committee. Source: 7, Nov. 1981, p. 170.

1214

Walker, Alice. *The Color Purple.* Harcourt. Challenged as an appropriate reading for Oakland, Calif. High School honors class (1984) due to the work's "sexual and social explicitness" and its "troubling ideas about race relations, man's relation-

Kurt Vonnegut, Jr.   (original photo by Jill Krementz)

ship to God, African history, and human sexuality." After nine months of haggling and delays, a divided Oakland Board of Education gave formal approval for the book's use. Rejected for purchase by the Hayward, Calif. school trustees (1985) because of "rough language" and "explicit sex scenes." Removed from the open shelves of the Newport News, Va. school library (1986) because of its "profanity and sexual references" and placed in a special section accessible only to students over the age of 18 or who have written permission from a parent. Challenged at the public libraries of Saginaw, Mich. (1989) because it was "too sexually graphic for a 12-year-old." Challenged as a summer youth program reading assignment in Chattanooga, Tenn. (1989) because of its language and "explicitness." Challenged as an optional reading assignment in the Ten Sleep, Wyo. schools (1990). Challenged as a reading assignment at the New Bern, N.C. High School (1992) because the main character is raped by her stepfather. Banned in the Souderton, Pa. Area School District (1992) as appropriate reading for tenth graders because it is "smut." Challenged on the curricular reading list at Pomperaug High School in Southbury, Conn. (1995) because sexually explicit passages aren't appropriate high school reading. Retained as an English course reading assignment in the Junction City, Oreg. high school (1995) after a challenge to Walker's Pulitzer Prize-winning novel caused months of controversy. Although an alternative assignment was available, the book was challenged due to "inappropriate language, graphic sexual scenes, and book's negative image of black men." Challenged at the St. Johns County Schools in St. Augustine, Fla. (1995). Retained on the Round Rock, Tex. Independent High School reading list (1996) after a challenge that the book was too violent. Challenged as part of the reading list for Advanced English classes at Northwest High School in High Point, N.C. (1996) because the book is "sexually graphic and violent." Source: 7, July 1984, p. 103; Sept. 1984, p. 156; Mar. 1985, p. 42; May 1985, pp. 75, 91; July 1985, p. 111; Nov. 1986, p. 209; May 1989, p. 77; Sept. 1989, p. 162; May 1990, p. 88; Sept. 1992, p. 142; Mar. 1993, p. 44; May 1993, p. 74.; July 1995, p. 98; Sept. 1995, pp. 135, 160-61; Jan. 1996, p. 14; May 1996, p. 99; Mar. 1997, p. 50.

1215

_____. *Warrior Marks.* Harcourt. Former Weslaco, Tex. (1995) librarian filed a federal lawsuit charging that she was fired for publicly discussing that city's efforts to ban Walker's work from the library. Source: 7, Sept. 1995, p. 153.

1216
Walker, Barbara G. *The Woman's Encyclopedia of Myths and Secrets.* Harper. Restricted to non-required assignments at the North Bend, Oreg. (1988) High School library because the book "is of no benefit to anyone." Source: 7, Jan. 1990, pp. 4-5.

1217
Walker, Margaret. *Jubilee.* Houghton; Bantam. Challenged in the Greenville, S.C. County school libraries (1977) by the Titan of the Fourth Province of the Knights of the Ku Klux Klan because the novel produces "racial strife and hatred." Source: 7, May 1977, p. 73.

1218
Wallace, Daisy, ed. *Witch Poems.* Holiday. Challenged at the Bozeman, Mont. elementary school libraries (1993) because it scared a kindergartner. Source: 7, Sept. 1993, p. 158.

1219
Wallace, Irving. *The Fan Club.* Bantam. The twenty-six branch librarians of Riverside County, Calif. (1974) were advised that the book was not selected for circulation, and patrons should be told the county selection committee could not in good conscience spend tax money on it; further, that it was not their policy to purchase "formula-written commercial fiction." In Oct. 1982, Malaysian police confiscated the works of Wallace because the books were considered "prejudicial to the public interest." Destroyed in Beijing, China (1988) and legal authorities threatened to bring criminal charges against the publishers. Source: 3, p. 91; 4, Jan. 1983, p. 45; 7, Jan. 1989, p. 15.

1220
Wambaugh, Joseph. *The Black Marble.* Dell. Banned from the Stroudsburg, Pa. High School library (1985) because it was "blatantly graphic, pornographic and wholly unacceptable for a high school library." Source: 7, May 1985, p. 79.

1221
_____. *The Delta Star.* Bantam; Morrow. Banned from the Stroudsburg, Pa. High School library (1985) because it was "blatantly graphic, pornographic and wholly unacceptable for a high school library." Source: 7, May 1985, p. 79.

1222
_____. *The Glitter Dome.* Bantam. Banned from the Stroudsburg, Pa. High School library (1985) because it was "blatantly graphic, pornographic and wholly unacceptable for a high school library." Source: 7, May 1985, 79.

1223
_____. *The New Centurions.* Dell; Little. Banned from the Stroudsburg, Pa. High School library (1985) because it was "blatantly graphic, pornographic and wholly unacceptable for a high school library." Source: 7, May 1985, p. 79.

1224
Warren, Patricia Nell. *The Front Runner.* Bantam. Challenged at the Three Rivers, Mich. Public Library (1982) because it "promotes homosexuality and perversion." Source: 7, Mar. 1983, p. 29.

1225
Warren, Robert Penn. *All the King's Men.* Harcourt; Random. Challenged at the Dallas, Tex. Independent School District high school libraries (1974). Source: 7, Jan. 1975, pp. 6-7.

1226
Watson, Jane Werner and Chambers, Sol. *The Golden Book of the Mysterious.* Golden. Challenged at the Winchester, Md. Elementary School (1988) because of the book's reference to witchcraft, sorcery and spells, fortune-telling, reincarnation, werewolves, vampires, and ghosts. Source: 7, July 1988, p. 120; Sept. 1988, p. 178.

1227
Waxman, Stephanie. *What Is a Girl? What Is a Boy?* Peace Pr. After the Minnesota Civil Liberties Union sued the Elk River, Minn. School Board (1983), the board reversed its decision to restrict this title to students who have written permission from their parents. Challenged at the Blue Mountain schools in Wells River, Vt. (1991). Placed in a special nonfiction section where an adult must request it for a child at the Lake Lanier Regional Library in Lawrenceville, Ga. (1994) after a group of parents complained that the book is not appropriate for young children. Moved to the nonfiction section of the Gwinnet-Forsyth, Ga. (1994) Regional Library. Source: 7, Sept. 1982, pp. 155-56; May 1983, p. 71; Sept. 1983, p. 153; Sept. 1991, p. 178; Nov. 1994, p. 187; Jan. 1995, p. 6.

1228
We the People–History of the U.S. D.C. Heath. Removed from the Mississippi state-approved textbook list (1981). Source: 7, July 1981, p. 93.

1229
Webb, James. *Fields of Fire.* Bantam. Challenged at the Fort Mill, S.C. High School (1988) because the book contains "offensive language and explicit sex scenes." School officials

decided to retain the novel, but to explore the possibility of setting up a "restricted" shelf for "controversial" books. Source: 7, July, 1988, p. 122; Sept. 1988, pp. 178-79.

1230
Welch, James. *Winter in the Blood.* Harper. Retained on the Round Rock, Tex. Independent High School reading list (1996) after a challenge that the book was too violent. Source: 7, May 1996, p. 99.

1231
Wells, Rosemary. *Shy Charles.* Dial. Challenged because the mother allegedly is portrayed too negatively, but retained at the Multnomah, Oreg. County Library (1991). Source: 7, Jan. 1992, p. 6.

1232
Wentworth, Harold, and Flexner, Stuart B. *Dictionary of American Slang.* Crowell. Returned to the publisher after a parent complained to the Stuart, Fla. Middle School (1979); removed from the Westminster, Colo. elementary and secondary school libraries (1981). Source: 7, July 1979, p. 75; Mar. 1982, pp. 42-43.

1233
Wertenbaker, Lael Tucker. *The World of Picasso.* Time-Life. Retained at Maldonado Elementary School in Tucson, Ariz. (1994) after being challenged by parents who objected to nudity and "pornographic," "perverted," and "morbid" themes. Source: 7, July 1994, p. 112.

1234
Westheimer, David. *Von Ryan's Express.* Doubleday; NAL. Challenged at the North Suburban District Library in Loves Park, Ill. (1977) because the novel contains "vulgar sexual expressions, profanity, and a discussion of a scene of gross immorality." Source: 7, July 1977, p. 99.

1235
Wharton, William. *Birdy.* Knopf; Penguin. Banned, but later returned to the shelves of the Mary E. Taylor Middle School in Camden, Maine (1988). The book was originally removed because it contained ten phrases and sentences which contained sexual material and "offensive" language. Source: 7, Jan. 1988, pp. 8, 28.

1236
White, Edmund, and Mars-Jones, Adam. *The Darker Proof: Stories from a Crisis.* NAL. Challenged at the Deschutes County Library in Bend, Oreg. (1993) because it "encourages and condones" homosexuality. Source: 7, Sept. 1993, pp. 158-59.

1237
White, Ellen Emerson. *Long Live the Queen.* Scholastic. Challenged in the Mount Vernon, Wash. school libraries (1991) because it contained a word they found objectionable. Source: 7, Mar. 1992, p. 41.

1238
White, Ryan and Cunningham, Ann Marie. *Ryan White: My Own Story.* Dial. Removed from the curriculum, but placed on library shelves, with restricted access, at the Stroudsburg, Pa. middle school (1996) because a section "uses a gutter term for sodomy and another approves of teen smoking." Source: 7, Mar. 1997, p. 37.

1239
Whitlock, Katherine. *Bridge of Respect: Creating Support for Lesbian and Gay Youth.* American Friends Service Committee. Challenged at the Muscatine, Iowa Public Library (1990) because it is "wrong to promote immorality." Source: 7, Nov. 1990, p. 225.

1240
Whitman, Walt. *Leaves of Grass.* Adler; Doubleday; Holt; Norton; Penguin. The District Attorney in Boston, Mass. (1881) threatened criminal prosecution unless the volume was expurgated. The book was withdrawn in Boston. Source: 1, p. 38; 3, p. 45; 9, Vol. I, p. 562, II, p. 610.

1241
Wiebe, Rudy. *The Story Makers.* Gage; Macmillan. Removed from the Halton County, Ontario School District (1984) because the short story anthology contains "The Sins of Jesus," by Isaac Babel. According to the complainants some Christians consider the story "blasphemous because the Lord Jesus appears as a slightly confused comic character who in the end seems to accept that he has made a mistake." Source: 7, Nov. 1984, p. 188.

1242
Wieler, Diane. *Bad Boy.* Delacorte. Challenged at the State College, Pa. area middle school libraries (1996). Three parents requested the book's removal, charging that it was full of profanity and portrayed underage drinking and other problems. In addition, the portrayal of the homosexual relationship between two secondary characters "conveys a wrong message." Source: 7, Nov. 1996, p. 211; Jan. 1997, p. 9.

1243
Wilde, Oscar. *The Happy Prince and Other Stories.* Penguin. Challenged at the Springfield, Oreg. Public Library (1988) because the stories were "distressing and morbid." Source: 7, Jan. 1989, p. 3.

1244

_____. *Salome.* Collins. Lord Chamberlain withheld the play license on the grounds that it introduced biblical characters (1892); book banned in Boston, Mass. (1895). Source: 3, p. 55.

1245

Wilder, Laura Ingalls. *Little House in the Big Woods.* Buccaneer; Harper; Transaction. Removed from the classrooms, but later reinstated, for third-graders at the Lincoln Unified School District in Stockton, Calif. (1996). Complainants also want the book removed from the library because it "promotes racial epithets and is fueling the fire of racism." Source: 7, Jan. 1997, p. 9; Mar. 1997, p. 50.

1246

_____. *Little House on the Prairie.* Buccaneer; Harper; Transaction. Challenged at the Lafourche Parish elementary school libraries in Thibodaux, La. (1993) because the book is "offensive to Indians." Banned in the Sturgis, S.Dak. elementary school classrooms (1993) due to statements considered derogatory to Native Americans. Source: 7, July 1993, pp. 124-25; Mar. 1994, p. 55,

1247

Willhoite, Michael. *Daddy's Roommate.* Alyson Pubns. Removed from the Brooklyn, N.Y. School District's curriculum (1992) because the school board objected to words that were "age inappropriate." Challenged at the Timberland Regional Libraries in Olympia, Wash. (1992) because the book promotes homosexuality and is offensive. Challenged at the Roswell, N.Mex. Public Library (1992) and the Dauphin County, Pa. Library System (1992) because the book's intent "is indoctrination into a gay lifestyle." Challenged at the Wayne County Public Library in Goldsboro, N.C. (1992), Grand Prairie, Tex. Memorial Library (1992), Fayetteville, N.C. (1992) and Tillamook, Oreg. (1992) because it "promotes a dangerous and ungodly lifestyle from which children must be protected." Restricted to adults at the Lake Lanier Regional Library System in Gwinnett County, Ga. (1992). Moved from the children's section to the adult section at the Manatee, Fla.

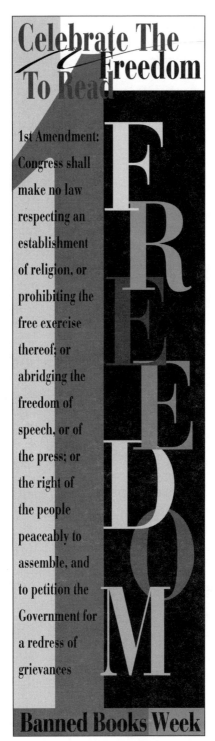

Celebrate The Freedom To Read

1st Amendment: Congress shall make no law respecting an establishment of religion, or prohibiting the free exercise thereof; or abridging the freedom of speech, or of the press; or the right of the people peaceably to assemble, and to petition the Government for a redress of grievances

FREEDOM

Banned Books Week

Public Library (1993) and the Elizabethtown, N.C. library (1993). Challenged as a reading in the Rosemount-Apple Valley-Eden, Minn. School District (1993). Moved from the children's section to the adult section of the Mercer County Library System in Lawrence, N.J. (1993). Challenged at the Alachua County Library in High Springs, Fla. (1993), Seekonk, Mass. library (1993), the North Brunswick, N.J. Public Library (1993), the Cumberland County Public, N.C. Library (1993), Chattanooga-Hamilton County, Tenn. Bicentennial Library (1993), Wicomico County Free Library in Salisbury, Md. (1993), Sussex, Wis. Public Library (1993) and Juneau, Alaska school libraries (1993). Challenged at the Mesa, Ariz. Public Library (1993) because it "is vile, sick and goes against every law and constitution." Retained at the Dayton and Montgomery County, Ohio Public Library (1993). Removed by Lane County Head Start officials in Cottage Grove, Oreg. (1994) from its anti-bias curriculum. Challenged at the Chandler, Ariz. Public Library (1994) because the book is a "skillful presentation to the young child about lesbianism/homosexuality." Removed from the children's section of the Fort Worth, Tex. Public Library (1994) because critics say it legitimizes gay relationships. Source: 7, May 1992, p. 83, p. 95; Sept. 1992, p. 162; Nov. 1992, pp. 197-99; Jan. 1993, pp. 7, 9, 10, 28; May 1993, pp. 69-71; July 1993, pp. 101, 106-107, 123-26; Sept. 1993, pp. 143-46; Nov. 1993, p. 179; Jan. 1994, pp. 13, 34-36; Mar. 1994, p. 69; July 1994, p. 115; Sept. 1994, pp. 147-48, 166; Nov. 1994, p. 187; Jan. 1995, pp. 4, 6, 8; Sept. 1995, p. 159.

1248

Williams, Chancellor. *The Destruction of African Civilization and The Origin of African Civilization.* Third World. Challenged at the Prince George County, Md. high school libraries (1993) because the two volumes promote "racism against white people." In a complaint filed with the state, the works were called "racist pornography" written "to provoke emotions and actions of racial prejudice, bias, hatred and hostility towards citizens and students in Maryland." Source: 7, Nov. 1993, p. 177.

1249
Williams, Garth. *The Rabbit's Wedding*. Harper. Removed from the "open" shelves to the "reserved" shelves at the Montgomery, Ala. Public Library (1959) because an illustration of the lapin couple, the buck was black while the doe was white. Such miscegenation, stated an editor in Orlando, Fla., was "brainwashing… as soon as you pick up the book and open its pages you realize these rabbits are integrated." The Home News of Montgomery, Ala., added that the book was integrationist propaganda obviously aimed at children in their formative years. Source: 2, p. 250.

1250
Williams, Jaston; Sears, Joe; and Howard, Eds. *Greater Tuna*. Samuel French. Challenged at the Grayslake, Ill. Community High School (1991). Source: 7, July 1991, pp. 129-30.

1251
Williams, Jay. *The Magic Grandfather*. Macmillan. Challenged at the Little Butte Intermediate School in Eagle Point, Oreg. (1989) because the book used swear words, and deals with magic and witches. Source: 7, Jan 1990, pp. 4-5.

1252
Willingham, Calder. *End as a Man*. Vanguard. New York Society for Suppression of Vice sought a ban (1947); seized in Philadelphia raid (1948). Source: 3, p. 96.

1253
Wilson, August. *Fences*. NAL. Challenged in the honors and academic English classes in Carlisle, Pa. schools (1993) because it is "demeaning to women." Teachers must send parents a letter warning about the work's content and explaining that their children may read alternate selections. Source: 7, July 1993, p. 127.

1254
Wilson, Colin. *The Sex Diary of Gerard Orme*. Dial; Pocket Bks. A bookseller in New Britain, Conn. (1964) was arrested for selling this title. Source: 3, p. 99.

1255
_____. *Witches*. A & W Pub. Challenged at the Albany, Oreg. Library (1986) because the book "is satanic in nature, thereby having tremendous drawing power to the curious and unsuspecting." Source: 7, July 1986, p. 136.

1256
Wilson, Edmund. *Memoirs of Hecate County*. Godine; Octagon. Confiscated by the New York City police from four Doubleday bookshops after the New York Society for Suppression of Vice charged that it was salacious and lascivious (1946); banned from the U.S. mail (1956). Source: 3, pp. 76-77; 9, Vol. IV, pp. 697-99.

1257
Winship, Elizabeth; Caparulo, Frank; and Harlin, Vivian K. *Human Sexuality*. Houghton. Challenged in the Fulton County, Ga. schools (1992) because the "book is a 'how-to' book. It's not only explicit, but it promotes promiscuity in a subtle way that the determined abstainer would have second thoughts about their position." The group alleged that the text "undermines parents' authority, encourages breaking the law, and tears down normal sexual barriers by co-ed, hardcore, adult subject matter covered." Removed from use in health classes by the Belleville, Mo. School District School Board (1994) after parents had complained that the book "didn't stress abstinence from sex by high school students," and because "it didn't say whether sexual relations before marriage, homosexuality, masturbation, or abortion are right or wrong." Banned in the Fulton County, Ga. high schools (1994) because the book was too graphic, out-of-date, and did too little to persuade students not to have sex. Source: 7, May 1992, pp. 82-83; May 1994, p. 87; Sept. 1994, p. 150.

1258
Winship, Elizabeth. *Perspectives on Health: Human Sexuality*. D. C. Heath. Retained by unanimous school board vote, two mothers nevertheless protested by removing their daughters from classes at an Argos, Ind. Community School (1994) using this textbook because they felt it is "too explicit and sends mixed messages about abstinence." They also objected to treatment of abortion and homosexuality. Source: 7, May 1994, p. 99.

1259
Winsor, Kathleen. *Forever Amber*. NAL. Temporary injunction issued against sale of the book in Springfield, Mass. (1946). Attorney General George Rowell cited as due cause for banning the book some seventy references to sexual intercourse; thirty-nine illegitimate pregnancies; seven abortions; ten descriptions of women undressing, dressing or bathing in the presence of men; five references to incest; thirteen references ridiculing marriage; and forty-nine "miscellaneous objectionable passages." Rowell lost his case, and Judge Donahue of the Massachusetts Supreme Court defined the book as "a soporific rather an aphrodisiac… while the novel was conducive to sleep, it was not conducive to a desire to sleep with a member of the opposite sex." Copies burned at British ports and by the public library in Birmingham, England (1946); banned in Ireland (1953). Source: 2, p. 95; 3, p. 93; 9, Vol. IV, pp. 696-98.

1260
Winthrop, Elizabeth. *The Castle in the Attic.* Bantam; Dell; Fawcett; Greenwillow. Challenged at the Medway, Maine schools (1995) because the book uses swear words and deals with sorcery. Source: 7, July 1995, p. 97.

1261
Witt, Mary A., et al. *The Humanities: Cultural Roots and Continuities.* Heath. Banned from classroom use, but returned to the Columbia High School library in Lake City, Fla. (1986) because of "offensive" language. The school board banned two sections of the text that contained modern adaptation of *The Miller's Tale,* by Chaucer and *Lysistrata,* by Aristophanes. In December 1986, four parents filed a lawsuit charging that their children's rights were violated when the textbook was banned from classroom use. On January 30, 1988, the U. S. District Court for the Middle District of Florida ruled that in *Virgil v. School Board of Columbia County* "the school board acted within its broad range of discretion in determining educational suitability" and thus may constitutionally ban a textbook because of sex and vulgarity. Upholding this ruling, the U. S. Court of Appeals for the Fourth Circuit ruled on January 16, 1989 that the school board did not violate students' constitutional rights when it removed the textbook. Source: 7, July 1986, p. 119; Nov. 1986, p. 207; Mar. 1987, p. 51; Nov. 1987, p. 223; May 1988, pp. 81, 98; Sept. 1988, p. 150; Mar. 1989, p. 52.

1262
Wolf, Eric. *Peasant Wars of the Twentieth Century.* Harper. Banned in South Korea (1985). Source: 4, April 1986, pp. 30-33.

1263
Wolfe, Thomas. *Of Time and the River.* Scribner. Four members of the Alabama State Textbook Committee (1983) called for the rejection of Wolfe's work for use in Alabama public schools. Source: 7, Mar. 1983, p. 39.

1264
Wolk, Robert L., and Henley, Arthur. *The Right to Lie.* Wyden. Challenged at the Plymouth-Canton school system in Canton, Mich. (1987) because the book is "a psychological guide to everyday deceit." Source: 7, May 1987, p. 110.

1265
Wood, Audrey. *Elbert's Bad Word.* Harcourt. Challenged in

> ## "To forbid us anything is to make us have a mind for it."
>
> ~ *Michel de Montaigne,*
> *Essays, 1595*

the Columbia County, Ga. school libraries (1992) because Elbert visits a friendly gardener who is a "practicing wizard." Source: 7, Nov. 1992, p. 197.

1266
Wood, Bari. *Amy Girl.* NAL. Removed from the shelves of the Northern Burlington County, N.J. Regional High School library (1988) because of its "descriptions of underage drinking and teenage sex." Source: 7, Mar. 1988, p. 46.

1267
Woodroofe, Patrick. *The Second Earth: The Pentateuch Retold.* Avery Pub. Removed from the Warrenton, Va. Junior High School library (1992) because a single parent complained about its "anti-Christian" ideas and its illustrations. Source: 7, May 1992, pp. 81-82.

1268
Woolley, Persia. *Queen of the Summer Stars.* Pocket Bks. Challenged, but retained at the Case Junior High School Library in Watertown, N.Y. (1995) because although the book contains scenes of sex, kidnapping, rape and incest, the themes of love, loyalty, honor and trust are more obvious to the reader. Source: 7, May 1995, p. 66; July 1995, pp. 109-10.

1269
Worth, Valerie. *Imp and Biscuit: The Fortune of Two Pugs.* Farrar. Challenged at the Mena, Ark. schools (1990) because the book contains "violence, voodoo and cannibalism." Source: 7, July 1990, p. 147.

1270
Wright, Peter. *Spycatcher.* Viking; Penguin. Banned in England (1987) because the author had violated his secrecy oath under the Official Secrets Act. After a two-and-a-half-year battle, the courts determined that three London newspapers could publish excerpts from the former intelligence agent's memoirs. Banned in India (1987). Source: 7, Nov. 1987, p. 229; May 1988, p. 93; Jan. 1989, p. 15.

1271
Wright, Richard. *Black Boy.* Harper. Restricted to students with parental approval at the Island Trees, N. Y. Union Free School District High School library in 1976; restriction lifted after the U.S. Supreme Court ruling on June 25, 1982 in *Board of Education, Island Trees Union Free School District No.*

26 et al. v. Pico et al., 457 U. S. 853 (1982). Challenged in the Lincoln, Nebr. school libraries (1987) because of the novel's "corruptive, obscene nature." Retained on the Round Rock, Tex. Independent High School reading list (1996) after a challenge that the book was too violent. Source: 7, May 1978, p. 57; Nov. 1982, p. 197; Nov. 1987, p. 225; May 1996, p. 99.

1272

_____. *Native Son.* Harper. Challenged in Goffstown, N.H. (1978); Elmwood Park, N.J. (1978) due to "objectionable" language; and North Adams, Mass. (1981) due to the book's "violence, sex, and profanity." Challenged at the Berrien Springs, Mich. High School in classrooms and libraries (1988) because of the novel is "vulgar, profane, and sexually explicit." Retained in the Yakima, Wash. schools (1994) after a five-month dispute over what advanced high school students should read in the classroom. Two parents raised concerns about profanity and images of violence and sexuality in the book and requested that it be removed from the reading list. Challenged as part of the reading list for Advanced English classes at Northwest High School in High Point, N.C. (1996) because the book is "sexually graphic and violent." Source: 7, May 1978, p. 57; July 1978, p. 98; Sept. 1981, p. 125; Nov. 1981, p. 170; Jan. 1989, p. 28; Nov. 1994, pp. 202-3; Mar. 1997, p. 50.

1273

Wyden, Peter, and Wyden, Barbara. *Growing Up Straight: What Every Thoughtful Parent Should Know about Homosexuality.* New American Library; Stein and Day. Challenged at the Deschutes County Library in Bend, Oreg. (1993) because it "encourages and condones" homosexuality. Source: 7, Sept. 1993, pp. 158-59.

1274

Yashima, Taro. *Crow Boy.* Puffin; Viking Child. Challenged by a school board member in the Queens, N.Y. school libraries (1994) because it "denigrate[s] white American culture, 'promotes racial separation, and discourages assimilation.'" The rest of the school board voted to retain the book. Source: 7, July 1994, pp. 110-11; Sept. 1994, p. 166.

1275

Yates, Elizabeth. *Amos Fortune, Free Man.* Dutton; Penguin.

A Note from the Editor

This "List of Books Some People Consider Dangerous" is a compilation of actual or attempted bannings, over the centuries, worldwide. All entries are books published in the English language and emphasis is on recent U.S. incidents involving popular titles. The verification source for each incident is listed.

The compilation is admittedly incomplete because it is impossible to document and record all prohibitions against free speech and expression. In fact, this list is limited to books and therefore does not include prohibitions against magazines, newspapers, films, broadcasts, play performances or exhibits. Moreover, the professional, economic, or emotional consequences of the curtailment of an author's free expression also are not documented.

At the 1986 American Library Association (ALA) Annual Conference, the ALA Intellectual Freedom Committee adopted the following operative definitions of some terms frequently used to describe the various levels of incidents which may or may not lead to censorship. This terminology is employed by the *Newsletter on Intellectual Freedom.*

Expression of Concern	An inquiry that has judgmental overtones
Oral Complaint	An oral challenge to the presence and/or appropriateness of the material in question
Written Complaint	A formal, written complaint filed with the institution (library, school, etc.) challenging the presence and/or appropriateness of specific material
Public Attack	A publicly disseminated statement challenging the value of the material, presented to the media and/or others outside the institutional organization in order to gain public support for further action
Censorship	A change in the access status of material, made by a governing authority or its representatives. Such changes include: exclusion, restriction, removal, or age/grade level changes

Temporarily removed from the classrooms as an optional reading assignment in the Montgomery County, Md. schools (1989) because the 1950 Newbery Award-winning book contained "racist dialogue, fostered stereotypes, and could be degrading to black children who read it." Source: 7, Mar. 1990, p. 62.

1276

Yep, Laurence. *Dragonwings*. Harper. Challenged at the Apollo-Ridge schools in Kittanning, Pa. (1992) because of the frequent use of the word "demon" in the book. The Newbery Award-winning book might encourage children to "commit suicide because they think they can be reincarnated as something or someone else." On Sept. 15, 1992, Judge Joseph Nickleach denied a request seeking to ban the book from the district's curriculum. In his opinion, Nickleach wrote: "The fact that religions and religious concepts are mentioned in school does not automatically constitute a violation of the establishment clause." Source: 7, Sept. 1992, pp. 142-43; Jan. 1993, p. 18.

1277

Young, Lawrence A. *Recreational Drugs*. Macmillan. Challenged in the Alameda County, Calif. Library (1982) because it allegedly encourages drug use. Source: 7, Sept. 1982, p. 169.

1278

Zindel, Paul. *My Darling, My Hamburger*. Bantam; Harper. Removed from the Frazee, Minn. School library (1973); Lyons, N.Y. Elementary School library (1976); and Hiawatha, Iowa Public Library (1979). Challenged in Champaign, Ill. (1980) and Jefferson County, Ky. (1982). Banned in the Dupree, S.Dak. High School English classes (1987) because of what the school board called "offensive language and vulgarity." Source: 7, Nov. 1973, p. 135; July 1976, p. 86; Mar. 1979, p. 27; May 1980, p. 61; Mar. 1983, p. 41; Jan. 1988, p. 12.

1279

_____. *Pigman*. Bantam; Harper. Challenged at the Hillsboro, Mo. School District (1985) because the novel features "liars, cheaters and stealers." Challenged as suitable curriculum material in the Harwinton and Burlington, Conn. schools (1990) because it contains profanity and subject matter that set bad examples and gives students negative views of life. Challenged at the Lynchburg, Va. middle and high school English classes (1992) because the novel contains twenty-nine instances of "destructive, disrespectful, antisocial and illegal behavior…placed in a humorous light, making it seem acceptable." Source: 7, Mar. 1985, p. 44; Mar. 1991, p 44; May 1991, p. 90; Sept. 1992, p. 164.

1280

Zola, Emile. *J'Accuse*. French & European. Listed on the *Index Librorum Prohibitorum* in Rome (1894); banned in Yugoslavia (1929) and in Ireland (1953). Source: 3, pp.51-52.

1281

_____. *Nana*. Airmont; French & European; Penguin. Listed on the *Index Librorum Prohibitorum* in Rome (1894); banned in Yugoslavia (1929) and in Ireland (1953). Source: 3, pp. 51-52.

Notable First Amendment Court Cases

The following are selected notable First Amendment cases:

They are arranged chronologically and involve decisions on a variety of court levels; e.g., United States District Courts, Courts of Appeal and the Supreme Court, as well as state appellate and supreme courts.

The legal citation is included for each case to help locate the actual Court case. For example, the citation— *Texas v. Johnson,* 57 S.Ct. 2533 (1989) — provides the following information: the name of the case, with the party appealing to the Court first, and the other listed second (*Texas v. Johnson*); the volume number (57); the name of the publication (S.Ct. is the abbreviation for the *Supreme Court Reporter*); the page number (2533); and the year the case was decided (1989).

Abbreviations:

U.S.	=	*United States Reports;*
S.Ct.	=	*Supreme Court Reporter;*
L. Ed.	=	*United States Supreme Court Reports Lawyers' Edition;*
L.Ed.2d.	=	*United States Supreme Court Reports Lawyers' Edition, Second Series;*
P.	=	*Pacific Reporter;*
N.Y.S.	=	*New York Supplement;*
N.W.	=	*North Western Reporter;*
F.2d	=	*Federal Reporter Second Series;*
F. Supp.	=	*Federal Supplement.*

Schenck v. United States, 249 U.S. 47, 39 S.Ct. 247, 63 L.Ed.2d. (1919)

Justice Oliver Wendell Holmes formulated his famous "clear and present danger test" for evaluating speech and other forms of expression under the First Amendment in this case. He said, "The question in every case is whether the words are used in such circumstances and are of such a nature as to create a clear and present danger that they will bring about the substantive evils that Congress has the right to prevent. It is a question of proximity and degree." In this case, the Court affirmed convictions for conspiracy to violate the 1917 Espionage Act by attempting to incite insubordination in the armed forces, and interfering with enlistment or recruitment. Defendants, during wartime, distributed a pamphlet that alleged that military conscription was an unconstitutional form of slavery.

Evans v. Shelma Union High School District of Fresno County, 222 P. 801 (Ca. 1924)

The California State Supreme Court decided that the Shelma Union High School District of Fresno County could purchase twelve copies of the Bible in the King James version for the high school library, the court declaring: "The mere act of purchasing a book does not carry with it any implication of adoption of the theory or dogma contained therein, or any approval of the book itself, except as a work of literature fit to be included in a reference library."

Near v. Minnesota, 283 U.S. 697, 51 S.Ct. 625, 75 L.Ed. 1357 (1931)

In this case, the Supreme Court interpreted the First Amendment to protect against prior restraints. "Prior restraints" are "pre-publication" restrictions on the dissemination of information and ideas.

Rosenberg v. Board of Education of City of New York, 92 N.Y.S.2d 344 (1949)

After considering the charge that *Oliver Twist* and the *Merchant of Venice* are "objectionable because they tend to engender hatred of the Jew as a person and as a race," the Supreme Court, Kings County, New York, decided that these two works cannot be banned from the New York City schools, libraries, or classrooms, declaring that the Board of Education "acted in good faith without malice or prejudice and in the best interests of the school system entrusted to their care and control, and, therefore, that no substantial reason exists which compels the suppression of the two books under consideration."

The New York Times v. Sullivan, 376 U.S. 254, 84 S.Ct. 710, 11 L.Ed.2d. 686 (1964)

The Court found that a public official may not recover damages for a defamatory statement, unless the official can prove that the statement was made with "actual malice," i.e., that it was known to be false or was made with reckless disregard for the truth.

Tinker v. Des Moines School District, 393 U.S. 503, 89 S.Ct. 733, 21 L.Ed.2d. 731 (1969)

The Supreme Court held that students "do not shed their constitutional rights at the schoolhouse gate" and that the First Amendment protects public school students' rights to express political and social views. In this case, students had worn black armbands to school in symbolic protest of the Vietnam War.

Brandenburg v. Ohio, 395 U.S. 444 (1969)

The Supreme Court established the modern version of the "clear and present danger" doctrine, holding that states only could restrict speech that "is directed to inciting or producing imminent lawless action, and is likely to incite or produce such action."

New York Times Company v. United States, 403 U.S. 713, 91 S.Ct. 2140, 29 L.Ed.2d. 822 (1971)

In the "Pentagon Papers" case, the U.S. government attempted to enjoin the *New York Times* and the *Washington Post* from publishing classified documents concerning the Vietnam War. Applying the doctrine of prior restraint from *Near v. Minnesota*, the Court found that the claims that publication of the documents would interfere with foreign policy and prolong the war were too speculative, and could not overcome the strong presumption against prior restraints.

Todd v. Rochester Community Schools, 200 N.W.2d 90 (Mich. App. 1972)

In deciding that *Slaughterhouse Five* could not be banned from the libraries and classrooms of the Michigan schools, the Court of Appeals of Michigan declared: "Vonnegut's literary dwellings on war, religion, death, Christ, God, government, politics, and any other subject should be as welcome in the public schools of this state as those of Machiavelli, Chaucer, Shakespeare, Melville, Lenin, Joseph McCarthy, or Walt Disney. The students of Michigan are free to make of *Slaughterhouse-Five* what they will."

Presidents Council, District 25 v. Community School Board No. 25 (New York City), 457 F.2d 289 (2d Cir. 1972); cert. denied, 409 U.S. 998, 93 S.Ct. 308, 34 L.Ed.2d 260 (1972)

This 1972 case was the first to consider whether a school board could remove books from a school library. The U.S. Court of Appeals upheld the school board's action revoking free access by junior high school students to *Down These Mean Streets* by Piri Thomas. Writing for the court, Judge Mulligan stated: "There is here no problem of freedom of speech or the expression of opinions on the part of parents, students or librarians. As we have pointed out, the discussion of the book or the problems which it encompasses or the ideas it espouses have not been prohibited by the board's action in removing the book... . To suggest that the shelving or unshelving of books presents a constitutional issue, particularly where there is no showing a curtailment of freedom of speech or thought, is a proposition we cannot accept."

Miller v. California, 413 U.S. 15, 93 S.Ct. 2607, 37 L.Ed.2d. 419 (1973)

In this case, the U.S. Supreme Court mapped out its famous three-part definition of obscenity. First, the average person, applying contemporary community standards, must find that the work, taken as a whole, appeals to prurient interests;

second, that it depicts or describes, in a patently offensive way, sexual conduct as defined by state law; and third, that the work, taken as a whole, lacks serious literary, artistic, political, or scientific value. The Court ruled that community standards and state statutes that describe sexual depictions to be suppressed could be used to prosecute Miller, who operated one of the largest West Coast mail order businesses dealing in sexually explicit materials.

Gertz v. Robert Welch, Inc., 418 U.S. 323, 94 S.Ct. 2997, 41 L.Ed.2d. 789 (1974)

The Court applied the rule in the *New York Times* case to public figures, finding that persons who have special promi-nence in society by virtue of their fame or notoriety, even if they are not public officials, must prove "actual malice" when alleging libel. Gertz was a prominent lawyer who alleged that a leaflet defamed him.

Minarcini v. Strongsville (Ohio) City School District, 541 F.2d 577 (6th Cir. 1976)

The Strongsville City Board of Education rejected faculty recommendations to purchase Joseph Heller's *Catch-22* and Kurt Vonnegut's *God Bless You, Mr. Rosewater* and ordered the removal of *Catch-22* and Vonnegut's *Cat's Cradle* from the library. The U.S. Court of Appeals for the Sixth Circuit ruled against the School Board, upholding the students' First Amendment right to receive information and the librarian's right to disseminate it. "The removal of books from a school library is a much more serious burden upon the freedom of classroom discussion than the action found unconstitutional in Tinker v. Des Moines School District."

Right to Read Defense Committee v. School Committee of the City of Chelsea, 454 F. Supp. 703 (D. Mass. 1978)

The Chelsea, Mass. School Committee decided to bar from the high school library a poetry anthology, *Male and Female Under 18,* because of the inclusion of an "offen-sive" and "damaging" poem, "The City to a Young Girl," written by a fifteen-year-old girl. Challenged in U.S. Dis-trict Court, Joseph L. Tauro ruled: "The library is 'a mighty resource in the marketplace of ideas.' There a stu-dent can literally explore the unknown, and discover areas of interest and thought not covered by the prescribed cur-riculum. The student who discovers the magic of the library is on the way to a life-long experience of self-edu-cation and enrichment. That student learns that a library is a place to test or expand upon ideas presented to him, in or out of the classroom. The most effective antidote to the poison of mindless orthodoxy is ready access to a broad sweep of ideas and philosophies. There is no danger from such exposure. The danger is mind control. The

committee's ban of the anthology Male and Female is enjoined."

Salvail v. Nashua Board of Education, 469 F. Supp. 1269 (D. N.H. 1979)

MS magazine was removed from a New Hampshire high school library by order of the Nashua School Board. The U.S. District Court decided for the student, teacher, and adult residents who had brought action against the school board, the court concluding: "The court finds and rules that the defendants herein have failed to demonstrate a substan-tial and legitimate government interest sufficient to warrant the removal of *MS* magazine from the Nashua High School library. Their action contravenes the plaintiffs' First Amend-ment rights, and as such it is plainly wrong."

Bicknell v. Vergennes Union High School Board, 475 F. Supp. 615 (D. Vt. 1979), aff'd, 638 F.2d 438 (2d Cir. 1980)

U.S. District Court Judge Albert W. Coffin dismissed a complaint filed by librarian Elizabeth Phillips, protesting the School Board's removal of *The Wanderer* and *Dog Day After-noon.* In finding for the school board, the court declared: "Although the court does not entirely agree with the policies and actions of the defendants we do not find that those poli-cies and actions directly or sharply infringe upon the basic constitutional rights of the students of Vergennes Union High School… neither the board's failure to purchase a work nor its decision to remove or restrict access to a work in the school library violate the First Amendment rights of the stu-dent plaintiffs before this court… Nor do we believe that school librarians have an independent First Amendment right to control the collection of the school library under the rubric of academic freedom." This ruling was affirmed by the U.S. Court of Appeals for the Second Circuit.

Loewen v. Turnipseed, 488 F. Supp. 1138 (N.D. Miss. 1980)

When the Mississippi Textbook Purchasing Board refused to approve *Mississippi: Conflict and Change* for use in Mississip-pi public schools, on the grounds that it was too concerned with racial matters and too controversial, the authors filed suit. U.S. District Judge Orma R. Smith ruled that the crite-ria used were not justifiable grounds for rejecting the book. He held that the controversial racial matter was a factor lead-ing to its rejection, and thus the authors had been denied their constitutionally guaranteed rights of freedom of speech and the press.

Zykan v. Warsaw (Indiana) Community School Corporation and Warsaw School Board of Trustees, 631 F.2d 1300 (7th Cir. 1980)

A student brought suit seeking to reverse school officials' decision to "limit or prohibit the use of certain textbooks, to remove a certain book from the school library, and to delete certain courses from the curriculum." The district court dismissed the suit. On appeal, the Court of Appeals for the Seventh Circuit ruled that the school board has the right to establish a curriculum on the basis of its own discretion, but it is forbidden to impose a "pall of orthodoxy." The right of students to file complaints was recognized, but the court held that the students' claims "must cross a relatively high threshold before entering upon the field of a constitutional claim suitable for federal court litigation."

Board of Education, Island Trees Union Free School District No. 26 v. Pico, 457 U.S. 853, 102 S.Ct. 2799, 73 L.Ed.2d 435 (1982)

In 1975, three school board members sought the removal of several books determined objectionable by a politically conservative organization. The following February, the board gave an "unofficial direction" that the books be removed from the school libraries, so that board members could read them. When the board action attracted press attention, the board described the books as "anti-American, anti-Christian, anti-Semitic, and just plain filthy." The nine books that were the subject of the lawsuit were *Slaughterhouse Five* by Kurt Vonnegut, Jr.; *The Naked Ape* by Desmond Morris; *Down These Mean Streets* by Piri Thomas; *Best Short Stories of Negro Writers* edited by Langston Hughes; *Go Ask Alice; Laughing Boy* by Oliver LaFarge; *Black Boy* by Richard Wright; *A Hero Ain't Nothin' But a Sandwich* by Alice Childress; and *Soul on Ice* by Eldrige Cleaver.

The board appointed a review committee that recommended that five of the books be returned to the shelves, two be placed on restricted shelves, and two be removed from the library. The full board voted to remove all but one book.

After years of appeals, the U.S. Supreme Court upheld (5-4) the students' challenge to the board's action. The Court held that school boards do not have unrestricted authority to select library books and that the First Amendment is implicated when books are removed arbitrarily. Justice Brennan declared in the plurality opinion: "Local school boards may not remove books from school library shelves simply because they dislike the ideas contained in those books and seek by their removal to prescribe what shall be orthodox in politics, nationalism, religion or other matters of opinion."

American Booksellers Assoc., Inc. v. Hudnut, 771 F.2d 323 (7th Cir. 1985) (Easterbrook, J.), affd., 475 U.S. 1001 (1986)

The city of Indianapolis passed a statute outlawing pornography, defined as the graphic, sexually explicit subordination of women, presenting women as sex objects, or as enjoying pain, humiliation, or servility. The court of appeals struck the law down, saying it impermissibly established an "approved" view of women and how they react in sexual encounters. The law therefore allowed sexually explicit words and images that adhered to that approved view, but banned sexually explicit words and images that did not adhere to the approved view. The court called this "thought control," saying the "Constitution forbids the state to declare one perspective right and silence opponents."

Mozert v. Hawkins County Board of Education, 827 F.2d 1058 (6th Cir. 1987)

Parents and students brought this action challenging the mandatory use of certain textbooks on the ground that the texts promoted values offensive to their religious beliefs. The U.S. Court of Appeals for the Sixth Circuit rejected the plaintiffs' claim, finding that the Constitution does not require school curricula to be revised substantially in order to accommodate religious beliefs.

Smith v. Board of School Commissioners of Mobile (Ala.) County, 827 F.2d 684 (11th Cir. 1987)

Parents and other citizens brought a lawsuit against the school board, alleging that the school system was teaching the tenets of an anti-religious religion called "secular humanism." The complainants asked that forty-four different elementary through high school level textbooks be removed from the curriculum. After an initial ruling in a federal district court in favor of the plaintiffs, the U.S. Court of Appeals for the Eleventh Circuit ruled that as long as the school was motivated by a secular purpose, it didn't matter whether the curriculum and texts shared ideas held by one or more religious groups. The Court found that the texts in question promoted important secular values (tolerance, self-respect, logical decision making) and thus the use of the textbooks neither unconstitutionally advanced a nontheistic religion nor inhibited theistic religions.

Hazelwood School District v. Kuhlmeier, 484 U.S. 260, 108 S.Ct. 562, 98 L.Ed.2d 592 (1988)

After a school principal removed two pages containing articles, among others, on teenage pregnancy and the impact of divorce on students from a newspaper produced as part of a high school journalism class, the student staff filed suit claiming violation of their First Amendment rights. The principal defended his action on the grounds that he was protecting the privacy of the pregnant students described, protecting younger students from inappropriate references to sexual activity and birth control, and protecting the school from a potential libel action.

The Supreme Court held that the principal acted reasonably and did not violate the students' First Amendment rights. A school need not tolerate student speech, the Court declared, "that is inconsistent with its 'basic educational mission,' even though the government could not censor similar speech outside the school." In addition, the Court found the newspaper was part of the regular journalism curriculum and subject to extensive control by a faculty member. The school, thus, did not create a public forum for the expression of ideas, but instead maintained the newspaper "as supervised learning experience for journalism students." The Court concluded that "educators do not offend the First Amendment by exercising editorial control over the style and content of student speech in school-sponsored expressive activities so long as their actions are reasonably related to legitimate pedagogical concerns." The Court strongly suggested that supervised student activities that "may fairly be characterized as part of the school curriculum," including school-sponsored publications and theatrical productions, were subject to the authority of educators. The Court cautioned, however, that this authority does not justify an educator's attempt "to silence a student's personal expression that happens to occur on the school premises."

Hustler v. Falwell, 485 U.S. 46 (1988)

Hustler magazine published a parody of a liquor advertisement in which Rev. Jerry Falwell described his "first time" as a drunken encounter with his mother in an outhouse. A unanimous Supreme Court held that a public figure had to show *New York Times* actual malice in order to recover for intentional infliction of emotional distress as a result of a parody in a magazine. The Court held that political cartoons and satire such as this parody "have played a prominent role in public and political debate. And although the outrageous caricature in this case "is at best a distant cousin of political cartoons," the Court could see no standard to distinguish among types of parodies that would not harm public discourse, which would be poorer without such satire.

Romano v. Harrington, 725 F. Supp. 687 (D. N.Y. 1989)

The U.S. District Court found in favor of a faculty adviser to a high school newspaper who claimed a violation of the First and Fourteenth Amendments when fired following the newspaper's publication of a student's article opposing the federal holiday for Martin Luther King, Jr. The Court held that educators may exercise greater editorial control over what students write for class than what they voluntarily submit to extracurricular publications.

Virgil v. School Board of Columbia County, 862 F.2d 1517 (11th Cir. 1989)

This case presented the question of whether the First Amendment prevents a school board from removing a previously approved textbook from an elective high school class because of objections to the material's vulgarity and sexual explicitness. The U.S. Circuit Court of Appeals concluded that a school board may, without contravening constitutional limits, take such action when the removal decision was "reasonably related" to the "legitimate pedagogical concern" of denying students access to "potentially sensitive topics." The written "stipulation concerning Board Reasons" cites explicit sexuality and excessively vulgar language in two selections contained in *Volume 1, The Humanities: Cultural Roots and Continuities* as the basis for removal of this textbook. The two selections are Chaucer's *The Miller's Tale* and Aristophanes's *Lysistrata*.

Texas v. Johnson, 491 U.S. 397, 109 S.Ct. 2533, 105 L.Ed.2d 342 (1989)

In this case the Supreme Court held that burning the United States flag was a protected form of symbolic political speech.

Concerned Women for America, Inc. v. Lafayette County, 883 F.2d 32 (5th Cir. 1989)

The County library that had permitted various groups to use its auditorium had created a designated public forum and thus could not deny access to groups whose meetings had political or religious content. Such a denial would be based on the content of speech and would be permissible only as the least restrictive means to serve a compelling interest. Preventing disruption or interference with general use of the library could be such an interest; library officials' first step to controlling such disruptions would be to impose reasonable regulations on the time, place, or manner of the auditorium's use, provided the regulations apply regardless of the subject matter of the speech.

U.S. v. Eichmann and U.S. v. Haggerty, 496 U.S. 310, 110 S.Ct. 2404, 110 L.Ed.2d 287 (1990)

The Supreme Court struck down a federal statute designed to allow the government to punish persons who burn United States flags. The Court held that the plain intent of the statute was to punish persons for political expression and that burning the flag inextricably carries with it a political message.

Simon & Schuster, Inc. v. Members of New York State Crime Victims Board, 502 U.S. 105 (1991)

The Supreme Court struck down New York's "Son of Sam Law," which required book publishers to turn over to the state, any proceeds from a book written by any person convicted of a crime, related to or about that crime. The Court said the law impermissibly singled out income only from the prisoner's expressive activity, and then only expressive activity relating to his crime, without necessarily compensating any victims of those crimes. The Court agreed that many important books—including *The Autobiography of Malcolm X*, Thoreau's *Civil Disobedience*, and works by Martin Luther King—perhaps might not have been published with such a law in place.

R.A.V. v. St. Paul, 112 S.Ct. 2538 (1992)

St. Paul, Minn. passed an ordinance that banned "hate speech," any expression, such as a burning cross or swastika, that might arouse anger, alarm, or resentment in others on the basis of race, color, religion, or gender. The Supreme Court struck the ordinance down as unconstitutionally discriminating based on the content of expression: the law banned only fighting words that insult based on race, religion or gender, while abusive invective aimed at someone on the basis of political affiliation or sexual orientation would be permissible. The law thus reflected only the city's special hostility towards certain biases and not others, which is what the First Amendment forbids.

Kreimer v. Bureau of Police for Morristown, 958 F.2d 1242 (3d Cir. 1992)

In detailed analysis, the court of appeals held that a municipal public library was a limited public forum, meaning open to the public for the specified purposes of exercising their First Amendment rights to read and receive information from library materials. Such exercise could not interfere with or disrupt the library's reasonable rules of operation. The court then upheld three library rules which: 1) required patrons to read, study, or otherwise use library materials while there; 2) prohibited noisy or boisterous activities which might disturb other patrons; and 3) permitted the removal of any patron whose offensive bodily hygiene was a nuisance to other patrons.

Lamb's Chapel v. Center Moriches Union Free School Dist., 508 U.S. 384 (1993)

The Court held that a school district that opened its classrooms after hours to a range of groups for social, civic, and recreational purposes, including films and lectures about a range of issues such as family values and child-rearing, could not deny access to a religious organization to discuss the same, permissible issues from a religious point of view.

Whether or not the classrooms were public fora, the school district could not deny use based on the speaker's point of view on an otherwise permissible topic.

Case v. Unified School District No. 233, 908 F. Supp. 864 (D. Kan. 1995)

When the Olathe, Kansas, School Board voted to remove the book *Annie on My Mind*, a novel depicting a lesbian relationship between two teenagers, from the district's junior and senior high school libraries, the federal district court in Kansas found they violated the students' rights under the First Amendment to the United States Constitution and the corresponding provisions of the Kansas State Constitution. Despite the fact that the school board testified that they had removed the book because of "educational unsuitability," which is within their rights under the Pico decision, it became obvious from their testimony that the book was removed because they disapproved of the book's ideology. In addition, it was found that the school board had violated their own materials selection and reconsideration policies, which weighed heavily in the judge's decision.

City of Ladue v. Gilleo, 114 S.Ct. 2038 (1994)

A federal court struck down a local ordinance banning the placement of signs on private property, in a challenge brought by a woman who had posted a sign on her lawn protesting the Persian Gulf War. The Court said lawn signs were a "venerable means of communication that is both unique and important," for which "no adequate substitutes exist."

McIntyre v. Ohio Election Commission, 115 S.Ct. 1511 (1995)

The Supreme Court struck down a state law banning distribution of anonymous campaign literature, emphasizing the long tradition of anonymous and pseudonymous political and literary speech and recognizing the right to exercise First Amendment rights anonymously as an "honorable tradition of advocacy and dissent."

Campbell v. St. Tammany Parish School Board, 64 F.3d 184 (5th Cir. 1995)

Public school district removed the book *Voodoo and Hoodoo*, a discussion of the origins, history, and practices of the voodoo and hoodoo religions that included an outline of some specific practices, from all district library shelves. Parents of several students sued and the district court granted summary judgment in their favor. The court of appeals reversed, finding that there was not enough evidence at that stage to determine that board members had an unconstitutional motivation, such as denying students access to ideas with which board members disagreed; the court remanded the case for a full trial at which all board members could be questioned about their reasons for removing the book. The court observed that "in light of the special role of the school library as a place where students may freely and voluntarily explore diverse topics, the school board's non-curricular decision to remove a book well after it had been placed in the public school libraries evokes the question whether that action might not be an attempt to 'strangle the free mind at its source.'" The court focused on some evidence that school board members had removed the book without having read it or having read only excerpts provided by the Christian Coalition. The parties settled the case before trial, returning the book to the libraries but on specially designated reserve shelves.

Rosenberger v. Rector of the University of Virginia, 115 S.Ct. 2510 (1995)

The Supreme Court held that a public university's refusal to fund a student-run religious newspaper violated free speech. The newspaper in question would have discussed news and events at the university, but from a religious viewpoint; since the school funded other newspapers, it could not deny funds to a religious newspaper. Such restrictions based on the viewpoint of a speaker are improper when the government spends money to fund a diversity of views from a variety of private speakers.

American Civil Liberties Union v. Reno, American Library Association v. United States Department of Justice, 929 F. Supp. 824 (E.D. Pa. 1996)

A three-judge federal panel used strong language to strike down the Communications Decency Act of 1996, which had banned the display, transmission, or sending of "indecent" or patently offensive speech over the Internet or other interactive computer service. In three opinions, the judges used forceful language in holding that the Internet should receive the same level of First Amendment protection as newspapers, books, and other printed material. The judges held the restrictions on "indecent" speech, passed in the name of protecting children from adult material, were overbroad and would impermissibly have the effect of reducing the level of communication on the Internet to what would be appropriate for children. The Supreme Court agreed to hear an appeal of the case in March 1997.

United States v. Thomas, 74 F.3d 701 (6th Cir. 1996)

One of the first major prosecutions for distributing legally obscene material over the Internet. The circuit court upheld the convictions of the operators of an adult BBS in Califor-

nia for distributing obscene material in Tennessee. The court refused to redefine "community" in the 3-prong obscenity test for speech sent by computer and held that the couple could be prosecuted in Tennessee, with its stricter "community standards," even though their computer was in California. The court emphasized that a BBS operator could control where the images were sent.

Denver Area Educational Telecommunications Consortium, Inc. v. FCC, 116 S.Ct. 2374 (1996)

In a decision that produced six opinions, the Supreme Court upheld a federal law permitting cable system operators to ban "indecent" or "patently offensive" speech on leased access channels. The Court also struck down a similar law for non-leased, public access channels, and struck down a law requiring indecent material to be shown on separate, segregated cable channels. The case is significant in that the Court affirmed that protecting children from some speech is a compelling state interest.

Cohen v. San Bernardino Valley College, 92 F.3d 968 (9th Cir. 1996)

Tenured professor of English was disciplined for violating the college's sexual harassment policy against creating a "hostile learning environment" for his in-class use of profanity, and discussions of sex, pornography, obscenity, cannibalism, and other controversial topics in a confrontational, devil's advocate style. The court held the policy unconstitutionally vague as applied to Cohen's in-class speech, calling it a "legalistic ambush." In-class speech did not fall within the policy's core definition of sexual harassment and Cohen, who had used this apparently sound and proper teaching style for year, did not know the policy would be applied to him or his teaching methods.

Finley v. National Endowment for the Arts, 1996 WL636040 (9th Cir. Cal.)

Congress had required that grant decisions by the National Endowment for the Arts (NEA) consider "general standards of decency and respect for the diverse beliefs and values of the American public." The standard was challenged by four artists, known as the "NEA Four." The court of appeals struck down this requirement for two reasons. First, the standard was vague and therefore posed the danger of "arbitrary and discriminatory application" by government officials whose personal beliefs were offended by some art. Second, the provision was an impermissible restriction on the arts, which are "at the core of a democratic society's cultural and political values."

Quotes on the First Amendment

"Freedom of thought and freedom of speech in our great institutions of learning are absolutely necessary ... the moment that either is restricted, liberty begins to wither and die and the career of a nation after that time is downwards."

— John Peter Altgeld

"Intellectual freedom, the essence of equitable library services, promotes no cause, furthers no movements, and favors no viewpoints. It only provides for free access to all expressions of ideas through which any and all sides of a question, cause, or movement may be explored. Toleration is meaningless without tolerance for what some may consider detestable. Librarians cannot justly permit their own preferences to limit their degree of tolerance in collection development, because freedom is indivisible."

Office for Intellectual Freedom, American Library Association. *Intellectual Freedom Manual.* Fourth edition. Chicago: American Library Association, 1992, p. 50.

"To permit every interest group, especially those who claim to be victimized by unfair expression, their own legislative exceptions to the First Amendment so long as as they succeed in obtaining a majority of legislative votes in their favor demonstrates the potentially predatory nature of what defendants seek through this Ordinance and defend in this lawsuit.

"It ought to be remembered by defendants and all others who would support such a legislative initiative that, in terms of altering sociological patterns, much as alteration may be necessary and desirable, free speech, rather than being the enemy, is a long-tested and worthy ally. To deny free speech in order to engineer social change in the name of accomplishing a greater good for one sector of our society erodes the freedoms of all and, as such, threatens tyranny and injustice for those subjected to the rule of such laws. The First Amendment protections presuppose the evil of such tyranny and prevent a finding by this Court upholding the Ordinance."

American Booksellers Association, Inc. et al. v. William H. Hudnut III.
U.S. District Court IP 84-791C at 47 (1984).

"Free speech has been on balance an ally of those seeking change. Governments that want stasis start by restricting speech... .Change in any complex system ultimately depends on the ability of outsiders to challenge accepted views and the reigning institutions. Without a strong guarantee of freedom of speech, there is no effective right to challenge what is."

American Booksellers Association, Inc. et al. v. William H. Hudnut III. (7th Cir. 1985)

"The layman's constitutional view is that what he likes is constitutional and that which he doesn't like is unconstitutional."

Hugo L. Black

"I fear more harm from everybody thinking alike than from some people thinking otherwise."

Charles G. Bolte

"Experience teaches us to be most on our guard to protect liberty when the government's purpose is beneficent. The greatest dangers to liberty lurk in insidious encroachments by men of zeal, well-meaning but without understanding."

United States Supreme Court Justice Louis D. Brandeis, dissenting *Olmstead v. United States,* 277 U.S. 438 (1928).

"Correctly applied, (the clear and present danger test) ... will preserve the right of free speech from suppression by tyrannous majorities and from abuse by irresponsible, fanatical minorities."

United States Supreme Court Justice Louis D. Brandeis.

"Those who won our independence by revolution were not cowards. They did not fear political change. They did not exalt order at the cost of liberty... .If there be time to expose through discussion the falsehood and fallacies, to avert the evil by the processes of education, the remedy to be applied is more speech, not enforce silence."

United States Supreme Court Justice Louis D. Brandeis, *Whitney v. California*

"Debate on public issues should be uninhibited, robust and wide-open and that ... may well include vehement, caustic, and sometimes unpleasantly sharp attacks on government and public officials."

United States Supreme Court Justice William Brennan, *New York Times v. Sullivan,* 376 U.S. 254, 84 S.Ct. 710, 11 L.Ed.2d 686 (1964)

"If there is a bedrock principle underlying the First Amendment, it is that the Government may not prohibit the expression of an idea simply because society finds the idea itself offensive or disagreeable."

United States Supreme Court Justice William Brennan, *Texas v. Johnson*

"Freedom of expression is the matrix, the indispensible condition, of nearly every other form of freedom."

Benjamin Nathan Cardozo, *Palko v. Connecticut,* 302 U.S. 319, 327 (1937)

"Everyone is in favor of free speech. Hardly a day passes without its being extolled, but some people's idea of it is that they are free to say what they like, but if anyone says anything back, that is an outrage."

Winston Churchill

"The fact is that censorship always defeats its own purpose, for it creates, in the end, the kind of society that is incapable of exercising real discretion... . In the long run it will create a generation incapable of appreciating the difference between independence of thought and subservience."

Henry Steel Commager

"Restriction of free thought and free speech is the most dangerous of all subversions. It is the one un-American act that could most easily defeat us."

Supreme Court Justice William O. Douglas, address, Author's Guild, December 3, 1952, on receiving the Lauterbach Award.

"... the ultimate welfare of the single human soul (is) the ultimate test of the vitality of the First Amendment."

United States Supreme Court Justice William O. Douglas, *Gillette v. United States,* 401 U.S. 437 (1971).

"One has the right to freedom of speech whether he talks to one person or to 1,000."

William O. Douglas

"A government that can give liberty in its constitution ought to have the power to protect liberty in its administration."

Frederick Douglass

"It is evident that any restriction of academic freedom acts in such a way to hamper the dissemination of knowledge among the people and thereby impedes national judgment and action."

Albert Einstein

"Don't join the book burners. Don't think you are going to conceal thoughts by concealing evidence that they ever existed."

Dwight D. Eisenhower, speech at Dartmouth College, June 14, 1953.

"The libraries of America are and must ever remain the home of free, inquiring minds. To them, our citizens—of all ages and races, of all creeds and political persuasions—must ever be able to turn with clear confidence that there they can freely seek the whole truth, unwarped by fashion and uncompromised by expediency. For in such whole and healthy knowledge alone are to be found and understood those majestic truths of man's nature and destiny that prove, to each succeeding generation, the validity of freedom."

Dwight D. Eisenhower, letter to the American Library Association's Annual Conference, Los Angeles, 1953.

"Students in school as well as out of schools are 'persons' under our Constitution. They are possessed of fundamental rights which the state must respect.... . It can hardly be argued that either students or teachers shed their constitutional rights to freedom of speech or expression at the schoolhouse gate."

Abe Fortas

"They that can give up essential liberty to obtain a little temporary safety deserve neither liberty nor safety."

Benjamin Franklin, *Historical Review of Pennsylvania,* 1759.

"In the long run of history, the censor and the inquisitor have always lost. The only sure weapon against bad ideas is better ideas. The source of better ideas is wisdom."

Alfred Whitney Griswold, *Essays on Education*

"To prohibit the reading of certain books is to declare the inhabitants to be either fools or slaves."

Claude Adrien Helvetius, *De l'Homme,* Vol. 1, sec. 4.

"We state these propositions neither lightly nor as easy generalizations. We here stake out a lofty claim for the value of books. We do so because we believe that they are good, possessed of enormous variety and usefulness, worthy of cherishing and keeping free. We realize that the application of these propositions may mean the dissemination of ideas and manners of expression that are repugnant to many persons. We do not state these propositions in the comfortable belief that what people read is unimportant. We believe rather that what people read is deeply important; that ideas can be dangerous; but that the suppression of ideas is fatal to a democratic society. Freedom itself is a dangerous way of life, but it is ours."

The Freedom to Read Statement. Concerned about threats to free communication of ideas, more than thirty librarians, publishers, and others conferred at Rye, New York, May 2-3, 1953. A committee was appointed to prepare a statement to be made public. This was endorsed officially by the American Library Association Council on June 25, 1953, and subsequently by the American Book Publishers Council (ABPC), American Booksellers Association, Book Manufacturers' Institute, and other national groups. In the light of later developments, a somewhat revised version was prepared after much consultation, and was approved in 1972 by the ALA Council, Association of American Publishers (successor to ABPC and American Educational Publishers Institute), and subsequently by many other book industry, communications, educational, cultural, and public service organizations.

"We must learn to welcome and not to fear the voices of dissent. We must dare to think about 'unthinkable things' because when things become unthinkable, thinking stops and action becomes mindless."

James William Fulbright

"When there is official censorship it is a sign that speech is serious. When there is none, it is pretty certain that the official spokesmen have all the loudspeakers."

Paul Goodman, *Growing Up Absurd*

"Our Constitution was not intended to be used by ... any group to foist its personal religious beliefs on the rest of us."

Katherine Hepburn

"The best test of truth is the power of the thought to get itself accepted in the competition of the market... . We should be eternally vigilant against attempts to check the expression that we loathe."

Justice Oliver Wendell Holmes, dissenting *Abrams v. United States,* 250 U.S. 616 (1919).

"The vast number of titles which are published each year—all of them are to the good, even if some of them may annoy or even repel us for a time. For none of us would trade freedom of expression and of ideas for the narrowness of the public censor. America is a free market for people who have something to say, and need not fear to say it."

Vice President Hubert Humphrey, as reported by the *New York Times,* March 9, 1967, p. 42. Humphrey addressed the National Book Awards ceremony in New York City, March 8, 1967, where during his speech more than 50 people walked out to protest the U.S. role in Vietnam.

"The right to be heard does not automatically include the right to be taken seriously."

Hubert H. Humphrey

"Did you ever hear anyone say 'That work had better be banned because I might read it and it might be very damaging to me?'"

Joseph Henry Jackson.

"Fear of corrupting the mind of the younger generation is the loftiest form of cowardice."

Holbrook Jackson.

"The First Amendment grew out of an experience which taught that society cannot trust the conscience of a majority to keep its religious zeal within the limits that a free society can tolerate. I do not think it any more intended to leave the conscience of a majority to fix its limits. Civil government cannot let any group ride roughshod over others simply because their consciences tell them to do so."

Robert H. Jackson.

"The very purpose of the Bill of Rights was to withdraw certain subjects from the vicissitudes of political controversy, to place them beyond the reach of majorities and officials and to establish them as legal principles to be applied by the courts... ."

Robert H. Jackson, 1943.

"Books and ideas are the most effective weapons against intolerance and ignorance."

~ *Lyndon Baines Johnson, commenting as he signed into law a bill providing increased Federal aid for library service, February 11, 1964.*

"We are not afraid to entrust the American people with unpleasant facts, foreign ideas, alien philosophies, and competitive values. For a nation that is afraid to let its people judge the truth and falsehood in an open market is a nation that is afraid of its people."

John F. Kennedy. Remarks made on the 20th anniversary of the Voice of America at H.E.W. Auditorium, February 26, 1962.

"People hardly ever make use of the freedom they have, for example, freedom of thought; instead they demand freedom of speech as a compensation."

Soren Kierkegaard.

"The first step in liquidating a people is to erase its memory. Destroy its books, its culture, its history. Then have somebody write new books, manufacture a new culture, invent a new history. Before long the nation will begin to forget what it is and what it was. The world around it will forget even faster."

Milan Kundera from "Memories of a Wistful Amnesiac," by Walter Goodman, *The New Leader*, Vol. 63, No. 23, December 15, 1980, p. 26ff.

"Censorship, like charity, should begin at home; but unlike charity, it should end there."

Clare Booth Luce.

"Every American librarian worthy of the name is today the champion of a cause. It is, to my mind, the noblest of all causes for it is the cause of man, or more precisely the cause of the inquiring mind by which man has come to be. But noblest or not, it is nevertheless a cause—a struggle—not yet won: a struggle which can never perhaps be won for good and all. There are always in any society, even a society founded in the love of freedom, men and women who do not wish to be free themselves and who fear the practice of freedom by others—men and women who long for the comfort of a spiritual and intellectual authority in their own lives and who would feel more comfortable if they could also impose such an authority on the lives of their neighbors. As long as such people exist—and they show no sign of disappearing from the earth, even the American earth—the fight to subvert freedom will continue. And as long as the fight to subvert freedom continues, libraries must be strong points of defense."

Archibald MacLeish. *Champion of a Cause.* Chicago: American Library Association, 1971, pp. 228-29.

"A popular government, without popular information, or the means of acquiring it, is but a prologue to a farce or a tragedy; or perhaps both. Knowledge will forever govern ignorance; and a people who mean to be their own governors, must arm themselves with the power which knowledge gives."

James Madison, letter to W. T. Barry, August 4, 1782, in *The Complete Madison.* New York: Harper, 1953, p. 337.

"It is impossible for ideas to compete in the marketplace if no forum for their presentation is provided or available."

Thomas Mann.

"Thanks to television, for the first time the young are seeing history made before it is censored by their elders."

Margaret Mead.

"If all mankind minus one were of one opinion, and only one person were of the contrary opinion, mankind would be no more justified in silencing that one person, than he, if he had the power, would be justified in silencing mankind."

John Stuart Mill, *On Liberty.*

"Who can compute what the world loses in the multitude of promising intellects combined with timid characters, who dare not follow out any bold, vigorous, independent train of thought, lest it should land them in something which would admit of being considered irreligious or immoral? … . No one can be a great thinker who does not recognize that as a thinker it is his first duty to follow his intellect to whatever conclusions it may lead… . "

John Stuart Mill, *On Liberty.*

"As good almost kill a man as kill a good book; who kills a man kills a reasonable creature, God's image; but he who destroys a good book kills reason itself."

John Milton, *Aeropagitica.*

"To forbid us anything is to make us have a mind for it."

Michel de Montaigne, *Essays,* 1595.

"You have not converted a man because you have silenced him."

John Morley.

*"Senator Smoot (Republican, Ut.)
Is planning a ban on smut
Oh rooti-ti-toot for Smoot of Ut.
And his reverent occiput.
Smite. Smoot, smite for Ut.,
Grit your molars and do your dut.,
Gird up your l—ns,
Smite h-p and th-gh,
We'll all be Kansas
By and By."*

Ogden Nash, "Invocation," 1931.

"When voices of democracy are silenced, freedom becomes a hollow concept. No man or woman should be sentenced to the shadows of silence for something he or she has said or written."

Allen H. Neuharth.

"The First Amendment forbids any law 'abridging the freedom of speech.' It doesn't say, 'except for commercials on children's television' or 'unless somebody says 'cunt' in a rap song or 'chick' on a college campus.'"

P. J. O'Rourke, *Parliament of Whores,* 1991.

"That is what pluralism is: a nation where people who are different from one another are all entitled to the same rights and opportunities; the same standing before the law; the same respect, given to and received from each other.

"It is shared values, not shared opinions, that keep a diverse and pluralistic nation from splintering. It is tolerance for our differences that binds us. It is the First Amendment that protects the individual mind and conscience against the authority of government and the tyranny of the majority."

Jean H. Ott, *Social Education,* October 1990, p. 356.

"The First Amendment's value is linked directly to its use. To preserve it, it must be shared. Unless it is everyone's, it can be no one's."

Jean Otto.

"He that would make his own liberty secure, must guard even his enemy from opposition; for if he violates this duty he establishes a precedent that will reach to himself."

Thomas Paine, *Dissertation on First Principles of Government,* p. 242.

"A censor is an expert in cutting remarks. A censor is a man who knows more than he thinks you ought to."

~ *Dr. Laurence Peter,* Peter's Quotations: Ideas for Our Time. *New York: Morrow, 1977, p. 97.*

"A free press is a cornerstone of our democracy. In the First Amendment to the Constitution, our Founding Fathers affirmed their belief that competing ideas are fundamental to freedom. We Americans cherish our freedom of expression and our access to multiple sources of news and information."

Ronald Reagan. Message of the President for National Newspaper Week, October 10-16, 1982.

"Where, after all, do universal human rights begin? In small places, close to home—so close and so small that they cannot be seen on any maps of the world. Yet they are the world of the individual persons; the neighborhood he lives in; the school or college he attends; the factory, farm or office where he works. Such are the places where every man, woman and child seeks equal justice, equal opportunity, equal dignity without discrimination. Unless these rights have meaning there, they have little meaning anywhere. Without concerned citizen action to uphold them close to home, we shall look in vain for progress in the larger world."

Eleanor Roosevelt.

"If in other lands the press and books and literature of all kinds are censored, we must redouble our efforts here to keep it free. Books may be burned and cities sacked, but truth, like the yearning for freedom, lives in the hearts of humble men and women. No people in all the world can be kept eternally ignorant or eternally enslaved."

Franklin Delano Roosevelt, Speech before the National Education Association, 1938.

"Free societies ... are societies in motion, and with motion comes tension, dissent, friction. Free people strike sparks, and those sparks are the best evidence of freedom's existence."

Salman Rushdie.

"The First Amendment cases of the 1990s and the twenty-first century will pit powerful emotional interests—such as privacy or nationalism—against our intellectual commitment to the value of information and the right of the public to freely receive information."

Bruce W. Sanford.

"All censorships exist to prevent anyone from challenging current conceptions and existing institutions. All progress is initiated by challenging current conceptions, and executed by supplanting existing institutions. Consequently the first condition of progress is the removal of censorship."

George Bernard Shaw, Preface to *Mrs. Warren's Profession*.

"The war between the artist and writer and government or orthodoxy is one of the tragedies of humankind. One chief enemy is stupidity and failure to understand anything about the creative mind. For a bureaucratic politician to presume to tell any artist or writer how to get his mind functioning is the ultimate in asininity. The artist is no more able to control his mind than is any outsider. Freedom to think requires not only freedom of expression but also freedom from the threat of orthodoxy and being outcast and ostracized."

Helen Foster Snow.

"Our nation's understanding and appreciation of the First Amendment is not passed along genetically. It must be reaffirmed and defended, over and over. Keep fighting and keep winning."

Paul Steinle.

"The sound of tireless voices is the price we pay for the right to hear the music of our own opinions."

Adlai Stevenson.

"Censorship reflects a society's lack of confidence in itself. It is the hallmark of an authoritarian regime ..."

Justice Potter Stewart, dissenting *Ginzberg v. United States*, 383 U.S. 463 (1966).

"The ultimate expression of free speech lies not in the ideas with which we agree, but in those ideas that offend and irritate us."

Chuck Stone.

"Once a government is committed to the principle of silencing the voice of opposition, it has only one way to go, and that is down the path of increasingly repressive measures, until it becomes a source of terror to all its citizens and creates a country where everyone lives in fear."

Harry S. Truman, message to Congress,
August 8, 1950.

"The burning of an author's books, imprisonment for opinion's sake, has always been the tribute that an ignorant age pays to the genius of its time."

Joseph Lewis, *Voltaire: The Incomparable Infidel.* 1929. Reprint. Darby, Pa.:
Darby Books, 1982.

"The values embodied in the First Amendment are not indigenous only to the USA. The drive of the human spirit to be free—and to be able to express that freedom—is a worldwide hope."

Christine Wells

"The books that the world calls immoral are the books that show the world its own shame."

Oscar Wilde.

"An idea that is not dangerous is unworthy of being called an idea at all."

Oscar Wilde.

"To suppress minority thinking and minority expression would tend to freeze society and prevent progress... . Now more than ever we must keep in the forefront of our minds the fact that whenever we take away the liberties of those whom we hate, we are opening the way to loss of liberty for those we love."

Wendell Lewis Willkie, *One World.*

"I believe in America because in it we are free — free to choose our government, to speak our minds, to observe our different religions. Because we are generous with our freedom, we share our rights with those who disagree with us."

~ *Wendell Lewis Willkie.*

"Every dogma has its day, but ideals are eternal."

Israel Zangwill

Suggested Activities

http://www.ala.org/bbooks

LINK your web site to the Banned Books Home Page. The address is http://www.ala.org/bbooks.

PRINT the message of Banned Books Week on bags to use during the week. The Camden County (New Jersey) College Library Learning Resource Center and the Merrick (New York) Library used the bag illustrated here to enclose all materials checked out that week.

ORGANIZE a reading and discussion series. Your series could focus on books banned in the past year, or it might examine banned books throughout history or by topic (religion, politics, sex, etc.).

ASSIGN a research paper for students, such as: "Censorship and the Democratic Society"; "Banned Authors"; "The Various Forms of Censorship." Make arrangements for the local or school newspaper to print the best paper.

STICK a "Book Banning Burns Me Up!" notice on your car. These bright red and yellow stickers (13" x 3³/₄") sell for 50¢ each from H. P. Kopplemann, Inc., Paperback Book Service, POB 145, Hartford, CT 06141; (800) 243-7724.

ASK the student or community newspaper to devote an issue to Banned Books Week. Suggest editorials on the importance of the Bill of Rights, the Constitution, and students' rights.

ILLUSTRATE flyers, posters, newsletters, and booklets with the clip art in this book which can be enlarged, reduced, or duplicated. Local print shops can assist you with printing specifications. There are essentially two kinds of printers: instant printers and commercial printers. Instant printers, usually able to do a job in a few days, are best used for simple, small jobs. Ask to see paper samples and, to save money, try to use what is in stock. Show the printer a sample of a comparable finished piece showing the quality you're looking for.

The larger the quantity of your order, the more economical it may be to use a commercial printer. To find a good commercial printer, ask local businesses whose printed pieces you admire which printer they use. Call the recommended printers and ask for a representative to call. Again, show them samples of comparable finished products and give them a budget range. The representatives will be able to advise you on paper stock, size, and color. Commercial printers require more lead time, so plan ahead.

HOLD a film festival of movies depicting censorship. *Storm Center,* a Bette Davis classic, is the story of a small town librarian (Davis) who refuses to remove a book on communism. The flaming conclusion should generate discussion and interest (1965, bw, 87m, Columbia/Phoenix). *Fahrenheit 451* shows a futuristic fascist society where the fireman's job is to burn books (1966, color, 112m, Rank/Anglo Enterprise/Vineyard). *1984* is the George Orwell classic about Big Brother and the subordination of the individual to the state (1955, bw, 91m, Holiday). *The Seven Minutes,* based on the Irving Wallace novel of the same title, tells the story of a bookseller arrested for distributing an "obscene" novel (1971, col., 102m, TCF). *Inherit the Wind* is a fictionalized account of the famous Scopes "monkey trial" starring Spencer Tracy as William Jennings Bryan (1960, bw, 127m, United Artists/Lomitas). End the festival with ALA's film *The Speaker,* which depicts a high school committee facing censorship after suggesting a speaker whose controversial theory about genetics is abhorrent to their parents and classmates (1977, col., 16mm, American Library Association).

STAGE a mock trial or moot court.

Put a banned book on trial and have students argue for and against the book. Select a jury that has not read the book. For mock trial materials and technical assistance, contact the following organizations:

1) The Constitutional Rights Foundation (601 South Kingsley Drive, Los Angeles, CA 90005; [213] 487-5590; Fax [213-386-0459]) has packets of mock trial material available for $3.95 each.

2) The National Institute for Citizen Education in the Law, Street Law Program (711 G Street, S. E., Washington, DC 20003; [202] 546-6644; Fax [202-546-6649]) has many mock trial scenarios compiled into case packets; they will send a bibliography of cases free upon request. Note that the mock trials they have are not on censorship, but can be used as examples.

3) The Center for Civic Education (5146 Douglas Fir Road, Calabasas, CA 91302; [800] 350-4223) develops curriculum materials to teach about the Constitution in upper elementary grades, and will send a catalog of items free upon request.

MARCH in a community parade. Staff at the Parlin-Ingersoll Library in Canton, Illinois, celebrated Banned Books Week by marching in the Friendship Festival parade dressed as famous banned books. Other Banned Books Week activities included the creation of a Banned Book Club, book discussions for children, and the distribution of an annotated list of banned books with the "hot books" logo.

GIVE away gags imprinted with the titles of banned books. The gags could also be worn as arm bands as in mourning, e.g., "Censorship = the death of ideas."

WEAR a bright red button sold by the American Society of Journalists and Authors, 1501 Broadway, Suite 302, New York, NY 10036; (212) 997-0947; Fax (212) 768-7414. 1—10, $1 each; 11—50, 75¢ each; 51—100, 50¢ each; 101—1000, 40¢ each; 1001+, 30¢ each. Please add $5.00 delivery charge on orders over $15.00.

SCREEN a banned film. Encourage your local television station or plan your own program using *Banned Films: Movies, Censors, and the First Amendment,* by Edward de Grazia and Roger K. Newman. This book will provide you with 122 examples of American and foreign films banned in the U.S. including *The Birth of the Nation, The Exorcist,* and *Carnal Knowledge.*

SPONSOR a poster contest for children illustrating the concept of free speech. Display the posters in your bookstore or library during Banned Books Week—Celebrating the Freedom to Read.

CREATE radio spots. Improve the spot with music! Ask the radio station's technician/engineer/disc jockey to help you select music and dub it into the radio spot. For example, one library used the theme from *Dragnet* for an effective attention-grabbing spot.

WEAR a T-shirt supporting the right to free speech.
The Washington Coalition Against Censorship has developed four different designs available in various colors and sizes. All profits support public education efforts by the Coalition. T-shirts are $15.00 each, plus $2.00 shipping per order. Call the Washington Coalition Against Censorship (6201 15th N.W. #640, Seattle, WA 98107; [206] 784-6418; Fax [206-789-0930]) to get ordering information.

REENACT the signing of the Constitution.
Follow with a discussion of the First Amendment and the rights it ensures.

CAUTION!
SOME PEOPLE CONSIDER THESE BOOKS DANGEROUS

AMERICAN HERITAGE DICTIONARY • THE BIBLE • ARE YOU THERE, GOD? IT'S ME, MARGARET • OUR BODIES, OURSELVES • TARZAN • ALICE'S ADVENTURES IN WONDERLAND • THE EXORCIST • THE CHOCOLATE WAR • CATCH-22 • LORD OF THE FLIES • ORDINARY PEOPLE • SOUL ON ICE • RAISIN IN THE SUN • OLIVER TWIST • A FAREWELL TO ARMS • THE BEST SHORT STORIES OF NEGRO WRITERS • FLOWERS FOR ALGERNON • ULYSSES • TO KILL A MOCKINGBIRD • ROSEMARY'S BABY • THE FIXER • DEATH OF A SALESMAN • MOTHER GOOSE • CATCHER IN THE RYE • THE MERCHANT OF VENICE • ONE DAY IN THE LIFE OF IVAN DENISOVICH • GRAPES OF WRATH • THE ADVENTURES OF HUCKLEBERRY FINN • SLAUGHTERHOUSE-FIVE • GO ASK ALICE

BANNED BOOKS WEEK— CELEBRATING THE FREEDOM TO READ

PRINT annotated, "Freedom to Read" bookmarks.
The Serra Cooperative Library System in California and the San Diego Booksellers Association printed bookmarks that included a short summary of banned books with a history of censorship efforts against them.

CO-SPONSOR an essay contest with the state library association, local school, or community group.
Possible topics include "What the First Amendment means to me" or "What does freedom to read mean?" Contestants can include eighth-graders, junior or senior high students. Use local newspaper editors/journalists or university faculty as judges and award banned books as prizes.

USE readership surveys to point out the hazards of censorship.
A serendipitous combination of promotions for a week long literacy celebration at the Carroll County Public Library, Maryland, and Banned Books Week resulted in an unprompted editorial in the local newspaper. As part of the literacy celebration, the library surveyed prominent citizens in the community on books that influenced their lives. When the list was published in the newspaper, it coincided with publicity on Banned Books Week from the People for the American Way. The editor noted that many of the "influential" books were also on the banned books list. His editorial "Literature's Worst Obscenity Is Banning, Burning Books" gave the library an added P.R. effort.

Read a Banned Book

SPONSOR a contest.
Possibilities include matching quotes and titles of the banned books; matching titles and authors; selecting banned authors or titles from lists or displays of books. Make sure your selections reflect the literary quality of the works and inspire contestants to read them. Award banned books to the winners.

BLOW UP Banned Books Week balloons.
Print your message on helium strength balloons. Use for decoration and/or distribute at schools, shopping areas, programs, etc.

COMMISSION a local storyteller or theater group to prepare a dramatic rendition of banned or challenged books.
Provide printed lists of appropriate material (books, videotapes, etc.) and take the show on the road—to schools, libraries, and community centers.

PRINT the easily removable camera-ready clip art to promote Banned Books Week.
Ask local newspaper and magazine editors to use the public service advertisements as fillers whenever space is available. Community newsletters and staff newsletters also are good places to run the ads. You may want to duplicate the ads for distribution to several sources. Be sure the duplication process (use photostats or print on heavy, enamel paper) produces good camera-ready art.

SCHEDULE provocative speakers to focus on intellectual freedom issues. The Merrick Library, New York, scheduled the Honorable James Buchanan, chairman of People for the American Way, to speak during Banned Books Week. Also during the week, a librarian from a nearby community spoke on her experience with the Secret Service. The ALA Office for Intellectual Freedom can provide suggestions for speakers: (800) 545-2433, ext. 4223.

SPONSOR a day at the state capitol for students, teachers, community leaders, seniors, or other people to learn about the democratic process—work with organizations such as the League of Women Voters.

ASK the student or community newspaper to devote an issue to Banned Books Week. Suggest editorials on the importance of the Bill of Rights, the Constitution, and students' rights.

Sigma Tau Delta, the International Honor Society at the University of Northern Colorado presented "Banned." This program was a collaboration of six directors and their individual ideas about censorship. It was created to present literature, poetry, musical lyrics, and drama that has been banned, censored or deemed dangerous by certain individuals.

INCLUDE study on banned books in your school's curriculum.

Ruth Bauerle, Assistant Professor of English at Ohio Wesleyan University, planned a fall semester seminar on "Banned Books: From Judy Blume to Molly Bloom." The coursework consisted of six reading units and several individual and/or group projects. The six-week seminar began with a background lecture on laws (Constitution, court cases) governing "censorship," and case histories of book withdrawals from libraries.

The reading units were followed by class discussion of the controversial elements in each book, the positive or negative merits in each work and whether each book met the court test of having social value. Role-playing was used in the first reading unit with students assuming the roles of a parent complaining about the book, a parent defending the right to read, the high school librarian, the high school English teacher, school board members, and high school students for and against the book.

The unit "themes" and titles were:

1) Young adult fiction — Judy Blume's *Are You There God? It's Me, Margaret; Deenie;* and *Tiger Eyes* and J. D. Salinger's *The Catcher in the Rye.*

2) Studs Terkel's *Working* was the second unit. As part of the study of this work, students were asked to "test" the common complaint of many dictionaries—including (or excluding) "bad" language. Students listed dirty, profane, and obscene expressions and then looked the words up in a variety of dictionaries.

3) National security censorship readings included: Victor Marchetti and John D. Marks, *The CIA and the Cult of Intelligence;* Philip Agee, *Inside the Company: CIA Diary;* and Frank Snepp, *Decent Interval.*

4) The fourth reading unit was on censored black writers. Bauerle explains this somewhat "illogical" grouping—the books were challenged or banned due to their content, not the color of the author—stating that the books provide realistic portrayals of the black experience and may have been censored because of the sordidness of that experience. Readings included Ralph Ellison, *Invisible Man;* Maya Angelou, *I Know Why the Caged Bird Sings;* Richard Wright, *Native Son;* and Gordon Park, *The Learning Tree.*

5) The class examined school texts (elementary—high school) for slanting, factual completeness, omissions in science and social science, e.g., creationism vs. evolution; controversial topics—women, minorities, Vietnam War, Watergate.

6) "Literary classics" that have been banned was the final unit and James Joyce's *Ulysses* was used. Group projects included interviewing librarians, county school superintendents, curriculum supervisors, and principals to see what censorship problems or complaints they've encountered and how the complaint was handled.

Individual projects included: researching a particular author or book (What has been the writer's experience with censorship? What was the writer's reaction? How many times has the book been challenged? Why was the book banned?). Students could also study a single censorship incident, e.g., the Island Trees case, the Louisiana creationism case, the Scopes trial, the Kanahwa County, the West Virginia controversy. In addition, students could examine positions taken by particular advocacy groups—People for the American Way, the ACLU, the Moral Majority, the American Library Association, the American Booksellers Association, the Association of American Publishers, etc.

BAG your banned books, and belongings, in style in a great heavy-duty canvas book bag! The Washington Coalition Against Censorship has T-shirts and tote bags, measuring approximately 15" x 16" with sturdy 22" handles. Call for order forms, or send $15.00 (plus $2.00 per order for shipping) with your order to: Washington Coalition Against Censorship, 6201 15th N.W., #640, Seattle, WA 98107; (206) 784-6418.

PIN your

commitment to your lapel. The Alaska Library Association sells pins (shown here) proclaiming "I Read Banned Books." The pin costs $3.00 (including shipping) and can be ordered from the Alaska Library Association, P.O. Box 81084, Fairbanks, AK 99708; Fax (907) 479-4784; e-mail: boba@muskox.alaska.edu. Proceeds benefit Alaska library-oriented organizations.

CONTACT the Constitutional Rights Foundation (601 South Kingsley Drive, Los Angeles, CA 90005; [213] 487-5590; Fax [213-386-0459]) for a catalog of materials on the U.S. Constitution and Bill of Rights.

COMBINE the message of Banned Books Week with your bookstore catalog. The Carleton College Alumni Bookstore (Minn.) added interesting reading to its catalog by including "Faculty Favorites," a list of five most meaningful or most highly treasured books in the lives of the faculty. *The Adventures of Huckleberry Finn* was one of the top ten and the clip art from the 1988 Resource Book was used as the cover of the catalog.

ENCOURAGE your governor, city council, and/or mayor to proclaim "Banned Books Week— Celebrating the Freedom to Read" in your state or community. For example, the state of Ohio and city of St. Louis did for the purpose of "informing our citizens as to the nature and magnitude of the threat censorship poses to our First Amendment rights of freedom of speech and pess, the cornerstone of American liberty." The St. Louis proclamation, which can serve as a prototype, is shown here.

SPONSOR a readout. The American Society of Authors and Journalists supported a spirited public rally on the steps of the New York Public Library. Members of the Society dramatized the dangers of book censorship by reading selections from banned books. The American Center of Poets, Playwrights, Editors, Essayists and Novelists, or P.E.N., sponsored a "Forbidden Books" evening

where well-known writers and actors read sections from banned books. In Virginia Beach, the public library led a storytelling and audience discussion program about banned children's books. In planning these programs, determine your audience, select a well-known place and time for the readout, provide some musical link between the readings, and make it visually interesting by, for instance, enlarging the jackets of banned books.

PARTICIPATE—Big Banned Books was the name of the Missoula Public Library's float, as Banned Books Week coincided with the University of Montana's homecoming parade, "The Big Band Era." The anti-censorship float featured library staff and friends dressed as characters from books that have been banned.

CREATE an

interesting photo for publicity. The North Salem Free Library in North Salem, New York, dressed three library employees (shown here) in "prison garb" borrowed from the local barbershop chorus. The "prisoners" were shown reading banned books.

HOLD — At the Ossining (New York) Public Library, actor Alan Arkin and author Sol Stein participated in an evening of celebrity readings.

Arkin read from *Catch 22* to a crowd of 250. At the Merrick (New York) Public Library patrons were invited to speak out against censorship by writing their own comments on sheets of newsprint beneath some famous quotes about censorship.

ORGANIZE a slide show that introduces Banned Books Week. Collect slides that help teach and explain the meaning of freedom.

The slides can show books written by or about persons who valued intellectual freedom. Examples could include: Thomas Jefferson, Benjamin Franklin, Maya Angelou, John Peter Zenger, Henry Thoreau, Judy Blume, James Baldwin, and Susan B. Anthony. Slides could also include clip art and book jackets. A short slide show can easily be shown during a class or

at a library. These shows are especially effective for large group presentations.

SPONSOR a community forum.

The forums serve both educational and participatory purposes. They allow the public to examine various aspects of the Constitution, its evolution, the underlying values involved, and its significance in contemporary society and to the individual citizen. By encouraging the audience to speak out on the constitutional issues, these sessions emphasize the citizen's role in the continuing development of the law. Organizers may choose from several different model formats, for example, mock legislative hearing, town hall meeting (Socratic discussion), mock trial, and debate. For planning assistance use *Speaking & Writing Truth: Community Forums on the First Amendment* by Robert S. Peck and Mary Manemann. This guide to planning mock legislative hearings, town hall meetings, mock trials or debates provides detailed suggestions on getting started and six First Amendment issues with scripts and legal memoranda ($4.95; add $2 handling). Order from Service Center, American Bar Association, 750 North Lake Shore Drive, Chicago, IL 60611; (312) 988-5522; (800) 285-2221. Order number PC 468-0004.

GIVE away a banned book! Parents and students from the Goochland High School

in Richmond, Virginia, were offered free copies of Stephen King's *Salem's Lot* after the school board banned it. The bookstore, Volume I, created a front window display featuring *Salem's Lot* and 20 other banned books. The *Richmond News-Dispatch* published a photograph of the display and interviewed the bookstore owner. In the first week, twenty-two copies were given away.

EXAMINE the role of the free press in contemporary society by hosting a community discussion.

The Society of Professional Journalists' Project Sunshine will help with suggestions on topics and speakers for your area. For more information, contact Greg Christopher, Society of Professional Journalists' Project Sunshine, 16 South Jackson Street, Greencastle, IN 46135-1514; (765) 653-3333 is their phone number; Fax: (765) 653-4631.

JOIN the Freedom to Read Foundation.

The Foundation is dedicated to the legal and financial defense of intellectual freedom, especially in libraries. Since its establishment in 1969, the Foundation has stood at the forefront of nearly all major battles to defend the right to read. Your contribution will help the Freedom to Read Foundation preserve First Amendment freedoms by challenging those who would remove or ban materials from library col-

newsletter on

intellectual freedom

IFC ALA

Editor: Judith F. Krug, Director
Office for Intellectual Freedom, American Library Association
Associate Editor: Henry F. Reichman

January 1997 □ Volume XLVI □ No. 1

ISSN 0028-9485

Internet decency fight moves to Supreme Court

Published by the ALA Intellectual Freedom Committee,
Ann K. Symons, Chairperson.

lections, and establishing, through the courts, legal precedents on behalf of intellectual freedom principles. For more information, contact the Freedom to Read Foundation, 50 East Huron Street, Chicago, IL 60611; (800) 545-2433, ext. 4226.

GO FOR THE "BURN" and kick off Banned Books Week with a fun run in your community. Print "Banned Books Week—The Censorship Challenge" race T-shirts for participants, volunteers and for sale to spectators. Keep the race distance short (under 3 miles) to involve as many people as possible. Check with your local running club on how to promote and organize the event. Or pick up a copy of the *Road Runners*

Club of America Handbook, available for $15 (postage included) from RRCA, 1150 South Washington, Suite 250, Alexandria, VA 22314; (703) 836-0558.

HOLD—Brown and Clark Booksellers in Mashpee, Massachusetts, held a "Whodunit/Duzzit" forum on censorship and book banning. Four local authors made presentations on self-censorship by authors, the role of "bestseller" lists and chain stores, and the future of electronic books. Coffee and snacks, e.g., Chocolate War Brownies and Uncensored Salsa, were served after the program. The bookstore had both in-store and window displays profiling banned books.

JOIN ARTICLE 19, a human rights group working to identify and oppose censorship throughout the world. The London-based organization is named after Article 19 of the United Nation's Universal Declaration of Human Rights ("everyone has the right to freedom of opinion and expression; this right includes freedom to hold opinions, without interference and to seek, receive, and impart information and ideas through any media regardless of frontiers.") Dues are $25; and members receive their Bulletin three times a year. Additional information can be obtained from ARTICLE 19, International Centre Against Censorship, 33 Islington High Street, London, N1 9LH, U.K.; (44 171) 278 9292; Fax (44 171) 713 1356.

PLAN a quiz. (Answers are on next page.)

In Bound Brook, N.J., middle school and high school librarian Lillian Keating planned a contest to commemorate the week — a daily quiz from a list of books that have been challenged or removed from libraries. The winner of the quiz received a gift certificate to a local bookstore.

The high school questions were:

Monday	What is a popular book in many high school English classes by Harper Lee that has been banned or challenged?
Tuesday	What is the part of the Bill of Rights that guarantees the freedom of religion, speech, press, assembly, and petition?
Wednesday	Who is the author of *The Chocolate War,* a novel about peer pressure which was banned and challenged?
Thursday	What was one of the most challenged titles in 1995? *The Adventures of_____.*
Friday	John _____, one of America's most famous novelists, has had many titles, banned and challenged, and continues to be challenged frequently.

The middle school questions were:

Monday	What was S. E. Hinton's famous novel? *The_____.*
Tuesday	*A Light in the Attic* and *Where the Sidewalk Ends* are frequently challenged. Who is the author?
Wednesday	Who wrote *Matilda,* a book found offensive for its disrespect for adults?
Thursday	What is the title of a spooky series that is often challenged? You may have read the stories when you were younger.
Friday	Who is the popular author of novels for young adults, such as *Forever* and *Deenie?*

HOLD a book discussion group with teenagers and their parents. Select banned titles that deal realistically with teen' issues. Have several people read each book. At the book discussion, have the teens discuss the book, followed by parents' reactions to the books and discussion by the teens. End the sessions with a brief description of the book selection policies and procedures for teens, stressing the importance of free access for young adults.

PETITION your neighbors and politicians to challenge censorship and cooperate with all persons or groups that resist abridgment of free expression and free access to ideas. In Connecticut, several hundred signatures were obtained on a petition protesting censorship which was then sent to the governor, state representatives, and members of the U.S. Congress.

DISTRIBUTE and place
table tent cards in cafeterias, reading rooms and study halls in schools and libraries that promote the freedom to read. The cards could even be personalized with a statement or story.

Have you read a banned book today?

SELECT a video. *The Video Sourcebook, Sixteenth Edition,* features 91,000 programs currently available on video and lists twelve videotapes on censorship. Those videos are: *Bags: Books Under Fire; Censorship in a Free Society; Censorship or Selection: Choosing Books for Public Schools; Free Press, Fair Trial: Inside the Anonymous Source; Is It Easy to Be Young?; It's Only Rock and Roll; Legacy of the Hollywood Blacklist; Life and Liberty … .For All Who Believe; See Evil;* and *What Johnny Can't Read.* The Sourcebook gives complete ordering information, program description, release date, and other information.

PURCHASE a variety of promotional materials (mugs, T-shirts, bumper stickers, tote bags, and buttons) from the American Booksellers Foundation for Free Expression and speak your mind every time you use them. Contact the American Booksellers Foundation for Free Expression, 828 South Broadway, Tarrytown, NY 10591; (914) 591-2665, ext. 289; Fax (914) 591-2716.

CONTACT your college public relations department.

Let them know about your Banned Books Week activities. Their media contacts are well-established and will usually result in better coverage.

PUBLICIZE the Bill of Rights with camera-ready art available from the Newspaper Association of America Foundation. Representing the winners in their 1991 college-level graphics competition, the ad packets are available for $10 from the Newspaper Association of America Foundation, NAA, P.O. Box 2527, Kearneysville, WV 25430; (800) 651-4622, Order Fulfillment Department, Item # 80079.

REWARD patrons who check out banned books during the week. The staff at the Dallas, Texas, Public Library gave library patrons gift certificates redeemable at a local bookstore each time a banned book was checked out.

ENLIST the help of a local business which has an electronic bulletin board on its property. The Algona, Iowa Public Library asked the Iowa State Bank to run a weeklong info-notice about Banned Books Week, and they agreed.

HUNT for banned books throughout the business community. The Bernardsville, New Jersey, Public Library worked with local retail businesses of all kinds to develop a "treasure" hunt of banned books, hiding the titles in plain sight in the display windows and areas of the stores. Patrons were invited to make the rounds of the stores and list all titles they discovered. Participating businesses included flower shops, paint stores, jewelry stores, travel agencies, and many others.

WORK with the local arts council to develop a proposal for Banned Books Week (BBW). Present the proposal well in advance of BBW to potential supporting agencies who might provide some funds for BBW programs and activities, especially if BBW is community-wide in focus, and multi-disciplinary in nature. The Hartland Art Council in Michigan successfully combined an "Authors Live at the Library" program with a banned books theme.

RUN a raffle, that can be entered only by visiting your Banned Books display. The Honolulu, Hawaii, Community College bookstore donated a backpack for the raffle; students checked out the display and entered the contest.

WORK with other libraries in your area to develop a "united front" for Banned Books Week; have each library responsible for one event, and schedule them to complement each other. A letter to the editor from four or five libraries, especially representing different constituencies, will be more effective than your library going it alone. Develop information packets that are available at all participating libraries, and say so in your press releases.

USE the public address system in your school or library to communicate about Banned Books Week. A First Amendment quote at the beginning of the day, or at peak times, would certainly give your patrons something to think about. This idea was submitted by Shannon Van Kirk who successfully used a public address announcement at the St. Cecilia Academy in Nashville, Tenn.

Answers to
Plan a Quiz...

The high school questions are:

Monday	*To Kill a Mockingbird*
Tuesday	1st Amendment
Wednesday	Robert Cormier
Thursday	*The Adventures of Huckleberry Finn*
Friday	Steinbeck

The middle school answers are:

Monday	*The Outsiders*
Tuesday	Shell Silverstein
Wednesday	Roald Dahl
Thursday	*Scary Stories to Tell in the Dark*
Friday	Judy Blume

PRINT a Banned Books Week calendar. The Merrick (New York) Library observed Banned Books Week by printing a calendar showing activities in the library, as well as holidays, events, etc. Each month of the calendar was illustrated with a quotation by a prominent artist, poet, philosopher, scientist, or statesman on the importance of the freedom to read. This Resource Book is a good source for quotations and clip art for your calendar.

DISTRIBUTE materials to high school students. The Paulsboro, New Jersey, High School librarian complied a list of challenged and banned books that the students would recognize. These were distributed to English, History, and Civics classes along with a copy of the First Amendment and the editorial from the Banned Books Week kit.

SUPPORT
the legal battle of the Little Sisters Bookstores and other gay and lesbian Canadian stores.
Since the 1980s, the stores have been waging an expensive legal battle with the Canadian government for seizing and confiscating books at the Canadian borders. To raise funds, they have published *Forbidden Passages: Writings Banned in Canada,* excerpts from a number of the confiscated materials. In the United States, the book can be obtained from Cleis Press, P.O. Box 8933, Pittsburgh, PA 15221. (412) 937-1555; Fax (412) 937-1567.

CONDUCT a poll. Alvin Schwartz's book *Scary Stories to Tell in the Dark* is among the top ten most censored books in the United States today. Conduct a poll of twenty-five adults asking them if and why they feel scary stories are harmful to children and teenagers. Then, poll twenty-five

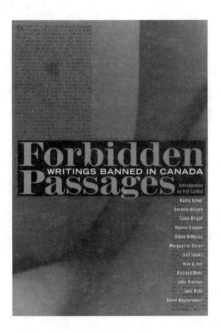

teenagers, asking them the same question. Make a visual contrasting the results of each poll.

PREPARE a speech. Many parents believe that Halloween promotes "evil" and should not be celebrated in schools. Research the origin of Halloween and prepare a persuasive speech about why it should or should not be celebrated by children.

USE a periodical index to locate as many articles as possible regarding book challenges in schools in the United States in the past five years. Draw a map of the United States and color in the states where you found challenges. Which state has the most challenges? How have each of the cases been resolved?

WRITE a ballad or a legend. Ballads and legends are often written about heroic people. For example, research John Peter Zenger's historic fight for First Amendment rights or select your favorite First Amendment advocate and write a ballad or a legend about him or her.

Display Ideas

This exhibit in Ohio used inexpensive brown Kraft paper and bags, paint, and a lot of ingenuity to package up the challenged books so they couldn't be read.

SPRAY PAINT — People Like Us, an exclusively gay and lesbian bookstore in Chicago, created a "graffiti" look in their Banned Books Week display. Using brown wrapping paper and black spray paint, the window presented a feeling of "something forbidden."

DISPLAY — The Illinois State Library displayed banned books behind brown paper, carefully ripped to illustrate the display.

DISPLAY a small collection of "dangerous" books in a prominent location under a sign that provocatively exclaims, "Don't Read These Books." Wrap "banned books" in brown paper, print the title and reason for the banning on individual cards, and tape a card to each book.

PAINT a poster for a window display on a window shade. R. Kent Fordyce, Book Buyer, Lambda Rising in Washington, D.C., wanted a strong image for the bookstore's banned books window display. "Some of the strongest visual art imagery appears in political posters, especially the designs from Third World radical artists. After prowling through five stores and leafing through a couple hundred posters, I found an image in the upper left hand corner of a poster from Latin America that I modified to produce our window's banner (shown here). The banner combined with a display of banned books and accompa-

nying blurbs taken from this book, stopped a lot of people who normally hurry past our store. Many, after reading the blurbs, came into the store to browse. I knew the banner was a success when someone overheard one 'punk' woman turn to another, point to the banner, and say, 'COOL!'"

DISPLAY — The University of New Mexico Bookstore displayed widely known books that have been challenged or banned in a small black "jail" built expressly for the purpose with red and black CENSORED signs woven through the "prison bars." University of Indiana - Purdue University, Indianapolis, Ind., bookstores placed books in bamboo bird cages with the sign "Banned Books Are for the Birds." The display window at Blue Ridge Books, Roanoke, Virginia, was bare during Banned Books Week, representing the attempts by various people or groups during the past year to keep books they deem objectionable from being read. People stood on the sidewalk outside the Main Street store and read excerpts from books recently challenged. Inside, store owners Bob and Teresa Lazo displayed books challenged or banned in the past 12 months.

DISPLAY books on and by persons who valued

intellectual freedom — Thomas Jefferson, Benjamin Franklin, Maya Angelou, John Peter Zenger, Henry Thoreau, Judy Blume, James Baldwin, Thomas Paine, Fredrick Douglass, Susan B. Anthony, John Thomas Scopes, etc.

DISPLAY — The Brown University Bookstore, Providence, Rhode Island, window display was based on a Fahrenheit 451 theme. A photostat was made and displayed on an easel with the quote, "The system was simple. Everyone understood it. Books were for burning...along with the houses in

This library posted comments from patrons about Banned Books Week.

A "caged book" showed patrons of this bookstore how it would feel to not have access to the many resources that have been challenged or banned.

which they were hidden." Books were depicted as though they were being burned at the stake. Banned books were glued to a post, then wrapped with rope. At the bottom of the display were more books and twigs, red, orange, and yellow acetate gave the appearance of fire at the base of the window. The bookstore also contacted local actors to participate in a highly successful public readout.

INTRIGUE

customers or patrons by painting a display window almost entirely black, leaving only a small peep hole; then paint the word "caution" in large red letters, which will encourage them to peer in and see books that have been banned or challenged in the past.

DISPLAY the dust jackets of banned books with accompanying cards explaining the challenge and listing a favorable review. The School of Library Science at the University of North Carolina found this to be a very effective display for their bulletin board.

DEMONSTRATE the inaccessibility of banned books by roping off a section of the bookstore or library and

IMPROVE

— Iron your Banned Books Week posters.

Barbara Ungar, co-owner of House of Books in Dallas, Texas, gave us these tips to eliminate all those nasty creases. Here's how:

1) First the poster arrives. At best, it's got some folds; at worst, it's a mess. You groan.

2) Cut two pieces of brown wrapping paper about the same size as the poster or a little larger.

3) Put one of those pieces on your counter.

4) Put the poster on the top of the wrapping paper, face down.

5) Put the other piece of brown paper on the top of the poster.

6) Put your iron on low heat (no steam, please!) and iron. This is just one of those booksellers' tips handed down through the ages, but it really and truly works.

Save and use previous years' posters to add to this year's poster to show your long-time support for Celebrating the Right to Read.

PROMOTE your books and displays. Chapter One Bookstore in Pittsford, New York, printed brown and white T-shirts depicting a gagged William Shakespeare and used a "Tom Sawyer" type fence (made from brown paper) with a knot hole and the inscription "Caution—if you look through here you may see some banned books!" Some booksellers placed bands or stickers on books, store bags, or receipts saying "banned."

FIND a container that could hold several grab bags. Stuff the bags with information and/or examples of banned authors, movies, and ideas. Then label each so they say "anti-Christian," "sexist," or "communistic." Place them in local libraries, bookstores, or offices. The outside display could say "Keep Away" or "Dangerous Reading."

IMAGINE eye-catching displays. The University of Wisconsin-Oshkosh displayed a full drawer of catalog cards being sucked into a vacuum cleaner alongside empty drawers with printed bands, "sanitized for your protection." In another display, "Censorship of ideas, a bad combination," UW-O "chained" books together with plastic chain links and combination locks (available from the hardware store).

Covering your window in newspaper with strategically placed viewing spots is an effective way to attract a crowd. Books that were challenged or banned were placed behind the newspaper window.

DISPLAY — Anne's Book Shop in Sharon, Massachusetts, had a store window painted "graffiti-style," "Warning! These Books Are Dangerous" with titles of banned books scattered over the glass. Inside the store, four shelves of books were covered with brown paper and ripped open. Red ribbons ("red tape") crisscrossed the display. Lots of books were sold from the display!

allow into the area only those customers or patrons with an entry ticket. The Harry W. Schwartz Bookshop in Milwaukee, Wisconsin, found this to be very effective.

CREATE a bulletin board display using a top ten list as used by David Letterman. Use this book to compile a list or try the following suggestions.

Ten most far-fetched (silliest, irrational, illogical) reasons to ban a book.

1) "Encourages children to break dishes so they won't have to dry them." (*A Light in the Attic* by Shel Silverstein)

2) "It caused a wave of rapes." (*Arabian Nights* or *Thousand and One Nights,* anonymous)

3) "If there is a possibility that something might be controversial, then why not eliminate it?" (*Bury My Heart at Wounded Knee* by Dee Brown)

4) Tarzan was "living in sin" with Jane. (*Tarzan* by Edgar Rice Burroughs)

5) It is a real "downer." (*Diary of Anne Frank* by Anne Frank)

This library in Arlington County, Va., put up "What Do You Think?" and large tablets of paper throughout its 1995 Banned Books Week exhibit. They prompted answers to questions such as "Who should have primary responsibility for determining what materials young people can have access to — the government or the family?"

You can build an exhibit out of articles on censorship from newspapers or magazines. This library also wrapped paper "Censored" labels around challenged library books.

6) The basket carried by Little Red Riding Hood contained a bottle of wine, which condones the use of alcohol. (*Little Red Riding Hood* by Jacob Grimm and Wilhelm K. Grimm)

7) One bunny is white and the other is black and this "brainwashes" readers into accepting miscegenation. (*The Rabbit's Wedding* by Garth Williams)

8) It is a religious book and public funds should not be used to purchase religious books. (*Evangelical Commentary on the Bible* by Walter A. Elwell, ed.)

9) A female dog is called a bitch. (*My Friend Flicka* by Mary O'Hara)

10) An unofficial version of the story of Noah's Ark will confuse children. (*Many Waters* by Madeline L'Engle)

DISPLAY a timeline of Constitutional Amendments on your bulletin board. Show different books that relate to the amendments.

CONSTRUCT

a "Graffiti Wall" made up of large sheets of paper upon which students are encouraged to "write" about their own thoughts and responses to censor-

This model of **The Canterbury Tales** *(right) was part of an elaborate Banned Books Week campaign at Marshall Public Library in Pocatello, Idaho.*

Pictured here are 9 of the 17 small displays depicting books listed in the Banned Books Resource Guide and an explanation of why the book was removed or challenged.

The Canterbury Tales

Serbs & Croats

The Egypt Game

Indian In My Cupboard

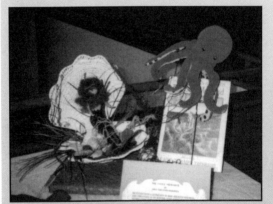

The Little Mermaid

I Know Why the Caged Bird Sings

Tar Beach

The Runaway

Halloween ABC

Banned Books Week at the Arlington County Public Library

by Jeffrey Slack,

**Young Adult
Library Associate**

The Arlington County (Virginia) Public Library took a unique approach to Banned Books Week by distributing specially designed, interactive "censored materials" packets. The three-person design committee was determined to not only inform patrons, but to learn from them as well — and to accomplish this in an innovative and eye-catching manner.

The idea had to sensitively address diverse political views in the community, the needs of seven library branches of greatly varying size, and a controversy that had erupted in the region concerning access to materials in public libraries.

The result was the creation of 700 folders that invited patrons to explore for themselves the issues of censorship and accessibility. Inside, thirteen loose pages introduced the concept of Banned Books Week, provided an overview of recent challenges, and presented case studies of five well-known challenged books, where patrons could draw their own conclusions. Also included was a bibliography of materials in the Arlington Library system for further study and a copy of the *Library Bill of Rights*. Patrons were then encouraged to share their thoughts by responding to questions on three enclosed cards. Almost 550 responses were received. These were then posted in each branch so others could

read them and comment further, thus allowing for a public dialogue on the issues.

All of these materials were bound in simple, brown, corrugated cardboard folders with closeable flaps. Each folder was sealed shut with a white sticker, across which was stamped in large red letters the warning "CENSORED." Curious participants could then break open the packets and delve inside, where the design and text revealed that the flaps were actually symbolic doors to the library and that attacks on the freedom to read go far beyond materials in "plain brown wrappers."

By enlisting assistance from throughout the library and community, the project became a team effort and illustrated how readily available materials can be combined for a unique effect. The folder design was adapted from a local art exhibit brochure and was produced by a nearby cardboard box manufacturer. The text and comment cards were generated in-house using a word processing program and laser printer. The American flag graphic on each page came from a simple software package. The rubber stamps were specially ordered from a local supplier. Printing and trimming were handled by the county's print shop. Posters for the displays were purchased through ALA. Final collating, stuffing and stickering were completed by the committee members (and numerous unsung colleagues and spouses).

Creation of the project entailed a substantial time commitment, even though the period from conceptualization to execution took only about two

Providing a space for patrons of your store or library to comment in writing draws attention and gets people thinking more deeply about censorship issues. This library in Arlington County, Va., exhibited posters with a censorship theme and large quotes blown up for easy reading from a distance.

"Censorship, like charity, should begin at home; but unlike charity, it should end there."

months. Approximately 200 total staff hours were involved (including time from non-committee members), with an additional 40 hours provided by volunteers. Expenses totalled approximately $350 (not including the cost of supplies on-hand), with most of the money coming from Friends of the Library funds committed to public programming. The largest costs were $196 for production of the 700 cardboard folders and $120 for printing and trimming the text. An additional $30 went for rubber stamps and stickers.

Between $30 and $50 was saved by using an existing cutting die for the folders, rather than paying for a new design. For library systems with smaller staffs and budgets, patron comment cards could be created and displayed at a very minimal cost. Alternative means of providing appealing background material would have to be developed, but the interactive approach could still be retained.

Most frequently overheard comment:

"But I've read this book; why was it banned?"

(continued on p. 160)

Response to the packets was tremendous and impassioned. By the final day, the last of the folders were picked up by patrons and the display at the Central branch had been enlarged three times to accommodate all of the responses. A broad range of viewpoints was articulated, but a clear message emerged: Censorship and restrictions would not readily be welcomed in Arlington.

When asked who should have primary responsibility for determining what materials young people can have access to—the government or the family—over three quarters of the respondents replied "the family." Of the remainder, over half suggested "the individual" as an alternate decision maker. The rest wanted governmental control or some mixture of government and family involvement. When asked if there are ever situations when it's right to censor or restrict books, more than two thirds responded that there should never be censorship; the other third presented instances when they felt censorship or limitations had some merit. And when asked if they had ever personally experienced censorship or restrictions, nearly ninety people recounted amazingly diverse stories from home and abroad.

Even more impressive than the number of participants who voluntarily took time to write was the intensity and depth of their responses. Regardless of how people felt, their answers in most cases illustrated understanding, commitment, and sensitivity often lacking in media coverage of this complex issue.

The direct involvement of the people who use the libraries was the true strength of this project. At a time when community interest was at a peak, Arlington was fortunate to have at hand a creative vehicle for patrons to respond to issues that were making front-page news. The library took a risk. And through Arlington County's commitment to employees, quality, diversity, and empowerment, the public affirmed its support of the library and the *Library Bill of Rights.*

Free societies... are societies in motion, and with motion comes tension, dissent, friction. Free people strike sparks, and those sparks are the best evidence of freedom's existence.
Salman Rushdie
BANNED BOOKS WEEK- Celebrating the Freedom to Read

The First Amendment's value is linked directly to its use. To preserve it, it must be shared. Unless it is everyone's, it can be no one's.
Jean Otto
BANNED BOOKS WEEK- Celebrating the Freedom to Read

You don't have to burn books to destroy a culture. Just get people to stop reading them.
Ray Bradbury
BANNED BOOKS WEEK- Celebrating the Freedom to Read

Censorship, like charity, should begin at home; but unlike charity, it should end there.
Clare Booth Luce
BANNED BOOKS WEEK- Celebrating the Freedom to Read

A Selected, Annotated Bibliography of First Amendment Resources

Adams, Thelma, ed. *Censorship and First Amendment Rights: A Primer.* Tarrytown, New York: American Booksellers Foundation for Free Expression, 1992. ISBN: 1-879556-05-7. $10. Case studies and resources for handling censorship, working with lawyers and lobbyists, etc., with an introduction by Anthony Lewis.

Article 19 Freedom of Expression Handbook: International and Comparative Law, Standards and Procedures. London: ARTICLE 19, Int. Centre Against Censorship, 1996. £12. The handbook brings together, by topic, summaries and analysis of relevant international jurisprudence as well as decisions from national courts around the world that declare strong protections of the rights to freedom of expression and access to information. The handbook's aims are: 1) to enable lawyers around the world to use international and comparative freedom of expression law in cases before national courts and to assess whether their client's case would be advanced by filing an application with an international body; 2) to inform journalists, writers and human rights campaigners and provide access to information under international and comparative law and standards, and to provide them with examples of how courts from a diversity of legal traditions have protected and promoted freedom of expression, often in the face of repressive government practices; 3) to provide a resource for academics, lawyers and others interested in comparative and international freedom of expression law and jurisprudence.

Brown, Jean E. *Preserving Intellectual Freedom: Fighting Censorship in Our Schools.* Urbana, Ill.: National Council of Teachers of English, 1995. ISBN: 0-8141-3671-0. $19.95. Stock no. 36710-0015. The author sheds light on the ways in which censorship arises; how it affects curricula, students and teachers; and how it can be fought. The book also takes a comprehensive look at the provisions and implications of the 1988 U.S. Supreme Court decision in Hazelwood v. Kuhlmeir, which held that a high school principal's censorship of a student newspaper did not violate students' First Amendment rights because the paper was not a public forum.

Censorship or Selection: Choosing Books for Public Schools, a dynamic, hour-long videotape of a twenty-two member panel responding to issues of how books get into classrooms and libraries and how they are sometimes removed. Encourage your local television station to screen the tape, or use it to create your own program. Available for $79.95 plus $6.00 for shipping and handling from PBS Video, 1320 Braddock Place, Alexandria, VA 22314; (800) 424-7963.

Coetzee, J. M. *Giving Offense: Essays on Censorship.* Chicago: Univ. of Chicago Pr., 1996. ISBN: 0-226-11174-1. $24.95. South African writer J. M. Coetzee presents a coherent, unorthodox analysis of censorship from the perspective of a writer who has lived and worked under its shadow.

DelFaltore, Joan. *What Johnny Shouldn't Read: Textbook Censorship in America.* New Haven, Conn.: Yale University Press, 1992. ISBN: 0-300-05709-1. $25. An enlightening treatise on how pressure groups affect textbook publishing, influencing schools throughout the country. The stories behind recent lawsuits show how local communities' concerns become national issues because of sophisticated pressure group tactics.

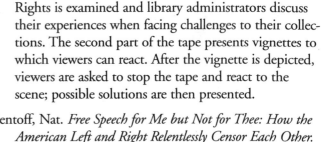

Demac, Donna A. *Liberty Denied: The Current Rise of Censorship in America.* 2nd ed. New Brunswick, N.J.: Rutgers Univ. Pr., 1992. ISBN: 0-934638-09-8. $6.95. Shows the extent of the assault on free expression in the past decade, making the point that the quiet eroding of individual rights poses a threat to the principles Americans hold dear.

Foerstel, Herbert N. *Banned in the U.S.A.: A Reference Guide to Book Censorship in Schools and Public Libraries.* Westport, Conn.: Greenwood Press, 1994. ISBN: 0-313-28517-9. $45.00. Virtually every aspect of book censorship is examined in this comprehensive source. Included in this readable survey are an evaluation of eight book-banning incidents from 1976 to 1992; a ranking and summary of the fifty most challenged books of the 1990s; and a series of interviews with frequently-challenged authors, such as Judy Blume, Katherine Paterson and Robert Cormier.

_____. *Free Expression and Censorship in America: An Encyclopedia.* Westport, Conn.: Greenwood Press, 1997. ISBN: 0-313-29231-0. $65.00. This comprehensive encyclopedia includes analysis of the First Amendment implications of major political issues of the 1990s including abortion, campaign finance, violence on television, homosexuality, and the Internet.

For Freedom's Sake, ALA Video/Library Video Network, 1996. 800-441-TAPE. ISBN: 1-56641-039-8. $130. The first part of this tape presents an overview of intellectual freedom in libraries today. The Library Bill of Rights is examined and library administrators discuss their experiences when facing challenges to their collections. The second part of the tape presents vignettes to which viewers can react. After the vignette is depicted, viewers are asked to stop the tape and react to the scene; possible solutions are then presented.

Hentoff, Nat. *Free Speech for Me but Not for Thee: How the American Left and Right Relentlessly Censor Each Other.* New York: Harper-Collins, 1993. ISBN: 0-06-099510-6. $13. Hentoff explores not only the "traditional" sources of censorship—religious fundamentalists and political right-wingers—but also censorship from the left, e.g., feminists who tried to prevent a pro-life women's group from participating in Yale University's Women's Center. He also takes on proponents of "hate speech" regulations as enemies of free expression.

Index on Censorship; $50 per year/6 issues; Index on Censorship, c/o Mercury Airfreight Int./Ltd. Inc., 2323 Randolph Ave., Avenue, NJ 07001; indexoncenso@gn.apc.org; http://www.oneworld.org/index_oc/ This bimonthly publication examines censorship from an international perspective. Special issues have been devoted to subjects such as film censorship and art censorship.

Intellectual Freedom Manual, Fifth Edition, compiled by the Office for Intellectual Freedom, American Library Association. Chicago: ALA, 1996. ISBN: 0-8389-0677-X. $35. Completely revised, the manual offers practical options for anticipating and responding to censorship pressures. It provides guidance on developing a materials selection policy, dealing with the political strategies of organized pressure groups and how to write effectively to a legislator. New features include two new interpretations to the Library Bill of Rights, updated recommendations for special libraries, information about legal decisions affecting school and public libraries, a new section on the Intellectual Freedom Network, and an updated intellectual freedom bibliography. It is an indispensable reference tool.

Jensen, Carl. *Censored: The News That Didn't Make the News.* New York: Four Walls, Eight Windows, 1996. ISBN: 1-56858-030-4. $13. This annual publication of Project Censored presents a report card for the American press, listing the least-reported news stories of the past year. In addition to summarizing the year's 25 most censored stories, the volume includes Censored Déjà Vu, censored stories from past years that have since reached the mainstream media; Junk Food News, a review of stories covered at the expense of real news; An Eclectic Chronology of Censorship from 605 B.C. to the present; Top Censored Books of the Year; Censored Resource Guide, a directory of media and anti-censorship organizations; an Alternative Writer's Market; and reprints of the top ten censored stories.

Marsh, Dave. *50 Ways to Fight Censorship.* New York: Thunder's Newsletter Press, 1991. ISBN: 1-56025-011-9. $5.95. A straightforward action guide for people who see real dangers in limiting expression, and want to do something about it, but don't know where to begin. These actions include forming anti-censorship groups, writing petitions, staging rallies, and organizing boycotts. To make follow-through easier and more effective, the book concludes with an extensive list of local and national resources for organized political action.

Newsletter on Intellectual Freedom. ALA, 50 E. Huron St. Chicago, IL 60611; (800) 545-2433, ext. 4223. $40. This bimonthly publication of the American Library Association reports censorship incidents across the country, summarizes recent court cases on the First Amendment, and includes a bibliography on intellectual freedom. It is the best source of information on the continuing battle to defend and extend First Amendment rights.

Nobel, William. *Bookbanning in America: Who Bans Books?—And Why?* Middlebury, Vt.: Paul S. Eriksson, 1990. ISBN: 1-56025-011-9. $5.95. Anecdotes, interviews, trial transcripts, and case histories show how and why bookbanning happens, beginning in 1650, through the Salman Rushdie affair.

Reichman, Henry F. *Censorship and Selection: Issues and Answers for Schools,* Rev. ed. Chicago: ALA, 1993. ISBN: 0-8389-0620-6. $18. The manual contains clear, concise, and useful information on the issues and solutions to censorship. Though its focus is primarily for schools, information is sufficiently general so libraries will find it useful. *Censorship and Selection* addresses how to develop viable policies ranging from how to handle complaints to the selection of learning materials. Specific recommendations for how to plan for potential crises are also included.

Robbins, Louise S. *Censorship and the American Library: The American Library Association's Response to Threats to Intellectual Freedom, 1939-1969.* Westport, Conn.: Greenwood Press, 1996. ISBN: 0-313-29644-8. $59.95. A study of the development of the American Library Association's intellectual freedom policies from 1939, when ALA first articulated its commitment to providing diverse viewpoints to library users, to 1969, when the Freedom to Read Foundation was founded.

Smith, Robert Ellis. *Our Vanishing Privacy.* Providence, R.I.: Privacy Journal, 1993. ISBN: 1-55950-100-6. $12.95. Loompanics. Smith is an outspoken advocate for personal freedom from unwelcome—and threatening—intrusions. He offers succinct guidance to statutes protecting individuals from unreasonable credit requirements and unnecessary job application questions.

Symons, Ann K. and Charles Harmon. *Protecting the Right to Read.* New York: Neal Schuman, 1995. ISBN: 1-55570-216-3. $39.95. This 'How-To' manual is designed to assist school and public librarians in developing and implementing intellectual freedom policies, handling a challenge to library resources, and providing Internet access.

Teaching Students about the First Amendment: A Bibliography compiled by Pat Scales, Library Media Specialist, Greenville (S.C.) Middle School

FICTION

Christian, Peggy. *The Bookstore Mouse.* Illus. by Gary A. Lippincott. San Diego: Harcourt Brace, 1995. ISBN: 0-

15-200203-0. $16.00. Cervantes, a mouse who lives in an antiquarian bookstore, embarks on a great adventure while trying to elude Milo the cat. When Cervantes discovers the power of words, he finds a special way to deal with Milo, and they both live a more enlightened life.

Diaz, Jorge. *The Rebellious Alphabet.* Illus. by Oivind S. Jorfald. New York: Henry Holt & Company, 1993. ISBN: 0-8050-2765-3. $14.95. For older readers, this illustrated fable tells the story of an illiterate dictator who bans reading and writing, but is outwitted by an old man who trains canaries to deliver printed messages to people.

Facklam, Margery. *The Trouble with Mothers.* New York: Clarion, 1989. ISBN: 0-89919-773-6. $13.95. Eighth-grader Luke Troy is devastated when his Mother, a teacher, writes an historical novel that is considered pornography by some people in the community where they live.

Hentoff, Nat. *The Day They Came to Arrest the Book.* New York: Dell, 1985. ISBN: 0-4409-1814-6. $3.99. Students in a high school English class protest the study of Huckleberry Finn until the editor of the school newspaper uncovers other cases of censorship and in a public hearing reveals the truth behind the mysterious disappearance of certain library books and the resignation of the school librarian.

Lasky, Kathryn. *Memoirs of a BookBat.* San Diego: Harcourt, Brace, 1994. ISBN: 0-15-215727-1. $10.95. Fourteen-year-old Harper Jessup, an avid reader, runs away because she feels that her individual rights are threatened when her parents, born again fundamentalists, lodge a public promotion of book censorship.

Meyer, Carolyn. *Drummers of Jericho.* San Diego: Harcourt Brace, 1995. ISBN: 0-15-200441-6. $4.95. When a fourteen-year-old Jewish girl joins the high school marching band and discovers that the band will play hymns and stand in the formation of a cross, she objects and major issues of individual rights are raised.

Miles, Betty. *Maudie, and Me and the Dirty Book.* New York: Knopf, 1994. ISBN: 0-3948-2595-0. $3.99. Eleven-year-old Kate Harris volunteers to read to first graders but her choice of book, The Birthday Dog, causes the children to ask questions about how puppies are born. When parents of the younger children raise objection, the principal suspends the reading project, and Kate

CENSORSHIP AND THE AMERICAN LIBRARY
The American Library Association's Response to Threats to Intellectual Freedom, 1939-1969
Louise S. Robbins

and her friends learn first-hand about censorship.

Peck, Richard. *The Last Safe Place on Earth.* New York: Delacorte, 1995. ISBN: 0-385-32052-3. $14.95. The Tobin family is satisfied that Walden Woods is a quiet, safe community to rear three children. Then, seven-year-old Marnie begins having nightmares after a teenage babysitter tells her that Halloween is "evil," and Todd and Diana, sophomores in high school, witness an organized group's attempt to censor books in their school library.

Thompson, Julian F. *The Trials of Molly Sheldon.* New York: Henry Holt, 1995. ISBN: 0-8050-3382-3. $15.95. When high schooler Molly Sheldon begins working for her father in his eclectic general store in central Vermont, she faces First Amendment issues for the first time in her life. Moralists try to censor the books that her father sells, and Molly is accused of being a witch.

Tolan, Stephanie S. *Save Halloween!* New York: William Morrow, 1993. ISBN: 0-688-12168-3. $14.00. When sixth-grader Johnna Filkings gets caught up in researching and writing a class pageant about Halloween, her father and uncle, fundamentalist ministers, disrupt the entire community by declaring Halloween evil.

NONFICTION

Faber, Doris and Harold. *We The People: The Story of the United States Constitution Since 1787.* New York: Scribner's, 1987. ISBN: 0-684-18753-1. $13.95. An historical account of the writing of the Constitution and the adoption of the Bill of Rights, including a discussion of the responsibility of the Supreme Court as an interpreter of this important document.

Gold, John C. *Board of Education v. Pico (1982).* New York: Twenty-First Century Books, 1994, ISBN: 0-8050-3660-1. $15.98. Traces the Pico case from its beginning in 1975 to the 1982 final Supreme Court decision that ordered the school board of the Island Trees Union Free School District No. 26 on Long Island, New York to return nine books to the library shelves.

Gottfried, Ted. *The American Media.* New York: Franklin Watts, 1997. ISBN: 0-531-11315-9. $22.70. Focusing on the history of the media in the United States, this book explores topics such as yellow journalism, censorship and freedom of the press. Index.

Greenberg, Keith. *Adolescent Rights: Are Young People Equal under the Law?* New York: Twenty-First Century Books, 1995. ISBN: 0-8050-3877-9. $15.98. Details adolescent rights from an historical and contemporary perspective and invites readers to form their own conclusions regarding specific issues.

Meltzer, Milton. *The Bill of Rights: How We Got It and What It Means.* New York: Crowell, 1990. ISBN: 0-690-04805-X. $14.89 A comprehensive discussion of the history of the Bill of Rights with specific references to contemporary challenges of the ten amendments.

Monroe, Judy. *Censorship.* New York: Crestwood House, 1990. ISBN: 0-89686-490-1 (The Facts About Series). An overview, in simple language, of the problems of censorship with textbooks, movies, music, and children's books.

Pascoe, Elaine. *Freedom of Expression: The Right to Speak out in America.* Brookfield, Conn.: Millbrook Press, 1992. ISBN: 1-56294-255-7. $16.90. Traces the First Amendment's roots in earlier societies, and examines how it has been tested and interpreted from colonial times to the present.

Rappaport, Doreen. *Tinker vs. Des Moines: Student Rights on Trial.* New York: HarperCollins, 1993. ISBN: 0-06-025117-4. $15.00. Part of the Be The Judge, Be The Jury series, this book deals with students' first and fourteenth amendment rights by recreating the trial of John Tinker and his classmates who were suspended from school in 1965 for protesting the Vietnam War by wearing black armbands.

Sherrow, Victoria. *Censorship in Schools.* Springfield, N.J.: Enslow Publishers, 1996. ISBN: 0-89490-728X. $19.95. A well-documented text that clearly defines censorship and traces the development of censorship in schools throughout history. There is detailed discussion of problems of free expression in schools today, including censorship of literature, textbooks, student newspapers, etc. Index.

Steele, Philip. *Censorship.* New York: New Discovery Books, 1992. ISBN: 0-02-735404-0 (Past and Present Series). A short (seven chapters) book that looks at the history of censorship in all forms—its religious, political and moral—aspects, and its impact on American society.

Stein, Richard. *Censorship: How Does It Conflict with Freedom?* New York: Twenty-First Century Books, 1995. ISBN: 0-8050-3879-5 (Issues of Our Time Series). $15.98. In six quick chapters, this easy-to-read text explains the First Amendment and applies the meaning of free expression to the use of printed materials, the arts, and the internet. Glossary. Index.

Crossword Puzzle

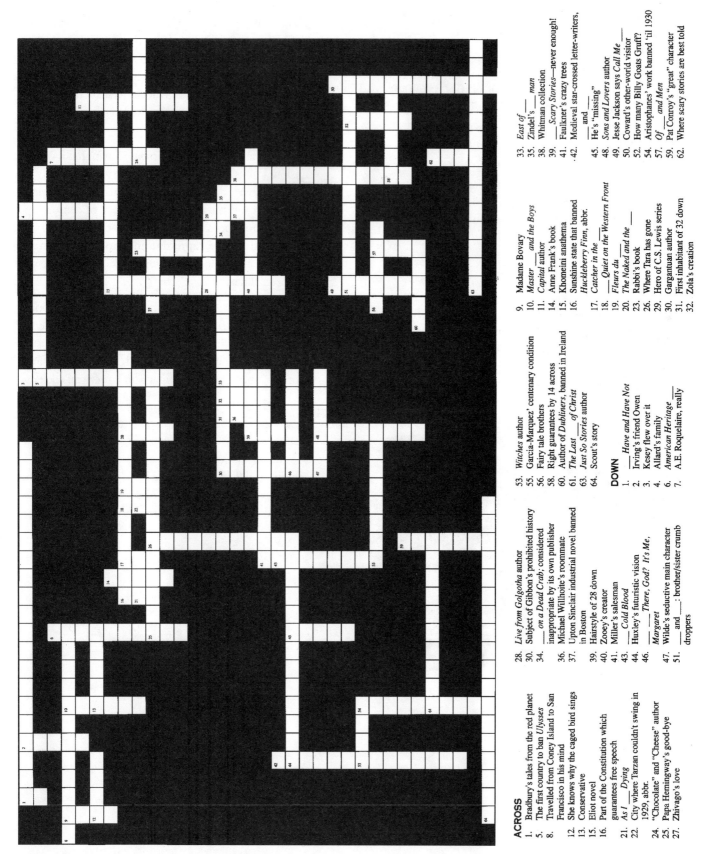

ACROSS

1. Bradbury's tales from the red planet
5. The first country to ban *Ulysses*
8. Travelled from Coney Island to San Francisco in his mind
12. She knows why the caged bird sings
13. Conservative
15. Eliot novel
16. Part of the Constitution which guarantees free speech
21. As I _____ *Dying*
22. City where Tarzan couldn't swing in 1929, abbr.
24. "Chocolate" and "Cheese" author
25. Papa Hemingway's good-bye
27. Zhivago's love
28. *Live from Golgotha* author
30. Subject of Gibbon's prohibited history
34. _____ *on a Dead Crab;* considered inappropriate by its own publisher
36. Michael Willhoite's roommate
37. Upton Sinclair industrial novel banned in Boston
39. Hairstyle of 28 down
40. Zooey's creator
41. Miller's salesman
43. _____ *Cold Blood*
44. Huxley's futuristic vision
46. _____ *There, God? It's Me, Margaret*
47. Wilde's seductive main character
51. _____ and _____: brother/sister crumb droppers
53. *Witches* author
55. Garcia-Marquez' centenary condition
56. Fairy tale brothers
58. Right guarantees by 14 across
60. Author of *Dubliners,* banned in Ireland
61. *The Last _____ of Christ*
63. *Just So Stories* author
64. Scout's story

DOWN

1. _____ *Have and Have Not*
2. Irving's friend Owen
3. Kesey flew over it
4. Allard's family
6. *American Heritage*
7. A.E. Roquelaire, really
9. *Madame Bovary*
10. *Master _____ and the Boys*
11. *Capital* author
14. Anne Frank's book
15. Khomeini anathema
16. Sunshine state that banned *Huckleberry Finn,* abbr.
17. *Catcher in the _____*
18. _____ *Quiet on the Western Front*
19. *Fleurs du _____*
20. *The Naked and the _____*
23. Rabbi's book
26. Where Tara has gone
29. Hero of C.S. Lewis series
30. Gargantuan author
31. First inhabitant of 32 down
32. Zola's creation
33. *East of _____*
35. Zindel's _____ *man*
38. Whitman collection
39. _____ *Scary Stories*—never enough!
41. Faulkner's crazy trees
42. Medieval star-crossed letter-writers, _____ and _____
45. He's "missing"
49. *Sons and Lovers* author
49. Jesse Jackson says *Call Me _____*
50. Coward's other-world visitor
52. How many Billy Goats Gruff?
54. Aristophanes' work banned 'til 1930
57. *Of _____ and Men*
59. Pat Conroy's "great" character
62. Where scary stories are best told

Answers on page 170

Selected List of Concerned National Organizations

American Association of School Administrators

1801 N. Moore St.
Arlington, VA 22209
Phone: 703-528-0700
Fax: 703-841-1543
http://www.aasa.org

American Booksellers Association

828 S. Broadway
Tarrytown, NY 10591
Phone: 914-591-2665
Fax: 914-591-2716
http://www.bookweb.org

American Booksellers Foundation for Free Expression

828 S. Broadway
Tarrytown, NY 10591
Phone: 914-591-2665, ext. 289
Fax: 914-591-2716
http://www.bookweb.org

American Federation of Teachers

555 New Jersey Ave., N.W.
Washington, DC 20001
Phone: 202-879-4400
Fax: 202-879-4576
http://www.aft.org

American Civil Liberties Union

132 W. 43rd St.
New York, NY 10036-6599
Phone: 212-944-9800
Fax: 212-869-9065
http://www.aclu.org

American Library Association
Office for Intellectual Freedom
50 E. Huron St.
Chicago, IL 60611-2795
Phone: 312-280-4223
Fax: 312-280-4227
http://www.ala.org/oif.html

American Society of Journalists and Authors
1501 Broadway, Suite 302
New York, NY 10036
Phone: 212-997-0947
Fax: 212-768-7414
http://www.asja.org

Americans for Religious Liberty
P.O. Box 6656
Silver Spring, MD 20916
Phone: 301-598-2447
Fax: 301-438-8424

Americans United for Separation of Church and State
1816 Jefferson Place
Washington, DC 20036
Phone: 202-466-3234
Fax: 202-466-2587
http://www.au.org

Article 19, International Centre Against Censorship
33 Islington High St.
London N1 9LH, U.K.
Phone: (44 171) 278 9292
Fax: (44 171) 713 1356

The Association for Supervision and Curriculum Development
1250 N. Pitt St.
Alexandria, VA 22314-1453
Phone: 703-549-9110
Fax: 703-299-8631
http://www.ascd.org

Association of American Publishers
1718 Connecticut, N.W., Suite 700
Washington, DC 20009-1148
Phone: 202-232-3335
Fax: 202-745-0694
http://www.publishers.org

Center for Democracy and Technology
1634 Eye St., N.W., Suite 1100
Washington, DC 20006
Phone: 202-637-9800
Fax: 202-637-0968
http://www.cdt.org

Council of Chief State School Officers
1 Massachusetts Ave., N.W.
Suite 700
Washington, DC 20001-1431
Phone: 202-408-5505
Fax: 202-408-8072
http://www.ccsso.org

Electronic Frontier Foundation
1550 Bryant St., Suite 725
San Francisco, CA 94103
Phone: 415-436-9333
Fax: 415-436-9993
http://www.eff.org

First Amendment Congress
University of Denver
2200 S. Josephine St.
Denver, CO 80208-4430
Phone: 303-744-7068
Fax: 303-871-4514

Freedom to Read Foundation
50 E. Huron St.
Chicago, IL 60611-2795
Phone: 312-280-4226
Fax: 312-280-4227
http://www.ala.org/alaorg/oif/ftrf_home.htm/

International Reading Association
800 Barksdale Road
P.O. Box 8139
Newark, DE 19714-8139
Phone: 302-731-1600
Fax: 302-731-1057
http://www.reading.org

National Association of Biology Teachers
11250 Roger Bacon Dr., #19
Reston, VA 20190-5202
Phone: 703-471-1134
Phone: 800-406-0775
Fax: 703-435-5582
http://www.nabt.org

National Association of College Stores
528 E. Lorain St.
Oberlin, OH 44074-1298
Phone: 216-775-7777
Phone: 800-622-7498
Fax: 216-775-4769
http://www.nacs.org

National Center for Science Education
P.O. Box 9477
Berkeley, CA 94709-9953
Phone: 415-528-2521

National Coalition Against Censorship
275 7th Ave.
New York, NY 10001
Phone: 212-807-6222
Fax: 212-807-6245
http://www.ncac.org

National Council for the Social Studies
3501 Newark St., N.W.
Washington, DC 20016-3167
Phone: 202-966-7840
Fax: 202-966-2061
http://www.ncss.org

National Council of Teachers of English
1111 West Kenyon Rd.
Urbana, IL 61801-1096
Phone: 217-328-3870
Fax: 217-328-1077
http://www.ncte.org

National Education Association Human and Civil Rights Division
1201 16th St., N.W.
Washington, DC 20036-3290
Phone: 202-822-7700
Fax: 202-822-7578
http://www.nea.org

National School Boards Association
1680 Duke St.
Alexandria, VA 22314-3493
Phone: 703-838-6722
Fax: 703-683-7590

People for the American Way
2000 M St., N.W., Suite 400
Washington, DC 20036
Phone: 202-467-4999
Fax: 202-293-2672
http://www.paw.org

This window exhibit at a Booksellers shop in Beechwood, Ohio, cover banned or challenged magazines such as Hemp Times, Playboy, *and* Mountain Astrologer *with the statement "Censorship, like charity, should begin at home; but unlike charity, it should end there".*

Answers to Crossword Puzzle

(p. 166)

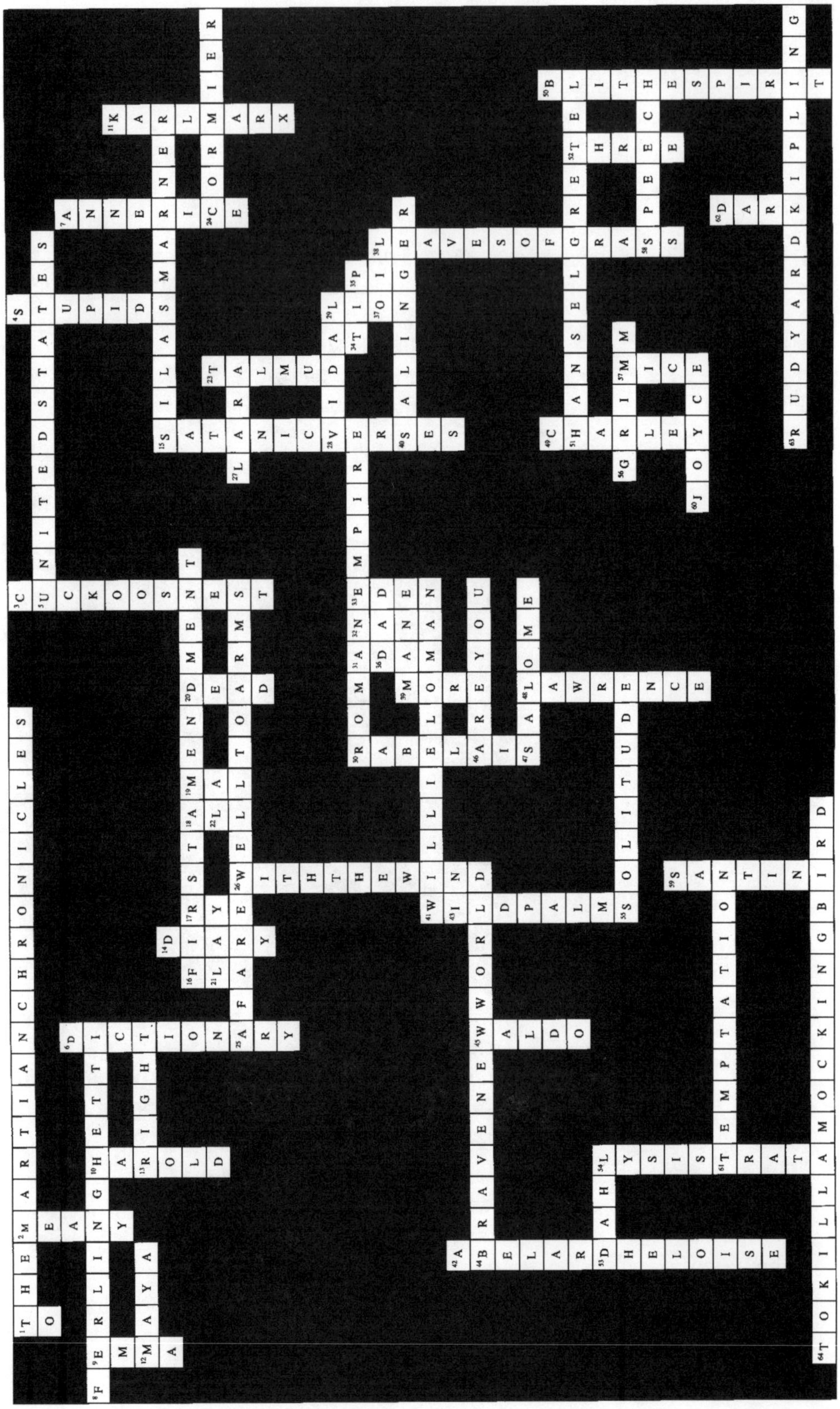

Suggestions for Dealing with Concerns about Library Resources

Be ready!

Introduction

Library policies and decisions are often challenged by individuals and groups concerned about the availability of a wide variety of library materials to everyone. Addressing these challenges requires a balance of carefully crafted library policy, knowledge and understanding of intellectual freedom principles, and sensitivity to community needs and concerns. It also requires effective communication. The following suggestions were prepared to help if such challenges arise.

Prevention

An ounce of prevention is worth a pound of cure when it comes to heading off controversy. Make sure all library staff and board members understand the library's policies and procedures for dealing with challenges. Provide customer service and other human relations training that will help staff deal effectively with sensitive matters.

- Make sure you have an up-to-date selection policy, reviewed regularly by the appropriate governing board, which includes a request for reconsideration form. It should apply to all library materials equally. If you do not have such a policy, samples are available from your regional library system, the state library, and the ALA Library and Research Center.

- Maintain a library service policy. This should cover registration policies, programming, and services in the library that involve access issues.

- Maintain a clearly defined method for reconsideration of library materials. The complaint must be filed in writing and the complainant must be properly identified before action is taken. A decision should be deferred until fully considered by appropriate administrative authority. The process should be followed, whether the complaint originates internally or externally.

- As a public institution, the library must develop and implement all policies within the legal framework that applies to it. Have your policies reviewed regularly by legal counsel for compliance with federal and state constitutional requirements, federal and state civil rights legislation, and other applicable federal and state legislation, including confidentiality legislation and applicable case law.

- Maintain a clearly defined method for reconsideration of library materials. The complaint must be filed in writing and the complainant must be properly identified before action is taken. A decision should be deferred until fully considered by appropriate administrative authority. The process should be followed, whether the complaint originates internally or externally.

- Maintain in-service training. Conduct periodic in-service training to acquaint staff, administration, and the governing authority with the materials selection policy and library service policy and procedures for handling complaints.

- Maintain lines of communication with civic, religious, educational, and political bodies of the community. Library board and staff participation in local civic organizations and presentations to these organizations should emphasize the library's selection process and intellectual freedom principles.

- Maintain a vigorous public information program on behalf of intellectual freedom. Newspaper, radio, television should be informed of policies governing resource selection and use, and of any special activities pertaining to intellectual freedom.

- Maintain familiarity with local municipal and state legislation pertaining to intellectual freedom and First Amendment rights.

Communicating Effectively

Following these practices will not preclude receiving complaints from pressure groups or individuals, but should provide a base from which to operate when these complaints are expressed. When a complaint is made a few simple communication techniques can go a long way toward defusing emotion and clearing up any misunderstanding. First, all people should be accorded respect and fair treatment.

One on one

- Greet the person with a smile. Communicate your openness to receive inquiries and that you take them seriously. Listen more than you talk.

- Practice "active listening." Take time to really listen and acknowledge the individual's concern. This can be as simple as "I'm sorry you're upset. I understand your concern."

- Stay calm and courteous. Upset parents are not likely to be impressed by talk about the First Amendment or *Library Bill of Rights*. Talk about freedom of choice, the library's role in serving all people and the responsibility of parents to supervise their own children's library use. Avoid library jargon such as intellectual freedom.

Q&A

Sample Questions and Answers

The following questions provide sample language to use when answering questions from the media and other members of the public. You will want to personalize your remarks for your library and community. Remember, keep it simple. Keep it human.

What is the role of libraries in serving children?

The same as it is for adults. Libraries provide books and other materials that will meet a wide range of ages and interests. Many libraries have special areas for children and teenagers. They also have many special programs, such as preschool storyhour, movies, puppet shows, and term paper clinics. In fact, more children participate in summer reading programs at libraries than play Little League baseball!

Why don't libraries restrict certain materials based on age like movie theaters or video stores?

Movie theaters and video stores are private businesses and

can make their own policies. Libraries are public institutions. They cannot limit access on the basis of age or other characteristics. Our library does provide copies of movie reviews and ratings, and we encourage parents to use them in guiding their children's library use.

How do libraries decide what to buy?

Every library has its own policies which are approved by its own board. Our library has adopted the *Library Bill of Rights*. We also have a mission statement that says our goal is to serve a broad range of community needs. Librarians are taught as part of their professional education to evaluate books and other materials and to select materials based on library policies.

What is the Library Bill of Rights?

The *Library Bill of Rights* is a policy statement adopted by the American Library Association to protect the right of all library users to choose for themselves what they wish to read or view. The policy is more than 50 years old and it has been adopted voluntarily by most libraries as a way of ensuring the highest quality library service to their communities.

Does that mean a child can check out Playboy or other materials intended for adults?

- Distribute facts, policy and other background materials in writing to all interested parties. Avoid giving personal opinions.

- Be prepared to give a clear and non-intimidating explanation of the library's procedure for registering a complaint and be clear about when a decision can be expected.

Dealing with the media

When a challenge occurs, realize it may attract media attention. How effectively you work with the media may well determine how big the story becomes and will help to shape public opinion.

Some suggestions:

- Have one spokesperson for the library. Make sure that reporters, library staff and the members of the board know who this is. Make it clear that no one other than this spokesperson should express opinions on behalf of the library.

- Prepare carefully for any contacts with the media. Know the most important message you want to deliver and be able to deliver it in 25 words or less. You will

want to review your library's borrowing and collection development policies and the American Library Association's *Library Bill of Rights*.

- Practice answering difficult questions and answers out loud. You may wish to invest in a session with a professional media consultant. The American Library Association offers this training at annual conferences.

- Keep to the high ground — no matter what. Don't mention the other side by name, either personal or corporate. Be careful to speak in neutral terms. Name calling and personalization are great copy for reporters but create barriers to communication.

- Do not let yourself be put on the defensive. Stay upbeat, positive — "Libraries are vital to democracy. We are very proud of the service our library provides." If someone makes a false statement, gently but firmly respond: "That's absolutely incorrect. The truth is the vast majority of parents find the library an extremely friendly, safe place for their children. We receive many more compliments from parents than we do complaints."

- Be prepared to tell stories or quote comments from

We believe in freedom of choice for all people but we also believe in common sense. It would be extremely unusual for a young child to check out that type of adult material. Most libraries are designed with special areas for children and teenagers. And there are librarians to provide assistance. We also provide suggested reading lists to help them make appropriate choices. Our goal is to provide the best possible service for young people, and we are very proud of what we offer. If you haven't been to our library recently, we encourage you to come down and see for yourself!

What should I do if I find something I don't approve of in the library?

Libraries offer a wide range of materials and not everyone is going to like or approve of everything. If you have a concern, simply ask to speak to a librarian. We do want to know your concerns, and we're confident we have or can get materials that meet your needs. The library also has a formal review process if you wish to put your concern in writing.

What does the library do if someone complains about something in its collection?

We take such concerns very seriously. First, we listen. We also have a formal review process where we ask you to fill out a special form designed to help us understand your

concerns. Anyone who makes a written complaint will receive a response in writing.

What can parents do to protect their children from materials they consider offensive?

Visit the library with your child. If that's not possible, ask to see the materials your child brings home. Set aside a special shelf for library materials. If there are materials on it you don't approve of, talk with your children about why you would rather they not read or view them. Most libraries provide suggested reading lists for various ages. And librarians are always glad to advise children and parents on selecting materials we think they would enjoy and find helpful.

I pay tax dollars to support the library. Why shouldn't I be able to control what my kids are exposed to?

You can control what your children are exposed to simply by going with them to visit the library or supervising what they bring home. The library has a responsibility to serve all taxpayers, including those you may not agree with — or who may not agree with you. We believe parents know what's best for their children, and each parent is responsible for supervising his or her child.

parents and children about how the library has helped them.

- Be strategic in involving others. For instance, board members, friends of libraries, community leaders, teachers and other supporters can assist by writing letters to the editor or an opinion column, meeting with a newspaper editorial board or other members of the media.

More tips

The following tips apply both when dealing with the media and when speaking to other audiences — community groups, trustees, staff:

- Never repeat a negative. Keep your comments upbeat and focused on service.

- Keep it simple. Avoid professional jargon. Try to talk in user-friendly terms your audience can relate to: Freedom of choice — not the *Library Bill of Rights*. "People with concerns" or "concerned parents" — not censors.

- Ask questions. Find out what the approach is, whether there will also be someone with an opposing view present. If you do not feel qualified to address the question or are uncomfortable with the approach, say so. Suggest other angles ("The real issue is freedom of choice…")

- Be clear whom you represent — yourself or your library.

- Know your audience. Make sure you know which newspaper, radio or TV station you're dealing with and who the audience is — whether they're parents, seniors, teenagers, their ethnic background, religious affiliation and anything else that will help you focus your remarks.

- Anticipate the standard "Who-What-When-Where and Why" questions and develop your answers beforehand. Keep your answers brief and to the point. Avoid giving too much information. Let the reporter ask the questions.

- Beware of manipulation. Some reporters may ask leading questions, something like "Isn't it true that … ?" Make your own statement.

- Don't rush. Pause to think about what you want to say and the best way to say it. Speak deliberately. It will make you sound more thoughtful and authoritative.

- Don't be afraid to admit you don't know. "I don't know" is a legitimate answer. Reporters do not want

incorrect information. Tell them you'll get the information and call back.

- Provide hand-outs with copies of relevant policies, statistics, other helpful information. You also may want to provide a written copy of your statement.

- Never say "No comment." A simple "I'm sorry I can't answer that" will suffice.

- Remember, nothing is "off the record." Assume that anything you say could end up on the front page or leading the news broadcast.

It's not just what you say

How you look and the tone of your voice can be as important as what you say — especially on radio and TV or before a live audience.

You want to sound and look professional, but also friendly and approachable. Studies have shown audiences are more likely to trust and believe you if they like how you look and sound.

Smile when you're introduced, if someone says something funny, if you want to show your enthusiasm for all the good things that your library is doing. On the flip side, be sure not to smile when you — or someone else — are making a serious point.

Dress and make up appropriately. There are many articles and books on what works for TV and speaking appearances.

On radio, use your voice as a tool to express your feelings — concern, enthusiasm, empathy. A smile can be "heard" on the radio.

Don't panic if you misspeak. Simply say "I'm sorry, I forgot what I was going to say." Or, "I'm sorry I was confused. The correct number is…" To err is human, and audiences are very forgiving of those who confess — but don't agonize over — their mistakes.

Key messages

When responding to a challenge, you will want to focus on three key points:

- Libraries provide ideas and information across the spectrum of social and political views.

- Libraries are one of our great democratic institutions. They provide freedom of choice for all people.

- Parents are responsible for supervising their own children's library use.

These simple, but sometimes overlooked essentials are the bulwark against challenges.

Tips for trustees

- First, remember your role. As a library trustee, you have a responsibility to speak your mind, and to argue forcibly for your point of view within the forum of the board. Once the board has made a decision, it is your responsibility to support the decision of the majority. If you disagree for whatever reason, do not speak out publicly. If, for reasons of conscience, you feel you cannot be silent, it is best to resign from the board before making your opposition public.

- Work with your library director to ensure that the necessary policies are in place and that they are reviewed regularly and thoroughly. Review and affirm your library's selection policy annually and make sure it is followed carefully.

- Insist that the entire board understand the library's collection policy and that it be involved in reviewing and reaffirming this policy on an annual basis.

- Be an effective advocate for the library. Use your contacts in the community to educate and mobilize others in support of the library.

- Bring what you hear back to the library director. Your roots in the community may be much deeper and of longer duration that those of the director. The things that people will tell you what they won't tell a director can provide valuable feedback.

- Be involved with the professional organizations serving library trustees on both the state and national levels.

- Remember the roots of the word "trustee." The community has placed its trust in you to act as an effective steward for the library. This means representing the interests of the entire community, not just a vocal minority.

Tips for children's and young adult librarians

- Make sure you and your staff are familiar with the library's collection policy and can explain it in a clear, easily understandable way.

- Take time to listen to and empathize with a parent's concern. Explain in a non-defensive way the need to protect the right of all parents to determine their own children's reading.

- Keep your director informed of any concerns expressed, whether you feel they have been successfully resolved or not.

- Join professional organizations to keep abreast of issues and trends in library service to children and families.

- Encourage parents or guardians to participate in choosing library materials for their young people and to make reading aloud a family activity. Host storytelling, book discussion groups and other activities that involve adults and youth.

- Offer "parent education" programs/workshops throughout the year. National Library Week in April and Children's Book Week in November provide timely opportunities. Suggested topics: how to select books and other materials for youth; how to raise a reader; how books and other materials can help children and teens cope with troubling situations; the importance of parents being involved in their children's reading and library use; concepts of intellectual freedom.

- Reach out to the media. Offer to write a newspaper column or host a radio or TV program discussing good books and other materials for children and teens. Give tips for helping families get the most from libraries.

- Build bridges. Offer to speak to parent and other groups on what's new at the library, good reading for youth, how to motivate children and teens to read, how to make effective use of the library and other topics of special interest.

Kids and Libraries
What You Should Know

Kids and curiosity go together. Children and teenagers have an unquenchable thirst for knowledge that usually pleases but sometimes frightens their parents. Why? How? The questions never seem to end!

Fortunately, there are libraries and librarians to help answer these unending questions, send kids on wondrous adventures and provide them with the resources they need today and to become informed, decision-making adults. And parents can relax knowing it is a friendly place for all families.

With so much available, how can you help your family make the best use of the library?

Here are answers to some commonly asked questions, along with suggestions for helping children become lifelong learners and library users.

What is the role of libraries and librarians in serving children?

Libraries are family-oriented public institutions charged with making a broad selection of materials available for everyone, including children and teenagers.

Most public libraries have special areas for children and teens with materials that appeal to various ages and interests. Libraries also offer summer reading programs, storytelling, book discussions and other special programs for young people. Programs such as these help kids learn to enjoy libraries and use them for their information and entertainment needs.

School libraries have a responsibility to support their school's curriculum and to provide materials that serve the diverse backgrounds, interests, maturity levels and reading levels of the entire student body.

How do librarians select their collections?

Each library has its own selection and collection development policies. Criteria may include popular demand, ensuring diversity in the collection, available space and budget. These policies must be approved by the library or school governing board, which is made up of community representatives.

The ultimate responsibility rests with the library director or school superintendent, who delegates selection to appropriate staff acting within the framework of the established policies. In schools, librarians work closely with teachers and school administrators to provide collections that support and supplement the school's curriculum.

The majority of books and other materials selected have been reviewed and recommended by professional librarians or reviewers. Purchases are also sometimes made on the recommendations of book discussion groups or requests by library users.

Selection is an inclusive process, where librarians seek materials that will provide a broad range of viewpoints and subject matter. This means that while library collections have thousands of items families want, like and need, they also will have materials that some parents may find offensive to them or inappropriate for their children.

Because an item is selected does not mean the librarian endorses or promotes it. He or she is simply helping the library to fulfill its mission of providing information from all points of view.

How are libraries different from movie theaters, book or video stores, which often have restrictions for children and teens?

As public institutions, libraries cannot discriminate based on age, sex, race or any other characteristic. Movie theaters are privately-owned businesses that can choose to show only children's movies or westerns. Similarly, video stores can decide not to rent certain movies to anyone under the age of 18.

Libraries must meet the diverse needs of everyone in their communities. They cannot overrule the rights and responsibilities of individuals by deciding who does or doesn't have access to library materials. Most libraries provide movie reviews and ratings for parents to use these in guiding their children's library use.

Can't parents tell the librarian what material they don't think children should have?

Decisions about what materials are suitable for particular children should be made by the people who know them best — their parents or guardians.

Children mature at different rates. They have different backgrounds and interests. And they have different reading levels and abilities. For instance, a video that one 10-year-old likes may not interest another. Or a parent may feel a particular library book is inappropriate for his daughter, while the same book may be a favorite of her classmate's family. These factors make it impossible for librarians to set any criteria for restricting use based on age alone. To do so would keep others who want and need materials from having access to them.

Like adults, children and teenagers have the right to seek and receive the information that they choose. It is the right and responsibility of parents to guide their own family's library use while allowing other parents to do the same.

Librarians are not authorized to act as parents. But they are happy to provide suggestions and guidance to parents and youngsters at any time.

What is the Library Bill of Rights?

The *Library Bill of Rights* is a policy adopted by the American Library Association to guide librarians in serving their communities or schools. This policy, based on the First Amendment, protects the rights of all library users to choose for themselves what they wish to read, listen to or view. It has been voluntarily adopted by many libraries to ensure that they serve everyone in their communities equally and fairly.

Under the First Amendment, children and teens have the same rights as adults to select the materials they wish to read, listen to or view. The *Library Bill of Rights* simply reminds libraries of their responsibilities to serve all the public, regardless of age.

How can parents help children and teens make the best use of the library?

1. Allow your kids to explore the library. Children and teens are naturally attracted to materials intended for them. They are generally not attracted to materials that are too advanced for their reading or maturity levels. By asking questions and learning to find their

The text shown below was printed in Coping With Challenges, *printed by the American Library Association. It can be copied and made available at your library or bookstore for parents or others* *concerned with children's reading materials. The entire text has been reprinted in this Resource Guide starting on page 175 in the section "Kids and Libraries: What You Should Know."*

Kids and Libraries

What you should know

Kids and curiosity go together. Children and teen-agers have an unquenchable thirst for knowledge that usually pleases but sometimes overwhelms their parents. Why? How? The questions never seem to end!

Fortunately, there are libraries and librarians to help answer these unending questions, send kids on wondrous adventures and provide them with the resources they need to learn and grow. And parents can relax knowing it is a friendly place for all families.

With so much available, how can you help your family make the best use of the library?

Here are answers to some commonly asked questions, along with suggestions for helping children become lifelong learners and library users.

What is the role of libraries and librarians in serving children?

Libraries are family-oriented public institutions charged with making a broad selection of materials available for everyone, including children and teenagers.

Most public libraries have special areas for children and teens with materials that appeal to various ages and interests. Libraries also offer summer reading programs, storytelling, book discussions and other special programs for young people. Programs such as these help kids learn to enjoy libraries and use them for their information and entertainment needs.

School libraries have a responsibility to support their school's curriculum and to provide materials that serve the diverse backgrounds, interests, maturity levels and reading levels of the entire student body.

How do librarians select their collections?

Each library has its own selection and collection development policies. Criteria may include popular demand, ensuring diversity in the collection, available space and budget. These policies must be approved by the library or school governing board, which is made up of community representatives.

The ultimate responsibility rests with the library director or school superintendent, who delegates selection to appropriate staff acting within the framework of the established policies. In schools, librarians work closely with teachers and school administrators to provide collections that support and supplement the school's curriculum.

The majority of books and other materials selected have been reviewed and recommended by professional librarians or reviewers. Purchases are also sometimes made on the recommendations of book discussion groups or requests by library users.

Selection is an inclusive process, where librarians seek materials that will provide a broad range of viewpoints and subject matter. This means that while library collections have thousands of items families want, like and need, they also will have materials that some parents may find offensive to them or inappropriate for their children.

Because an item is selected does not mean the librarian endorses or promotes it. He or she is simply helping the library to fulfill its mission of providing information from all points of view.

How are libraries different from movie theaters, book or video stores, which often have restrictions for children and teens?

As public institutions, libraries cannot discriminate based on age, sex, race or any other characteristic. Movie theaters are privately-owned businesses that can choose to show only children's movies or westerns. Similarly, video stores can decide not to rent certain movies to anyone under the age of 18.

Libraries must meet the diverse needs of everyone in their communities. They cannot overrule the rights and responsibilities of individuals by deciding who does or doesn't have access to library materials. Most libraries provide movie reviews and ratings for parents to use these in guiding their children's library use.

Can't parents tell the librarian what material they don't think children should have?

Decisions about what materials are suitable for particular children should be made by the people who know them best – their parents or guardians.

Children mature at different rates. They have different backgrounds and interests. And they have different reading levels and abilities. For instance, a video that one 10-year-old likes may not interest another. Or a parent may feel a particular library book is inappropriate for his daughter, while the same book may be a favorite of her classmate's family. These factors make it impossible for librarians to set any criteria for restricting use based on age alone. To do so would keep others who want and need materials from having access to them.

Like adults, children and teenagers have the right to seek and receive the information that they choose. It is the right and responsibility of parents to guide their own family's library use while allowing other parents to do the same.

Librarians are not authorized to act as parents. But they are happy to provide suggestions and guidance to parents and youngsters at any time.

What is the Library Bill of Rights?

The Library Bill of Rights is a policy adopted by the American Library Association to guide librarians in serving their communities or schools. This policy, based on the First Amendment, protects the rights of all library users to choose for themselves what they wish to read, listen to or view. It has been voluntarily adopted by many libraries to ensure that they serve everyone in their communities equally and fairly.

Under the First Amendment, children and teens have the same rights as adults to select the materials they wish to read, listen to or view. The Library Bill of Rights simply reminds libraries of their responsibilities to serve all the public, regardless of age.

How can parents help children and teens make the best use of the library?

1 Allow your kids to explore the library. Children and teens are naturally attracted to materials intended for them. They are generally not attracted to materials that are too advanced for their reading or maturity levels. By asking questions and learning to find their own answers, young people learn to think for themselves, to compare and contrast differing opinions and to analyze what they see and hear, rather than blindly following others.

2 Ask your librarian for suggestions about materials that are appropriate for your children's ages, maturity levels, knowledge and interests. Read books and brochures that review materials for children or teens. Review those materials yourself to determine if they are what you think your children may like or need. While librarians and resource lists can provide guidance, you know your children and family needs best.

3 Discuss your family rules regarding library use with your children. If you are concerned they will not respect your wishes, it is your responsibility to visit the library with them.

4 When you can't go along, show an interest in what your children bring home from the library. Have a special shelf for library materials and take time to familiarize yourself with them. Ask your children in a non-threatening way to share what they found at the library. Praise their independence and responsibility in caring for library materials and returning them on time.

5 If you feel an item is inappropriate for your children, use this as an opportunity to express your views and provide guidance. When you return the material, simply ask the librarian to help you find something else from among the many choices available.

6 Be aware that many young people seek information from libraries that they are embarrassed or afraid to ask an adult. A factual library book, unlike hearsay from friends, can ease their fears or even keep them safe from harm. Remember that just because a child is reading or viewing something, it doesn't mean he's participating or approves of it. If you have a concern, take the opportunity to discuss it with him or her.

7 Be a role model for library use. Nothing teaches children better than seeing you use and enjoying the wide range of materials available.

8 Establish a family routine of going to the library on a regular basis. Visiting the library once a week or once a month encourages young people to use the library both for learning and pleasure, and teaches them how to find what they need—an invaluable skill for school and a lifetime of learning.

9 Get to know your public and school librarians. Their expertise can help you and your children get the most out of libraries.

10 Ask for the item you want. If the library doesn't already own it, the librarian may be able to locate similar materials, borrow it from another library or add it to the collection.

For more information about how your library can meet your family's needs, talk to your librarian.

Add your library's name here

own answers, young people learn to think for themselves, to compare and contrast differing opinions and to analyze what they see and hear, rather than blindly following others.

2. Ask your librarian for suggestions about materials that are appropriate for your children's ages, maturity levels, knowledge and interests. Read books and brochures that review materials for children or teens. Review those materials yourself to determine if they are what you think your children may like or need. While librarians and resource lists can provide guidance, you know your children's and family's needs best.

3. Discuss your family rules regarding library use with your children. If you are concerned they will not respect your wishes, it is your responsibility to visit the library with them.

4. When you can't go along, show an interest in what your children bring home from the library. Have a special shelf for library materials and take time to familiarize yourself with them. Ask your children in a non-threatening way to share what they found at the library. Praise their independence and responsibility in caring for library materials and returning them on time.

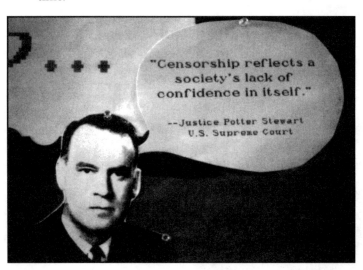

"Censorship reflects a society's lack of confidence in itself."

--Justice Potter Stewart
U.S. Supreme Court

5. If you feel an item is inappropriate for your children, use this as an opportunity to express your views and provide guidance. When you return the material, simply ask the librarian to help you find something else from among the many choices available.

6. Be aware that many young people seek information from libraries that they are embarrassed or afraid to ask an adult. A factual library book, unlike hearsay from friends, can ease their fears or even keep them safe from harm. Remember that just because a child is reading or viewing something, it doesn't mean he's participating in or approves of it. If you have a concern, take the opportunity to discuss it with him or her.

7. Be a role model for library use. Nothing teaches children better than seeing you use and enjoy the wide range of materials available.

8. Establish a family routine of going to the library on a regular basis. Visiting the library once a week or once a month encourages young people to use the library both for learning and pleasure, and teaches them how to find what they need — an invaluable skill for school and a lifetime of learning.

9. Get to know your public and school librarians. Their expertise can help you and your children get the most out of libraries.

10. Ask for the item you want. The librarian may be able to locate similar materials, borrow it from another library or add it to the collection.

For more information about how your library can meet your family's needs, talk to your librarian.

Title Index

Note:
The bibliographic entries are numbered sequentially and the entry number, rather than the page number, is listed below.

Topical Index

Note:
The bibliographic entries are numbered sequentially and the entry number, rather than the page number, is listed below.

Selected titles in this book have been indexed in the following categories: Biographical Works, Black Literature, Children's Literature, Gay and Lesbian Literature, Novels, Occult Books, Plays, Poetry, Reference Books, Religious Titles, Sex Education Titles, Textbooks, and Young Adult Literature.

Neither this list nor any of the categories is all-inclusive and comprehensive. Rather, this index is meant to assist in the development of displays, articles, editorials, and presentations.

Children's Literature

Gay and Lesbian Literature

Novels

Textbooks

Young Adult Literature

Geographic Index

Use this image for your Banned Books Week celebration materials. Use the graphic on bookbags, table tent cards and the rest of your press materials.

The First Amendment

Congress shall make no law respecting an establishment of religion, or prohibiting the free exercise thereof; or abridging the freedom of speech, or of the press, or the right of the people peaceably to assemble, and to petition the Government for a redress of grievances.

Clip Art

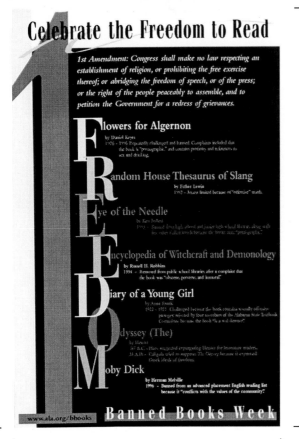

These reduced copies of the 1997 Banned Books Week posters can be used on flyers or ads for your Banned Books Week celebration.

Clip Art

This camera-ready art can support and enhance your public relations efforts. Simply copy these pages or selected items to illustrate flyers, posters, newsletters and bibliographies; to decorate invitations to readings or forums; and to tie together the look of your Banned Books Week celebration.